MOTIVATION
AND
PERSONALITY

Under the editorship of
Wayne G. Holtzman
and Gardner Murphy

MOTIVATION AND PERSONALITY

SECOND EDITION

Abraham H. Maslow

LATE, BRANDEIS UNIVERSITY

HARPER & ROW, PUBLISHERS
NEW YORK, EVANSTON, AND LONDON

MOTIVATION AND PERSONALITY, SECOND EDITION

LIBRARY OF CONGRESS CATALOG CARD NUMBER: 76-113490

This book was made possible
by the generosity of my brothers
Harold, Paul, and Lew
of the Universal Container Corporation

CONTENTS

PREFACE

I have tried in this revision to incorporate the main lessons of the last sixteen years. These lessons have been considerable. I consider it a real and extensive revision—even though I had to do only a moderate amount of rewriting—because the main thrust of the book has been modified in important ways which I shall detail below.

When this book appeared in 1954 it was essentially an effort to build *upon* the classical psychologies available rather than to repudiate them or to establish another rival psychology. It attempted to enlarge our conception of the human personality by reaching into the "higher" levels of human nature. (The title I had first planned to use for the book was *Higher Ceilings for Human Nature*.) If I had had to condense the thesis of this book into a single sentence, I would have said that, in *addition* to what the psychologies of the time had to say about human nature, man also had a higher nature and that this was instinctoid, i.e., part of his essence. And if I could have had a second sentence, I would have stressed the profoundly holistic nature of human nature in contradiction to the analytic–dissecting–atomistic–Newtonian approach of the behaviorisms and of Freudian psychoanalysis.

Or to say it another way, I certainly accepted and built upon the available *data* of experimental psychology and psychoanalysis. I accepted also the empirical and experimental spirit of the one, and the unmasking and depth-probing of the other, while yet rejecting the *images* of man which they generated. That is, this book represented a different philosophy of human nature, a new image of man.

However, what I took then to be an argument within the family of psychologists has in my opinion turned out since then to be rather a local manifestation of a new *Zeitgeist,* a new general comprehensive philosophy of life. This new "humanistic" *Weltanschauung* seems to be a new and far more hopeful and encouraging way of conceiving any and every area of human knowledge: e.g., economics, sociology, biology, and every profession: e.g., law, politics, medicine, and all of the social institutions: e.g., the family, education, religion, etc. I have acted upon this personal conviction in revising this book, writing into the psychology presented herein, the belief that it is an aspect of a much broader world view and of a comprehensive life-philosophy, which is already partly worked out, at least to the point of plausibility, and must, therefore, be taken seriously.

I must say a word about the irritating fact that this veritable revolution (a new image of man, of society, of nature, of science, of ultimate values, of philosophy, etc., etc.) is still almost completely overlooked by much of the intellectual community, especially that portion of it that controls the channels of communication to the educated public and to youth. (For this reason I have taken to calling it the Unnoticed Revolution.)

Many members of this community propound an outlook characterized by a profound despair and cynicism which sometimes degenerates into corrosive malice and cruelty. In effect they deny the possibility of improving human nature and society, or of discovering intrinsic human values, or of being life-loving in general.

Doubting the realness of honesty, of kindness, of generosity, of affection, they go beyond a reasonable skepticism or a withholding of judgment into an active hostility when confronted by people whom they sneer at as fools,"Boy Scouts," squares, innocents, do-gooders, or Pollyannas. This active debunking, hating and rending goes beyond contempt; it sometimes looks like an outraged counterattack against what they consider to be an insulting effort to fool them, to take them in, to pull their legs. The psychoanalyst would, I think, see in it a dynamics of rage and revenge for past disappointments and disillusionments.

This subculture of despair, this "more corrosive than thou" attitude, this counter-morality in which predation and hopelessness are real and good will is not, is flatly contradicted by the humanistic psychologies, and by the kind of preliminary data presented in this book and in many of the writings listed in the Bibliography. While it is still necessary to be very cautious about affirming the preconditions for "goodness" in human nature (see Chapters 7, 9, 11, 16), it is already possible to reject firmly the despairing belief that human nature is ultimately and basically depraved and evil. Such a belief is no longer a matter of taste merely. It can now be maintained only by a determined blindness and ignorance, by a refusal to consider the facts. It must therefore be considered to be a personal projection rather than a reasoned philosophical or scientific position.

The humanistic and holistic conceptions of science presented in the first two chapters and in Appendix B have been powerfully corroborated by many developments of the past decade, but especially by Michael Polanyi's great book *Personal Knowledge* (376). My own book, *The Psychology of Science* (292), carries forward very similar theses. These books are in blunt contradiction to the classical, conventional philosophy of science still too widely prevalent, and they offer a far better substitute for scientific work with persons.

The book is holistic throughout, but a more intensive and perhaps more difficult treatment is contained in Appendix B. Holism is obviously true—after all, the cosmos is one and interrelated; any society is one and interrelated; any person is one and interrelated, etc.—and yet the holistic outlook has a hard time being implemented and being used as it should be, as a way of looking at the world. Recently I have become more and more inclined to think that the atomistic way of thinking is a form of mild psychopathology, or is at least one aspect of the syndrome of cognitive immaturity. The holistic way of thinking and seeing seems to come quite naturally and automatically to healthier, self-actualizing people, and seems to be extraordinarily difficult for less evolved, less mature, less healthy people. To date this is only an impression, of course, and I do not want to push it too hard. Yet I feel justified in presenting it here as a hypothesis to be checked, something which should be relatively easy to do.

The motivation theory presented in Chapters 3 through 7, and to some extent throughout the book, has had an interesting history. First presented in 1942 to a psychoanalytic society, it was an effort to integrate into a single theoretical structure the partial truths I saw in Freud, Adler, Jung, D. M. Levy, Fromm, Horney, and Goldstein. I had learned from my own scattered experiences in therapy that each of these writers was correct at various times and for various persons. My question was essentially the clinical one: which earlier deprivations produce neurosis? Which psychological medicines cure neurosis? Which prophylaxis prevents neurosis? In which order are the psychological medicines demanded? Which are most powerful? Which most basic?

It is fair to say that this theory has been quite successful in a clinical, social and personological way, but not in a laboratory and experimental way. It has fitted very well with the personal experience of most people, and has often given them a structured theory that has helped them to make better sense of their inner lives. It seems for most people to have a direct, personal, subjective plausibility. And yet it still lacks experimental verification and support. I have not yet been able to think of a good way to put it to the test in the laboratory.

Part of the answer to this puzzle came from Douglas McGregor (332), who applied this theory of motivation to the industrial situation. Not only did he find it useful in ordering his data and his observations, but also these data served retroactively as a source of validation and verification for the theory. It is from *this* area, rather than from the laboratory, that empirical support is now coming. (The Bibliography contains a sampling of such reports.)

The lesson I had learned from this and from subsequent validation from other areas of life was this: when we talk about the needs of human beings, we talk about the essence of their lives. How *could* I have thought that this essence could be put to the test in some animal laboratory or some test tube situation? Obviously it needs a life situation of the total human being in his social environment. This is where confirmation or disconfirmation will come from.

Chapter 4 betrays its clinical-therapeutic origins by its stress on neurosis producers rather than on motivations which do not make trouble for the psychotherapist, e.g., inertia and laziness, sensory pleasures, and the need for sensory stimulations and for activity, the sheer zest for life, or the lack of it, the proneness to hope or to hopelessness, the tendency to regress more or less easily under fear, anxiety, scarcity, etc., not to mention the highest human values which are also motivators: beauty, truth, excellence, completion, justice, order, consistency, harmony, etc.

These necessary complements to Chapters 3 and 4 are discussed in Chapters 3, 4, and 5 of my *Toward a Psychology of Being* (295), in the chapter on Lower Grumbles, Higher Grumbles and Metagrumbles in my *Eupsychian Management* (291), and in A Theory of Metamotivation: the Biological Rooting of the Value-Life (314).

Human life will never be understood unless its highest aspirations are taken into account. Growth, self-actualization, the striving toward health, the quest for identity and autonomy, the yearning for excellence (and other ways of phrasing the striving "upward") must by now be accepted beyond question as a widespread and perhaps universal human tendency.

And yet there are also other regressive, fearful, self-diminishing tendencies as well, and it is very easy to forget them in our intoxication with "personal growth," especially for inexperienced youngsters. I consider that a necessary prophylactic against such illusions is a thorough knowledge of psychopathology and of depth psychology. We must appreciate that many people choose the worse rather than the better, that growth is often a painful process and may for this reason be shunned, that we are afraid of our own best possibilities in addition to loving them (314) and that we are all of us profoundly ambivalent about truth, beauty, virtue, loving them and fearing them too (295). Freud is still required reading for the humanistic psychologist (his facts, not his metaphysics). I should like also to recommend an extraordinarily sensitive book by Hoggart (196) which will certainly help us to understand compassionately the pull toward the vulgar, the trivial, the cheap and the fake in the less educated people he writes about.

Chapter 4, and Chapter 6 on "The Instinctoid Nature of Basic Needs," constitute for me the foundation of a system of intrinsic human values, human goods that validate themselves, that are intrinsically good and desirable and that need no further justification. This is a hierarchy of values which are to be found in the very essence of human nature itself. These are not only wanted and desired by all human beings, but also needed in the sense that they are necessary to avoid illness and psychopathology. To say the same thing in another vocabulary, these basic needs and the metaneeds (314) are also the intrinsic reinforcers, the unconditioned stimuli which can be used as a basis upon which can be erected all sorts of instrumental learnings and conditionings. That is to say that in order to get these intrinsic goods, animals and men are willing to learn practically anything that will achieve for them these ultimate goods.

I want to be sure to mention here, even though I do not have the space for expanding upon the idea, that it is legitimate and fruitful to regard instinctoid basic needs and the metaneeds as *rights* as well as needs. This follows immediately upon granting that human beings have a right to be human in the same sense that cats have a right to be cats. In order to be fully human, these need and metaneed gratifications are necessary, and may therefore be considered to be natural rights.

The hierarchy of needs and metaneeds has been helpful to me in another way. I find that it serves as a kind of smorgasbord table from which people can choose in accordance with their own tastes and appetites. That is to say, that in any judging of the motivations for a person's behavior, the character of the judge also has to be taken into account. He *chooses* the motivations to which he will attribute the behavior, for instance, in accord with his generalized optimism or pessimism. I find the latter choice to be made far more frequently today, so frequently that I find it useful to name the phenomenon "downlevelling of the motivations." Briefly put, this is the tendency to prefer, for explanatory purposes, the lower needs to the middle needs, and the middle needs to the higher. A purely materialistic motivation is preferred to a social or metamotivated one, or to a mixture of all three. It is a kind of paranoid-like suspicion, a form of devaluation of human nature, which I see often but which, to my knowledge, has not been sufficiently described. I think that any complete theory of motivation must include this additional variable.

And of course I am sure that the historian of ideas would find it very easy to find many examples, in different cultures and in different times, of either a general trend to downlevelling or uplevelling of human motivations. At the moment of writing, the trend in our culture is very clearly toward widespread downlevelling. The lower needs are being heavily overused for explanatory purposes and the higher and metaneeds are being badly underused. In my opinion this tendency rests far more on preconception than an empirical fact. I find the higher needs and metaneeds to be far more determinative than my subjects themselves suspect, and certainly far, far more than contemporary intellectuals dare admit. Obviously, this is an empirical and scientific question, and just as obviously it is far too important a matter to be left to cliques and in-groups.

I had added to Chapter 5 on gratification theory a section on the pathology of gratification. Certainly this is something that we were not prepared for fifteen or twenty years ago, that pathological consequences might ensue after having attained what one had been *trying* to attain, and which was supposed to bring happiness. We have learned with Oscar Wilde to beware of what we wish—for the tragedy may come about that our wishes may be granted. This seems to be possible at *any* of the motivational levels, whether the material, or the interpersonal, or the transcendent.

We can learn from this unexpected finding that the gratification of the basic needs does not in itself automatically bring about a system of values in which to believe and to which one may commit himself. Rather, we have learned that one of the possible consequences of basic need gratifications may be boredom, aimlessness, anomie and the like. Apparently we function best when we are striving for something that we lack, when we wish for something that we do not have, and when we organize our powers in the service of striving toward the gratification of that wish. The state of gratification turns out to be not necessarily a state of guaranteed happiness or contentment. It is a moot state, one that raises problems as well as solving problems.

This discovery implies that for many people the *only* definition of the meaningful life that they can think of is "to be lacking something essential and to be striving for it." But we know that self-actualizing people, even though all their basic needs have already been gratified, find life to be even *more* richly meaningful because they can live, so to speak, in the realm of Being (295). The ordinary, widespread philosophy of a meaningful life is, therefore, a mistaken one, or at least an immature one.

Just as important for me has been the growing realization of what I have been calling Grumble Theory (291). In brief, what I have observed is that need gratifications lead to only temporary happiness which in turn tends to be succeeded by another and (hopefully) higher discontent. It looks as if the human hope for eternal happiness can never be fulfilled. Certainly happiness does come and is obtainable and is real. But it looks as if we must accept its intrinsic transience, especially if we focus on its more intense forms. Peak experiences do not last, and *cannot* last. Intense happiness is episodic, not continuous.

But this amounts to a revision of the theory of happiness that has ruled us for three thousand years and that has determined our concepts of heaven, of the Garden of Eden, of the good life, the good society, the good person. Our love stories have traditionally ended "And they lived happily ever after." And so also have our theories of social improvement and social revolution. So also, for instance, have we been over-sold—and consequently disillusioned—by the very real though limited improvements in our society. We were over-sold on the benefits of labor unionism, of women's suffrage, of the direct election of Senators, of the graded income tax, and of many other improvements that we have built into, e.g., the amendments to the Constitution. Each one of them was supposed to bring a millenium, eternal happiness, the final solution of all problems. The result has tended to be disillusionment after the fact. But disillusionment means that there had been illusions. And this seems to be the clear point to make, that we may reasonably expect improvements to take place. But we can no longer reasonably expect perfection to come to pass, or permanent happiness to be achieved.

I must call attention also to what has been overlooked almost universally even though now it seems very obvious, namely that the blessings we have already achieved come to be taken for granted, to be forgotten, to drop out of consciousness, and finally, even, not to be valued any more —at least until they are taken away from us (see also 483). For instance, it is characteristic of the American culture as I write this preface in January, 1970, that the undoubted advancements and improvements that have been struggled for and achieved through 150 years are being flicked aside by many thoughtless and shallow people as being all a fake, as being of no value whatsoever, as being unworthy of fighting for or protecting, or valuing, just because the society is not yet perfect.

The present struggle for women's "liberation" will serve as a single example (I could have chosen dozens of others) to illustrate this complex but important point, and to show how many people tend to think in a dichotomous and splitting way rather than in a hierarchical and integrative way. In general it may be said that today, in our culture, the young girl's dream, a dream beyond which she cannot see, is most often of a man who falls in love with her, who gives her a home, and who gives her a baby. In her fantasies she then lives happily ever after. But the fact of the matter is that no matter how much one longs for a home or for a baby, or for a lover, that sooner or later one can become sated with these blessings, will take them for granted, and will start to feel restless and discontented as if something were lacking, as if something more had to be attained. The frequent mistake then is to turn upon the home and the baby and the husband as something of a fake, or perhaps even a trap or an enslavement, and then to long for the higher needs and higher gratifications in an either/or way, e.g., for professional work, for freedom to travel, for personal autonomy, and the like. The main point of Grumble Theory, and of Hierarchical–Integrative Theory of Needs, is that it is immature and unwise to think of these as mutually exclusive alternatives. It is best to think of the discontented woman as profoundly wishing to hang on to everything that she has and then—like the labor unionists—asking for *more!* That is to say that she generally would like to keep all her blessings and have additional ones as well. But even here it is as if we have not yet learned this eternal lesson, that whatever she yearns for, a career or whatever, when it is achieved the whole process will repeat itself. After the period of happiness, excitement, and fulfillment comes the inevitable taking it all for granted, and becoming restless and discontented again for *More!*

I offer for thought the real possibility that if we become fully aware of these human traits, if we can give up the dream of permanent and un-interrupted happiness, if we can accept the fact that we will be only transiently ecstatic and then inevitably discontented and grumbling for more, that then we may be able to teach the general population what self-actualizing people do automatically, i.e., to be able to count their blessings, to be grateful for them, and to avoid the traps of making either/or choices. It is possible for a woman to have all the specifically female fulfillments (being loved, having the home, having the baby) and *then,* without giving up any of the satisfactions already achieved, go on beyond femaleness to the full humanness that she shares with males, for example, the full development of her intelligence, of any talents that she may have, of her own particular idiosyncratic genius, of her own individual fulfillment.

The main thrust of Chapter 6, "The Instinctoid Nature of Basic Needs," has shifted considerably. The great advances of the last decade or so in the science of genetics has forced us to assign somewhat more determin-ing power to the genes than we did fifteen years ago. Most important of these discoveries for the psychologists has been, I think, the various things that can happen to the X and Y chromosomes: doubling, tripling, loss, etc.

Chapter 9, "Is Destructiveness Instinctoid?," has also been consider-ably changed by these new discoveries.

Perhaps these developments in genetics may help to make my posi-tion more clear and communicable than it apparently has been. Cur-rently, debate on the role of heredity and environment is almost as simplistic as it has been for the last fifty years. It still alternates between a simplistic theory of instincts on the one hand, total instincts of the sorts found in animals, and on the other hand, a complete rejection of the whole instinctual point of view in favor of a total environmentalism. Both positions are easily refuted, and in my opinion are so untenable as to be called stupid. In contrast with these two polarized positions the theory set forth in Chapter 6 and throughout the remainder of the book gives a third position, namely that there are *very weak* instinct-remnants left in the human species, nothing that could be called full instincts in the animal sense. These instinct-remnants and instinctoid tendencies are so weak that culture and learning easily overwhelm them and must be considered to be far more powerful. In fact, the techniques of psycho-analysis and other uncovering therapies, let alone the "quest for identity," may all be conceived as the very difficult and delicate task of discovering through the overlay of learning, habit, and culture, what our instinct-remnants and instinctoid tendencies, our weakly indicated essential nature may be. In a word, man has a biological essence, but this is very weakly and subtly determined, and needs special hunting techniques to discover it; we must discover, individually and subjectively, our animal-ity, our specieshood.

What this amounts to is the conclusion that human nature is extremely malleable in the sense that it is easy for culture and environ-ment to kill off altogether or to diminish genetic potential, although it cannot create or even increase this potential. So far as society is con-cerned, this seems to me to be an extremely strong argument in favor of absolute equality of opportunity for every baby born into the world. It is also an especially powerful argument in favor of the good society, since human potentials are so easily lost or destroyed by the bad environ-ment. This is quite apart from the contention already put forward that the sheer fact of membership in the human species constitutes *ipso facto* a right to become fully human, i.e., to actualize all the human potentials possible. *Being* a human being—in the sense of being born to the human species—must be defined also in terms of *becoming* a human being. In this sense a baby is only potentially a human being, and must grow into humanness in the society and the culture, the family.

Ultimately this point of view will force us to take far more seriously than we do the fact of individual differences, as well as species member-ship. We will have to learn to think of them in this new way as being, 1) very plastic, superficial, easily changed, easily stamped out, but pro-ducing thereby all sorts of subtle pathologies. This leads to the delicate task, 2) of trying to uncover the temperament, the constitution, the hidden *bent* of each individual so that he can grow unhampered in his own individual style. This attitude will require far greater attention than has been given by the psychologists to the subtle psychological and physiological costs and sufferings of denying one's true bent, sufferings that are not necessarily conscious or easily seen from the outside. This, in turn, means much more careful attention to the operational meaning of "good growth" at every age level.

Finally, I must point out that we shall have to prepare ourselves in principle for the shaking consequences of giving up the alibi of social injustice. The more we continue to reduce social injustice, the more we shall find this replaced by "biological injustice," by the fact that babies are born into the world with different genetic potentials. If we get to the point of giving full opportunity to every baby's good potentials, then this means accepting poor potentials as well. Whom shall we blame when a baby is born with a bad heart, or weak kidneys, or with neurological defects? If only nature is there to blame, what will this mean for the self-esteem of the individual "unfairly" treated by nature itself?

In this chapter, and also in other papers, I have introduced the concept of "subjective biology." I have found this to be a very helpful tool in bridging the gap between the subjective and the objective, the phenomenological and the behavioral. I hope this discovery, that one can and must study one's own biology introspectively and subjectively, will be of help to others, especially to biologists.

Chapter 9 on Destructiveness has been extensively reworked. I have subsumed it under the more inclusive category of the psychology of evil, hoping to demonstrate by this careful treatment of one aspect of evil, that the whole problem is empirically and scientifically workable. Bringing it under the jurisdiction of empirical science means for me that we can confidently look forward to steadily increased understanding which always has meant being able to do something about it.

Aggression, we have learned, is both genetically and culturally determined. Also I consider extremely important the distinction between healthy and unhealthy aggression.

Just as aggression cannot be blamed entirely on *either* society *or* inner human nature, so also is it already clear that evil in general is neither a social product alone or a psychological product alone. This may sound too obvious to be mentioned, but there are today many people who not only believe in these untenable theories but who act upon them as well.

I have introduced in Chapter 10, "The Expressive Component of Behavior," the concept of Apollonian controls, i.e., desirable controls which do not endanger gratification but rather enhance it. I consider this concept to be profoundly important both for pure psychological theory and for applied psychology. It has enabled me to differentiate between (sick) impulsivity and (healthy) spontaneity, a distinction very badly needed today, especially by young people, and by many others who tend to think of *any* controls as necessarily repressive and evil. I hope this insight will be as helpful to others as it has been to me.

I have not taken the time to bring this conceptual tool to bear upon the old problems of freedom, ethics, politics, happiness, and the like, but

I think its relevance and power will be obvious to any serious thinker in these fields. The psychoanalyst will notice that this solution overlaps to some extent with Freud's integration of pleasure principle and reality principle. To think through the similarities and differences will, I think, be a profitable exercise for the theorist of psychodynamics.

In Chapter 11 on self-actualization I have removed one source of confusion by confining the concept very definitely to older people. By the criteria I used, self-actualization does not occur in young people. In our culture at least, youngsters have not yet achieved identity, or autonomy, nor have they had time enough to experience an enduring, loyal, post-romantic love relationship, nor have they generally found their calling, the altar upon which to offer themselves. Nor have they worked out their *own* system of values; nor have they had experience enough (responsibility for others, tragedy, failure, achievement, success) to shed perfectionistic illusions and become realistic; nor have they generally made their peace with death; nor have they learned how to be patient; nor have they learned enough about evil in themselves and others to be compassionate; nor have they had time to become post-ambivalent about parents and elders, power and authority; nor have they generally become knowledgeable and educated enough to open the possibility of becoming wise; nor have they generally acquired enough courage to be unpopular, to be unashamed about being openly virtuous, etc.

In any case, it is better psychological strategy to separate the concept of mature, fully-human, self-actualizing people in whom the human potentialities have been realized and actualized from the concept of health at *any* age level. This translates itself, I have found, into "good-growth-toward-self-actualization," a quite meaningful and researchable concept. I have done enough exploration with college age youngsters to have satisfied myself that it *is* possible to differentiate "healthy" from "unhealthy." It is my impression that healthy young men and women tend to be still growing, likeable, and even lovable, free of malice, secretly kind and altruistic (but very shy about it), privately affectionate of those of their elders who deserve it. Young people are unsure of themselves, not yet formed, uneasy because of their minority position with their peers (their private opinions and tastes are more square, straight, metamotivated, i.e., virtuous, than average). They are secretly uneasy about the cruelty, meanness, and mob spirit so often found in young people, etc.

Of course I do not know that this syndrome inevitably grows into the self-actualization I have described for older people. Only longitudinal studies can determine this.

I have described my self-actualizing subjects as transcending nationalism. I could have added that they also transcend class and caste. This is true in my experience even though I would expect a priori that affluence and social dignity are apt to make self-actualization more probable.

Another question which I did not anticipate in my first report has been this: Are these people capable of living only with "good" people and in a good world only? My retrospective impression, which of course remains to be checked, is that self-actualizing people are essentially *flexible,* and can adapt themselves realistically to any people, any environment. I think they are ready to handle good people *as* good people, while also being able to handle bad people *as* bad people.

Another addition to the description of self-actualizing people emerged from my study of "grumbles" (291) and the widespread tendency to undervalue one's already achieved need-gratifications, or even to devalue them and throw them away. Self-actualizing persons are relatively exempted from this profound source of human unhappiness. In a word, they are capable of "gratitude." The blessedness of their blessings remains conscious. Miracles remain miracles even though occurring again and again. The awareness of undeserved good luck, of gratuitous grace, guarantees for them that life remains precious and never grows stale.

My study of self-actualizing persons has worked out very well—to my great relief, I must confess. It was, after all, a great gamble, doggedly pursuing an intuitive conviction and, in the process, defying some of the basic canons of scientific method and of philosophical criticism. These were, after all, rules which I myself had believed and accepted, and I was very much aware that I was skating on thin ice. Accordingly, my explorations proceeded against a background of anxiety, conflict, and self-doubt.

Enough verifications and supports have accumulated in the last few decades (see Bibliography) so that this kind of basic alarm is no longer necessary. And yet I am very much aware that these basic methodological and theoretical problems still confront us. The work that *has* been done is a bare beginning. We are now ready for far more objective, consensual and impersonal team methods of selecting self-actualizing (healthy, fully-human, autonomous) individuals for study. Cross-cultural work is clearly indicated. Follow-ups, from the cradle to the grave, will furnish the only truly satisfactory validation, at least in my opinion. Sampling the total population is clearly necessary in addition to selecting, as I did, the equivalent of Olympic gold medal winners. Nor do I think we can ever understand irreducible human evil until we explore more fully than I did the "incurable" sins and the shortcomings of the best human beings we can find.

Such studies I am convinced will change our philosophy of science (292), of ethics and values (314), of religion (293), of work, management and interpersonal relations (291), of society (312), and who knows what else. In addition, I think that great social and educational changes could occur almost immediately if, for instance, we could teach our young people to give up their unreal perfectionism, their demands for perfect human beings, a perfect society, perfect teachers, perfect parents, perfect politicians, perfect marriages, perfect friends, perfect organizations, etc., none of which exist and simply can not exist—that is, except for transient moments of peak-experience, of perfect fusion, etc. Such expectations we already know, even with our inadequate knowledge, are illusions and, therefore, must inevitably and inexorably breed disillusionment along with attendant disgust, rage, depression and revenge. The demand for "Nirvana *Now!*" is itself a major source of evil, I am finding. If you demand a perfect leader or a perfect society, you thereby give up choosing between better and worse. If the imperfect is defined as evil, then everything becomes evil, since everything is imperfect.

I believe also, on the positive side, that this great frontier of research is our most likely source of knowledge of the values intrinsic to human nature. Here lies the value system, the religion-surrogate, the idealism-satisfier, the normative philosophy of life that all human beings seem to need, to yearn for, and without which they become nasty and mean, vulgar and trivial.

Psychological health not only feels good subjectively but is also correct, true, real. In this sense, it is "better" than sickness and superior to it. Not only is it correct and true, but it is more perspicuous, seeing more truths as well as higher truths. That is, the lack of health not only feels awful but is a form of blindness, a cognitive pathology as well as moral and emotional loss. Furthermore, it is a form of crippling, of loss of capacities, of lesser ability to do and to achieve.

Healthy persons exist even though not in great numbers. Health with all its values—truth, goodness, beauty, etc.—having been demonstrated to be possible is, therefore, in principle an attainable reality. For those who prefer seeing to being blind, feeling good to feeling bad, wholeness to being crippled, it can be recommended that they seek psychological health. One remembers the little girl who, when asked why goodness was better than evil, answered, "Because it's *nicer.*" I think we can do better than that: the same line of thinking can demonstrate that living in a "good society" (brotherly, synergic, trusting, Theory Y) is "better" than living in a jungle society (Theory X, authoritarian, adversary, Hobbesian) *both* because of biological, medical and Darwinian survival values, and growth values, both subjective and objective (314). The same is true of a good marriage, a good friendship, good parents. Not only are these desired (preferred, chosen), but they are also, in specific senses, "desirable." I realize that this can make considerable trouble for professional philosophers, but I am confident that they will manage.

The demonstration that wonderful people *can* and do exist—even though in very short supply, and having feet of clay—is enough to give us courage, hope, strength to fight on, faith in ourselves and in our own possibilities for growth. Also, hope for human nature, however sober, should help us toward brotherliness and compassion.

I have decided to omit the last chapter of the first edition of this book, "Toward a Positive Psychology"; what was 98 percent true in 1954 is only two-thirds true today. A positive psychology is at least available today though not very widely. The humanistic psychologies, the new transcendent psychologies, the existential, the Rogerian, the experiential, the holistic, the value-seeking psychologies, are all thriving and available, at least in the United States, though unfortunately not yet in most departments of psychology, so that the interested student must seek them out or just stumble across them. For the reader who would like to taste for himself, I think a good sampling of the people, the ideas and the data is most easily available in the various books of readings by Moustakas (344), Severin (419), Bugental (69), and Sutich and Vich (441). For addresses of the appropriate schools, journals, societies, I would recommend the Eupsychian Network, an appendix in my book, *Toward a Psychology of Being* (see 295).

For uneasy graduate students I would still recommend this last chapter in the first edition, which is probably available in most university libraries. Also recommended is my *Psychology of Science* for the same reasons. For those who are willing to take these questions seriously enough to work hard at them, the great book in the field is Polanyi's *Personal Knowledge* (376).

This revised edition is an example of the increasingly firm rejection of traditionally value-free science—or rather of the futile effort to have a value-free science. It is more frankly normative than it was, more confidently affirming science to be a value-instigated search by value-seeking scientists who can, I claim, uncover intrinsic and ultimate and species-wide values in the structure of human nature itself.

To some this will seem like an assault upon the science that they love and revere, and which I do too. I accept that their fear is sometimes well founded. There are many, especially in the social sciences, who see total political commitment (by definition in the absence of full information) as the only conceivable alternative to value-free science and mutually exclusive with it. Embracing the one means for them necessarily rejecting the other.

That this dichotomizing is sophomoric is proven at once by the simple fact that it is best to get correct information even when you are fighting an enemy, even when you are avowedly a politician.

But quite beyond this self-defeating foolishness, and addressing ourselves to this very serious question at the highest levels of which we are capable, I believe it can be shown that normative zeal (to do good, to help mankind, to better the world) is quite compatible with scientific objectivity and indeed even makes conceivable a better, a more powerful science with a far wider jurisdiction than it now has when it tries to be value-neutral (leaving values to be arbitrarily affirmed by non-scientists on non-factual grounds). This is achieved simply by enlarging our conception of objectivity to include not only "spectator-knowledge" (laissez-faire, uninvolved knowledge, knowledge about, knowledge from the outside) but also experential knowledge (85) and what I may call love-knowledge or Taoistic knowledge.

The simple model of Taoistic objectivity comes from the phenomenology of disinterested love and admiration for the Being of the other (B-love). For instance, loving one's baby, or friend, or profession, or even one's "problem" or field in science, can be so complete and accepting that it becomes non-interfering, non-intrusive, i.e., liking it just as it is and as it will become with no impulse to change it or improve it. It takes great love to be able to leave something alone, to let it be and to become. One can love one's child that purely, letting him become what is in him to become. But—and this is the point of my argument—one can love the truth *in the same way*. One can love it enough to trust also its *becoming*. It is possible to love one's baby even before it is born, and to wait with bated breath and with great happiness to see what kind of person it will be, and now to love that future person.

A priori plans for the child, ambitions for it, prepared roles, even hopes that it will become this or that—all these are non-Taoistic. They represent demands upon the child that it become what the parent has already decided it *should* become. Such a baby is born into an invisible straitjacket.

Similarly, it is possible to love the truth yet to come, to trust it, to be happy and to marvel as its nature reveals itself. One can believe that the uncontaminated, unmanipulated, unforced, undemanded truth will be more beautiful, more pure, more *truly* true than that same truth would have been had we forced it to conform to a priori expectations or hopes or plans or current political needs. Truth also can be born into an "invisible straitjacket."

Normative zeal *can* be wrongly understood and *can* distort the truth-to-come by a priori demands, and I am afraid that some scientists do just this, in effect giving up science for politics. But this is not at all a necessity for the more Taoistic scientist who can love the truth-yet-to-be-born enough to assume that it will be for the best and, for this reason, will let-it-be, precisely for the sake of his normative zeal.

I too believe this: that the purer the truth, and the less contaminated it is by doctrinaires whose minds are made up in advance, the better it will be for the future of mankind. I trust that the world will be more bene-fited by the truth of the future than by the political convictions which I hold today. I trust what will be known more than I trust my present knowledge.

This is a humanistic-scientific version of "Not my will but Thine be done." My fears and hopes for mankind, my eagerness to do good, my desire for peace and brotherhood, my normative zeal—all these I feel are best served if I remain modestly open to the truth, objective and disinterested in the Taoistic sense of refusing to pre-judge the truth or to tamper with it, and if I continue to trust that the more I know the better helper I can become.

At many points in this book, and in many publications since, I have assumed that the actualization of a person's real potentialities is condi-tioned upon the presence of basic-need satisfying parents and other people, upon all those factors now called "ecological," upon the "health" of the culture, or the lack of it, upon the world situation, etc. Growth toward self-actualization and full-humanness is made possible by a com-plex hierarchy of "good preconditions." These physical, chemical, bio-logical, interpersonal, cultural conditions matter for the individual finally to the extent that they do or do not supply him with the basic human necessities and "rights" which permit him to become strong enough, and person enough, to take over his own fate.

As one studies these preconditions, one becomes saddened by the ease with which human potentiality can be destroyed or repressed, so that a fully-human person can seem like a miracle, so improbable a happening as to be awe-inspiring. And simultaneously one is heartened by the fact that self-actualizing persons do in fact exist, that they are therefore possible, that the gauntlet of dangers can be run, that the finish line can be crossed.

The investigator here is almost certain to be caught in a cross-fire of accusations both interpersonal and intrapsychic, about being either "optimistic" or "pessimistic," depending on where he is focusing at the moment. So also will he be accused from one side of being hereditarian, from the other of being environmentalist. Political groups will certainly try to plaster him with one or another label, depending on the headlines of the moment.

The scientist of course will resist these all-or-none tendencies to dichotomize and rubricize, and will continue to think in terms of degree, and to be holistically aware of many, many determinants acting simultaneously. He will try as hard as he can to be receptive to the data, differentiating them as clearly as he can from his wishes, hopes, and fears. It is now quite clear that these problems—what is the good person and what is the good society—fall well within the jurisdiction of empirical science, and that we may confidently hope to advance knowledge in these areas (316).

This book focuses much more on the first problem—the fully-human person, than on the second problem—what kind of society makes him possible. I have written a good deal on the subject since 1954 when this book first appeared, but have refrained from trying to incorporate these findings into this revised edition. Instead I will refer the reader to some of my writings on the subject (291, 301, 303, 311a, 311b, 312, 315) and also urge as strongly as I can the necessity of becoming acquainted with the rich research literature on normative social psychology (called variously Organizational Development, Organization Theory, Management Theory, etc.). The implications of these theories, case reports and researches seem to me to be profound, offering as they do a real alternative, for instance, to the various versions of Marxian theory, of democratic and authoritarian theories, and of other available social philosophies. I am again and again astonished that so few psychologists are even aware of the work of, for instance, Argyris (15, 16), Bennis (42, 43, 45), Likert (275), and McGregor (332), to mention only a few of the well-known workers in the field. In any case, anyone who wishes to take seriously the theory of self-actualization must also take seriously this new kind of social psychology. If I were to choose a single journal to recommend to the person who wishes to keep in touch with the current developments in this area, it would be the *Journal of Applied Behavioral Sciences,* in spite of its totally misleading title.

Finally, I wish to say a word about this book as a transition to humanistic psychology, or what has come to be called Third Force. Immature though it yet is from a scientific point of view, humanistic psychology has already opened the doors to study of all those psychological phenomena which can be called transcendent or transpersonal, data which were closed off in principle by the inherent philosophical limitations of behaviorism and Freudianism. Among such phenomena I include not only higher and more positive states of consciousness and of personality, i.e., transcending materialism, the skin-bounded ego, atomistic-splitting-divisive-adversary attitudes, etc., but also a conception of values (eternal verities) as part of a much enlarged self. Already a new *Journal of Transpersonal Psychology* has begun publishing on these subjects.

It is possible already to start *thinking* about the transhuman, a psychology and a philosophy which transcends the human species itself. This is yet to come.

A. H. M.

W. P. Laughlin Charitable Foundation

ACKNOWLEDGMENTS

I wish first to express my deep thanks to Bill Laughlin and the W. P. Laughlin Charitable Foundation for granting me a resident fellowship which gave me the time and freedom to do this revision. Theoretical work of this kind—thinking problems through to their depths—is a full-time job. Without this fellowship I would not have undertaken it. I wish also to acknowledge with thanks the fellowship granted to me for the year 1967–1968 by the Fund for the Advancement of Education of the Ford Foundation. I used this year to work out the theory of humanistic education.

Mrs. Kay Pontius did not only all the secretarial work that the book entailed but helped with the Bibliography, editing, proofreading, and many other jobs. This was all done efficiently, intelligently, and cheerfully. I wish to acknowledge her hard work and to thank her for it. I wish also to thank Mrs. Hilda Smith, my former secretary at Brandeis University, for her help in getting this work started before I left the university. Mrs. Marylyn Morrell generously helped with the Bibliography. George Middendorf of Harper & Row suggested to me this revised edition and now I am glad that he did.

I have acknowledged many of my intellectual debts in my other books, and in the Bibliography of this book, and will not repeat them here. I wish to thank the many friends—too many to mention—who helped me by listening, by conversations, and by debating. Thinking through theoretical problems can be much helped by trying them out on friends. My wife, Bertha, who got this kind of sounding board treatment every day, almost always managed to be patient and helpful. I wish here to thank her for her help and to marvel at her patience.

I

A PSYCHOLOGICAL APPROACH TO SCIENCE

A psychological interpretation of science begins with the acute realization that science is a human creation, rather than an autonomous, nonhuman, or *per se* "thing" with intrinsic rules of its own. Its origins are in human motives, its goal are human goals, and it is created, renewed, and maintained by human beings. Its laws, organization, and articulations rest not only on the nature of the reality that it discovers, but also on the nature of the human nature that does the discovering. The psychologist, especially if he has had any clinical experience, will quite naturally and spontaneously approach any subject matter in a personal way by studying people, rather than the abstractions they produce, scientists as well as science.

The misguided effort to make believe that this is not so, the persistent attempt to make science completely autonomous and self-regulating and to regard it as a disinterested game, having intrinsic, arbitrary chesslike rules, the psychologist must consider unrealistic, false, and even anti-empirical.

In this chapter, I wish first to spell out some of the more important truisms on which this thesis is based. Some implications and consequences of the thesis will then be presented.

1

THE PSYCHOLOGY OF SCIENTISTS

THE MOTIVES OF SCIENTISTS

Scientists are motivated, like all other members of the human species, by species-wide needs for food, etc.; by needs for safety, protection, and care; by needs for gregariousness and for affection-and-love relations; by needs for respect, standing, and status, with consequent self-respect; and by a need for self-actualization or self-fulfillment of the idiosyncratic and species-wide potentialities of the individual person. These are the needs that are best known to psychologists for the simple reason that their frustration produces psychopathology.

Less studied but knowable through common observation are the cognitive needs for sheer knowledge (curiosity) and for understanding (the philosophical, theological, value-system-building explanation need).

Finally, least well known are the impulses to beauty, symmetry, and possibly to simplicity, completion, and order, which we may call aesthetic needs, and the needs to express, to act out, and to motor completion that may be related to these aesthetic needs.

To date it seems as if all other needs or desires or drives are either means to the basic ends listed above, or are neurotic, or else are products of certain kinds of learning processes.

Obviously the cognitive needs are of most concern to the philosopher of science. It is man's persistent curiosity that is most responsible for science in its natural-history stage, and it is his equally persistent desire to understand, explain, and systematize that generates science in its more theoretical and abstract levels. However, it is this latter theoretical urge that is more specifically a *sine qua non* for science, for sheer curiosity is seen often enough in animals (172, 174).

But the other motives are certainly also involved in science at all its stages. It is too often overlooked that the original theorizers of science often thought of science primarily as a means to help the human race. Bacon (24), for instance, expected much amelioration of disease and poverty from science. It has been shown that even for Greek science where pure unmanual contemplation of the Platonic sort was a strong tradition, the practical and humanistic trend was also fairly strong. The feeling of identification and belongingness with people in general, and even more strongly the feeling of love for human beings may often be the primary motivation in many men of science. Some people go into science, as they might into social work or medicine, in order to help people.

And then finally we must recognize that any other human need may serve as a primary motivation for going into science, for working at it, or for staying in it. It may serve as a living, a source of prestige, a means of self-expression, or as a satisfaction for any one of many neurotic needs.

In most persons, a single primary all-important motive is less often found than a combination in varying amounts of *all* motivations working simultaneously. It is safest to assume that in any single scientist his work is motivated not only by love, but also by simple curiosity, not only by prestige, but also by the need to earn money, etc.

THE SYNERGIC NATURE OF RATIONALITY AND IMPULSE

In any case it is now quite clear that it is obsolete to dichotomize reason and animality, for reason is quite as animal as eating, at any rate in the human animal. Impulse is not necessarily in contrast with intelligent judgment, for intelligence is itself an impulse. In any case, it begins to appear more and more clearly that in the healthy human being, rationality and impulse are synergic, and strongly tend to come to similar conclusions rather than contrasting ones. The nonrational is not necessarily irrational or antirational; it is more often prorational. A chronic discrepancy or antagonism between conation and cognition is usually itself a product of social or individual pathology.

Man's need for love or for respect is quite as "sacred" as his need for the truth. "Pure" science has no more intrinsic virtue than "humanistic" science, nor has it any less. Human nature dictates both and they need not even be dichotomized. It is easily possible to have fun in science and at the same time to do good. The Greek respect for reason was not wrong but only too exclusive. Aristotle did not see that love is quite as human as reason.

The occasional instances in which there is temporary conflict between cognitive need gratification and emotional need gratificaton set us a problem of integration, coördination, and pacing, rather than of conflict and opposition. It *can* happen that the pure, objective, disinterested nonhumanistic curiosity of the pure scientist may jeopardize the gratification of other equally important human needs, e.g., safety. I refer here not only to the obvious atom bomb example but also to the more general fact that science itself implies a value system. After all, the limit to which the "pure" scientist approaches is not an Einstein or a Newton but rather the Nazi "scientist" of the concentration-camp experiments or the "mad" scientist of Hollywood. A fuller, more humanistic and transcendental definition of truth and science may be found in (66, 292, 376). Science for science's sake can be just as sick as art for art's sake.

THE PLURALISTIC NATURE OF SCIENCE

People seek for as many different satisfactions in scientific work as they do in their social lives, in their jobs, or in their marriages. There is something in science for all, old and young, bold and timid, duty-bound or fun loving. Some seek in it immediately humanistic ends; others delight precisely in its impersonal, nonhuman qualities. Some seek lawfulness primarily; others stress content and want to know more about "important" things even if less precisely and elegantly. Some like trail breaking and pioneering; others prefer the settler's work, the organizing, the tidying, and the policing of territory already won. Some seek safety in science; others adventure and excitement. No more than we can describe the ideal wife can we describe the ideal science or scientist, or method or question or activity or research. Just as we can approve of marriage in general and still leave individual choices to individual tastes, so also can we be pluralistic in science.

We can differentiate out in science at least the following functions:

1. Its problem-seeking, question-asking, hunch-encouraging, hypotheses-producing function
2. Its testing, checking, confirming and disconfirming, and verifying function; its trying out and testing of hypotheses; its repetition and checking of experiments; its piling up of facts; making facts more reliable
3. Its organizing, theorizing, structuring function; its search for larger and larger generalizations
4. Its history-collecting, scholarly function
5. Its technological side; instruments, methods, techniques
6. Its administrative, executive, and organizational side
7. Its publicizing and educational functions
8. Its applications to human uses
9. Its appreciation, enjoyment, celebration, and glorification

This multiplicity of function implies necessarily a division of labor, for few individuals could combine within themselves all these skills. Division of labor calls for different kinds of people, different tastes, different capacities and skills.

Tastes reflect and express character and personality. This is not less true for tastes in fields of science, e.g., physics vs. anthropology, than for areas within the field, e.g., ornithology vs. genetics. It is also true, though probably in a lower degree, for choice of particular problem within a field, e.g., retroactive inhibition vs. insight, as well as for choice of method, materials, degree of precision, degree of applicability or practicability, closeness to current human concerns, etc.

We all complement and need each other in science. If everyone preferred physics to biology, scientific advance would be impossible. It is fortunate that we have different tastes in scientific pursuits in the same way that it is fortunate that not all of us love the same climate or the same musical instrument. Because some like violins, and others like clarinets or drums, the orchestra becomes possible. So does science in its broadest sense become possible through differences in taste. Science *needs* all kinds of people (I say this rather than, "Science can *tolerate* all kinds of people") just as art does, or philosophy, or politics, since each person can ask different questions and see different worlds. Even the schizophrenic can be peculiarly useful, for his illness sensitizes him in certain special ways.

The monistic pressure is a real danger in science because of the fact that often "knowledge about the human species" really means only "knowledge about oneself." We are too prone to project our own tastes, prejudices, and hopes upon the universe. For instance, the physicist, the biologist, and the sociologist have already demonstrated that they are fundamentally different in important respects by their choice of field (401). We may quite reasonably expect them, because of this basic difference in taste, to have different definitions of science, of method, and of the goals and values of science. Clearly we need the same kind of tolerance and acceptance of individual differences among scientists as we do in other human realms.

SOME IMPLICATIONS OF A PSYCHOLOGICAL APPROACH TO SCIENCE

THE STUDY OF THE SCIENTIST

The study of scientists is clearly a basic, even necessary, aspect of the study of science. Since science as an institution is partly a magnified projection of certain aspects of human nature, any increment in the knowledge of these aspects will be automatically multiplied many times. For instance, every science and every theory within every science will be affected by improved knowledge of (1) the nature of bias and objectivity, (2) the nature of the abstracting process, (3) the nature of creativity, (4) the nature of enculturation and of the scientist's resistance to enculturation, (5) the contamination of perception by wishes, hopes, anxieties, expectations, (6) the nature of the scientist's role or status, (7) anti-intellectualism in our culture, (8) the nature of belief, conviction, faith, certainty, etc. Of course even more primary are the questions we have already mentioned, particularly about the motivations and aims of scientists (292, 458).

SCIENCE AND HUMAN VALUES

Science is based on human values and is itself a value system (66). Human emotional, cognitive, expressive, and aesthetic needs give science its origins and its goals. The gratification of any such need is a "value." This is true of the love of safety as it is of the love of truth, or of certainty. The aesthetic satisfactions of succinctness, parsimony, elegance, simplicity, precision, neatness, are values to the mathematician and to the scientist as they are to the craftsman, to the artist, or the philosopher.

These are quite apart from the fact that as scientists we share the basic values of our culture and probably will always have to, at least to some extent, e.g., honesty, humanitariansm, respect for the individual, social service, democratic respect for the right of the individual to make his own decisions even when mistaken, the preservation of life and health, the relief of pain, giving credit where credit is due, sharing credit, sportsmanship, "fairness," etc.

Clearly "objectivity" and "disinterested observations" are phrases that need redefining (292). "Excluding values" meant originally excluding theological and other authoritarian dogmas that prejudged the facts. This exclusion is quite as necessary today as it was at the time of the Renaissance because we still want our facts as uncontaminated as possible. If organized religion today is only a feeble threat to science in our country, we still have strong political and economic dogmas to contend with.

UNDERSTANDING VALUES

However, the only way we now know of preventing contamination of our perception of nature, of society, or of ourselves, by human values, is to be very conscious of these values at all times, to understand their influence on perception, and with the aid of such understanding to make the necessary corrections. (By contamination, I mean the confusion of psychic determinants with reality determinants, when it is the latter we seek to perceive.) The study of values, of needs and wishes, of bias, of fears, of interests, and of neurosis must become a basic aspect of all scientific studies.

Such a statement must include also the most generalized tendencies of all human beings to abstract, to classify, to see similarities and differences, and in general, to pay selective attention to reality and to shuffle and reshuffle it in accordance with human interests, needs, wishes, and fears. To organize our perceptions under various rubrics ("to rubricize") in this way is desirable and useful in some ways and is undesirable and harmful in other ways, for, while it throws some aspects of reality into sharp relief, it simultaneously throws other aspects of reality into shadow. We must understand that while nature gives us clues to classification, and that it sometimes has "natural" lines of cleavage, often these clues are only minimal or ambiguous. We must often create or impose a classification upon nature. This we do in accordance not only with nature's suggestions but also in accordance with our own human nature, our own unconscious values, biases, and interests. Granted that the ideal of science is to reduce to a minimum these human determinants of theory, this will never be achieved by denying their influence, but only by knowing them well.

It should reassure the uneasy pure scientist to know that the point of all this disquieting talk about values is to achieve more efficiently *his* goal, i.e., the improvement of our knowledge of nature, the decontamination of our knowledge of the known by study of the knower (376, 377).

HUMAN AND NONHUMAN LAWS

The laws of human psychology and of nonhuman nature are in some respects the same, but are in some respects utterly different. The fact that humans live in the natural world does not mean that their rules and laws need to be the same. The human being, living in the real world, certainly has to make concessions to it, but this in itself is not a denial of the fact that the human being has intrinsic laws, which are not those of natural reality. Wishes, fears, dreams, hopes, all behave differently from pebbles, wires, temperatures, or atoms. A philosophy is not constructed in the same way as a bridge. A family and a crystal must be studied in different ways. All our talk about motives and values does not imply a wish to subjectivize or psychologize nonhuman nature, but of course, we *must* psychologize *human* nature.

This nonhuman reality is independent of the wishes and needs of human beings, being neither beneficent nor malevolent, having no purposes, aims, goals, or functions (only living beings have purposes), no conative and no affective tendencies. This is the reality that would persist if all human beings disappeared—a not impossible happening.

To know this reality as it is rather than as we should like it to be, is desirable from *any* point of view, either of "pure," disinterested curiosity, or of concern for predicting and controlling reality for immediate human ends. Kant was certainly correct in claiming that we can never fully know nonhuman reality, yet it *is* possible to get closer to it, to know it more truly, or less truly.

THE SOCIOLOGY OF SCIENCE

The study of the sociology of science and of scientists deserves more attention than it is now getting. If scientists are determined in part by cultural variables, then so also are the products of these scientists. To what extent science needs the contribution of men of other cultures, to what extent the scientist must stand aloof from his culture in order to perceive more validly, to what extent he must be an internationalist rather than, e.g., an American, to what extent the products of scientists are determined by their class and caste affiliation—these are questions of the type that must be asked and answered for fuller understanding of the "contaminating" effect of culture upon perception of nature.

THE VARIOUS APPROACHES TO KNOWLEDGE OF REALITY

Science is only one means of access to knowledge of natural, social, and psychological reality. The creative artist, the philosopher, the literary humanist, or for that matter, the ditch digger, can also be the discoverer of truth, and should be encouraged as much as the scientist.[1] They should not be seen as mutually exclusive or even as necessarily separate from each other. The scientist who is also something of a poet, philosopher, and even a dreamer, is almost certainly an improvement on his more constricted colleagues.

If we are led by this psychological pluralism to think of science as an orchestation of diverse talents, motives, and interests, the line between the scientist and the nonscientist grows shadowy. The philosopher of science who occupies himself with criticism and analysis of the concepts of

---

[1] Perhaps the main differences today between the idealized artist and the idealized scientist can be phrased in the following way: the former is usually a specialist in knowledge or discovery of the idiographic (the unique, the idiosyncratic, the individual), whereas the latter is a specialist in the nomothetic (the generalized, the abstract). Second, the artist is closer to the scientist as problem discoverer, questioner, or hypothesizer than to the scientist as problem solver, checker, and certainty maker. These last functions are ordinarily the exclusive responsibility of the scientist. In this respect, he is more like the businessman, or the athlete, or the surgeon in being pragmatic and in dealing with what is verifiable, testable. There are results by which his claims can be judged. If he is supposed to be turning out bicycles, then one can count the bicycles. But the teacher, the artist, the professor, the therapist, the minister can make the same mistakes for forty years, achieve nothing, and still feel virtuous and effective. The classical example is the therapist who made the same mistake through his whole life time and then called it "rich clinical experience."

science is surely closer to the scientist who is also interested in pure theory than the latter is to the purely technological scientist. The dramatist or poet who presents an organized theory of human nature is certainly closer to the psychologist than the latter is to the engineer. The historian of science may be either a historian or a scientist, it does not matter which. The clinical psychologist or the physician who makes a careful study of the individual case may get more nutrition from the novelist than from his abstracting, experimenting brothers.

I see no way of sharply defining off scientists from nonscientists. One cannot even use as a criterion the pursuit of experimental research, because so many people who are down on the payrolls as scientists have never performed and never will perform a true experiment. The man who teaches chemistry in a junior college considers himself a chemist even though he has never discovered anything new in chemistry, but has simply read the chemical journals and repeated the experiments of others in a cookbook fashion. He may be less a scientist than a bright 12-year-old student who is systematically curious in his basement, or a skeptical housewife who checks on the doubtful claims of advertisers.

In what respect does the chairman of a research institute remain a scientist? His time may be completely occupied with administration and organizational work to the day he dies. Yet he will wish to call himself a scientist.

If the ideal scientist combines within himself the creative hypothesizer, the careful checker-experimenter, the philosopical system builder, the historical scholar, the technologist, the organizer, the educator-writer-publicist, the applier, and the appreciator, then we can easily conceive that the ideal team might be composed of at least nine individual specialists in these different functions, *no one of whom need himself be a scientist in the rounded sense*!

But while this makes the point that the scientist-nonscientist dichotomy is too simple, we must also take into account the general finding that he who overspecializes is usually not much good for anything in the long run, since he suffers as a whole human being. The generalized, rounded, and healthy person can do most things better than the generalized, crippled human being, i.e., the person who tries to be *too* pure a thinker by stifling his impulses and emotions paradoxically winds up being a sick man who can think only in a sick fashion, i.e., he becomes a bad thinker. In a word we may expect the scientist who is also a bit of an artist to be a better scientist than his colleague who is not also a bit of an artist.

If we use the case-history method, this becomes very clear. Our great scientific figures ordinarily have had extensive interests and certainly have not been narrow technologists. From Aristotle to Einstein, from Leonardo to Freud, the great discoverer has been versatile and many-sided, with humanistic, philosophical, social, and aesthetic interests.

We must conclude that a psychological pluralism in science teaches us that there are many paths to knowledge and truth, that the creative artist, the philosopher, the literary humanist, either as individuals or as aspects within the single individual, can also be discoverers of truth.

PSYCHOPATHOLOGY AND THE SCIENTIST

All other things being equal, we may expect the scientist (or artist, or machinist, or executive) who is happy, secure, serene, and healthy to be a better scientist (or artist, or machinist, or executive) than if he were unhappy, insecure, troubled, and unhealthy. The neurotic person distorts reality, makes demands upon it, imposes premature conceptualizations upon it, is afraid of the unknown and of novelty, is too much determined by his intrapersonal needs to be a good reporter of reality, is too easily frightened, is too eager for other people's approval, etc.

There are at least three implications of this fact. First of all the scientist (or better, truth seeker in general) ought to be psychologically healthy rather than unhealthy to do his best work. Secondly, it may be expected that as a culture improves, thereby improving the health of all its citizens, truth seeking should improve, and third, we should expect that psychotherapy would improve the individual scientist in his individual function.

We already acknowledge as a fact that better social conditions tend to help the searcher for knowledge by our pressure for academic freedom, tenure, better salaries, etc.[2]

---

[2] For those readers who recognize that this is a revolutionary statement, and who feel the obligation to read further, I would urge struggling through *the* great book in the field, *Personal Knowledge* by Michael Polanyi (376). If you have not studied this book, you dare not consider yourself prepared for the next century. If you don't have the time, the will, or the strength for this giant of a book, then I recommend my *Psychology of Science: A Reconnaissance* (292), which has the virtue of being short and readable while making similar points. This chapter, these two books, and the other books touted in their bibliographies represent well enough the new humanistic *Zeitgeist* as it is reflected in the field of science.

2

PROBLEM CENTERING VS. MEANS CENTERING IN SCIENCE

Through the last decade or two, more and more attention has been given to the shortcomings and sins of "official" science. With the one major exception of Lynd's brilliant analysis (282), discussion of the sources of these failings has, however, been neglected. This chapter will attempt to show that many of the weaknesses of orthodox science and particularly of psychology are consequences of a means- or technique-centered approach to the defining of science.

By means centering, I refer to the tendency to consider that the essence of science lies in its instruments, techniques, procedures, apparatus, and its methods rather than in its problems, questions, functions, or goals. In its unsophisticated form, means centering confuses scientists with engineers, physicians, dentists, laboratory technicians, glass blowers, urinanalysts, machine tenders, etc. Means centering at the highest intellectual levels usually takes the form of making synonyms of science and scientific method.

OVERSTRESS ON TECHNIQUE

Inevitable stress on elegance, polish, technique, and apparatus has as a frequent consequence a playing down of meaningfulness, vitality, and significance of the problem and of creativeness in general. Almost any candidate for the Ph.D. in psychology will understand what this means

11

in practice. A methodologically satisfactory experiment, whether trivial or not, is rarely criticized. A bold, ground-breaking problem, because it may be a "failure," is too often criticized to death before it is ever begun. Indeed criticism in the scientific literature seems usually to mean only criticism of method, technique, logic, etc. I do not recall seeing, in the literature with which I am familiar, any paper that criticized another paper for being unimportant, trivial, or inconsequential.[1]

The tendency is growing therefore to say that the dissertation problem itself does not matter—only so it be well done. In a word, it need no longer be a contribution to knowledge. The Ph.D. candidate is required to know the techniques of his field and the already accumulated data in it. It is not usually stressed that good research ideas are also desirable. As a consequence it is possible for completely and obviously uncreative people to become "scientists."

At a lower level—in the teaching of science in the high school and college—similar results can be seen. The student is encouraged to identify science with directed manipulations of apparatus, and with rote procedures learned out of a cook book—in a word, following other people's leads and repeating what other people have already discovered. Nowhere is he taught that a scientist is different from a technician or from a reader of books about science.

It is easy to misunderstand the point of these contentions. I do not wish to underplay method; I wish only to point out that even in science, means may easily be confused with ends. It is only the goals or ends of science that dignify and validate its methods. The working scientist must, of course, be concerned with his techniques, but only because they can help him achieve his proper ends, i.e., the answering of important questions. Once he forgets this, be becomes like the man spoken of by Freud who spent all his time polishing his glasses instead of putting them on and seeing with them.

Means centering tends to push into a commanding position in sci-

---

[1] "But even the scholars were likely to work most at big monographs on little subjects. Original research they called it. What mattered was that the facts that they found had not been known before, not that they were worth knowing. Some oher specialist might sooner or later make use of them. The specialists in all the universities wrote for one another, with the patience of mound builders, for mysterious ends." (Van Doren, C., *Three Worlds*, Harper & Row, 1936, p. 107.)

"Or they sit all day at swamps with anglerods and, on that account, think themselves profound, but whoever fishes where there are no fish I do not even call him superficial." (Nietzsche, F., *Thus Spake Zarathustra*, Modern Library, 1937, p. 117.)

A "sportsman" is a man who sits and *watches* athletes.

ence the technicians, and the "apparatus men," rather than the "question askers" and the problem solvers.* Without wishing to create an extreme and unreal dichotomy, it is still possible to point out a difference between those who know only *how* to do and those who also know *what* to do. These former individuals, of whom there are always a large number, tend inevitably to become a class of priests in science, authorities on protocol, on procedure, and, so to speak, on ritual and ceremonial. While such people have been no more than a nuisance in the past, now that science becomes a matter of national and international policy, they may become an active danger. This trend is doubly dangerous because laymen understand manipulators far more easily than they do creators and theorists.

Means centering tends strongly to overvalue quantification indiscriminately and as an end in itself. This must be true because of the greater stress of means-centered science on *how* statements are made rather than on what is said. Elegance and precision are then counterposed to pertinence and breadth of implication.

Means-centered scientists tend, in spite of themselves, to fit their problems to their techniques rather than the contrary. Their beginning question tends to be Which problems can I attack with the techniques and equipment I now possess? rather than what it should more often be, Which are the most pressing, the most crucial problems I could spend my time on? How else explain the fact that most run-of-the-mill scientists spend their life-times in a small area whose boundaries are defined, not by a basic question about the world, but by the limits of a piece of apparatus or of a technique?[2] In psychology, few people see any humor in the concept of an "animal psychologist" or a "statistical psychologist," i.e., individuals who do not mind working with *any* problem so long as they can use, respectively, their animals or their statistics. Ultimately this must remind us of the famous drunk who looked for his wallet, not where he had lost it, but under the street lamp, "because the light is better there," or of the doctor who gave all his patients fits because that was the only sickness he knew how to cure.

Means centering tends strongly to create a hierarchy of sciences, in which, quite perniciously, physics is considered to be more "scientific" than biology, biology than psychology, and psychology than sociology. Such an assumption of hierarchy is possible only on the basis of elegance, success, and precision of technique. From the point of view of a problem-

2 "We tend to do the things that we know how to do, instead of trying to do the things that we ought to do." (Anshen, R., ed., *Science and Man*, Harcourt, Brace & World, 1942, p. 466.)

centered science, such a hierarchy would never be suggested, for who could maintain that questions about unemployment, or race prejudice, or love are, in any intrinsic way, less important than questions about stars, or sodium, or kidney function?

Means centering tends to compartmentalize the sciences too strongly, to build walls between them that divide them into separate territories. Jacques Loeb, when asked whether he was a neurologist, a chemist, a physicist, a psychologist, or a philosopher, answered only, "I solve problems." Certainly this ought to be a more usual answer. And it would be well for science if it had more men like Loeb. But these desiderata are clearly discouraged by the philosophy that makes the scientist into a technician and an expert rather than a venturesome truth seeker, into one who *knows* rather than one who is *puzzled*.

If scientists looked on themselves as question askers and problem solvers rather than specialized technicians, there would now be something of a rush to the newest scientific frontier, to the psychological and social problems about which we know least and should know most. Why is it that there is so little traffic across these departmental borders? How does it happen that a hundred scientists prosecute physical or chemical research for every dozen who pursue the psychological problems? Which would be better for mankind, to put a thousand fine minds to producing better bombs (or even better penicillin) or to set them to work on the problems of nationalism or psychotherapy or exploitation?

Means centering in science creates too great a cleavage between scientists and other truth seekers, and between their various methods of searching after truth and understanding. If we define science as a search for truth, insight, and understanding, and as a concern with important questions, we must be hard put to it to differentiate between the scientists on the one hand, and the poets, artists, and philosophers on the other hand.[3] Their avowed problems may be the same. Ultimately, of course, a semantically honest differentiation should be made, and it must be admitted that it would have to be mostly on the basis of difference in method and in techniques of guarding against mistakes. And yet it would clearly be better for science if this gap between the scientist and the poet and the philosopher were less abysmal than it is today. Means centering simply puts them into different realms; problem centering would conceive of them as mutually helpful collaborators. The biographies of most great

3 "You must love the questions themselves"—Rilke.

"We have learned all the answers, all the answers:
It is the questions that we do not know."—A. MacLeish, *The Hamlet of A. MacLeish*, Houghton Mifflin.

scientists show that the latter is more nearly true than the former. Many of the greatest scientists have themselves been also artists and philosophers, and have often derived as much sustenance from philosophers as from their scientific colleagues.

MEANS CENTERING AND SCIENTIFIC ORTHODOXY

Means centering tends inevitably to bring into being a scientific orthodoxy, which in turn creates a heterodoxy. Questions and problems in science can rarely be formulated, classified, or put into a filing system. The question of the past are no longer questions, but answers. The questions of the future have not yet come into existence. But it *is* possible to formulate and classify the methods and techniques of the past. These then are termed the "laws of scientific method." Canonized, crusted about with tradition, loyalty, and history, they tend to become binding upon the present day (rather than merely suggestive or helpful). In the hands of the less creative, the timid, the conventional, these "laws" become virtually a demand that we solve our present problems *only* as our forefathers solved theirs.

Such an attitude is especially dangerous for the psychological and social sciences. Here the injunction to be truly scientific is usually translated as: Use the techniques of the physical and life sciences. Hence we have the tendency among many psychologists and social scientists to imitate old techniques rather than to create and invent the new ones made necessary by the fact that their degree of development, their problems, and their data are intrinsically different from those of the physical sciences. Tradition in science can be a dangerous blessing. Loyalty is an unqualified peril.

DANGERS OF SCIENTIFIC ORTHODOXY

One main danger of scientific orthodoxy is that it tends to block the development of new techniques. If the laws of scientific method have already been formulated, it remains only to apply them. New methods, new ways of doing things, must inevitably be suspect, and have usually been greeted with hostility, e.g., psychoanalysis, Gestalt psychology, Rorschach testing. The expectation of such hostility probably is partly to blame for the fact that there have not yet been invented the relational, holistic, and syndrome logics, statistics, and mathematics demanded by the new psychological and social sciences.

Ordinarily, the advance of science is a collaborative product. How else could limited individuals make important, even great, discoveries? When there is no collaboration, the advance is apt to stop dead until there shows up some giant who needs no help. Orthodoxy means the denial of help to the heterodox. Since few (of the heterodox, as well as of the orthodox) are geniuses, this implies continuous, smooth advance only for orthodox science. We may expect heterodox ideas to be held up for long periods of weary neglect or opposition, to break through rather suddenly (if they are correct), and then to become in turn orthodox.

Another, probably more important, danger of the orthodoxy fostered by means centering is that it tends to limit more and more the jurisdiction of science. Not only does it block the development of new techniques; it also tends to block the asking of many questions, on grounds that the reader might well expect by now, that such questions cannot be answered by currently available techniques, e.g., questions about the subjective, questions about values, questions about religion. It is only such foolish grounds that make possible that unnecessary confession of defeat, that contradiction in terms, the concept of the "unscientific problem," as if there were *any* question that we dared not ask, and try to answer. Surely, anyone who had read and understood the history of science would not dare to speak of an *unsolvable* problem; he would speak only of problems which had not yet been solved. Phrased in this latter way, we have a clear incentive to action, to further exercise of ingenuity and inventiveness. Phrased in terms of current scientific orthodoxy, i.e., What can we do with scientific method (as we know it)? we are encouraged to the opposite, i.e., to voluntarily imposed self-limitations, to abdication from huge areas of human interest. This tendency can go to the most incredible and dangerous extremes. It has even happened in recent discussions of congressional efforts to set up national research foundations, that some physicists suggested the exclusion from its benefits of all the psychological and social sciences on the grounds that they were not "scientific" enough. On what possible basis could this statement have been made if not an exclusive respect for polished and successful techniques, and a complete lack of awareness of the question-asking nature of science and its rooting in human values and motives? How shall I as a psychologist translate this and other similar jibes from my physicist friends? Ought I to use their techniques? But these are useless for my problems. How would that get the psychological problems solved? Ought they not be solved? Or ought scientists to abdicate from the field completely and give it back to the theologians? Or is there perhaps an *ad hominem* sneer? Is it implied that the psychologists are stupid and the physicists intelligent? But on what grounds can such an inherently improbable statement be made? Impressions? Then I must report *my* impression that there are as many fools in any one scientific group as in any other. Which impression is more valid?

I am afraid that I can see no other possible explanation except one that covertly gives the primary place to technique—perhaps the only place.

Means-centered orthodoxy encourages scientists to be "safe and sound" rather than bold and daring. It makes the normal business of the scientist seem to be moving ahead inch by inch on the well-laid-out road rather than cutting new paths through the unknown. It forces conservative rather than radical approaches to the not-yet-known. It tends to make him into a settler rather than a pioneer.[4]

The proper place for the scientist—once in a while at least—is in the midst of the unknown, the chaotic, the dimly seen, the unmanageable, the mysterious, the not-yet-well-phrased. This is where a problem-oriented science would have him be as often as necessary. And this is where he is discouraged from going by a means-stressing approach to science.

Overstress on methods and techniques encourages scientists to think (1) that they are more objective and less subjective than they actually are, and (2) that they need not concern themselves with values. Methods are ethically neutral; problems and questions may not be, for sooner or later, they involve all the knotty arguments about values. One way of avoiding the problem of values is to stress the techniques of science rather than the goals of science. Indeed, it seems probable that one of the main roots of the means-centered orientation in science is the strenuous effort to be as objective (nonvalued) as possible.

But as we have seen in Chapter 1, science was not, is not, and cannot be completely objective, which is to say, independent of human values. Furthermore, it is highly debatable whether it ought even to *try* to be (that is, *completely* objective rather than as objective as it is possible for human beings to be). All the mistakes listed in this chapter and in the previous one attest to the dangers of attempting to neglect the shortcomings of human nature. Not only does the neurotic pay a huge subjective price for his vain attempt, but ironically enough, he also becomes progressively a poorer and poorer thinker.

Because of this fancied independence of values, standards of worth

---

[4] "Geniuses are panzer-spearheads; their lightning advance into no-man's-land necessarily leaves their flanks unprotected." (Koestler, A., *The Yogi and the Commissar*, Macmillan, 1945, p. 241.)

become steadily more blurred. If means-centering philosophies were extreme (which they rarely are), and if they were quite consistent (which they dare not be for fear of obviously foolish consequences), there would be no way to distinguish between an important experiment and an unimportant one. There could be only technically well-prosecuted experiments and technically poorly prosecuted experiments.[5] Using only methodological criteria, the most trivial research could demand as much respect as the most fruitful one. Of course, this does not actually happen in an extreme way, but this is only because of appeal to criteria and standards other than methodological ones. However, although this mistake is rarely seen in a blatant form, it *is* often enough seen in a less obvious form. The journals of science are full of instances that illustrate the point, that what is not worth doing, is not worth doing well.

If science were no more than a set of rules and procedures, what difference would there be between science on the one hand, and on the other, chess, alchemy, "umbrellaology," or the practice of dentistry?[6]

[5] "A scientist is called 'great' not so much because he has solved a problem as because he has posed a problem the solution of which . . . will make for real progress." (Cantril, H., An inquiry concerning the characteristics of man, *J. abnorm. social Psychol.,* 1950, *45,* 491–503.)

"The formulation of a problem is far more often essential than its solution, which may be merely a matter of mathematical or experimental skill. To raise new questions, new possibilities, to regard old problems from a new angle requires creative imagination and marks real advance in science." (Einstein, A., and Infeld, L., *The Evolution of Physics,* Simon and Schuster, 1938.)

[6] Sir Richard Livingstone, of Corpus Christi College, Oxford, has defined a technician as "a man who understands everything about his job except its ultimate purpose and its place in the order of the universe." Someone else, in similar vein, has defined an expert as a person who avoids all the small errors as he sweeps on to the grand fallacy.

3

PREFACE TO MOTIVATION THEORY

In this chapter are presented sixteen propositions about motivation that must be incorporated into any sound motivation theory. Some of these propositions are so true as to be platitudinous. These I feel need re-emphasis. Others may be found less acceptable and more debatable.

THE INDIVIDUAL AS AN INTEGRATED WHOLE

Our first proposition states that the individual is an integrated, organized whole. This theoretical statement is usually accepted piously enough by psychologists, who then often proceed calmly to ignore it in their actual experiments. That it is an experimental reality as well as a theoretical one must be realized before sound experimentation and sound motivation theory are possible. In motivation theory this proposition means many specific things. For instance, it means the whole individual is motivated rather than just a part of him. In good theory there is no such entity as a need of the stomach or mouth, or a genital need. There is only a need of the individual. It is John Smith who wants food, not John Smith's stomach. Furthermore satisfaction comes to the whole individual and not just to a part of him. Food satisfies John Smith's hunger and not his stomach's hunger.

Dealing with John Smith's hunger as a function merely of his gastrointestinal tract has made experimenters neglect the fact that when an individual is hungry he changes not only in his gastrointestinal function, but in many, perhaps even in most other functions of which he is capable. His perceptions change (he will perceive food more readily than he will at other times). His memories change (he is more apt to remember a good meal at this time than at other times). His emotions change (he is more tense and nervous than he is at other times). The content of his thinking changes (he is more apt to think of getting food than of solving an algebraic problem). And this list can be extended to almost every other faculty, capacity, or function, both physiological and psychic. In other words, when John Smith is hungry, he is hungry all over; he is different as an individual from what he is at other times.

HUNGER AS PARADIGM

The choice of hunger as a paradigm for all other motivation states is both theoretically and practically unwise and unsound. It can be seen upon closer analysis that the hunger drive is more a special case of motivation than a general one. It is more isolated (using this word as used by the Gestalt and Goldsteinian psychologists) than other motivations; it is less common than other motivations; and finally, it is different from other motivations in that it has a known somatic base, which is unusual for motivational states. What are the more common immediate motivations? We can find these easily enough by introspecting during the course of an average day. The desires that flit through consciousness are most often desires for clothes, automobiles, friendliness, company, praise, prestige, and the like. Customarily these have been phrased as secondary or cultural drives and have been regarded as of a different order from the truly "respectable" or primary drives, i.e., the physiological needs. In actuality these are far more important for us and they are far more common. It would therefore be well to make one of them paradigm rather than the hunger drive.

The common assumption has been that all drives will follow the example set by the physiological drives. It is fair to predict now that this will never be. Most drives are not isolable, nor can they be localized somatically, nor can they be considered as if they were the only things happening in the organism at the time. The typical drive or need or desire is not and probably never will be related to a specific, isolated, localized somatic base. The typical desire is much more obviously a need of the whole person. It would be far better to take as a model for research such a drive, let us say, as the desire for money rather than the sheer hunger drive, or even better, rather than any partial goal, a more fundamental one, like the desire for love. Considering all the evidence now in hand, it is probably true that we could never understand fully the need for love no matter how much we might know about the hunger drive. Indeed a stronger statement is possible, namely, that from a full knowledge of the need for love we can learn more about general human motivation (including the hunger drive) than we could from a thorough study of the hunger drive.

It is well in this connection to recall the critical analysis of the concept of simplicity that has been made so often by the Gestalt psychologists. The hunger drive, which seems simple when compared with the drive of love, is actually not so simple in the long run (160). The appearance of simplicity can be obtained by selecting isolated cases, activities that are relatively independent of the wholeness of the organism. An important activity can easily be shown to have dynamic relationships with almost everything else of importance in the person. Why then take an activity that is not at all average in this sense, an activity that is selected out for special attention only because it is easier to deal with by our customary (but not necessarily correct) experimental technique of isolation, reduction, or of independence from other activities? If we are faced with the choice of dealing with either (1) experimentally simple problems that are however trivial or invalid, or (2) experimental problems that are fearfully difficult but important, we should certainly not hesitate to choose the latter.

MEANS AND ENDS

If we examine carefully the average desires that we have in daily life, we find that they have at least one important characteristic, i.e., that they are usually means to an end rather than ends in themselves. We want money so that we may have an automobile. In turn we want an automobile because the neighbors have one and we do not wish to feel inferior to them, so that we can retain our own self-respect and so that we can be loved and respected by others. Usually when a conscious desire is analyzed we find that we can go behind it, so to speak, to other, more fundamental aims of the individual. In other words, we have here a situation that parallels very much the role of symptoms in psychopathology. The symptoms are important, not so much in themselves, but for what they ultimately mean, that is, for what their ultimate goals or effects may be. The study of symptoms in themselves is quite unimportant, but the study of the dynamic meaning of symptoms is important because it is fruitful—for instance, making possible psychotherapy. The particular desires that pass through our consciousness dozens of times a day are not in themselves so important as what they stand for, where they lead, what they ultimately mean upon deeper analysis.

It is characteristic of this deeper analysis that it will always lead ultimately to certain goals or needs behind which we cannot go; that is, to certain need-satisfactions that seem to be ends in themselves and seem not to need any further justification or demonstration. These needs have the particular quality in the average person of not being seen directly very often but of being more often a kind of conceptual derivation from the multiplicity of specific conscious desires. In other words then, the study of motivation must be in part the study of the ultimate human goals or desires or needs.

These facts imply another necessity for sound motivation theory. Since these goals are not often seen directly in consciousness, we are at once forced into the necessity of dealing with the whole problem of unconscious motivation. Careful study of the conscious motivational life alone will often leave out much that is as important as or even more important than what can be seen in consciousness. Psychoanalysis has often demonstrated that the relationship between a conscious desire and the ultimate unconscious aim that underlies it need not be at all direct. Indeed the relationship may actually be a negative one, as in reaction formations. We may then assert that sound motivation theory cannot possibly afford to neglect the unconscious life.

DESIRE AND CULTURE

There is now sufficient anthropological evidence to indicate that the fundamental or ultimate desires of all human beings do not differ nearly as much as do their conscious everyday desires. The main reason for this is that two different cultures may provide two completely different ways of satisfying a particular desire, let us say, for self-esteem. In one society, one obtains self-esteem by being a good hunter; in another society by being a great medicine man or a bold warrior, or a very unemotional person and so on. It may then be that, if we think of ultimates, the one individual's desire to be a good hunter has the same dynamics and the same fundamental aim as the desire of the other individual to be a good medicine man. We may then assert that it would be more useful for psychologists to combine these two seemingly disparate conscious desires into the same category rather than to put them into different categories on purely behavioral grounds. Apparently ends in themselves are far more universal than the roads taken to achieve those ends, for these roads are determined locally in the specific culture. Human beings are more alike than one would think at first.

MULTIPLE MOTIVATIONS

We have learned from the study of psychopathology that a conscious desire or a motivated behavior has another peculiarity that is allied to the one we have just discussed, viz., that it may serve as a kind of channel through which other purposes may express themselves. There are several ways of showing this. For instance, it is well known that sexual behavior and conscious sexual desires may be tremendously complex in their underlying, unconscious purposes. In one individual sexual desire may actually mean the desire to assure himself of his masculinity. It may in other individuals represent fundamentally a desire to impress, or a desire for closeness, friendliness, for safety, for love or for any combination of these. Consciously the sexual desire in all these individuals may have the same content, and probably all of them would make the mistake of thinking that they seek only sexual gratification. But we now know that this is not correct, that it is useful in understanding these individuals to deal with what the sexual desire and behavior represent fundamentally rather than what the individual consciously thinks they represent. (This holds true for either preparatory or consummatory behavior.)

Another line of evidence supporting this same point is the finding that a single psychopathological symptom may represent at one and the same time several different, even opposing desires. A hysterically paralyzed arm may represent the fulfillment of simultaneous wishes for revenge, for pity, for love, and for respect. To take either the conscious wish in the first example or the overt symptom in the second in a purely behavioral fashion means that we arbitrarily throw out the possibility of a total understanding of the behavior and of the motivational state of the individual. Let us emphasize that it is unusual, *not* usual, that an act or a conscious wish have but one motivation.

MOTIVATING STATES

In a certain sense almost any organismic state of affairs whatsoever is in itself also a motivating state. If we say that a person feels rejected, what do we mean? A static psychology would be content to put a period to this statement. But a dynamic psychology would imply very many more things by this statement with full empirical justification. Such a feeling has repercussions throughout the whole organism both in its somatic and psychic aspects. For instance, it means also tension and strain and un-happiness. Furthermore, quite apart from the current relationships with the rest of the organism, such a state of affairs automatically and of necessity leads to many other happenings, e.g., compulsive desires to win back affection, defensive efforts of various kinds, piling up of hostility, etc.

It is clear then that we will explain the state of affairs implied in the statement, "This person feels rejected," only if we add many, many more statements about what happens to him because he feels rejected. In other words, the feeling of rejection is itself a motivating state. Current conceptions of motivation proceed ordinarily, or at least seem to pro-ceed, on the assumption that a motivational state is a special, a peculiar state, sharply marked off from the other happenings in the organism. Sound motivational theory should, on the contrary, assume that motiva-tion is constant, never ending, fluctuating, and complex, and that it is an almost universal characteristic of practically every organismic state of affairs.

RELATIONSHIPS OF MOTIVATIONS

Man is a wanting animal and rarely reaches a state of complete satis-faction except for a short time. As one desire is satisfied, another pops up to take its place. When this is satisfied, still another comes into the foreground, etc. It is a characteristic of the human being throughout his whole life that he is practically always desiring something. We are faced then with the necessity for studying the relationships of all the motiva-tions to each other and we are concomitantly faced with the necessity of giving up the motivational units in isolation if we are to achieve the broad understanding that we seek for. The appearance of the drive or desire, the actions that it arouses, and the satisfaction that comes from attaining the goal object, all taken together, give us only an artificial, isolated, single instance taken out of the total complex of the motiva-tional unit. This appearance practically always depends on the state of satisfaction or dissatisfaction of all other motivations that the total or-ganism may have, i.e., on the fact that such and such other prepotent desires have attained states of relative satisfaction. Wanting anything in itself implies already existing satisfactions of other wants. We should never have the desire to compose music or create mathematical systems, or to adorn our homes, or to be well dressed if our stomachs were empty most of the time, or if we were continually dying of thirst, or if we were continually threatened by an always impending catastrophe, or if every-one hated us.

Proper respect has never been paid by the constructors of motivation theories to either of these facts: first, that the human being is never satisfied except in a relative or one-step-along-the-path fashion, and second, that wants seem to arrange themselves in some sort of hierarchy of prepotency.

LIST OF DRIVES

We should give up the attempt once and for all to make atomistic lists of drives or needs. For several different reasons such lists are theoretically unsound. First of all they imply an equality of the various drives that are listed, an equality of potency and probability of appearance. This is incorrect because the probability of any one desire emerging into consciousness depends on the state of satisfaction or dissatisfaction of other prepotent desires. There are great differences in probability of appearance of the various particular drives.

Secondly such a listing implies an isolatedness of each of these drives from each of the others. Of course they are not isolated in any such fashion.

Third, such a listing of drives, since it is usually made on the behavioral basis, neglects completely all that we know about the dynamic nature of drives, e.g., that their conscious and unconscious aspects may be different, that a particular desire may actually be a channel through which several other desires express themselves, etc.

Such listings are foolish also because drives do not range themselves in an arithmetical sum of isolated, discrete members. They arrange themselves rather in a hierarchy of specificity. What is meant by this is that the number of drives one chooses to list depends entirely on the degree of specificity with which one chooses to analyze them. The true picture is not one of a great many sticks lying side by side, but rather of a nest of boxes in which one box contains three others, and in which each of these three contains ten others, and in which each of these ten contains fifty others, and so on. Or another analogy might be that of a description of a histological section under various degrees of magnification. Thus we can speak of a need for gratification or equilibrium; or more specifically of a need to eat; or still more specifically of a need to fill the the stomach; or still more specifically of a desire for proteins; or still more specifically of a desire for a particular protein; and so on. Too many of the listings that we now have available have combined indiscriminately needs at various levels of magnification. With such a confusion it is understandable that some lists should contain three or four needs and others contain hundreds of needs. If we wished, we could have such a list of drives contain anywhere from one to one million drives, depending entirely on the specificity of analysis. Furthermore, it should be recognized that if we attempt to discuss the fundamental desires they should be clearly understood as sets of desires, as fundamental categories or *collections* of desires. In other words, such an enumeration of fundamental goals would be an abstract classification rather than a cataloguing list (12).

Furthermore, all the lists of drives that have ever been published seem to imply mutual exclusiveness among the various drives. But there is not mutual exclusiveness. There is usually such an overlapping that it is almost impossible to separate quite clearly and sharply any one drive from any other. It should also be pointed out in any critique of drive theory that the very concept of drive itself probably emerges from a preoccupation with the physiological needs. It is very easy in dealing with these needs to separate the instigation, the motivated behavior, and the goal object. But it is not easy to distinguish the drive from the goal object when we talk of a desire for love. Here the drive, the desire, the goal object, the activity seem all to be the same thing.

CLASSIFICATION OF MOTIVATIONAL LIFE

The weight of evidence now available seems to me to indicate that the only sound and fundamental basis on which any classification of motivational life may be constructed is that of the fundamental goals or needs, rather than on any listing of drives in the ordinary sense of instigation (the "pulls" rather than the "pushes"). It is only the fundamental goals that remain constant through all the flux that a dynamic approach forces upon psychological theorizing. Considerations that we have already discussed should support this statement without much further proof. Certainly motivated behavior is not a good basis for classification, since we have seen that it may express many things. The specific goal object is not a good basis for classification for the same reason. A human being having a desire for food, then behaving in the proper fashion to get it and then chewing and eating it may actually be seeking safety rather than food. An individual going through the whole process of sexual desire, courting behavior, and consummatory love making may actually be seeking self-esteem rather than sexual gratification. The drive as it appears introspectively in consciousness, the motivated behavior, and even the explicitly apparent goal objects or effects sought for are none of them a sound foundation on which to base a dynamic classification of the motivational life of the human being. If only by the process of logical exclusion alone we are finally left with the largely unconscious fundamental goals or needs as the only sound foundations for classification in motivation theory.[1]

MOTIVATION AND ANIMAL DATA

Academic psychologists have relied largely on animal experimentation in working in the field of motivation. It is a truism to say that a white rat is not a human being, but unfortunately it is necessary to say it again, since too often the results of animal experiments are considered the basic data on which we must base our theorizing of human nature.[2] Animal data certainly can be of great use, but only when they are used cautiously and wisely.

There are certain further considerations that are pertinent to my contention that motivation theory must be anthropocentric rather than animalcentric. First let us discuss the concept of instinct, which we can define rigidly as a motivational unit in which the drive, motivated behavior, and the goal object or the goal effect are all appreciably determined by heredity. As we go up the phyletic scale there is a steady trend toward disappearance of the instincts so defined. For instance, in the white rat it is fair to say that, by our definition, there are found the hunger instinct, the sex instinct, the maternal instinct. In the monkey the sexual instinct has definitely disappeared, the hunger instinct has clearly been modified in various ways, and only the maternal instinct is undoubtedly present. In the human being, by our definition, they have all three disappeared, leaving in their place conglomerations of hereditary reflexes, hereditary drives, autogenous learning, and cultural learning in the motivated behavior and in the choice of goal objects (see Chapter 6). Thus if we examine the sexual life of the human being we find that sheer drive itself is given by heredity but that the choice of object and the choice of behavior must be acquired or learned in the course of the life history.

[1] See *Explorations in Personality* by Murray and others for fuller discussion of some of these points (346).

[2] For instance P. T. Young (492) arbitrarily excluded the concept of purpose or goal from motivation theory because we cannot ask a rat for his purpose: Is it necessary to point out that we *can* ask a human being for his purpose? Instead of rejecting purpose or goal as a concept because we cannot ask the rat about it, it would seem much more sensible to reject the rat because we cannot ask him about his purpose.

As we go up the phyletic scale appetites become more and more important and hungers less and less important. That is to say there is much less variability, for instance, in the choice of food in the white rat than there is in the monkey, and there is less variability in the monkey than there is in the human being (302).

Finally as we go up the phyletic scale and as the instincts drop away there is more and more dependence on the culture as an adaptive tool. If then we have to use animal data let us realize these facts, and for instance, let us prefer the monkey to the white rat as a subject for motivation experiments if only for the simple reason that we human beings are much more like monkeys than we are like white rats. Harlow and many other primatologists have amply demonstrated (172, 202).

ENVIRONMENT

So far I have spoken only of the nature of the organism itself. It is now necessary to say at least a word about the situation or environment in which the organism finds itself. We must certainly grant at once that human motivation rarely actualizes itself in behavior except in relation to the situation and to other people. Any theory of motivation must of course take account of this fact, including not only in the environment but also in the organism itself, the role of cultural determination.

Once this is granted it remains to caution the theorizer against too great preoccupation with the exterior, with the culture, the environment, or the situation. Our central object of study here is, after all, the organism or the character structure. It is easy to go to the extreme in situation theory of making the organism just one additional object in the field, equivalent with perhaps a barrier, or some object that he tries to obtain. We must remember that the individual partly *creates* his barriers and his objects of value, that they must be defined partially in terms set by the particular organism in the situation. I know of no way of defining or describing a field universally in such a way that this description can be independent of the particular organism functioning within it. It certainly must be pointed out that a child who is trying to attain a certain object of value to him, but who is restrained by a barrier of some sort, determines not only that the object is of value, but also that the barrier is a barrier. Psychologically there is no such thing as a barrier; there is only a barrier for a particular person who is trying to get something that he wants.

It is my impression that extreme or exclusive situation theory flourishes best when it is based on inadequate theories of motivation. For instance, any purely behavioral theory needs situation theory to give it any sense at all. A motivation theory that is based on existing drives rather than on goals or needs also needs a strong situation theory if it is not to fall. However, a theory that stresses constant fundamental needs finds them to be relatively constant and more independent of the particular situation in which the organism finds itself. For not only does the need organize its action possibilities, so to speak, in the most efficient way feasible and with a great deal of variation, but it also organizes and even creates the external reality. Another way of saying this is, if we accept Koffka's distinction between the geographical and psychological environment, that the only satisfactory way of understanding how a geographical environment becomes a psychological environment is to understand that the principle of organization of the psychological environment is the current goal of the organism in that particular environment.

Sound motivation theory must then take account of the situation, but must never become pure situation theory; that is, unless we are explicitly willing to give up our search for an understanding of the nature of the constancy of the organism in favor of understanding the world it lives in.

To avoid unnecessary argument, let me stress that we are now concerned, not with behavior theory, but with motivation theory. Behavior is determined by several classes of determinants, of which motivation is one and environmental forces is another. The study of motivation does not negate or deny the study of situational determinants, but rather supplements it. They both have their places in a larger structure.

INTEGRATION

Any motivation theory must take account not only of the fact that the organism behaves ordinarily as an integrated whole, but also of the fact that sometimes it does not. There are specific isolated conditionings and habits to account for, segmental responses of various kinds, and a host of phenomena of dissociation and lack of integration that we know about. The organism furthermore can even react in a nonunitary fashion in daily life as when we do many things at the same time.

Apparently the organism is most unified in its integration when it is successfully facing either a great joy or creative moment or else a major problem or a threat or emergency. But when the threat is overwhelming or when the organism is too weak or helpless to manage it, it tends to disintegrate. On the whole when life is easy and successful, the organism can simultaneously do many things and turn in many directions.

It is my belief that a fair share of the phenomena that seem to be specific and isolated actually are not. Often it is possible to demonstrate with deeper analysis that they take a meaningful place in the whole structure, e.g., conversion hysterical symptoms. This apparent lack of integration may sometimes be simply a reflection of our own ignorance, but we also know enough now to be sure that isolated, segmental, or unintegrated responses are possible under certain circumstances. Furthermore is is now becoming more and more clear that such phenomena are not necessarily to be regarded as weak or bad or pathological. Rather they are often to be regarded as evidence of one of the most important capacities of the organism, viz., to deal with unimportant or with familiar or with easily conquered problems in a partial, specific, or segmental fashion so that the main capacities of the organism are still left free for the more important or more challenging problems that it faces (160).

NONMOTIVATED BEHAVIOR

It seems to me quite clear, in spite of near universal acceptance of the contrary by psychologists, that *not* all behaviors or reactions are motivated, at least not in the ordinary sense of seeking need gratifications, i.e., seeking for what is lacked or needed. The phenomena of maturation, of expression, and of growth or self-actualization are all instances of exceptions to the rule of universal motivation, and had much better be considered expression rather than coping. They will be discussed at length below, especially in Chapters 10 and 14.

In addition, Norman Maier (284) has forcibly called our attention to a distinction often implied by the Freudians but never made sharp and unmistakable by them. Most neurotic symptoms or trends amount to basic-need-gratification-bent impulses that have somehow got stymied or misdirected or confused with other needs or fixated on the wrong means. Other symptoms, however, are no longer gratification-bent but are simply protective or defensive. They have no goal but to prevent further hurt or threat or frustration. The difference is like that between the fighter who still hopes to win and the one who has no hope of winning, trying only to lose as painlessly as possible.

Since giving up and hopelessness are very definitely of considerable relevance to prognosis in therapy, to expectations of learning, even probably to longevity, Maier's differentiation, as well as Klee's interpretation of it (233), must be handled by any definitive motivation theory.

POSSIBILITY OF ATTAINMENT

Dewey (108) and Thorndike (449) have stressed one important aspect of motivation that has been completely neglected by most psychologists, namely, possibility. On the whole we yearn consciously for that which might conceivably be actually attained. That is to say that we are much more realistic about wishing than the psychoanalysts might allow, absorbed as they are with unconscious wishes.

As a man's income increases he finds himself actively wishing for and striving for things that he never dreamed of a few years before. The average American yearns for automobiles, refrigerators, and television sets because they are real possibilities; he does not yearn for yachts or planes because they are in fact not within the reach of the average American. It is quite probable that he does not long for them *unconsciously* either.

Attention to this factor of possibility of attainment is crucial for understanding the differences in motivations between various classes and castes within our own population and between it and other poorer countries and cultures.

INFLUENCE OF REALITY

Related to this problem is that of the influence of reality on unconscious impulses. For Freud, an id impulse is a discrete entity having no intrinsic relatedness to anything else in the world, not even other id impulses.

> We can come nearer to the id with images, and call it a chaos, a cauldron of seething excitement. . . . These instincts fill it with energy, but it has no organization and no unified will, only an impulsion to obtain satisfaction for the instinctual needs, in accordance with the pleasure principle. The laws of logic—above all, the law of contradiction—do not hold for processes in the id. Contradictory impulses exist side by side without neutralizing each other or drawing apart; at most they combine in compromise formations under the overpowering economic pressure towards discharging their energy. There is nothing in the id which can be compared to negation, and we are astonished to find in it an exception to the philosophers' assertion that space and time are necessary forms of our mental acts. . . .
>
> Naturally, the id knows no values, no good and evil, no morality. The economic, or, if you prefer, the quantitative factor, which is so closely bound up with the pleasure-principle, dominates all its processes. Instinctual cathexes seeking discharge—that, in our view, is all that the id contains. (Freud, Sigmund, *New Introductory Lectures on Psychoanalysis*, W. W. Norton, 1933, pp, 103–105.)

To the extent that these impulses are controlled, modified, or held back from discharge by reality conditions, they become part or the ego rather than the id.

> One can hardly go wrong in regarding the ego as that part of the id which has been modified by its proximity to the external world and the influence that the latter has had on it, and which serves the purpose of receiving stimuli and protecting the organism from them, like the cortical layer with which a particle of living substance surrounds itself. This relation to the external world is decisive for the ego. The ego has taken over the task of representing the external world for the id and so of saving it; for the id, blindly striving to gratify its instincts in complete disregard of the superior strength of outside forces, could not otherwise escape annihilation. In the fulfillment of this function, the ego has to observe the external world and preserve a true picture of it in the memory traces left by its perceptions, and, by means of the reality-test, it has to eliminate any element in this picture of the external world which is a contribution from internal sources of excitation. On behalf of the id, the ego controls the path of access to motility, but it interpolates between desire and action, the procrastinating factor of thought, during which it makes use of the residues of experience stored up in memory. In this way it dethrones the pleasure-principle, which exerts undisputed sway over the processes in the id, and substitutes for it the reality-principle, which promises greater security and greater success. (*Ibid.,* p. 106.)

It is, however, John Dewey's contention that all impulses in the adult—or at least the characteristic impulse—are integrated with and affected by reality. In a word, this is the equivalent of maintaining that there are no id impulses, or, reading between the lines, if there are, that they are intrinsically pathological rather than intrinsically healthy.

This contradiction is noted here, even though no empirical solution can be offered, because it is a crucial, head-on difference.

As it appears to us, the question is not whether there exist id impulses of the sort Freud describes. Any psychoanalyst will testify to the occurrence of fantasy impulses that exist without regard to reality, common sense, logic, or even personal advantage. The question is, are they evidences of sickness or of regression, or are they revelation of the inmost core of the healthy human being? At what point in the life history does the infantile fantasy begin to be modified by perception of reality? Is it the same for all, neurotic and healthy alike? Can the efficiently functioning human being maintain completely free of such influence any hidden corner of his impulse life? Or if it does turn out that such impulses, completely intraorganismic in origin, *do* exist in all of us, then we must ask,

When do they appear? Under what conditions? Are they necessarily the troublemakers that Freud assumed them to be? *Must* they be in opposition to reality?

KNOWLEDGE OF HEALTHY MOTIVATION

Most of what we know of human motivation comes not from psychologists but from psychotherapists treating patients. These patients are a great source of error as well as of useful data, for they obviously constitute a poor sample of the population. The motivational life of neurotic sufferers should, even in principle, be rejected as a paradigm for healthy motivation. Health is not simply the absence of disease or even the opposite of it. Any theory of motivation that is worthy of attention must deal with the highest capacities of the healthy and strong man as well as with the defensive maneuvers of crippled spirits. The most important concerns of the greatest and finest people in human history must all be encompassed and explained.

This understanding we shall never get from sick people alone. We must turn our attention to healthy men as well. Motivation theorists must become more positive in their orientation.

4

A THEORY
OF HUMAN
MOTIVATION

INTRODUCTION

This chapter is an attempt to formulate a positive theory of motivation that will satisfy the theoretical demands listed in the previous chapter and at the same time conform to the known facts, clinical and observational as well as experimental. It derives most directly, however, from clinical experience. This theory is, I think, in the functionalist tradition of James and Dewey, and is fused with the holism of Wertheimer, Goldstein, and Gestalt psychology, and with the dynamicism of Freud, Fromm, Horney, Reich, Jung, and Adler. This integration or synthesis may be called a holistic-dynamic theory.

THE BASIC NEEDS

THE PHYSIOLOGICAL NEEDS

The needs that are usually taken as the starting point for motivation theory are the so-called physiological drives. Two recent lines of research make it necessary to revise our customary notions about these needs: first, the development of the concept of homeostasis, and second, the finding that appetites (preferential choices among foods) are a fairly efficient indication of actual needs or lacks in the body.

Homeostasis refers to the body's automatic efforts to maintain a constant, normal state of the blood stream. Cannon (78) has described this process for (1) the water content of the blood, (2) salt content, (3) sugar content, (4) protein content, (5) fat content, (6) calcium content, (7) oxygen content, (8) constant hydrogen-ion level (acid-base balance), and (9) constant temperature of the blood. Obviously this list could be extended to include other minerals, the hormones, vitamins, etc.

Young (491, 492) has summarized the work on appetite in its relation to body needs. If the body lacks some chemical, the individual will tend (in an imperfect way) to develop a specific appetite or partial hunger for that missing food element.

Thus it seems impossible as well as useless to make any list of fundamental physiological needs, for they can come to almost any number one might wish, depending on the degree of specificity of description. We cannot identify all physiological needs as homeostatic. That sexual desire, sleepiness, sheer activity and exercise, and maternal behavior in animals are homeostatic has not yet been demonstrated. Furthermore, this list would not include the various sensory pleasures (tastes, smells, tickling, stroking), which are probably physiological and which may become the goals of motivated behavior. Nor do we know what to make of the fact that the organism has simultaneously a tendency to inertia, laziness and least effort and *also* a need for activity, stimulation, and excitement.

In the previous chapter it was pointed out that these physiological drives or needs are to be considered unusual rather than typical because they are isolable, and because they are localizable somatically. That is to say, they are relatively independent of each other, of other motivations, and of the organism as a whole, and second, in many cases, it is possible to demonstrate a localized, underlying somatic base for the drive. This is true less generally than has been thought (exceptions are fatigue, sleepiness, maternal responses) but it is still true in the classic instances of hunger, sex, and thirst.

It should be pointed out again that any of the physiological needs and the consummatory behavior involved with them serve as channels for all sorts of other needs as well. That is to say, the person who thinks he is hungry may actually be seeking more for comfort, or dependence, than for vitamins or proteins. Conversely, it is possible to satisfy the hunger need in part by other activities such as drinking water or smoking cigarettes. In other words, relatively isolable as these physiological needs are, they are not completely so.

Undoubtedly these physiological needs are the most prepotent of all needs. What this means specifically is that in the human being who is missing everything in life in an extreme fashion, it is most likely that the major motivation would be the physiological needs rather than any others. A person who is lacking food, safety, love, and esteem would most probably hunger for food more strongly than for anything else.

If all the needs are unsatisfied, and the organism is then dominated by the physiological needs, all other needs may become simply nonexistent or be pushed into the background. It is then fair to characterize the whole organism by saying simply that it is hungry, for consciousness is almost completely preëmpted by hunger. All capacities are put into the service of hunger-satisfaction, and the organization of these capacities is almost entirely determined by the one purpose of satisfying hunger. The receptors and effectors, the intelligence, memory, habits, all may now be defined simply as hunger-gratifying tools. Capacities that are not useful for this purpose lie dormant, or are pushed into the background. The urge to write poetry, the desire to acquire an automobile, the interest in American history, the desire for a new pair of shoes are, in the extreme case, forgotten or become of secondary importance. For the man who is extremely and dangerously hungry, no other interests exist but food. He dreams food, he remembers food, he thinks about food, he emotes only about food, he perceives only food, and he wants only food. The more subtle determinants that ordinarily fuse with the physiological drives in organizing even feeding, drinking, or sexual behavior, may now be so completely overwhelmed as to allow us to speak at this time (but *only* at this time) of pure hunger drive and behavior, with the one unqualified aim of relief.

Another peculiar characteristic of the human organism when it is dominated by a certain need is that the whole philosophy of the future tends also to change. For our chronically and extremely hungry man, Utopia can be defined simply as a place where there is plenty of food. He tends to think that, if only he is guaranteed food for the rest of his life, he will be perfectly happy and will never want anything more. Life itself tends to be defined in terms of eating. Anything else will be defined as unimportant. Freedom, love, community feeling, respect, philosophy, may all be waved aside as fripperies that are useless, since they fail to fill the stomach. Such a man may fairly be said to live by bread alone.

It cannot possibly be denied that such things are true, but their *generality* can be denied. Emergency conditions are, almost by definition, rare in the normally functioning peaceful society. That this truism can be forgotten is attributable mainly to two reasons. First, rats have few motivations other than physiological ones, and since so much of the research upon motivation has been made with these animals, it is easy to carry the rat picture over to the human being. Second, it is too often not realized that culture itself is an adaptive tool, one of whose main functions is to make the physiological emergencies come less and less often. In most of the known societies, chronic extreme hunger of the emergency type is rare, rather than common. In any case, this is still true in the United States. The average American citizen is experiencing appetite rather than hunger when he says, "I am hungry." He is apt to experience sheer life-and-death hunger only by accident and then only a few times through his entire life.

Obviously a good way to obscure the higher motivations, and to get a lopsided view of human capacities and human nature, is to make the organism extremely and chronically hungry or thirsty. Anyone who attempts to make an emergency picture into a typical one, and who will measure all of man's goals and desires by his behavior during extreme physiological deprivation is certainly being blind to many things. It is quite true that man lives by bread alone—when there is no bread. But what happens to man's desires when there *is* plenty of bread and when his belly is chronically filled?

At once other (*and higher*) *needs emerge* and these, rather than physiological hungers, dominate the organism. And when these in turn are satisfied, again new (and still higher) needs emerge, and so on. This is what we mean by saying that the basic human needs are organized into a hierarchy of relative prepotency.

One main implication of this phrasing is that gratification becomes as important a concept as deprivation in motivation theory, for it releases the organism from the domination of a relatively more physiological need, permitting thereby the emergence of other more social goals. The physiological needs, along with their partial goals, when chronically gratified cease to exist as active determinants or organizers of behavior. They now exist only in a potential fashion in the sense that they may emerge again to dominate the organism if they are thwarted. But a want that is satisfied is no longer a want. The organism is dominated and its behavior organized only by unsatisfied needs. If hunger is satisfied, it becomes unimportant in the current dynamics of the individual.

This statement is somewhat qualified by a hypothesis to be discussed more fully later, namely, that it is precisely those individuals in whom a certain need has always been satisfied who are best equipped to tolerate deprivation of that need in the future, and that furthermore, those who have been deprived in the past will react differently to current satisfactions than the one who has never been deprived.

THE SAFETY NEEDS

If the physiological needs are relatively well gratified, there then emerges a new set of needs, which we may categorize roughly as the safety needs (security; stability; dependency; protection; freedom from fear, from anxiety and chaos; need for structure, order, law, limits; strength in the protector; and so on). All that has been said to the physiological needs is equally true, although in less degree, of these desires. The organism may equally well be wholly dominated by them. They may serve as the almost exclusive organizers of behavior, recruiting all the capacities of the organism in their service, and we may then fairly describe the whole organism as a safety-seeking mechanism. Again we may say of the receptors, the effectors, of the intellect, and of the other capacities that they are primarily safety-seeking tools. Again, as in the hungry man, we find that the dominating goal is a strong determinant not only of his current world outlook and philosophy but also of his philosophy of the future and of values. Practically everything looks less important than safety and protection (even sometimes the physiological needs, which, being satisfied, are now underestimated). A man in this state, if it is extreme enough and chronic enough, may be characterized as living almost for safety alone.

Although in this chapter we are interested primarily in the needs of the adult, we can approach an understanding of his safety needs perhaps more efficiently by observation of infants and children, in whom these needs are much more simple and obvious. One reason for the clearer appearance of the threat or danger reaction in infants is that they do not inhibit this reaction at all, whereas adults in our society have been taught to inhibit it at all costs. Thus even when adults do feel their safety to be threatened, we may not be able to see this on the surface. Infants will react in a total fashion and as if they were endangered, if they are disturbed or dropped suddenly, startled by loud noises, flashing light, or other unusual sensory stimulation, by rough handling, by general loss of support in the mother's arms, or by inadequate support.[1]

In infants we can also see a much more direct reaction to bodily illnesses of various kinds. Sometimes these illnesses seem to be immediately and *per se* threatening, and seem to make the child feel unsafe. For

[1] As the child grows up, sheer knowledge and familiarity as well as better motor development make these dangers less and less dangerous and more and more manageable. Throughout life it may be said that one of the main conative functions of education is this neutralizing of apparent dangers through knowledge, e.g., I am not afraid of thunder because I know something about it.

instance, vomiting, colic, or other sharp pains seem to make the child look at the whole world in a different way. At such a moment of pain, it may be postulated that, for the child, the whole world suddenly changes from sunniness to darkness, so to speak, and become a place in which anything at all might happen, in which previously stable things have suddenly become unstable. Thus a child who because of some bad food is taken ill may for a day or two develop fear, nightmares, and a need for protection and reassurance never seen in him before his illness. The recent work on the psychological effects of surgery on children demonstrates this richly (270).

Another indication of the child's need for safety is his preference for some kind of undisrupted routine or rhythm. He seems to want a predictable, lawful, orderly world. For instance, injustice, unfairness, or inconsistency in the parents seems to make a child feel anxious and unsafe. This attitude may be not so much because of the injustice *per se* or any particular pains involved, but rather because this treatment threatens to make the world look unreliable, or unsafe, or unpredictable. Young children seem to thrive better under a system that has at least a skeletal outline of rigidity, in which there is a schedule of a kind, some sort of routine, something that can be counted upon, not only for the present but also far into the future. Child psychologists, teachers, and psychotherapists have found that permissiveness within limits, rather than unrestricted permissiveness is preferred as well as *needed* by children. Perhaps one could express this more accurately by saying that the child needs an organized and structured world rather than an unorganized or unstructured one.

The central role of the parents and the normal family setup are indisputable. Quarreling, physical assault, separation, divorce, or death within the family may be particularly terrifying. Also parental outbursts of rage or threats of punishment directed to the child, calling him names, speaking to him harshly, handling him roughly, or actual physical punishment sometimes elicit such total panic and terror that we must assume more is involved than the physical pain alone. While it is true that in some children this terror may represent also a fear of loss of parental love, it can also occur in completely rejected children, who seem to cling to the hating parents more for sheer safety and protection than because of hope of love.

Confronting the average child with new, unfamiliar, strange, unmanageable stimuli or situations will too frequently elicit the danger or terror reaction, as for example, getting lost or even being separated from the parents for a short time, being confronted with new faces, new situations, or new tasks, the sight of strange, unfamiliar, or uncontrollable objects, illness, or death. Particularly at such times, the child's frantic clinging to his parents is eloquent testimony to their role as protectors (quite apart from their roles as food givers and lover givers).[2]

From these and similar observations, we may generalize and say that the average child and, less obviously, the average adult in our society generally prefers a safe, orderly, predictable, lawful, organized world, which he can count on and in which unexpected, unmanageable, chaotic, or other dangerous things do not happen, and in which, in any case, he has powerful parents or protectors who shield him from harm.

That these reactions may so easily be observed in children is in a way proof that children in our society feel too unsafe (or, in a world, are badly brought up). Children who are reared in an unthreatening, loving family do *not* ordinarily react as we have described. In such children the danger reactions are apt to come mostly to objects or situations that adults too would consider dangerous.

The healthy and fortunate adult in our culture is largely satisfied in his safety needs. The peaceful, smoothly running, stable, good society ordinarily makes its members feel safe enough from wild animals, extremes of temperature, criminal assault, murder, chaos, tyranny, and so on. Therefore, in a very real sense, he no longer has any safety needs as active motivators. Just as a sated man no longer feels hungry, a safe man no longer feels endangered. If we wish to see these needs directly and clearly we must turn to neurotic or near-neurotic individuals, and to the economic and social underdogs, or else to social chaos, revolution, or breakdown of authority. In between these extremes, we can perceive the expressions of safety needs only in such phenomena as, for instance, the common preference for a job with tenure and protection, the desire for a saving account, and for insurance of various kinds (medical, dental, unemployment, disability, old age).

Other broader aspects of the attempt to seek safety and stability in the world are seen in the very common preference for familiar rather than unfamiliar things (309), or for the known rather than the unknown. The tendency to have some religion or world philosophy that organizes

---

[2] A test battery for safety might be confronting the child with a small exploding firecracker, a bewhiskered face, or a hypodermic injection, having the mother leave the room, putting him upon a high ladder, having a mouse crawl up to him, and so on. Of course I cannot seriously recommend the deliberate use of such tests, for they might very well harm the child being tested. But these and similar situations come up by the score in the child's ordinary day-to-day living and may be observed.

the universe and the men in it into some sort of satisfactorily coherent, meaningful whole is also in part motivated by safety seeking. Here too we may list science and philosophy in general as partially motivated by the safety needs (we shall see later that there are also other motivations to scientific, philosophical, or religious endeavor).

Otherwise the need for safety is seen as an active and dominant mobilizer of the organism's resources only in real emergencies, e.g., war, disease, natural catastrophes, crimes waves, societal disorganization, neurosis, brain injury, breakdown of authority, chronically bad situations.

Some neurotic adults in our society are, in many ways, like the unsafe child in their desire for safety, although in the former it takes on a somewhat special appearance. Their reaction is often to unknown, psychological dangers in a world that is perceived to be hostile, overwhelming, and threatening. Such a person behaves as if a great catastrophe were almost always impending, i.e., he is usually responding as if to an emergency. His safety needs often find specific expression in a search for a protector, or a stronger person on whom he may depend, perhaps a Fuehrer.

The neurotic individual may be described with great usefulness as a grown-up person who retains his childhood attitudes toward the world. That is to say, a neurotic adult may be said to behave as if he were actually afraid of a spanking, or of his mother's disapproval, or of being abandoned by his parents, or having his food taken away from him. It is as if his childish attitudes of fear and threat reaction to a dangerous world had gone underground, and untouched by the growing up and learning processes, were now ready to be called out by any stimulus that would make a child feel endangered and threatened.[3] Horney (197) especially has written well about "basic anxiety."

The neurosis in which the search for safety takes its clearest form is in the compulsive-obsessive neurosis. Compulsive-obsessives try frantically to order and stabilize the world so that no unmanageable, unexpected, or unfamiliar dangers will ever appear. They hedge themselves about with all sorts of ceremonials, rules, and formulas so that every possible contingency may be provided for and so that no new contingencies may appear. They are much like the brain-injured cases, described by Goldstein, who manage to maintain their equilibrium by avoiding everything unfamiliar and strange and by ordering their restricted world in such a neat, disciplined, orderly fashion that everything in the world can be

---

[3] Not all neurotic individuals feel unsafe. Neurosis may have at its core a thwarting of the affection and esteem needs in a person who is generally safe.

counted on. They try to arrange the world so that anything unexpected (dangers) cannot possibly occur. If, through no fault of their own, something unexpected does occur, they go into a panic reaction as if this unexpected occurrence constituted a grave danger. What we can see only as a none-too-strong preference in the healthy person, e.g., preference for the familiar, becomes a life-and-death necessity in abnormal cases. The healthy taste for the novel and unknown is missing or at a minimum in the average neurotic.

The safety needs can become very urgent on the social scene whenever there are real threats to law, to order, to the authority of society. The threat of chaos or of nihilism can be expected in most human beings to produce a regression from any higher needs to the more prepotent safety needs. A common, almost an expectable reaction, is the easier acceptance of dictatorship or of military rule. This tends to be true for all human beings, including healthy ones, since they too will tend to respond to danger with realistic regression to the safety need level, and will prepare to defend themselves. But it seems to be most true of people who are living near the safety line. They are particularly disturbed by threats to authority, to legality, and to the representatives of the law.

THE BELONGINGNESS AND LOVE NEEDS

If both the physiological and the safety needs are fairly well gratified, there will emerge the love and affection and belongingness needs, and the whole cycle already described will repeat itself with this new center. Now the person will feel keenly, as never before, the absence of friends, or a sweetheart, or a wife, or children. He will hunger for affectionate relations with people in general, namely, for a place in his group or family, and he will strive with great intensity to achieve this goal. He will want to attain such a place more than anything else in the world and may even forget that once, when he was hungry, he sneered at love as unreal or unnecessary or unimportant. Now he will feel sharply the pangs of loneliness, of ostracism, of rejection, of friendlessness, of rootlessness.

We have very little scientific informaiton about the belongingness need, although this is a common theme in novels, autobiographies, poems, and plays and also in the newer sociological literature. From these we know in a general way the destructive effects on children of moving too often; of disorientation; of the general over-mobility that is forced by industrialization; of being without roots, or of despising one's roots, one's origins, one's group; of being torn from one's home and family, and friends and neighbors; of being a transient or a newcomer rather than a native. We still underplay the deep importance of the neighborhood, of one's territory, of one's clan, of one's own "kind," one's class, one's gang, one's familiar working colleagues. I will content myself with recommending a single book that says all this with great poignancy and conviction (196) and that helps us understand our deeply animal tendency to herd, to flock, to join, to belong. Perhaps also, Ardrey's *Territorial Imperative* (14) will help to make all of this conscious. Its very rashness was good for me because it stressed as crucial what I had been only casual about and forced me to think seriously about the matter. Perhaps it will do the same for the reader.

I believe that the tremendous and rapid increase in T-groups and other personal growth groups and intentional communities may in part be motivated by this unsatisfied hunger for contact, for intimacy, for belongingness and by the need to overcome the widespread feelings of alienation, aloneness, strangeness, and loneliness, which have been worsened by our mobility, by the breakdown of traditional groupings, the scattering of families, the generation gap, the steady urbanization and disappearance of village face-to-faceness, and the resulting shallowness of American friendship. My strong impression is also that *some* proportion of youth rebellion groups—I don't know how many or how much—is motivated by the profound hunger for groupiness, for contact, for real togetherness in the face of a common enemy, *any* enemy that can serve to form an amity group simply by posing an external threat. The same kind of thing was observed in groups of soldiers who were pushed into an unwonted brotherliness and intimacy by their common external danger, and who may stick together throughout a lifetime as a consequence. Any good society must satisfy this need, one way or another, if it is to survive and be healthy.

In our society the thwarting of these needs is the most commonly found core in cases of maladjustment and more severe pathology. Love and affection, as well as their possible expression in sexuality, are generally looked upon with ambivalence and are customarily hedged about with many restrictions and inhibitions. Practically all theorists of psychopathology have stressed thwarting of the love needs as basic in the picture of maladjustment. Many clinical studies have therefore been made of this need, and we know more about it perhaps than any of the other needs except the physiological ones. Suttie (442) has written an excellent analysis of our "taboo on tenderness."

One thing that must be stressed at this point is that love is not synonymous with sex. Sex may be studied as a purely physiological need. Ordinarily sexual behavior is multidetermined, that is to say, determined not only by sexual but also by other needs, chief among which are the love and affection needs. Also not to be overlooked is the fact that the love needs involve both giving *and* receiving love.

THE ESTEEM NEEDS

All people in our society (with a few pathological exceptions) have a need or desire for a stable, firmly based, usually high evaluation of themselves, for self-respect, or self-esteem, and for the esteem of others. These needs may therefore be classified into two subsidiary sets. These are, first, the desire for strength, for achievement, for adequacy, for mastery and competence, for confidence in the face of the world, and for independence and freedom.[4] Second, we have what we may call the desire for reputation or prestige (defining it as respect or esteem from other people), status, fame and glory, dominance, recognition, attention, importance, dignity, or appreciation. These needs have been relatively stressed by Alfred Adler and his followers, and have been relatively neglected by Freud. More and more today, however, there is appearing widespread appreciation of their central importance, among psychoanalysts as well as among clinical psychologists.

Satisfaction of the self-esteem need leads to feelings of self-confidence, worth, strength, capability, and adequacy, of being useful and necessary in the world. But thwarting of these needs produces feelings of inferiority, of weakness, and of helplessness. These feelings in turn give rise to either basic discouragement or else compensatory or neurotic trends. An appreciation of the necessity of basic self-considence and an understanding of how helpless people are without it can be easily gained from a study of severe traumatic neurosis (222).[5]

From the theologians' discussion of pride and *hubris,* from the Frommian theories about the self-perception of untruth to one's own

[4] Whether or not this particular desire is universal we do not know. The crucial question, especially important today, is, Will men who are enslaved and dominated inevitably feel dissatisfied and rebellious? We may assume on the basis of commonly known clinical data that a man who has known true freedom (not paid for by giving up safety and security but rather built on the basis of adequate safety and security) will not willingly or easily allow his freedom to be taken away from him. But we do not know for sure that this is true for the person born into slavery. See discussion of this problem in Ref. 145.

[5] For more extensive discussion of normal self-esteem, as well as for reports of various researches, see the bibliography on page 61. Also see the work of McClelland and his co-workers (326, 327, 328). Also (473).

nature, from the Rogerian work with self, from essayists like Ayn Rand (388), and from other sources as well, we have been learning more and more of the dangers of basing self-esteem on the opinions of others rather than on real capacity, competence, and adequacy to the task. The most stable and therefore most healthy self-esteem is based on *deserved* respect from others rather than on external fame or celebrity and unwarranted adulation. Even here it is helpful to distinguish the actual competence and achievement that is based on sheer will power, determination and responsibility, from that which comes naturally and easily out of one's own true inner nature, one's constitution, one's biological fate or destiny, or as Horney puts it, out of one's Real Self rather than out of the idealized pseudo-self (199).

THE NEED FOR SELF-ACTUALIZATION

Even if all these needs are satisfied, we may still often (if not always) expect that a new discontent and restlessness will soon develop, unless the individual is doing what *he,* individually, is fitted for. A musician must make music, an artist must paint, a poet must write, if he is to be ultimately at peace with himself. What a man *can* be, he *must* be. He must be true to his own nature. This need we may call self-actualization. See Chapter 11 for fuller description.

This term, first coined by Kurt Goldstein (160), is being used in this book in a much more specific and limited fashion. It refers to man's desire for self-fulfillment, namely, to the tendency for him to become actualized in what he is potentially. This tendency might be phrased as the desire to become more and more what one idiosyncratically is, to become everything that one is capable of becoming.

The specific form that these needs will take will of course vary greatly from person to person. In one individual it may take the form of the desire to be an ideal mother, in another it may be expressed athletically, and in still another it may be expressed in painting pictures or in inventions.[6] At this level, individual differences are greatest.

---

[6] Clearly creative behavior, like painting, is like any other behavior in having multiple determinants. It may be seen in innately creative people whether they are satisfied or not, happy or unhappy, hungry or sated. Also it is clear that creative activity may be compensatory, ameliorative, or purely economic. It is my impression (from informal experiments) that it is possible to distinguish the artistic and intellectual products of basically satisfied people from those of basically unsatisfied people by inspection alone. In any case, here too we must distinguish, in a dynamic fashion, the overt behavior itself from its various motivations or purposes.

The clear emergence of these needs usually rests upon some prior satisfaction of the physiological, safety, love, and esteem needs.

THE PRECONDITIONS FOR THE BASIC NEED SATISFACTIONS

There are certain conditions that are immediate prerequisites for the basic need satisfactions. Danger to these is reacted to as if it were direct danger to the basic needs themselves. Such conditions as freedom to speak, freedom to do what one wishes so long as no harm is done to others, freedom to express oneself, freedom to investigate and seek for information, freedom to defend oneself, justice, fairness, honesty, orderliness in the group are examples of such preconditions for basic need satisfactions. Thwarting in these freedoms will be reacted to with a threat or emergency response. These conditions are not ends in themselves but they are *almost* so since they are so closely related to the basic needs, which are apparently the only ends in themselves. These conditions are defended because without them the basic satisfactions are quite impossible, or at least, severely endangered.

If we remember that the cognitive capacities (perceptual, intellectual, learning) are a set of adjustive tools, which have, among other functions, that of satisfaction of our basic needs, then it is clear that any danger to them, any deprivation or blocking of their free use, must also be indirectly threatening to the basic needs themselves. Such a statement is a partial solution of the general problems of curiosity, the search for knowledge, truth, and wisdom, and the ever-persistent urge to solve the cosmic mysteries. Secrecy, censorship, dishonesty, blocking of communication threaten *all* the basic needs.

We must therefore introduce another hypothesis and speak of degrees of closeness to the basic needs, for we have already pointed out that *any* conscious desires (partial goals) are more or less important as they are more or less close to the basic needs. The same statement may be made for various behavior acts. An act is psychologically important if it contributes directly to satisfaction of basic needs. The less directly it so contributes, or the weaker this contribution is, the less important this act must be conceived to be from the point of view of dynamic psychology. A similar statement may be made for the various defense or coping mechanisms. Some are directly related to the protection or attainment of the basic needs, others are only weakly and distantly related. Indeed, if we wished, we could speak of more basic and less basic defense mechanisms, and then affirm that danger to the more basic defenses is more threatening than danger to less basic defenses (always remembering that this is so only because of their relationship to the basic needs).

THE DESIRES TO KNOW AND TO UNDERSTAND

The main reason we know little about the cognitive impulses, their dynamics, or their pathology, is that they are not important in the clinic, and certainly not in the clinic dominated by the medical-therapeutic tradition, i.e., getting rid of disease. The florid, exciting, and mysterious symptoms found in the classical neuroses are lacking here. Cognitive psychopathology is pale, subtle, and easily overlooked, or defined as normal. It does not cry for help. As a consequence we find nothing on the subject in the writings of the great inventors of psychotherapy and psychodynamics, Freud, Adler, Jung, etc.

Schilder is the only major psychoanalyst I know in whose writings curiosity and understanding are seen dynamically.[7] Among the academic psychologists Murphy, Wertheimer, and Asch (19, 142, 466) have treated the problem. So far, we have mentioned the cognitive needs only in passing. Acquiring knowledge and systematizing the universe have been considered as, in part, techniques for the achievement of basic safety in the world, or for the intelligent man, expressions of self-actualization. Also freedom of inquiry and expression have been discussed as preconditions of satisfaction of the basic needs. Useful though these formulations may be, they do not constitute definitive answers to the questions as to the motivational role of curiosity, learning, philosophizing, experimenting, etc. They are at best no more than partial answers.

Above and beyond these negative determinants for acquiring knowledge (anxiety, fear), there are some reasonable grounds for postulating positive *per se* impulses to satisfy curiosity, to know, to explain, and to understand (295).

1. Something like human curiosity can easily be observed in the higher animals. The monkey will pick things apart, will poke his finger into holes, will explore in all sorts of situations where it is improbable that hunger, fear, sex, comfort status, etc., are involved. Harlow's experiments (174) have amply demonstrated this in an acceptably experimental way.

2. The history of mankind supplies us with a satisfactory number of

---

[7] "However, human beings have a genuine interest in the world, in action, and in experimentation. They derive a deep satisfaction when they venture into the world. They do not experience reality as a threat to existence. Organisms, and especially human organisms, have a genuine feeling of safety and security in this world. Threats come merely from specific situations and deprivations. Even then, discomfort and danger are experienced as passing points, which finally leads to a new security and safety in touch with the world." (412, p. 220).

instances in which man looked for facts and created explanations in the face of the greatest danger, even to life itself. There have been innumerable humbler Galileos.

3. Studies of psychologically healthy people indicate that they are, as a defining characteristic, attracted to the mysterious, to the unknown, to the chaotic, unorganized, and unexplained. This seems to be a *per se* attractiveness; these areas are in themselves and of their own right interesting. The contrasting reaction to the well known is one of boredom.

4. It may be found valid to extrapolate from the psychopathological. The compulsive-obsessive neurotic (and neurotic in general), Goldstein's brain-injured soldiers, Maier's fixated rats (285), all show (at the clinical level of observation) a compulsive and anxious clinging to the familiar and a dread of the unfamiliar, the anarchic, the unexpected, the un-domesticated. On the other hand, there are some phenomena that may turn out to nullify this possibility. Among these are forced unconventionality, a chronic rebellion against any authority whatsoever, Bohemianism, the desire to shock and to startle, all of which may be found in certain neurotic individuals, as well as in those in the process of deacculturation.

Perhaps also relevant here are the perseverative detoxifications described in Chapter 10, which are, behaviorally at any rate, an attraction to the dreadful, to the not understood and to the mysterious.

5. Probably there are true psychopathological effects when the cognitive needs are frustrated (295, 314). The following clinical impression are also pertinent.

6. I have seen a few cases in which it seemed clear to me that the pathology (boredom, loss of zest in life, self-dislike, general depression of the bodily functions, steady deterioration of the intellectual life, of tastes, etc.)[8] were produced in intelligent people leading stupid lives in stupid jobs. I have at least one case in which the appropriate cognitive therapy (resuming parttime studies, getting a position that was more intellectually demanding, insight) removed the symptoms.

I have seen *many* women, intelligent, prosperous, and unoccupied, slowly develop these same symptoms of intellectual inanition. Those who followed my recommendation to immerse themselves in something worthy of them showed improvement or cure often enough to impress me with the reality of the cognitive needs. In those countries in which access to the news, to information, and to the facts were cut off, and in those where official theories were profoundly contradicted by obvious facts, at least

---

[8] This syndrome is very similar to what Ribot (396) and later Myerson (349) called "anhedonia" but which they ascribed to other sources.

some people responded with generalized cynicism, mistrust of *all* values, suspicion even of the obvious, a profound disruption of ordinary inter-personal relationships, hopelessness, loss of morale, etc. Others seem to have responded in the more passive direction with dullness, submission, loss of capacity, coarctation, and loss of initiative.

7. The needs to know and to understand are seen in late infancy and childhood, perhaps even more strongly than in adulthood. Further-more this seems to be a spontaneous product of maturation rather than of learning, however defined. Children do not have to be taught to be curious. But they *may* be taught, as by institutionalization, *not* to be curious, e.g., Goldfarb (158).

8. Finally, the gratification of the cognitive impulses is subjectively satisfying and yields end-experience. Though this aspect of insight and understanding has been neglected in favor of achieved results, learning, etc., it nevertheless remains true that insight is usually a bright, happy, emotional spot in any person's life, perhaps even a high spot in the life span.

The overcoming of obstacles, the occurrence of pathology upon thwarting, the widespread occurrence (cross-species, cross-cultural), the never-dying (though weak) insistent pressure, the need of gratification of this need as a prerequisite for the fullest development of human poten-tialities, the spontaneous appearance in the early history of the indi-vidual, all these point to a basic cognitive need.

This postulation, however, is not enough. Even after we know, we are impelled to know more and more minutely and microscopically on the one hand, and on the other, more and more extensively in the direc-tion of a world philosophy, theology, etc. The facts that we acquire, if they are isolated or atomistic, inevitably get theorized about, and either analyzed or organized or both. This process has been phrased by some as the search for meaning. We shall then postulate a desire to understand, to systematize, to organize, to analyze, to look for relations and meanings, to construct a system of values.

Once these desires are accepted for discussion, we see that they too form themselves into a small hierachy in which the desire to know is prepotent over the desire to understand. All the characteristics of a hierarchy of prepotency that we have described above seem to hold for this one as well.

We must guard ourselves against the too easy tendency to separate these desires from the basic needs we have discussed above, i.e., to make a sharp dichotomy between cognitive and conative needs. The desire to know and to understand are themselves conative, i.e., having a striving character, and are as much personality needs as the basic needs we have already discussed. Furthermore, as we have seen, the two hierarchies are interrelated rather than sharply separated; and as we shall see below, they are synergic rather than antagonistic. For further development of this section, see (295, 314).

THE AESTHETIC NEEDS

We know even less about these than about the others, and yet the testimony of history, of the humanities, and of aestheticians forbids us to bypass this uncomfortable (to the scientist) area. I have attempted to study this phenomenon on a clinical-personological basis with selected individuals, and have at least convinced myself that in *some* individuals there is a truly basic aesthetic need. They get sick (in special ways) from ugliness, and are cured by beautiful surroundings; they *crave* actively, and their cravings can be satisfied *only* by beauty (314). It is seen almost universally in healthy children. Some evidence of such an impulse is found in every culture and in every age as far back as the cavemen.

Much overlapping with conative and cognitive needs makes it impossible to separate them sharply. The needs for order, for symmetry, for closure, for completion of the act, for system, and for structure may be indiscriminately assigned to *either* cognitive, conative, or aesthetic, or even to neurotic needs. For myself I have thought of this area of study as a meeting ground for Gestalters and dynamic psychologists. What, for instance, does it mean when a man feels a strong conscious impulse to straighten the crookedly hung picture on the wall?

FURTHER CHARACTERISTICS
OF THE BASIC NEEDS

THE DEGREE OF FIXITY OF THE HIERARCHY OF BASIC NEEDS

We have spoken so far as if this hierarchy were a fixed order, but actually it is not nearly so rigid as we may have implied. It is true that most of the people with whom we have worked have seemed to have these basic needs in about the order that has been indicated. However, there have been a number of exceptions.

1. There are some people in whom, for instance, self-esteem seems to be more important than love. This most common reversal in the hierarchy is usually due to the development of the notion that the person

who is most likely to be loved is a strong or powerful person, one who inspires respect or fear, and who is self-confident or aggressive. Therefore such people who lack love and seek it may try hard to put on a front of aggressive, confident behavior. But essentially they seek high self-esteem and its behavior expressions more as a means to an end than for its own sake; they seek self-assertion for the sake of love rather than for self-esteem itself.

2. There are other apparently innately creative people in whom the drive to creativeness seems to be more important than any other counter-determinant. Their creativeness might appear not as self-actualization released by basic satisfaction, but in spite of lack of basic satisfaction.

3. In certain people the level of aspiration may be permanently deadened or lowered. That is to say, the less prepotent goals may simply be lost, and may disappear forever, so that the person who has experienced life at a very low level, i.e., chronic unemployment, may continue to be satisfied for the rest of his life if only he can get enough food.

4. The so-called psychopathic personality is another example of permanent loss of the love needs. These are people who, according to the best data available, have been starved for love in the earliest months of their lives and have simply lost forever the desire and the ability to give and to receive affection (as animals lose sucking or pecking reflexes that are not exercised soon enough after birth).

5. Another cause of reversal of the hierarchy is that when a need has been satisfied for a long time, this need may be underevaulated. People who have never experienced chronic hunger are apt to underestimate its effects and to look upon food as a rather unimportant thing. If they are dominated by a higher need, this higher need will seem to be the most important of all. It then becomes possible, and indeed does actually happen, that they may, for the sake of this higher need, put themselves into the position of being deprived in a more basic need. We may expect that after a long-time deprivation of the more basic need there will be a tendency to reëvaluate both needs so that the more prepotent need will actually become consciously prepotent for the individual who may have given it up lightly. Thus a man who has given up his job rather than lose his self-respect, and who then starves for six months or so, may be willing to take his job back even at the price of losing his self-respect.

6. Another partial explanation of *apparent* reversals is seen in the fact that we have been talking about the hierarchy of prepotency in terms of consciously felt wants or desires rather than of behavior. Looking at behavior itself may give us the wrong impression. What we have claimed

is that the person will *want* the more basic of two needs when deprived in both. There is no necessary implication here that he will act upon his desires. Let us stress again that there are many determinants of behavior other than the needs and desires.

7. Perhaps more important than all these exceptions are the ones that involve ideals, high social standards, high values, and the like. With such values people become martyrs; they will give up everything for the sake of a particular ideal, or value. These people may be understood, at least in part, by reference to one basic concept (or hypothesis), which may be called increased frustration-tolerance through early gratification. People who have been satisfied in their basic needs throughout their lives, particularly in their earlier years, seem to develop exceptional power to withstand present or future thwarting of these needs simply because they have strong, healthy character structure as a result of basic satisfaction. They are the strong people who can easily weather disagreement or opposition, who can swim against the stream of public opinion, and who can stand up for the truth at great personal cost. It is just the ones who have loved and been well loved, and who have had many deep friendships who can hold out against hatred, rejection, or persecution.

I say all this in spite of the fact that a certain amount of sheer habituation is also involved in any full discussion of frustration tolerance. For instance, it is likely that those persons who have been accustomed to relative starvation for a long time are partially enabled thereby to withstand food deprivation. What sort of balance must be made between these two tendencies, of habituation on the one hand, and of past satisfaction breeding present frustration tolerance on the other hand, remains to be worked out by further research. Meanwhile we may assume that both are operative, side by side, since they do not contradict each other. In respect to this phenomenon of increased frustration tolerance, it seems probable that the most important gratifications come in the first few years of life. That is to say, people who have been made secure and strong in the earliest years, tend to remain secure and strong thereafter in the face of whatever threatens.

DEGREES OF RELATIVE SATISFACTION

So far, our theoretical discussion may have given the impression that these five sets of needs are somehow in such terms as the following: If one need is satisfied, then another emerges. This statement might give the false impression that a need must be satisfied 100 percent before the next need emerges. In actual fact, most members of our society who are normal are partially satisfied in all their basic needs and partially unsatisfied in all their basic needs at the same time. A more realistic description of the hierarchy would be in terms of decreasing percentages of satisfaction as we go up the hierarchy of prepotency. For instance, if I may assign arbitrary figures for the sake of illustration, it is as if the average citizen is satisfied perhaps 85 percent in his physiological needs, 70 percent in his safety needs, 50 percent in his love needs, 40 percent in his self-esteem needs, and 10 percent in his self-actualization needs.

As for the concept of emergence of a new need after satisfaction of the prepotent need, this emergence is not a sudden, saltatory phenomenon, but rather a gradual emergence by slow degrees from nothingness. For instance, if prepotent need A is satisfied only 10 percent, then need B may not be visible at all. However, as this need A becomes satisfied 25 percent, need B may emerge 5 percent, as need A becomes satisfied 75 percent, need B may emerge 50 percent, and so on.

UNCONSCIOUS CHARACTER OF NEEDS

These needs are neither necessarily conscious nor unconscious. On the whole, however, in the average person, they are more often unconscious than conscious. It is not necessary at this point to overhaul the tremendous mass of evidence that indicates the crucial importance of unconscious motivation. What we have called the basic needs are often largely unconscious although they may, with suitable techniques, and with sophisticated people, become conscious.

CULTURAL SPECIFICITY AND GENERALITY OF NEEDS

This classification of basic needs makes some attempts to take account of the relative unity behind the superficial differences in specific desires from one culture to another. Certainly in any particular culture an individual's conscious motivation content will usually be extremely different from the conscious motivational content of an individual in another society. However, it is the common experience of anthropologists that people, even in different societies, are much more alike than we would think from our first contact with them, and that as we know them better we seem to find more and more of this commonness. We then recognize the most startling differences to be superficial rather than basic, e.g., differences in style of hairdress, clothes, tastes in food, etc. Our classification of basic needs is in part an attempt to account for this unity behind the apparent diversity from culture to culture. No claim is made yet that it is ultimate or universal for all cultures. The claim is made only that it is relatively *more* ultimate, *more* universal, *more* basic than the superficial conscious desires, and makes a closer approach to common human characteristics. Basic needs are more common human than are superficial desires or behaviors.

MULTIPLE MOTIVATIONS OF BEHAVIOR

These needs must be understood *not* to be exclusive or single determiners of certain kinds of behavior. An example may be found in any behavior that seems to be physiologically motivated, such as eating, sexual play, or the like. The clinical psychologists have long since found that any behavior may be a channel through which flow various impulses. Or to say it in another way, most behavior is overdetermined or multimotivated. Within the sphere of motivational determinants any behavior tends to be determined by several or *all* of the basic needs simultaneously rather than by only one of them. The latter would be more an exception than the former. Eating may be partially for the sake of filling the stomach, and partially for the sake of comfort and amelioration of other needs. One may make love not only for pure sexual release, but also to convince oneself of one's masculinity, or to make a conquest, to feel powerful, to win more basic affection. As an illustration, I may point out that it would be possible (theoretically if not practically) to analyze a single act of an individual and see in it the expression of his physiological needs, his safety needs, his love needs, his esteem needs, and self-actualization. This contrasts sharply with the more naïve brand of trait psychology in which one trait or one motive accounts for a certain kind of act, i.e., an aggressive act is traced solely to a trait of aggressiveness.

MULTIPLE DETERMINANTS OF BEHAVIOR

Not all behavior is determined by the basic needs. We might even say that not all behavior is motivated. There are many determinants of behavior other than motives. For instance, one other important class of determinants is the so-called external field. Theoretically, at least, behavior may be determined completely by the external field, or even by specific, isolated, external stimuli, as in association of ideas, or certain conditioned reflexes. If in response to the stimulus word "table," I immediately perceive a memory image of a table, or think of a chair, this response certainly has nothing to do with my basic needs.

Secondly, we may call attention again to the concept of degree of closeness to the basic needs or degree of motivation. Some behavior is highly motivated, other behavior is only weakly motivated. Some is not motivated at all (but all behavior is determined).

Another important point is that there is a basic difference between expressive behavior and coping behavior (functional striving, purposive goal seeking). An expressive behavior does not try to do anything; it is simply a reflection of the personality. A stupid man behaves stupidly, not because he wants to, or tries to, or is motivated to, but simply because he *is* what he is. The same is true when I speak in a bass voice rather than tenor or soprano. The random movements of a healthy child, the smile on the face of a happy man even when he is alone, the springiness of the healthy man's walk, and the erectness of his carriage are other examples of expressive, nonfunctional behavior. Also the *style* in which a man carries out almost all his behavior, motivated as well as unmotivated, is most often expressive (8, 486).

We may then ask, is *all* behavior expressive or reflective of the character structure? The answer is No. Rote, habitual, automatized, or conventional behavior may or may not be expressive. The same is true for most stimulus-bound behaviors.

It is finally necessary to stress that expressiveness of behavior and goal-directedness of behavior are not mutually exclusive categories. Average behavior is usually both. See Chapter 10 for a fuller discussion.

ANIMAL AND HUMAN CENTERING

This theory starts with the human being rather than any lower and presumably simpler animal. Too many of the findings that have been made in animals have been proved to be true for animals but not for the human being. There is no reason whatsoever why we should start with animals in order to study human motivation. The logic or rather illogic behind this general fallacy of pseudo simplicity has been exposed often enough by philosophers and logicians as well as by scientists in each of the various fields. It is no more necessary to study animals before one can study man than it is to study mathematics *before* one can study geology or psychology or biology.

MOTIVATION AND THE THEORY OF PSYCHOPATHOGENESIS

The conscious motivational content of everyday life has, according to the foregoing, been conceived to be relatively important or unimportant accordingly as it is more or less closely related to the basic goals. A desire for ice cream might actually be an indirect expression of a desire for love. If it is, this desire for ice cream becomes extremely important motivation. If, however, the ice cream is simply something to cool the mouth with, or a casual appetitive reaction, the desire is relatively unimportant. Everyday conscious desires are to be regarded as symptoms, as *surface indicators of more basic needs*. If we were to take these superficial desires at their face value we would find ourselves in a state of complete confusion that could never be resolved, since we would be dealing seriously with symptoms rather than with what lay behind the symptoms.

Thwarting of unimportant desires produces no psychopathological results; thwarting of basically important needs does produce such results. Any theory of psychopathogenesis must then be based on a sound theory of motivation. A conflict or a frustration is not necessarily pathogenic. It becomes so only when it threatens or thwarts the basic needs or partial needs that are closely related to the basic needs.

THE ROLE OF GRATIFIED NEEDS

It hase been pointed out above several times that our needs usually emerge only when more prepotent needs have been gratified. Thus gratification has an important role in motivation theory. Apart from this, however, needs cease to place an active determining or organizing role as soon as they are gratified.

What this means is that, e.g., a basically satisfied person no longer has the needs for esteem, love, safety, etc. The only sense in which he might be said to have them is in the almost metaphysical sense that a sated man has hunger, or a filled bottle has emptiness. If we are interested in what *actually* motivates us, and not in what has, will, or might motivate us, then a satisfied need is not a motivator. It must be considered for all practical purposes simply not to exist, to have disappeared. This point should be emphasized because it has been either overlooked or contradicted in every theory of motivation I know. The perfectly healthy, normal, fortunate man has no sex needs or hunger needs, or needs for safety, or for love, or for prestige, or self-esteem, except in stray moments of quickly passing threat. If we were to say otherwise, we should also have to affirm that every man had all the pathological reflexes, e.g., Babinski, etc., because if his nervous system were damaged, these would appear.

It is such considerations as these that suggest the bold postulation that a man who is thwarted in any of his basic needs may fairly be envisaged simply as a sick man or at least less than fully human. This is a fair parallel to our designation as sick of the man who lacks vitamins or minerals. Who will say that a lack of love is less important than a lack of vitamins? Since we know the pathogenic effects of love starvation, who is to say that we are invoking value questions in an unscientific or illegitimate way, any more than the physician does who diagnoses and treats pellagra or scurvy? If I were permitted this usage, I should then say simply that a healthy man is primarily motivated by his needs to develop and actualize his fullest potentialities and capacities. If a man has any other basic needs in any active, chronic sense, he is simply an unhealthy man. He is as surely sick as if he had suddenly developed a strong salt hunger or calcium hunger.[9]

If this statement seems unusual or paradoxical, the reader may be assured that this is only one among many such paradoxes that will appear as we revise our ways of looking at man's deeper motivations. When we ask what man wants of life, we deal with his very essence.

FUNCTIONAL AUTONOMY

Gordon Allport (6, 7) has expounded and generalized the principle that means to an end may become ultimate satisfactions themselves, connected only historically to their origins. They may *come* to be wanted for their own sake. This reminder of the tremendous importance of learning and change on the motivational life superimposes upon everything that has gone before an enormous additional complexity. There is no contradiction between these two sets of psychological principles; they complement each other. Whether or not any needs so acquired may be considered true *basic* needs by the criteria so far used is a question for further research.

In any case, we have already seen that higher *basic* needs may become, after long gratification, independent both of their more powerful prerequisites and of their own proper satisfactions, i.e., an adult who was love-satisfied in his early years becomes *more* independent than average with regard to safety, belongingness, and love gratification at the present time. I prefer to think of the character structure as the most important single instance of functional autonomy in psychology. It is the strong, healthy, autonomous person who is most capable of withstanding loss of love and popularity. But this strength and health have been ordinarily produced in our society by early chronic gratifications of safety, love, belongingness, and esteem needs. Which is to say that these aspects of the person have become functionally autonomous, i.e., independent of the very gratifications that created them.

[9] If we were to use the word sick in this way, we should then also have to face squarely the relations of man to his society. One clear implication of our definition would be that (1) since a man is to be called sick who is basically thwarted, and (2) since such basic thwarting is made possible ultimately only by forces outside the individual, then (3) sickness in the individual must come ultimately from a sickness in the society. The good or healthy society would then be defined as one that permitted man's highest purposes to emerge by satisfying all his basic needs.

5

THE ROLE
OF BASIC
NEED GRATIFICATION
IN PSYCHOLOGICAL
THEORY

This chapter explores some of the many theoretical consequences of the approach to human motivation set forth in the last chapter, and should serve as a positive or healthy balance to the current one-sided stress on frustration and pathology.

We have seen that the chief principle of organization in human motivational life is the arrangement of basic needs in a hierarchy of less or greater priority or potency. The chief dynamic principle animating this organization is the emergence in the healthy person of less potent needs upon gratification of the more potent ones. The physiological needs, when unsatisfied, dominate the organism, pressing all capacities into their service and organizing these capacities so that they may be most efficient in this service. Relative gratification submerges them and allows the next higher set of needs in the hierarchy to emerge, dominate, and organize the personality, so that instead of being, e.g., hunger obsessed, it now becomes safety obsessed. The principle is the same for the other sets of needs in the hierarchy, i.e., love, esteem, and self-actualization.

It is also probably true that higher needs may occasionally emerge, not after gratification, but rather after forced or voluntary deprivation, renunciation, or suppression of lower basic needs and gratifications (asceticism, sublimation, strengthening effects of rejection, discipline, persecution, isolation, etc.). We know very little about either the frequency or the nature of these events, although they are reported to be common in

59

Eastern cultures. In any case, such phenomena do not contradict the theses of this book, since it is not claimed that gratification is the only source of strength or of other psychological desiderata.

Gratification theory is obviously a special, limited, or partial theory, not capable of independent existence or validity. It may achieve such validity only when structured with, at least, (1) frustration theory, (2) learning theory, (3) theory of neurosis, (4) theory of psychological health, (5) theory of values, and (6) theory of discipline, will, responsibility, etc. This chapter attempts to trace only one thread through the complex web of psychological determinants of behavior, the subjective life, and the character structure. Meanwhile, in lieu of a more rounded picture, it is freely granted that there are determinants other than basic need gratification, that basic need gratification may be necessary but it is certainly not sufficient, that gratification and deprivation each have both desirable and undesirable consequences, and that basic need gratification differs from neurotic need gratification in important respects.

SOME GENERAL CONSEQUENCES OF SATIATING A NEED

The most basic consequence of satiation of any need is that this need is submerged and a new and higher need emerges.[1] Other consequences are epiphenomena of this fundamental fact. Examples of these secondary consequences are

1. Independence of and a certain disdain for the old satisfiers and goal objects, with a new dependence on satisfiers and goal objects that hitherto had been overlooked, not wanted, or only casually wanted. This exchange of old satisfiers for new ones involves many tertiary consequences. Thus there are changes in interests. That is, certain phenomena become interesting for the first time and old phenomena become boring, or even repulsive. This is the same as saying that there are changes in human values. In general, there tend to be: (1) overestimation of the satisfiers of the most powerful of the ungratified needs; (2) underestimation of the satisfiers of the less powerful of the ungratified needs (and of the strength of these needs); and (3) underestimation and even devaluation of the satisfiers of the needs already gratified (and of the strength of these needs). This shift in values involves, as a dependent phenomenon, reconstruction in philosophy of the future, of the Utopia, of the heaven and hell, of the

---

[1] All these statements apply to basic needs only.

good life, and of the unconscious wish-fulfillment state of the individual in a crudely predictable direction.

In a word, we tend to take for granted the blessings we already have, especially if we don't have to work or struggle for them. The food, the security, the love, the admiration, the freedom that have always been there, that have never been lacking or yearned for tends not only to be unnoticed but also even to be devalued or mocked or destroyed. This phenomenon of failing to count one's blessings is, of course, not realistic and can therefore be considered to be a form of pathology. In most instances it is cured very easily, simply by experiencing the appropriate deprivation or lack, e.g., pain, hunger, poverty, loneliness, rejection, injustice, etc.

This relatively neglected phenomenon of postgratification forgetting and devaluation is, in my opinion, of very great potential importance and power. Further elaborations can be found in the chapter, On Low Grumbles, High Grumbles, and Metagrumbles, in my *Eupsychian Management: A Journal* (291), in various writings by F. Herzberg (193), and in Colin Wilson's concept of the "St. Neot Margin" (481, 483).

In no other way can we make sense of the puzzling way in which affluence (economic and psychological) can make possible *either* growth to loftier levels of human nature *or* the various forms of value pathology just hinted at, and spelled out in the newspaper headlines of recent years. Long ago, Adler in many of his writings (2, 3, 13) talked of the "pampered style of life" and perhaps we should use this term to differentiate pathogenic gratifications from healthy, necessary ones.

2. With this change in values go changes in the cognitive capacities. Attention, perception, learning, remembering, forgetting, thinking, all are changed in a crudely predictable direction because of the new interests and values of the organism.

3. These new interests, satisfiers, and needs, are not only new, but in certain senses are also higher (see Chapter 7). When the safety needs are gratified, the organism is released to seek for love, independence, respect, self-respect, etc. The easiest technique for releasing the organism from the bondage of the lower, more material, more selfish needs is to gratify them. (Needless to say, there are other techniques as well.)

4. Gratification of any need whatsoever, so long as this be a true gratification, i.e., of a basic rather than of a neurotic or pseudo need, helps to determine character formation (see below). Furthermore, any true need gratification tends toward the improvement, strengthening, and healthy development of the individual. That is, gratification of any basic

need in so far as we can speak of it in isolation, is a move in the healthy direction, away from the neurotic direction. It is in this sense undoubtedly that Kurt Goldstein spoke of *any* specific need gratification as being in the long run a step toward self-actualization.

5. Specific need gratifications and satiations have in addition to these general results certain specific *ad hoc* results as well. For instance, other factors being equal, a satisfaction of the safety needs brings specifically a subjective feeling of safety more restful sleep, loss of feeling of danger, greater boldness, courage, etc.

LEARNING AND BASIC NEED GRATIFICATION

A first consequence of exploring the effects of need gratification must be a growing dissatisfaction with the overexpanded role attributed to purely associative learning by its proponents.

In general, gratification phenomena, e.g., any loss of appetite after satiation, the change in quantity and type of defensiveness after safety need gratification, etc., demonstrate (1) *disappearance* with increased exercise (or repetition, use, or practice) and (2) *disappearance* with increased reward (or satisfaction, praise, or reinforcement). Furthermore, not only do gratification phenomena such as those listed in the table at the end of this chapter flout the laws of association in spite of the fact that they are acquired changes in adaptation, but examination shows also that arbitrary association is not involved except in a secondary fashion. Any definition of learning must therefore be insufficient if it stresses simply changes in the connection between stimuli and responses.

The task of need gratification is almost entirely limited to intrinsically appropriate satisfiers. In the long run, there can be no casual and arbitrary choice, except for nonbasic needs. For the love-hungry, there is only one genuine, long-run satisfier, i.e., honest and satisfying affection. For the sex-starved, food-starved, or water-starved person, only sex, food, or water will ultimatelly serve. This is the sort of intrinsic appropriateness stressed by Wertheimer (465), Köhler (238), and other recent Gestalt psychologists, such as Asch, Arnheim, Katona, etc., as a central concept in all fields of psychology. Here, no fortuitous collocation or accidental or arbitrary juxtaposition will do. Nor will signals or warnings or associates of the satisfiers do (350); only the satisfiers themselves gratify needs. We must speak with Murphy of canalization rather than mere association.

The essence of this critique of associative, behavioristic learning theory is that it takes entirely for granted the ends (purposes, goals) of the organism. It deals entirely with the manipulation of *means* to unstated ends. In contrast, the theory of basic needs presented here is a theory of the ends and ultimate values of the organism. These ends are intrinsically, and in themselves, valuable to the organism. It will therefore do anything necessary to achieve these goals, even to learning arbitrary, irrelevant, trivial or silly procedures that an experimenter may set up as the only way to get to these goals. These tricks are of course expendable, and are discarded (extinguished) when they no longer buy intrinsic satisfactions (or intrinsic reinforcements).

It seems quite clear then that the behavioral and subjective changes listed on pages 97–101 cannot possibly be explained by the laws of associative learning alone. Indeed, it is more likely that they play only a secondary role. If a mother kisses her child often, the drive itself disappears and the child learns *not* to crave kisses (268). Most contemporary writers on personality, traits, attitudes, and tastes speak of them as habit aggregations, acquired according to the laws of associative learning, but it now seems advisable to reconsider and correct this usage.

Not even in the more defensible sense of acquisition of insight and understanding (Gestalt learning) can character traits be considered to be wholly learned. This broader, Gestalt approach to learning, partly because of its coolness to the findings of psychoanalysis, is yet too limited in its rationalistic stress on the cognition of intrinsic structure in the outside world. We need a stronger tie to the conative and affective process *within* the person than is afforded either by associative learning or Gestalt learning. (But see also the writings of Kurt Lewin (274), which were undoubtedly helping to solve this problem.)

Without attempting any detailed discussion at this time, I would tentatively suggest what can be described as character learning, or intrinsic learning, which takes as its centering point changes in the character structure rather than in behavior. Among its main components are (1) the educative effects of unique (nonrepetitive) and of profound personal experiences, (2) the *affective* changes produced by repetitive experience (309), (3) the conative changes produced by gratification–frustration experiences, (4) the broad attitudinal, expectational, or even philosophical changes produced by certain types of early experience (266), (5) the determination by constitution of the variation in selective assimilation of any experience by the organism, etc.

Such considerations point to a closer rapprochement between the concepts of learning and character formation, until ultimately, as this writer believes, it may become fruitful for psychologists to define typical paradigmatic learning as *change in personal development, in character structure,* i.e., as movement toward self-actualization and beyond (308, 315, 317).

NEED GRATIFICATION AND
CHARACTER FORMATION

Certain a priori considerations strongly connect need gratification with the development of some, perhaps even many, character traits. Such doctrine would be no more than the logical opposite of an already well-established relationship between frustration and psychopathology.

If it is easy to accept basic need frustration as one determinant of hostility, it is quite as easy to accept the opposite of frustration, i.e., basic need gratification, as an a priori determinant of the opposite of hostility, i.e., friendliness. One is as strongly implied by psychoanalytic findings as the other. And even though explicit theoretical formulation is still lacking, psychotherapeutic *practice* accepts our hypothesis in its stress on implicit reassurance, support, permissiveness, approval, acceptance, that is to say, the ultimate gratification of the deep-lying needs of the patient for safety, love, protection, respect, worth, etc. Especially is this true with children, in whom love hunger, independence hunger, safety hunger, etc., are often, without further ado, treated directly with replacement or gratification therapy, i.e., by feeding them respectively love, independence, or safety (anaclitic therapy). But see also Ref. 1 for the limitations of such therapy.

It is a pity that there is so small a body of experimental material. What there is, however, is very impressive, e.g., the experiments of Levy (264–269). The general pattern of these experiments was to take a group of animals at birth, e.g., puppies, and submit them to either satiation of a need or partial frustration of it, for example, the suckling need.

Experiments of this type were made with pecking in chicks, suckling in human babies, activity in various species of animals. In all cases, it was discovered that a need that was fully gratified ran its typical course and then, depending on its nature, either disappeared altogether, e.g., suckling, or else maintained a certain low optimum level for the rest of the life span, e.g., activity. Those animals in which the need was frustrated developed various semipathological phenomena, of which the most relevant for us were persistence of the need past its normal time of disappearance, and secondly, greatly increased activity of the need.

The full relevance of childhood gratification to adult character formation is suggested especially by Levy's work with love (263, 268). It seems quite clear that many traits characteristic of the healthy adult are positive consequences of childhood gratification of the love needs, e.g., ability to allow independence to the loved one, the ability to withstand lack of love, the ability to love without giving up autonomy, etc.

To phrase this opposition in theory as clearly and flatly as I can, what it amounts to is that a mother loving her child well produces in the child (by her rewards, reinforcements, repetition, exercise, etc.) a *reduction* of the strength of love need through later life, a lowered probability of, e.g., kissing, a lesser amount of clinging to her, etc. The best way to teach a child to go seeking in all directions for affection and to have a constant craving for it is partially to *deny* him love (268). This is another illustration of the functional autonomy principle (see page 98) that forced Allport to be skeptical about contemporary learning theory.

Every teacher of psychology meets this theory of character traits as learned whenever he speaks of basic need-gratification with children, or of free choice experimentation. "If you pick up the child when he wakes from his dream, won't he learn to cry whenever he wants to be picked up (since you reward the crying)?" "If you allow the child to eat what he chooses, won't he be spoiled?" "If you pay attention to the child's antics, won't he learn to be silly in order to attract your attention?" "If you give the child his way, won't he want his way always?" These questions can*not* be answered by learning theories alone; we must *also* invoke gratification theory and the theory of functional autonomy to round out the picture. For more data, see the general literature of dynamic child psychology and psychiatry, especially that bearing on the permissive regime, e.g., Ref. 296.

Another type of data supporting the relationship between need gratification and character formation is available in the directly observable clinical effects of gratification. Such data are available to every person working directly with people, and can be confidently expected in almost every therapeutic contact.

The easiest way to convince ourselves of this is to examine the direct and immediate effects of gratification of the basic needs, beginning with the most potent. So far as the physiological needs are concerned, we in our culture do not regard as character traits, food satiation or water satiation, although under other cultural conditions we might. Even at this physiological level, however, we get some borderline cases for our thesis. Certainly, if we may speak of the needs for rest and sleep, we may therefore also speak of their frustration and its effects (sleepiness, fatigue, lack of energy, loginess, perhaps even laziness, lethargy, etc.), and gratification (alertness, vigor, zest, etc.). Here are immediate consequences of simple need gratification which, if they be not accepted character traits, are at least of definite interest to the student of personality. And while we are not accustomed yet to thinking so, the same can be said for the sex need, e.g., the category sex-obsessed and the contrasting one of sex-gratification for which we have as yet no respectable vocabulary.

At any rate, when we speak of the safety needs we are on much firmer ground. Apprehensiveness, fear, dread and anxiety, tension, nervousness, and jitteriness are all consequences of safety-need frustration. The same type of clinical observation clearly shows corresponding effects of safety-need gratification (for which as usual we lack adequate vocabulary), e.g., lack of anxiety, lack of nervousness, relaxedness, confidence in the future, assurance, security, etc. Whatever words we use, there is a character difference between the man who feels safe and the one who lives his life out as if he were a spy in enemy territory.

So it is for the other basic emotional needs for belongingness, for love, for respect, and for self-esteem. Gratification of these needs permits the appearance of such characteristics as affectionateness, self-respect, self-confidence, security, etc.

One step removed from these immediate characterological consequences of need gratification are such general traits as kindliness, generosity, unselfishness, bigness (as opposed to pettiness), equanimity, serenity, happiness, contentment, and the like. These seem to be consequences of the consequences, by-products of general need gratification, i.e., of generally improving psychological life condition, of surplus, plenty, affluence.

It is obvious that learning, in both its restricted and broader forms, also plays a role of importance in the genesis of these and other character traits. Whether it is a more powerful determiner, the data available today do not permit us to say, and this would ordinarily be brushed aside as a fruitless question. And yet the consequences of greater stress on one or the other are so contrasting that we must at least be aware of the problem. Whether character education can take place in the classroom, whether books, lectures, catechisms, and exhortations are the best tools to use, whether sermons and Sunday schools can produce good human beings, or rather whether the good life produces the good man, whether love, warmth, friendship, respect, and good treatment of the child are more consequential for his later character structure—these are the alternatives presented by adherence to one or the other theory of character formation and of education.

THE CONCEPT OF GRATIFICATION HEALTH

Let us say that person A has lived for several weeks in a dangerous jungle where he has managed to stay alive by finding occasional food and water. Person B not only stays alive but also has a rifle and a hidden cave with a closable entrance. Person C has all of these and has two more men with him as well. Person D has the food, the gun, the allies, the cave, and in addition, has with him his best-loved friend. Finally, Person E, in the same jungle, has all of these, and in addition is the well-respected leader of his band. For the sake of brevity we may call these men, respectively, the merely surviving, the safe, the belonging, the loved, and the respected.

But this is not only a series of increasing basic need gratifications; it is as well *a series of increasing degrees of psychological health.*[2] It is clear that, other things being equal, a man who is safe and belongs and is loved will be healthier (by *any* reasonable definition) than a man who is safe and belongs, but who is rejected and unloved. And if in addition, he wins respect and admiration, and because of this, develops his self-respect, then he is still *more* healthy, self-actualizing, or fully human.

It would seem that degree of basic need gratification is positively correlated with degree of psychological health. Can we go further and affirm the limit of such a correlation, namely, that complete gratification of basic needs and ideal health are the same? Gratificaton theory would at least *suggest* such a possibility. (But see 315.) Although of course, the answer to such a question waits upon future research, even the bare statement of such a hypothesis directs our gaze to neglected facts and bids us ask again old and unanswered questions.

For instance, we must of course grant that there are other paths to health as well. And yet it is fair to ask as we choose life paths for our children, just how often health is achieved through ascetism, through renunciation of basic needs, through discipline, and through tempering in the fire of frustration, tragedy, and unhappiness, i.e., what are the relative frequencies of gratification health and frustration health?

This theory also confronts us with the prickly problem of selfishness, as raised by Wertheimer and his students, who have tended to identify

---

[2] It is pointed out further on that this same continuum of increasing degree of need gratification may also be used as the basis for a possible classification of personalities. Taken as steps or levels of maturing or personal growth toward self-actualization, through the individual's life span, it supplies a schema for a developmental theory roughly approximating and paralleling Freud's and Erikson's developmental system (123, 141).

all needs as *ipso facto* selfish and ego-centered. It is true that self-actualization, the ultimate need, is defined by Goldstein and in this book in a highly individualistic way, and yet empirical study of very healthy people shows them to be at the same time extremely individual and healthily selfish and extremely compassionate and altruistic, as will be seen in Chapter 11.

When we posit the concept of gratification health (or happiness health), we implicitly align ourselves thereby with those writers, Goldstein, Jung, Adler, Angyal, Horney, Fromm, May, Buhler, Rogers, and increasingly, others, who postulate some positive growth tendency in the organism which, from within, drives it to fuller development.[3]

For if we assume that the healthy organism is, paradigmatically, basic need-gratified and therefore released for self-actualization, then we have thereby also assumed that this organism develops from within by intrinsic growth tendencies, in the Bergsonian sense, rather than from without, in the behavioristic sense of environmental determinism. The neurotic organism is one that lacks basic need satisfactions that can come only from other people. It is therefore more dependent on other people and is less autonomous and self-determined, i.e., more shaped by the nature of the environment and less shaped by its own intrinsic nature. Such relative independence of environment as is found in the healthy person does not, of course, mean lack of commerce with it; it means only that in these contacts the person's *ends* and his own nature are the primary determinants, and that the environment is primarily a means to the person's self-actualizing ends. This is truly psychological freedom (398).

OTHER PHENOMENA DETERMINED IN PART BY NEED GRATIFICATION

What follows is a brief listing of a few of the more important hypotheses that are suggested by gratification theory. Others are listed on pages 72–79.

PSYCHOTHERAPY

It could probably be maintained that basic need gratification is primary in the dynamics of actual cure or improvement. Certainly it must be granted that at minimum, it is *one* such factor and an especially impor-

---

3 There are literally dozens and hundreds of such writers and researchers. A full list would be a very long catalogue and I mention here only a few of the older generation. The membership list of the American Association of Humanistic Psychology is more inclusive. So is the list of contributors in (344, 419, 69, 441).

tant one because so far neglected. This thesis will be discussed more fully in Chapter 15.

ATTITUDES, INTEREST, TASTES, AND VALUES

Several examples were given of the ways in which interests were determined by the gratification and frustration of needs. Also see Maier (284). It would be possible to go *much* further with this, ultimately involving necessarily a discussion of morality, values, and ethics, insofar as these are more than etiquette, manners, folkways, and other local social habits. The current fashion is to treat attitudes, tastes, interests, and indeed values of *any* kind as if they had no determinant other than local cultural associative learning, i.e., as if they were determined wholly by arbitrary environmental forces. But we have seen that it is necessary to invoke also intrinsic requiredness, and the effects of gratification of organismic needs.

CLASSIFICATION OF PERSONALITY

If we think of gratification of the hierarchy of basic emotional needs as a straight-line continuum, we are furnished with a helpful (even though imperfect) tool for classifying types of personality. If most people have similar organismic needs, each person can be compared with any other in the degree to which these needs are satisfied. This is a holistic or organismic principle because it classifies whole persons on a single continuum rather than parts or aspects of persons on a multiplicity of unrelated continua.

BOREDOM AND INTEREST

What, after all, is boredom but overgratification? And yet here too, we may find unsolved and unperceived problems. Why does repeated contact with painting A, woman A, music A produce boredom; while the same number of contacts with painting B, woman B, music B produces enhanced interest and heightened pleasure?

HAPPINESS, JOY, CONTENTMENT, ELATION, ECSTASY

What role does need gratification play in the production of the positive emotions? Students of emotion have too long confined their studies to the affective effects of frustration (259).

SOCIAL EFFECTS

In the table below are listed various ways in which gratification seems to have good social effects. That is, it is put forward as a thesis for further investigation that satisfying man's basic needs (all things being equal, putting aside certain puzzling exceptions, and for the moment neglecting the desirable effects of deprivation and of discipline) improves him not only in character structure but as a citizen on the national and international scene as well as in his face-to-face relationships. The possible implications for political, economic, educational, historical, and sociological theory are both tremendous and obvious (17, 104, 356, 488).

FRUSTRATION LEVEL

In a certain sense, paradoxical though it may seem, need gratification is a determinant of need frustration. This is true because higher needs will not even appear in consciousness until lower, prepotent needs are gratified. And in a sense, until they exist consciously, they cannot produce feelings of frustration. The merely surviving man will not worry much over the higher things of life, the study of geometry, the right to vote, the good name of his city, respect; he is primarily concerned with more basic goods. It takes a certain amount of gratification of lower needs to elevate him to the point where he is civilized enough to feel frustrated about the larger personal, social, and intellectual issues.

As a consequence, we may grant that most men are doomed to wish for what they do not have, and yet definitely *not* feel that it is useless to work for greater satisfaction quanta for all. Thus we learn simultaneously not to expect miracles from any single social reform (e.g., women suffrage, free education, secret ballot, labor unions, good housing, direct primaries), and yet not to underrate the reality of slow advance.

If a man must feel frustrated or worried, it is better for society that he worry about ending war than about being cold or hungry. Clearly raising the frustration level (if we may speak of higher and lower frustrations) has not only personal but also social consequences. Approximately the same may be said of the level of guilt and shame.

EMERGENCE OF FUN, PLEASANT AIMLESSNESS,
CASUAL AND RANDOM BEHAVIOR

Long remarked upon by philosophers, artists, and poets, this whole area of behavior has been strangely neglected by the scientific psychologists. Possibly this is because of the widely accepted dogma that all behavior is motivated. Without wishing at this moment to argue this (in the writer's opinion) mistake, there can yet be no question about the observation that, immediately after satiation, the organism allows itself to give up pressure, tension, urgency, and necessity, to loaf, laze, and relax, to putter, to be passive, to enjoy the sun, to ornament, decorate, and polish the pots and pans, to play and have fun, to observe what is of no importance, to be casual and aimless, to learn incidentally rather than with purpose; in a word, to be (relatively) unmotivated. Need gratification permits the emergence of unmotivated behavior (see Chapter 14 for fuller discussion).

GRATIFICATION-PRODUCED PATHOLOGY

Life in recent years has certainly taught us something about the pathology of *material* (lower need) affluence, of such outcomes as boredom, selfishness, feelings of eliteness, and of "deserved" superiority, of fixation at a low level of immaturity, of the destruction of brotherhood. Clearly, living the material or lower need life is not in itself satisfying for any length of time.

But now we are being confronted by a new possibility of pathology of psychological affluence; that is, of suffering from the consequences (apparently) of being loved and cared for devotedly, of being adored, admired, applauded, and listened to self-effacedly, of being given the center of the stage, of having loyal servants, of having every here-and-now wish granted, even of being the objects of self-sacrifice and self-abnegation.

It is true that we just don't know much about these new phenomena, certainly not in any developed scientific sense. All we have are strong suspicions, widespread clinical impressions, the slowly hardening opinion of child psychologists and educators that merely and only basic-need gratification is not enough, but that some experience with firmness, toughness, frustration, discipline, and limits is also needed by the child. Or to say it another way, basic need gratification had better be defined more carefully because it so easily slips over into unbridled indulgence, self-abnegation, total permissiveness, over protection, toadyism. Love and respect for the child must at the very least be integrated with love and respect for oneself as a parent and for adulthood in general. Children are certainly persons, but they are not experienced persons. They must be counted on to be unwise about many things, and positively stupid about some.

Gratification-produced pathology may also turn out to be in part what could be called metapathology (314), an absence of values, of meaningfulness and of fulfillment in life. It is believed by many humanists and existential psychologists—not yet with sufficient data to be sure, however—that gratification of all the basic needs does not *automatically* solve the problem of identity, of a value system, of a calling in life, of the meaning of life. For some people at least, especially young people, these are separate and additional life-tasks beyond the gratification of the basic needs.

Finally, I mention again the little understood facts that human beings seem almost never to be permanently satisfied or content (291) and—deeply connected with this—that we tend to get used to our blessings, to forget them, to take them for granted, even to cease to value them. For many people—we don't know how many—even the highest pleasures may grow stale and may lose their newness (483), and can be made properly valuable again only by some experience of deprivation, frustration, threat, or even tragedy. For such people, especially those with little zest in experiencing, with low vitality, with weak ability to have peak-experiences, with strong blocks against enjoying and against pleasure, it may be *necessary* to experience loss of their blessings in order to be able to appreciate them again.

FUNCTIONAL AUTONOMY OF HIGHER NEEDS

Although it is generally true that we move to higher need levels after gratification of the lower needs, it yet remains an observable phenomenon that once having attained these higher need levels and the values and tastes that go with them they may become autonomous, no longer depending on lower need gratifications. Such persons may even despise and spurn the lower need gratifications that made possible their "higher life," in about the same spirit that third-generation wealth becomes ashamed of first- generation wealth, or as the educated children of immigrants may be ashamed of their cruder parents.

SOME PHENOMENA THAT ARE IN LARGE PART DETERMINED BY BASIC NEED GRATIFICATION

A. Conative-Affective

1. Feelings of physical sating and glut—food, sex, sleep, etc.—and, as *by-products*—well-being, health, energy, euphoria, physical contentment
2. Feelings of safety, peace, security, protection, lack of danger and threat
3. Feelings of belongingness, of being one of a group, of identification with group goals and triumphs, of acceptance, or having a place, at-homeness
4. Feelings of loving and being loved, of being loveworthy, of love identification
5. Feelings of self-reliance, self-respect, self-esteem, confidence, trust in

oneself; feeling of ability, achievement, competence, success, ego strength, respectworthiness, prestige, leadership, independence

6. Feelings of self-actualization, self-fulfillment, self-realization, of more and more complete development and fruition of one's resources and potentialities and consequent feeling of growth, maturity, health, and autonomy

7. Satisfied curiosity, feeling of learning and of knowing more and more

8. Satisfied understanding, more and more philosophical satisfaction; movement toward larger and larger, more and more inclusive and unitary philosophy or religion; increased perception of connections and relations; awe; value commitment

9. Satisfied beauty need, thrill, sensuous shock, delight, ectasy, sense of symmetry, rightness, suitability, or perfection

10. Emergence of higher needs

11. Temporary or long-run dependence on and independence of various satisfiers; increasing independence of and disdain for lower needs and lower satisfiers

12. Aversion and appetite feelings

13. Boredom and interest

14. Improvement in values; improvement in taste; better choosing

15. Greater possibility of and greater intensity of pleasant excitement, happiness, joy, delight, contentment, calm, serenity, exultation; richer and more positive emotional life

16. More frequent occurrence of ecstasy, peak experiences, orgasmic emotion, exaltation, and of mystic experience

17. Changes in aspiration level

18. Changes in frustration level

19. Movement toward metamotivation (314) and being-values (293)

B. Cognitive

1. Keener, more efficient, more realistic cognition of all types; better reality-testing

2. Improved intuitive powers; more successful hunches

3. Mystic experience with illuminations and insights

4. More reality-object-and-problem centering; less projection and ego centering; more transpersonal and transhuman cognitions (295, 317)

5. Improvement in world view and in philosophy (in sense of becoming more true, more realistic, less destructive of self and others, more comprehensive, more integrated and holistic, etc.)

6. More creativeness, more art, poetry, music, wisdom, science
7. Less rigid robotlike conventionality; less stereotyping, less compulsive rubricizing (see Chapter 13); better perception of individual uniqueness through screen of man-made categories and rubrics; less dichotomizing
8. Many of the more basic, deeper attitudes (democratic, basic respect for all human beings, affection for others, love and respect for children, fellowship with women, etc.)
9. Less preference and need for the familiar, especially for important things; less fear of the novel and unfamiliar
10. More possibility of incidental or latent learning
11. Less need for the simple; more pleasure in the complex

C. Character Traits

1. More calmness, equanimity, serenity, peace of mind (opposite of tension, nervousness, unhappiness, feeling miserable)
2. Kindness, kindliness, sympathy, unselfishness (opposite of cruelty)
3. Healthy generosity
4. Bigness (opposite of pettiness, meanness, smallness)
5. Self-reliance, self-respect, self-esteem, confidence, trust in oneself
6. Feelings of safety, peacefulness, lack of danger
7. Friendliness (opposite of character-based hostility)
8. Greater frustration tolerance
9. Tolerance of, interest in, and approval of individual differences and therefore loss of prejudice and generalized hostility (but not loss of judgment); greater feeling of brotherhood, comradeship, brotherly love, respect for others
10. More courage; less fear
11. Psychological health and all its by-products; movement away from neurosis, psychopathic personality, and perhaps psychosis
12. More profoundly democratic (fearless and realistic respect for others who are worthy of it)
13. Relaxation; less tense
14. More honesty, genuineness, and straightforwardness; less cant, less phoniness
15. Stronger will; more enjoyment of responsibility

D. Interpersonal

1. Better citizen, neighbor, parent, friend, lover
2. Political, economic, religious, educational growth and openness

3. Respect for women, children, employees, and other minorities or groups with less power
4. More democratic, less authoritarian (303)
5. Less unwarranted hostility and more friendliness, more interest in others, easier identification with others
6. Better taste in friends, sweethearts, leaders, etc., better judge of people; better chooser
7. Nicer person, more attractive; more beautiful
8. Better psychotherapist

E. Miscellaneous

1. Changed picture of heaven, hell, Utopia, good life, success and failure, etc.
2. Move toward higher values; toward higher "spiritual life"
3. Changes in all expressive behavior, e.g., smile, laugh, facial expression, demeanor, walk, handwriting; movement toward more expressive behavior and less coping behavior
4. Energy changes, lassitude, sleep, quiet, rest, alertness
5. Hopefulness, interest in future (opposite of loss of morale, apathy, anhedonia)
6. Changes in dream life, fantasy life, early memories (9)
7. Changes in (character-based) morality, ethics, values
8. Move away from win–lose, adversary, zero–sum–game way of life

6

THE INSTINCTOID
NATURE
OF BASIC NEEDS

INSTINCT THEORY REEXAMINED

REASONS FOR REEXAMINING INSTINCT THEORY

The theories of basic needs sketched out in previous chapters suggest and even call for a reconsideration of instinct theory, if only because of the necessity for differentiating between more and less basic, more and less healthy, more and less natural. Furthermore, we ought not to postpone indefinitely an examination of certain related questions unavoidably raised by this and other theories of basic needs (353, 160), e.g., the implied discarding of cultural relativity, the implied theory of constitutionally given values, the unmistakable narrowing of the jurisdiction assigned to associative, means learning, etc.

There are, in any case, a considerable number of other theoretical, clinical, and experimental considerations pointing in this same direction, i.e., the desirability of reevaluating instinct theory and perhaps even of resurrecting it in some form or other. These all support a certain skepticism with regard to the current, almost exclusive stress by psychologists, sociologists, and anthropologists on the plasticity, flexibility, and adaptability of the human being and on his ability to learn. Human beings seem to be far more autonomous and self-governed than current psychological theory allows for.

1. The homeostasis concept of Cannon (78), the death instinct of Freud (138), etc.

2. The appetite or free choice or cafeteria experiments (492, 491)

3. The instinct-satiation experiments of Levy (264–269), as well as his work on maternal overprotection (263) and affect hunger

4. The various psychoanalytic discoveries about the deleterious effects of overdemanding toilet training and hasty weaning in children

5. The host of observations that have led many educators, nursery school workers, and practical child psychologists to lean toward more reliance on self-choice in their dealings with children

6. The system of concepts explicitly underlying Rogerian therapy

7. The many neurological and biological data reported by the vitalists (112), by emergent evolutionists (46), by the modern experimental embryologists (435), and by such holists as Goldstein (160), on spontaneous readjustment of the organism after damage

These and other researches to be mentioned combine to suggest strongly that the organism is more trustworthy, more self-protecting, self-directing, and self-governing than it is usually given credit for. In addition, we may add that various recent developments have shown the theoretical necessity for the postulation of some sort of positive growth or self-actualization tendency within the organism, which is different from its conserving, equilibrating, or homeostatic tendency, as well as from the tendency to respond to impulses from the outside world. This kind of tendency to growth or self-actualization, in one or another vague form, has been postulated by thinkers as diverse as Aristotle and Bergson, and by many other philosophers. Among psychiatrists, psychoanalysts, and psychologists it has been found necessary by Goldstein, Bühler, Jung, Horney, Fromm, Rogers, and many others.

Perhaps, however, the most important influence in favor of reexamining instinct theory is the experience of the psychotherapists, especially the psychoanalysts. In this area, the logic of facts, however unclearly seen, has been unmistakable; inexorably, the therapist has been forced to differentiate more basic from less basic wishes (or needs, or impulses). It is as simple as this: the frustration of some needs produces pathology, the frustration of other needs does not. The gratification of these needs produces health, of others not. These needs are inconceivably stubborn and recalcitrant. They resist all blandishments, substitutions, bribes, and alternatives; nothing will do for them but their proper and intrinsic gratifications. Consciously or unconsciously they are craved and sought forever. They behave always like stubborn, irreducible, final, unanalyzable facts that must be taken as given or as starting points not to be questioned. It should be an overwhelmingly impressive point that almost every school of psychiatry, psychoanalysis, clinical psychology, social work, or child therapy has *had* to postulate some doctrine of instinctlike needs no matter how much they disagreed on every other point.

Inevitably, such experiences remind us of species characteristics, of constitution, and of heredity rather than of superficial and easily manipulated habits. Wherever a choice has had to be made between the horns of this dilemma, the therapist has almost always chosen the instinct rather than the conditioned response or the habit as his basic building block. This is of course unfortunate, for as we shall see, there are other intermediate and more valid alternatives from among which we may now make a more satisfying choice, i.e., there are more than two horns to the dilemma.

But it does seem clear that, from the point of view of the demands of general dynamic theory, the instinct theory, as presented especially by McDougall and Freud, had certain virtues that were not sufficiently appreciated at the time, perhaps because its mistakes were so much more evident. Instinct theory accepted the fact that man was a self-mover; that his own nature as well as his environment helped to decide his behavior; that his own nature supplied him with a ready-made framework of ends, goals, or values; that most often, under good conditions, what he wants is what he needs (what is good for him) in order to avoid sickness; that all men form a single biological species; that behavior is senseless unless one understands its motivations and its goals; and that on the whole, organisms left to their own resources often display a kind of biological efficiency, or wisdom, that needs explaining.

MISTAKES OF INSTINCT THEORY

It will be our contention here that many of the mistakes of the instinct theorists, while profound and deserving of rejection, were by no means intrinsic or inevitable, and that, furthermore, a fair number of these mistakes were shared by both the instinctivists and their critics.

1. The semantic and logical errors were most flagrant. The instinctivists were accused deservedly of *ad hoc* creation of instincts to explain behavior they could not understand, or whose origins they could not determine. But of course, being properly forewarned, *we* need not hypostatize, confuse labels with facts, or propound invalid syllogisms. We know *much* more about semantics today.

2. We now know so much more about ethnology, sociology, and

genetics that we can avoid both the simple ethnocentrism and class-centrism and the simple social Darwinism that brought the early instinc-tivists to grief.

We must now also recognize that the recoil from the ethnological naïveté of the instinctivists was so extreme and sweeping as to constitute in itself a mistake, i.e., cultural relativity. This doctrine, so influential and so widely accepted during the last two decades, is now being very widely criticized (148). Certainly it is now again respectable to seek for crosscul-tural, species characteristics, as the instinctivists did. Apparently we must (and can) avoid both ethnocentrism and an overstated cultural relativism. For instance, it seems quite clear that instrumental behavior (means) are far more relative to local cultural determinants than are the basic needs (ends).

3. Most anti-instinctivists, e.g., Bernard, Watson, Kuo, and others, in the 1920s and 1930s criticized instinct theory on the ground that in-stincts could not be described in specific stimulus-response terms. What this boils down to is the accusation that instincts do not conform to simple behavioristic theory. This is true; they do not indeed. Such a criticism, however, is not taken seriously today by dynamic and humanistic psychol-ogists, who uniformly consider that it is impossible to define *any* impor-tant human whole quality or whole activity in stimulus-response terms alone.

Such an attempt can breed little more than confusion. We can take as a single typical instance the confounding of reflex with the classical lower animal instinct. The former is a pure motor act; the latter is this and a great deal more, i.e., predetermined impulse, expressive behavior, coping behavior, goal object, and affect.

4. Even on logical grounds alone, there is no reason why we should be forced to choose between the full instinct, complete in all its parts, and the noninstinct. Why may there not be instinct remnants, instinctlike aspects of impulse alone or of behavior alone, difference of degree, partial instincts?

Too many writers used the word instinct indiscriminately to cover need, aim, ability, behavior, perception, expression, value, and emotional concomitants, singly or in combination. The result was a hodgepodge of loose usage in which almost every known human reaction was characterized as instinctive by one or another writer, as Marmor (289) and Bernard (47) have pointed out.

Our main hypothesis is that human *urges* or *basic needs* alone may be innately given to at least some appreciable degree. The pertinent be-havior or ability, cognition or affection need not also be innate, but may be (by our hypothesis) learned, canalized, or expressive. (Of course, many of man's *abilities* or *capacities* are strongly determined or made possible by hereditary, e.g., color vision, etc., but they are of no concern to us at this point.) This is to say that the hereditary component of basic needs may be seen as simple conative lack, tied to no intrinsic goal-achieving behavior, as blind, directionless demands, like Freud's id impulses. (We shall see below that the satisfiers of these basic needs seem also to be intrinsic in a definable way.) What has to be learned is goal-bent (coping) behavior.

It was a severe mistake of both the instinctivists and their opponents to think in black and white dichotomous terms instead of in terms of degree. How could it be said that a complex set of reactions was either *all* determined by heredity or *not at all* determined by heredity? There is no structure, however simple, let alone any whole reaction, that has genic determinants alone. Even Mendel's sweet peas needed air and water and food. For that matter even the genes themselves have an environment, i.e., neighboring genes.

At the other extreme it is also obvious that nothing is completely free of the influence of heredity, for man is a biological species. This fact, determined by heredity, is a precondition of every human action, ability, cognition, etc., i.e., everything that a human being can do is made possible by the fact that he is a member of the human species. This membership is hereditary.

One confusing consequence of this invalid dichotomy is the tendency to define any activity as noninstinctive if *any* learning can be demonstrated; or contrawise, to define an activity as instinctive if *any* hereditary influence at all can be demonstrated. Since for most, perhaps all, urges, abilities, or emotions it is easy to demonstrate both kinds of determination, such arguments must be forever insoluble.

The instinctivists and anti-instinctivists both were all or nothing; we of course need not be. This is an avoidable mistake.

5. The paradigm for instinct theorists was the animal instinct. This led to various mistakes, e.g., failing to look for instincts unique to the human species. The one most misleading lesson, however, that was learned from the lower animals was the axiom that instincts were powerful, strong, unmodifiable, uncontrollable, unsuppressible. However this may be for salmon, or frogs, or lemmings, it is not true for humans.

If, as we feel, basic needs have an appreciable hereditary base, we may very well have blundered when we looked for instincts with only the naked eye and considered an entity instinctive only when it was obviously and unmistakably independent of and more powerful than all environmental forces. Why should there not be needs that, though instinctoid, yet are easily repressed, suppressed, or otherwise controlled, and that are easily masked or modified or even suppressed by habits, suggestions, by cultural pressures, by guilt, and so on (as, for instance, seems to be true for the love need)? That is to say, why not *weak* instincts?

It may be that the motive power behind the culturalists' attack on instinct theory comes largely from this mistaken identification of instinct with overpowering strength. The experience of every ethnologist contradicts such an assumption, and attack is therefore understandable. But if we were properly respectful of both the cultural and the biological (as this writer is), and if further we considered culture to be a stronger force than instinctoid need (as this writer does), then it would not seem a paradox but an obvious matter of course that it should be maintained (as this writer maintains) that we ought to protect the weak, subtle, and tender instinctoid needs if they are not to be overwhelmed by the tougher, more powerful culture, rather than the other way about. This could be so even though these same instinctoid needs are in another sense strong, i.e., they persist, they demand gratification, their frustration produces highly pathological consequences, etc.

To make the point, a paradox may help. I think of uncovering, insight, depth therapies—which include practically all but the hypnosis and behavior therapies—to be, from one point of view, an uncovering, a recovering, a strengthening of our weakened and lost instinctoid tendencies and instinct-remnants, our painted-over animal selves, our subjective biology. This ultimate purpose is even more nakedly stated in the so-called personal growth workshops. These—both the therapies and the workshops—are expensive, painful, long drawn-out efforts. ultimately taking a whole lifetime of struggle, patience and fortitude, and even then they may fail. But how many cats or dogs or birds need help to discover how to be a cat or a dog or a bird? Their impulse-voices are loud, clear and unmistakable, where ours are weak, confused and easily overlooked so that we need help to hear them.

This explains why animal naturalness is seen most clearly in self-actualizing people, least clearly in neurotic or "normally sick" people. I might go so far as to say that sickness often consists of just *exactly* the loss of one's animal nature. The clearest specieshood and animality is thus paradoxically seen in the *most* spiritual, the *most* saintly and sagacious, the *most* (organismically) rational.

6. An even worse mistake derives from this focusing on animal instincts. For inscrutable reasons that only the intellectual historian may be able to unravel, western civilization has generally believed that the animal

in us was a bad animal, and that our most primitive impulses are evil, greedy, selfish, and hostile.[1]

The theologians have called it original sin, or the devil. The Freudians have called it id, and philosophers, economists, and educators all have called it by various names. Darwin was so identified with this view that he saw only competition in the animal world, completely overlooking the coöperation that is just as common, and that Kropotkin saw so easily.

One expression of this world view has been to identify this animal within us with wolves, tigers, pigs, vultures, or snakes rather than with better, or at least milder, animals like the deer or elephant or dog or chimpanzee. This we may call the bad-animal interpretation of our inner nature, and point out that if we *must* reason from animals to men, it would be better if we chose those who were closest to us, i.e., the anthropoid apes. Since these are, on the whole, pleasant and likable animals sharing with us many characteristics that we call virtuous, the bad-animal outlook is not supported by comparative psychology (306).

7. Still another possibility must be kept in mind with regard to the assumption of unchangeability and unmodifiability of hereditary traits. It is this: even if a trait be primarily determined by genic heredity, it may yet be modifiable—even perhaps *easily* modifiable or controllable if we are fortunate enough in our discoveries. If we assume cancer to have a strong hereditary component, this need not stop anyone from hunting for a means to control it. If only on a priori grounds, we could also admit the possibility that IQ may turn out to be measurably hereditary and at the same time improvable by education and by psychotherapy.

---

[1] Is it not possible that the primitive and unconscious side of man's nature might be more effectively tamed, even radically transformed? If not, civilization is doomed [p. 5]. Beneath the decent facade of consciousness with its disciplined, moral order and its good intentions, lurk the crude instinctive forces of life, like monsters of the deep— devouring, begetting, warring endlessly. They are for the most part unseen, yet on their urge and energy life itself depends: without them living beings would be as inert as stones. But were they left to function unchecked, life would lose its meaning, being reduced once more to mere birth and death, as in the teeming world of primordial swamps [p. 1]. The instinctive forces that caused the dynamic upheaval in Europe, and obliterated in a decade the work of centuries of civilization. . . . [p. 3]. So long as the religious and social forms are able to contain and in some measure to satisfy the inner and outer life needs of the individuals who make up the community, the instinctive forces lie dormant and for the most part we forget their very existence. Yet at times they awaken from their slumber, and then the noise and tumult of their elemental struggle breaks in upon our ordered lives and rouses us rudely from our peace and contentment. Nevertheless we try to blind ourselves into believing that man's rational mind has conquered not only the world of nature around him, but also the world of natural instinctive life within" (p. 2). (Harding, M. E., *Psychic Energy*, Pantheon, 1947.)

8. We must make room for far more variability in the realm of instincts than was allowed by the instinct theorists. The needs to know and to understand seem to be *obviously* potent only in intelligent individuals. They seem to be practically absent or at least very rudimentary in the feeble-minded. Levy (263) has shown that the maternal impulse varies so widely in women as to be not detectable in some. The special talents, which very likely have genic determinants, e.g., as in music, mathematics, art (411), are absent in most people.

The instinctoid impulses can disappear altogether, as apparently animal instincts cannot. For example, in the psychopathic personality the needs for being loved and loving have disappeared, and so far as we know today, this is usually a permanent loss, i.e., the psychopathic personality is usually incurable by any known psychotherapeutic technique. We also have older examples from studies (119) on unemployment in an Austrian village, etc., to indicate that long unemployment may crush morale so badly as to destroy certain needs. Such destroyed needs may not return in some even when environmental conditions improve. Similar material has been obtained from the Nazi concentration camps. Bateson's and Mead's (34) observations on the Balinese may also be pertinent. The adult Balinese is not a loving person in our western sense and need not be. Since the motion pictures from Bali show that the infants and children cry and bitterly resent the lack of affection, we can only conclude that this loss of affectionate impulse is an acquired loss.

9. We have seen that instincts and flexible, cognitive adaptation to the novel tend to be mutually exclusive in the phyletic scale. The more of one we find, the less of the other we may expect. Because of this the vital and even tragic mistake (in view of the historical consequences) has been made from time immemorial, of dichotomizing instinctive impulse and rationality in the human being. It has rarely occurred to anyone that they might *both* be instinctoid in the human being, and more important, that their results or implied goals might be identical and synergic rather than antagonistic.

It is our contention that the impulses to know and to understand may be exactly as conative as the needs to belong or to love.

In the ordinary instinct-reason dichotomy or contrast, it is a badly defined instinct and a badly defined reason that are opposed to each other. If they were correctly defined in accordance with modern knowledge, they would be seen as not contrasting or opposing or even as strongly different from each other. Healthy reason as definable today, and healthy instinctoid impulses point in the same direction and are *not* in opposition to each other in the healthy person (although they *may* be antagonistic in the unhealthy). As a single example, all the scientific data now available indicate that it is psychiatrically desirable for children to be protected, accepted, loved, and respected. But this is precisely what children (instinctively) desire. It is in this very tangible and scientifically testable sense that we assert instinctoid needs and rationality to be probably synergic and not antagonistic. Their apparent antagonism is an artifact produced by an exclusive preoccupation with sick people. If this turns out to be true, we shall have thereby resolved the age-old problem of which should be master, instinct or reason, a question now as obsolete as, e.g., Which should be the boss in a good marriage, the husband or the wife?

10.   From instinct theory, as understood in its heyday, flowed many social, economic, and political consequences of the most conservative and even antidemocratic nature, as is conclusively demonstrated by Pastore (372) especially in his analysis of McDougall and Thorndike (the writer would add Jung and perhaps Freud). These arose from the (mistaken) identification of heredity with fate, inexorable, irresistible, and unmodifiable.

This conclusion was erroneous as we shall see. *Weak* instinctoid needs a beneficent culture for their appearance, expression, and gratification, and are easily blasted by bad cultural conditions. Our society, for instance, must be considerably improved before weakly hereditary needs may expect gratification.

In any case Pastore's (372) correlation is shown to be not an intrinsic one by the recently revealed necessity to use two continua and not just one. The continuum liberal-conservative has given way to the two continua of socialist-capitalist *and* democratic-authoritarian even in scientific questions. There may now be counted environmentalist-authoritarian-socialist or environmentalist-democratic-socialist, or environmentalist-democratic-capitalist, etc.

In any case to accept as intrinsic an antagonism between instincts and society, between individual interests and social interests was a terrific begging of the question. Possibly its main excuse was that in the sick society and in the sick individual, it actually tends to be true. But, as Benedict (40, 291, 312) has proved, it *need* not be true. And in the good society, or at least in the kind she describes, it *cannot* be true. Individual and social interests under healthy social conditions are synergic and *not* antagonistic. The false dichotomy persists only because erroneous conceptions of individual and social interests are the natural ones under bad individual and social conditions.

11.   One lack in instinct theory, as in most other theories of motivation, was the failure to realize that impulses are dynamically related to

each other in a hierarchy of differential strength. If impulses are treated independently of each other, various problems must remain unsolved, and many pseudo problems are created. For instance, the essentially holistic or unitary quality of the motivational life is obscured, and the insoluble problem of making lists of motives is created. In addition, the value or choice principle is lost that permits us to say one need is higher than another, or more important than another or even more basic than another. By far the most important single consequence of this atomizing of the motivational life is to open the door to instincts toward Nirvana, death, quiescence, homeostasis, complacency, equilibrium. This is so because the *only* thing that a need, taken discretely, can do is to press for gratification, which is to say, its own obliteration.

This neglects the obvious fact that the gratification of any need, while putting that need to rest, allows other weaker needs that have been pushed aside to come to the foreground to press their claims. Needing never ceases. The gratification of one need uncovers another.

12. Coordinate with the bad-animal interpretation of instincts was the expectation that they would be seen most clearly in the insane, the neurotic, the criminal, the feeble-minded, or the desperate. This follows naturally from the doctrine that conscience, rationality, and ethics are no more than an acquired veneer, completely different in character from what lies beneath, and are related to that underneath as manacles to prisoner. From this misconception follows the phrasing of civilization and all its institutions—school, church, court, legislation—as bad-animality-restraining forces.

This mistake is so crucial, so tragedy laden, that it may be likened in historical importance to such mistakes as the belief in divine right of kings, in the exclusive validity of any one religion, in the denial of evolution, or in the belief that the earth is flat. Any belief that makes men mistrust themselves and each other unnecessarily, and to be unrealistically pessimistic about human possibilities, must be held partly responsible for every war that has ever been waged, for every racial antagonism, and for every religious massacre.

This false theory of human nature, curiously enough, has been upheld by both instinctivists and anti-instinctivists to this day. Those who hope for a better future for the human species, the optimists, the Humanists, the Unitarians, the liberals, the radicals, and environmentalists in general tend to reject the instinct theory with horror because, so misinterpreted, it seems to condemn all human beings to irrationality, to war, and to divisiveness and antagonism in a jungle world.

The instinctivists, similarly misinterpreting, but refusing to struggle against unavoidable fate, have generally given up optimism with no more than a shrug of the shoulders. Some people, of course, have renounced it eagerly.

We are reminded here of the alcoholism into which some go eagerly, and some go reluctantly; the ultimate effects are often similar. This explains why Freud can be found in the same camp with Hitler on many issues and why such wonderful individuals as Thorndike and McDougall could be forced to Hamiltonian and antidemocratic conclusions by the sheer logic of bad-animal instinctivism.

Recognize instinctoid needs to be not bad, but neutral or good, and a thousand pseudo problems solve themselves and fade out of existence.

As a single instance, the training of children would be revolutionized even to the point of not using a word with so many ugly implications as training. The shift to acceptance of legitimate animal demands would push us toward their gratification rather than toward their frustration.

In our culture, the averagely deprived child, not yet completely acculturated, i.e., not yet deprived of all his healthy and desirable animality, keeps on pressing for admiration, for safety, autonomy, for love, etc., in whatever childish ways he can invent. The ordinary reaction of the sophisticated adult is to say, "Oh! he's just showing off" or, "He's only trying to get attention," and thereupon to banish him from the adult company. That is to say, this diagonisis is customarily interpreted as an injunction *not* to give the child what he is seeking, *not* to notice, *not* to admire, *not* to applaud.

If however, we should come to consider such pleas for acceptance, love, or admiration as legitimate demands or *rights*, of the same order as complaints of hunger, thirst, cold, or pain, we should automatically become gratifiers rather than frustrators. A single consequence of such a regime would be that both children and parents would have more fun, would enjoy each other more, and would surely therefore love each other more.

This ought not be misinterpreted as implying complete and indiscriminate permissiveness. Some minimum of enculturation, i.e., training, discipline, acquisition of culturally demanded habits, preparation for the future, awareness of the needs of others, would still be necessary, although in an atmosphere of basic-need gratification such necessary training should make no particular trouble. No permissiveness is implied, furthermore, with respect to neurotic needs, addiction needs, habit needs, familiarization needs, fixations, acting out or any other noninstinctoid needs. Finally we must remind ourselves of the occasionally desirable effects of frustration, tragedy, and unhappiness.

BASIC NEEDS AS INSTINCTOID

All the foregoing considerations encourage us to the hypothesis that basic needs are in some sense, and to some appreciable degree, constitutional or hereditary in their determination. Such a hypothesis cannot be directly proved today, since the direct genetic or neurological techniques that are needed do not yet exist. Other forms of analysis, e.g., behavioral, familial, social, ethnological, are generally of more service in disproving, rather than in proving the hereditary hypothesis, except in unequivocal cases, and our hypothesis is by no means unequivocal.

In the following pages and in (298) are presented such available data and theoretical considerations as can be marshaled in support of the instinctoid hypothesis.

1. The chief argument in favor of offering new hypotheses is the failure of the old explanation. The instinct theory was drummed out by a complex of environmentalistic and behavioristic theories that rested almost entirely on associative learning as a basic, almost an all-sufficient tool of explanation.

On the whole it may fairly be said that this approach to psychology has failed to solve the problems of dynamics, e.g., of values, ends, and of essential needs, their gratification and frustration, and the consequences thereof, e.g., health, psychopathology, psychotherapy.

It is not necessary to go into a detailed argument to substantiate this conclusion. It is sufficient to note that clinical psychologists, psychiatrists, psychoanalysts, social workers, and all other clinicians use behavioristic theory almost not at all. They proceed stubbornly in an *ad hoc* way to build an extensive practical structure on inadequate theoretical foundations. They tend to be practical men rather than theorists. Be it noted that to the extent that theory *is* used by the clinicians it is a crude and unorganized dynamic theory in which instincts play a fundamental role, e.g., modified Freudian theory.

In general nonclinical psychologists agree in admitting as instinctoid only such psychological impulses as hunger, thirst, etc. On this basis, and with the aid of the conditioning process alone, it is assumed that all higher needs are derived or learned.

That is to say, we learn to love our parents supposedly because they feed us and in other ways reward us. Love, for this theory, is the by-product of a satisfactory business or barter arrangement, or, as the advertising people might say, it is synonymous with customer satisfaction.

No single experiment known to the writer has ever been performed that shows this to be true for the needs for love, safety, belongingness, respect, understanding, etc. It has always been simply assumed without further ado. This assumption may have survived only for that reason— that it has in fact never been closely examined.

Certainly the data of conditioning do not support such a hypothesis: on the contrary, such needs behave far more like the unconditioned responses on which conditioning is originally based than like secondary conditioned responses. In operant conditioning, which is based entirely on "intrinsic reinforcers," these instinctoid givens are simply taken for granted, and it is *all* called a learning theory.

As a matter of fact, the theory runs into many difficulties even at the common-observation level. Why is the mother so eager to give out rewards? What are *her* rewards? How rewarding are the nuisances of pregnancy and the pains of parturition? If indeed the relationship is at bottom a *quid pro quo* arrangement, why should she enter into such a poor business deal. Furthermore, why do clinicians unanimously affirm that a baby needs not only food, warmth, good handling, and other such rewards, but also love, as if this were something over and above the rewards? Can this be no more than redundancy? Is the efficient and un-loving mother more loved than the inefficient (or poverty-stricken) and loving mother?

Many other disquieting questions suggest themselves. What exactly is a reward—even a physiological reward? We must assume that it is a physiological pleasure, since the theory in question purports to prove that all other pleasures are derived from physiological ones. But are safety gratifications physiological, e.g., being held gently, not roughly handled, not dropped sharply, not frightened, etc.? Why do cooing to the infant, smiling at it, holding it in one's arms, paying attention to the young child, kissing him, embracing him, etc., *seem* to please him? In what sense are *giving*, rewarding, feeding the child, sacrificing for it, rewarding to the giver?

Evidence is accumulating that indicates the *manner* of rewarding to be as effective (or as rewarding) as the reward itself. What does this mean for the concept of reward? Do regularity and dependability of feeding reward the hunger need? Or some other? Which need is rewarded by permissiveness? By respect for the child's needs? By weaning or toilet training the child when *he* wishes? Why do institutionalized children develop psychopathologically so often, no matter how well cared for they may be, i.e., physiologically rewarded (158)? If love hunger is ultimately a request for food why can it not be stilled by food?

Murphy's concept of canalization (350) is highly useful at this point. He points out that arbitrary associations may be made between an unconditioned stimulus and any other stimulus because this latter arbitrary stimulus is only a signal and not itself a satisfier. When one deals with physiological needs, like hunger, *signals will not do—only satisfiers will do. Only* food will allay hunger. In a fairly stable world, such signal learning will take place and be useful, e.g., the dinner bell. But a far more important kind of learning that is *not* merely associative in nature is canalization, i.e., learning which objects are proper satisfiers and which are not, and which of the satisfiers are *most* satisfying or most to be preferred for other reasons.

The relevance to our argument lies in the writer's observation that healthy gratification of love needs, respect needs, understanding needs, and the like is by canalization, i.e., by some intrinsically proper gratification and not by arbitrary associations. Where the latter do occur, we speak of neurosis and of neurotic needs, e.g., fetishism.

Very important here are various experiments by Harlow and his colleagues at the Wisconsin Primate Laboratories (175–178). In one famous experiment, monkey babies were deprived of their mothers and offered instead a wire dummy at which they could feed, and another one covered with terry cloth but which offered no food. The babies chose as mother-surrogates the latter cuddly ones to which they could cling rather than the former "wire mothers" even though that was where they got their food. These motherless though well fed monkeys grew up to be extremely abnormal in various ways, including the complete loss of their own maternal "instincts." Apparently food and shelter are far from enough even for monkeys.

2. The ordinary biological criteria of instinct do not help us much, partly because we lack data, but also because we must now permit ourselves considerable doubt about these criteria themselves. (See, however, Howells' challenging papers [201, 202], which indicate a new possibility of by-passing the difficulty.)

As we have seen above, a serious mistake of the early instinct theorists was to overstress man's continuity with the animal world, without at the same time stressing the profound differences between the human species and all others. We can now see clearly in their writings the unquestioned tendency to define and list instincts in a universal animal way, i.e., so as to cover any instinct in any animal. Because of this, any impulse found in men and *not* in other animals was often thought, *ipso facto,* to be noninstinctive. Of course it is true that any impulse or need found in man *and* all other animals, e.g., feeding, breathing, is thereby proved to be instinctive beyond the need for any further evidence. This does not, however, disprove the possibility that some instinctoid impulses may be found only in the human species, or as appears to be the case with the love impulse, in common with chimpanzees alone of all the animal world. Homing pigeons, salmon, cats, etc., each have instincts peculiar to the species. Why could not the human species also have characteristics peculiar to it?

The commonly accepted theory has been that instincts steadily drop out as we go higher in the phyletic scale, to be replaced by an adaptability based on a vastly improved ability to learn, to think, and to communicate. If we define an instinct, in lower animal style, as a complex of innately predetermined urge, readiness to perceive, instrumental behavior and skill, and goal object (and possibly even affective accompaniment if we could ever find a way of observing it), then this theory seems to be true. Among the white rats, we find by this definition a sexual instinct, a maternal instinct, a feeding instinct (among others). In monkeys, the maternal instinct remains, the feeding instinct is modified and modifiable, and the sexual instinct is gone, leaving behind only an instinctlike urge. The monkey has to learn to choose his sexual mate and has to learn to perform the sexual act efficiently (304). The human being has *none* of these (or any other) instincts left. The sexual and feeding urges remain, and perhaps even the maternal urge (263) although very faintly, but instrumental behavior, skills, selective perception, and goal objects must be learned (mostly in the sense of canalization). He has no instincts, only instinct remnants.

3. The cultural criterion of instinct ("Is the reaction in question independent of culture?") is a crucial one, but unfortunately the data are as yet equivocal. It is the opinion of this writer that as far as they go, they either support or are compatible with the theory under consideration. However, it must be admitted that others, examining the same data, could conceivably come to an opposite conclusion.

Since the writer's field experience has been confined to a short stay with but one Indian group, and since the issue rests with the future findings of ethnologists rather than of psychologists, we shall not here consider the matter further.

4. One reason for considering basic needs to be instinctoid in nature has already been mentioned. Frustration of these needs is psychopathogenic, all clinicians agree. This is not true for neurotic needs, for habits, for addictions, for the preferences of familiarization, for instrumental or means needs, and it is true only in a special sense for the act-completion needs, for the needs for stimulation of the senses, and for the talent-

capacity-expression needs. (At least this variety of needs *can* be differentiated on operational or on pragmatic grounds and *should* be differentiated for various theoretical and practical reasons.)

If society creates and inculcates all values, why is it that only *some* and not others are psychopathogenic when thwarted? We learn to eat three times a day, say thank you, use forks and spoons, table and chair. We are forced to wear clothes and shoes, to sleep in a bed at night, and to speak English. We eat cows and sheep but not dogs and cats. We keep clean, compete for grades, and yearn for money. And yet any and all of these powerful habits can be frustrated without hurt and occasionally even with positive benefit. Under certain circumstances, as on a canoe or camping trip, we acknowledge their extrinsic nature by dropping them all with a sigh of relief. But this can *never* be said for love, for safety, or for respect.

Clearly, therefore, the basic needs stand in a special psychological and biological status. There is something different about them. They *must* be satisfied or else we get sick.

5. The gratification of basic needs leads to consequences that may be called variously desirable, good, healthy, self-actualizing. The words desirable and good are used here in a biological rather than in an a priori sense and are susceptible to operational definition. These consequences are those that the healthy organism itself tends to choose, and strives toward under conditions that permit it to choose.

These psychological and somatic consequences have already been sketched out in the chapter on basic need gratification and need not be examined further here except to point out that there is nothing esoteric or nonscientific about this criterion. It can easily be put on an experimental basis, or even on an engineering basis, if we remember only that the problem is not very different from choosing the right oil for a car. One oil is better than another if, with it, the car works better. It is the general clinical finding that the organism, when fed safety, love, and respect, works better, i.e., perceives more efficiently, uses intelligence more fully, thinks to correct conclusions more often, digests food more efficiently, is less subject to various diseases, etc.

6. The requiredness of basic need gratifiers differentiates them from all other need gratifiers. The organism itself, out of its own nature, points to an intrinsic range of satisfiers for which no substitute is possible as is the case, for instance, with habitual needs, or even with many neurotic needs. This requiredness is also responsible for the fact that the need is finally tied to its satisfiers by canalization rather than by arbitrary associations (350).

7. The effects of psychotherapy are of considerable interest for our purpose. It seems to the writer to be true for all major types of psychotherapy that, to the degree that they consider themselves successful, they foster, encourage, and strengthen what we have called basic, instinctoid needs, while they weaken, or expunge altogether the so-called neurotic needs.

Especially for those therapies that explicitly claim only to leave the person what he essentially and deep-down *is,* e.g., the therapies of Rogers, Jung, Horney, etc., is this an important fact, for it implies that the personality has some intrinsic nature of its own, and is not created *de novo* by the therapist, but is only *released* by him to grow and develop in its own style. If insight and the dissolution of repression make a reaction disappear, this reaction may reasonably thereafter be considered to have been foreign and not intrinsic. If insight makes it stronger, we may thereafter consider it to be intrinsic. Also, as Horney (143) has reasoned, if the release of anxiety causes the patient to become more affectionate and less hostile, does this not indicate that affection is basic to human nature, while hostility is not?

There is here in principle, a gold mine of data for the theory of motivation, of self-actualization, of values, of learning, of cognition in general, of interpersonal relations, of acculturation and de-acculturation, etc. Unfortunately these data on the implications of therapeutic change have not yet been accumulated.

8. The clinical and theoretical study of the self-actualizing man, as far as it has gone, indicates unequivocally the special status of our basic needs. On the satisfaction of these needs, and no other, is the healthy life conditioned (see Chapter 11). Furthermore, these individuals are readily seen to be impulse-accepting as the instinctoid hypothesis would demand rather than impulse-rejecting or repressing. On the whole, however, we must say for this kind of research that like the research on therapeutic effects, it is yet to be done.

9. Within anthropology, the first rumbles of dissatisfaction with cultural relativism came from field workers who felt that it implied more profound and irreconcilable difference between peoples than actually existed. The first and most important lesson that the writer learned from a field trip was that Indians are first of all people, individuals, human beings, and only secondarily Blackfoot Indians. By comparison with similarities, the differences, though undoubtedly there, seemed superficial. Not only they but all other peoples reported in the literature semed to have pride, to prefer to be liked, to seek respect and status, to avoid anxiety. Furthermore the constitutional differences observable in our own

culture are observable all over the world, e.g., differences in intelligence, in forcefulness, in activity or lethargy, in calmness or emotionality, etc.

Even where differences have been seen they may confirm the feeling of universality since they are very often immediately understandable as reactions of the sort that *any* human being would be prone to in similar circumstances, e.g., reactions to frustration, to anxiety, to bereavement, to triumph, to approaching death.

It is granted that such feelings are vague, unquantifiable, and hardly scientific. Yet, taken together with other hypotheses presented above, as well as further on, e.g., the weak voice of instinctoid basic needs, the unexpected detachment and autonomy of self-actualizing people and their resistance to acculturation, the separability of the concepts of health and adjustment, it seems fruitful to reconsider the culture-personality relationship so as to give a greater importance to determination by intra-organismic forces, at any rate in the healthier person.

If he is shaped without regard to this structuring, it is true that no bones are broken and no obvious or immediate pathology results. It is, however, completely accepted that the pathology *will come,* if not obviously, then subtly, and if not sooner, then later. It is not too inaccurate to cite the ordinary adult neurosis as an example of such early violence to the intrinsic (though weak) demands of the organism.

The resistance of the person to enculturation in the interests of his own integrity and of his own intrinsic nature is then, or should be, a respectable area of study in the psychological and social sciences. A person who gives in eagerly to the distorting forces in his culture, i.e., a well-adjusted man, may occasionally be less healthy than a delinquent, a criminal, a neurotic who may be demonstrating by his reactions that he has spunk enough left to resist the breaking of his psychological bones.

From this same consideration, furthermore, arises what seems at first to be a topsy-turvy, hind-end-to paradox. Education, civilization, rationality, religion, law, government, have all been interpreted by most as being primarily instinct-restraining and suppressing forces. But if our contention is correct that instincts have more to fear from civilization than civilization from instincts, perhaps it ought to be the other way about (if we still wish to produce better men and better societies): perhaps it should be at least one function of education, law, religion, etc., to safeguard, foster, and encourage the expression and gratification of the instinctoid needs for safety, for love, for self-esteem, for self-actualization.

10. This point of view helps to resolve and transcend many old philosophical contradictions, e.g., biology vs. culture, innate vs. learned, the subjective vs. the objective, the idosyncratic vs. the universal, etc. This

is so because the uncovering, self-searching psychotherapies and the personal growth, "soul-searching" techniques, are also a path to discovering one's objective, biological nature, one's animality and specieshood, i.e., one's Being.

Most psychotherapists of whatever school assume that they are uncovering or releasing a more basic and truer and more real personality as they cut down through the neurosis, i.e., to a core or nucleus that was somehow there all the time but was overlaid, concealed, inhibited by the sick surface layers. Horney's phrasing (199) shows this very clearly, when she speaks of getting through the pseudo-self to the Real Self. Self-actualization phrasings also stress the making real or actual of what the person already is, though in a potential form. The search for Identity means very much the same thing, as does "becoming what one truly is." As does also becoming "fully-functioning" or "fully-human," or individuated, or authentically oneself (166), etc.

Obviously, a central task here is to become aware of what one *is,* biologically, temperamentally, constitutionally as a member of a particular species. This is certainly what all the varieties of psychoanalysis try to do, to help one to become conscious of one's needs, impulses, emotions, pleasures, and pains. But this is a kind of phenomenology of one's own inner biology, of one's animality and specieshood, a discovery of biology by *experiencing* it, what one might call subjective biology, introspected biology, experienced biology or something of the sort.

But this amounts to subjective discovery of the objective, i.e., the species-specific characteristics of humanness. It amounts to individual discovery of the general and the universal, a personal discovery of the impersonal or transpersonal (and even the transhuman). In a word, the instinctoid can be studied *both* subjectively and objectively, via "soul-searching" *and* via the more usual external observation of the scientist. Biology is not only an objective science; it can also be a subjective one.

If I may paraphrase Archibald MacLeish's poem a little, I could say:

A person doesn't mean:
A person is.

7

HIGHER
AND LOWER
NEEDS

DIFFERENCES BETWEEN HIGHER
AND LOWER NEEDS

This chapter will demonstrate that there are real psychological and operational differences between those needs called "higher" and those called "lower." This is done in order to establish that the organism itself dictates hierarchies of values, which the scientific observer reports rather than creates. It is necessary thus to prove the obvious because so many still consider that values can never be more than the arbitrary imposition upon data of the writer's own tastes, prejudices, intuitions, or other unproved or unprovable assumptions. In the latter half of the chapter some of the consequences of this demonstration will be drawn.

The casting out of values from psychology not only weakens it, and prevents it from reaching its full growth, but also abandons mankind to supernaturalism, to ethical relativism, or to nihilistic valuelessness. But if it could be demonstrated that the organism itself chooses between a stronger and a weaker, a higher and a lower, then surely it would be impossible to maintain that one good has the same value as any other good, or that it is impossible to choose between them, or that one has no natural criterion for differentiating good from evil. One such principle of choice has already been set forth in Chapter 4. The basic needs arrange themselves in a fairly definite hierarchy on the basis of the principle of relative potency. Thus the safety need is stronger than the love need, because it dominates the organism in various demonstrable ways when both needs are frustrated. In this sense, the physiological needs (which are themselves ordered in a subhierarchy) are stronger than the safety needs, which are stronger than the love needs, which in turn are stronger than the esteem needs, which are stronger than those idiosyncratic needs we have called the need for self-actualization.

This is an order of choice or preference. But it is also an order that ranges from lower to higher in various other senses that are listed in this chapter.

1. *The higher need is a later phyletic or evolutionary development.* We share the need for food with all living things, the need for love with (perhaps) the higher apes, the need for self-actualization with nobody. The higher the need the more specifically human it is.

2. *Higher needs are later ontogenetic developments.* Any individual at birth shows physical needs, and probably also, in a very inchoate form, needs safety, e.g., it can probably be frightened or startled, and probably thrives better when its world shows enough regularity and orderliness so that it can be counted on. It is only after months of life that an infant shows the first signs of interpersonal ties and selective affection. Still later we may see fairly definitely the urges to autonomy, independence, achievement, and for respect and praise over and above safety and parental love. As for self-actualization, even a Mozart had to wait until he was three or four.

3. *The higher the need the less imperative it is for sheer survival, the longer gratification can be postponed, and the easier it is for the need to disappear permanently.* Higher needs have less ability to dominate, organize, and press into their service the autonomic reactions and other capacities of the organism, e.g., it is easier to be single-minded, mono-maniac, and desperate about safety than about respect. Deprivation of higher needs does not produce so desperate a defense and emergency reaction as is produced by lower deprivations. Respect is a dispensable luxury when compared with food or safety.

4. *Living at the higher need level means greater biological efficiency, greater longevity, less disease, better sleep, appetite, etc.* The psychosomatic researchers prove again and again that anxiety, fear, lack of love, domination, etc., tend to encourage undesirable physical as well as undesirable psychological results. Higher need gratifications have survival value and growth value as well.

5. *Higher needs are less urgent subjectively.* They are less perceptible, less unmistakable, more easily confounded with other needs by suggestion, imitation, by mistaken belief or habit. To be able to recognize

one's own needs, i.e., to know what one really wants, is a considerable psychological achievement. This is doubly true for the higher needs.

6. *Higher need gratifications produce more desirable subjective results, i.e., more profound happiness, serenity, and richness of the inner life.* Satisfactions of the safety needs produce at best a feeling of relief and relaxation. In any case they cannot produce, e.g., the ecstasy, peak experiences, and happy delirium of satisfied love, or such consequences as serenity, understanding, nobility, etc.

7. *Pursuit and gratification of higher needs represent a general healthward trend, a trend away from psychopathology.* The evidence for his statement is presented in Chapter 5.

8. *The higher need has more preconditions.* This is true if only because prepotent needs must be gratified before it can be. Thus it takes more quanta of satisfactions for the love need to appear in consciousness than for the safety need. In a more general sense, it may be said that life is more complex at the level of the higher needs. The search for respect and status involves more people, a larger scene, a longer run, more means, and partial goals, more subordinate and preliminary steps than does the search for love. The same may be said in turn of this latter need when compared with the search for safety.

9. *Higher needs require better outside conditions to make them possible.* Better environmental conditions (familial, economic, political, educational, etc.) are all more necessary to allow people to love each other than merely to keep them from killing each other. *Very* good conditions are needed to make self-actualizing possible.

10. *A greater value is usually placed upon the higher need than upon the lower by those who have been gratified in both.* Such people will sacrifice more for the higher satisfaction, and furthermore will more readily be able to withstand lower deprivation. For example, they will find it easier to live ascetic lives, to withstand danger for the sake of principle, to give up money and prestige for the sake of self-actualization. Those who have known both universally regard self-respect as a higher, more valuable subjective experience than a filled belly.

11. *The higher the need level, the wider is the circle of love identification, i.e., the greater is the number of people love-identified with, and the greater is the average degree of love identification.* We may define love identification as, in principle, a merging into a single hierarchy of prepotency of the needs of two or more people. Two people who love each other well will react to each other's needs and their own indiscriminately. Indeed the other's need *is* his own need.

12. *The pursuit and the gratification of the higher needs have desir-*

able civic and social consequences. To some extent, the higher the need the less selfish it must be. Hunger is highly egocentric; the only way to satisfy it is to satisfy oneself. But the search for love and respect necessarily involves other people. Moreover, it involves satisfaction for these other people. People who have enough basic satisfaction to look for love and respect (rather than just food and safety) tend to develop such qualities as loyalty, friendliness, and civic consciousness, and to become better parents, husbands, teachers, public servants, etc.

13. *Satisfaction of higher needs is closer to self-actualization than is lower-need satisfaction.* If the theory of self-actualization be accepted, this is an important difference. Among other things, it means that we may expect to find, in people living at the higher need level, a larger number and greater degree of the qualities found in self-actualizing people.

14. *The pursuit and gratification of the higher needs leads to greater, stronger, and truer individualism.* This may seem to contradict the previous statement that living at higher need levels means more love identification, i.e., more socialization. However it may sound logically, it is nevertheless an empirical reality. People living at the level of self-actualization are, in fact, found simultaneously to love mankind most and to be the most developed idiosyncratically. This completely supports Fromm's contention that self-love (or better, self-respect) is synergic with rather than antagonistic to love for others. His discussion of individuality, spontaneity, and robotization is also relevant (145).

15. *The higher the need level the easier and more effective psychotherapy can be: at the lowest need levels it is of hardly any avail.* Hunger cannot be stilled by psychotherapy.

16. *The lower needs are far more localized, more tangible, and more limited than are the higher needs.* Hunger and thirst are much more obviously bodily than is love, which in turn is more so than respect. In addition, lower need satisfiers are much more tangible or observable than are higher need satisfactions. Furthermore, they are more limited in the sense that a smaller quantity of gratifiers is needed to still the need. Only so much food can be eaten, but love, respect, and cognitive satisfactions are almost unlimited.

SOME CONSEQUENCES OF
THIS DIFFERENTIATION

Such a point of view, namely, that (1) the higher needs and lower needs have different properties and (2) that these higher needs as well as the lower needs must be included in the repertory of basic and given human nature (*not* as different from and opposed to it) must have many and revolutionary consequences for psychological and philosophical theory. Most civilizations, along with their theories of politics, education, religion, etc., have been based on the exact contradictory of this belief. On the whole, they have assumed the biological animal, and instinctoid aspects of human nature to be severely limited to the physiological needs for food, sex, and the like. The higher impulses for truth, for love, for beauty were assumed to be intrinsically different in nature from these animal needs. Furthermore, these interests were assumed to be antagonistic, mutually exclusive, and in perpetual conflict with each other for mastery. All culture, with all its instruments, is seen from such a point of view as on the side of the higher and against the lower. It is therefore necessarily an inhibitor and a frustrator, and is at best an unfortunate necessity.

Recognizing the higher needs to be instinctoid and biological, precisely as biological as the need for food, has many repercussions of which we can list only a few.

1. Probably most important of all is the realization that the dichotomy between cognitive and conative is false and must be resolved. The needs for knowledge, for understanding, for a life philosophy, for a theoretical frame of reference, for a value system, these are themselves conative, a part of our primitive and animal nature (we are very special animals).

Since we know also that our needs are not completely blind, that they are modified by culture, by reality, and by possibility, it follows that cognition plays a considerable role in their development. It is John Dewey's claim that the very existence and definition of a need depends on the cognition of reality, of the possibility or impossibility of gratification.

If the conative is in its nature also cognitive, and if the cognitive is in its nature also conative, the dichotomy between them is useless and must be discarded except as a sign of pathology.

2. Many age-old philosophical problems must be seen in a new light. Some of them perhaps may even be seen to be pseudo problems resting on misconceptions about human motivational life. Here may be included, for instance, the sharp distinction between selfishness and unselfishness. If our instinctoid impulses, for instance, to love, arrange it so that we get more personal "selfish" pleasure from watching our children eat a goody than from eating it ourselves, then how shall we define "selfish" and how differentiate it from "unselfish"? Is the man who risks his life for the truth any less selfish than the man who risks his life for food, if the need for truth is as animal as the need for food?

Obviously also hedonistic theory must be recast if animal pleasure, selfish pleasure, personal pleasure can come equally from gratification of the needs for food, sex, truth, beauty, love, or respect. This implies that a higher-need hedonism might very well stand where a lower-need hedonism would fall.

The romantic-classic opposition, the Dionysian-Apollonian contrast, must certainly be modified. In at least some of its forms, it has been based on the same illegitimate dichotomy between lower needs as animal, and higher needs as nonanimal or antianimal. Along with this must go considerable revision of the concepts of rational and irrational, the contrast between rational and impulsive, and the general notion of the rational life as opposed to the instinctive life.

3. The philosopher of ethics has much to learn from a close examination of man's motivational life. If our noblest impulses are seen not as checkreins on the horses, but as themselves horses, and if our animal needs are seen to be of the same nature as our highest needs, how can a sharp dichotomy between them be sustained? How can we continue to believe that they could come from different sources?

Furthermore, if we clearly and fully recognize that these noble and good impulses come into existence and grow potent primarily as a consequence of the prior gratification of the more demanding animal needs, we should certainly speak less exclusively of self-control, inhibition, discipline, etc., and more frequently of spontaneity, gratification, and self-choice. There seems to be less opposition than we thought between the stern voice of duty and the gay call to pleasure. At the highest level of living, i.e., of Being, duty *is* pleasure, one's "work" is loved, and there is no difference between working and vacationing.

4. Our conception of culture and of man's relation to it must change in the direction of "synergy," as Ruth Benedict (40, 291, 312) called it. Culture can be basic need-gratifying (314, 315) rather than need-inhibiting. Furthermore it is created not only for human needs but by them. The culture–individual dichotomy needs reexamination. There should be less exclusive stress on their antagonism and more on their possible collaboration and synergy.

5. The recognition that man's best impulses are appreciably intrinsic, rather than fortuitous and relative, must have tremendous implication for value theory. It means, for one thing, that it is no longer either necessary or desirable to deduce values by logic or to try to read them off from authorities or revelations. All we need do, apparently, is to observe and research. Human nature carries within itself the answer to the questions, how can I be good; how can I be happy: how can I be fruitful? The organism tells us what it needs (and therefore what it values) by sickening when deprived of these values and by growing when not deprived.

6. A study of these basic needs has shown that though their nature is to an appreciable extent instinctoid, in many ways they are not like the instincts we know so well in lower animals. Most important of all these differences is the unexpected finding that in contradiction to the age-old assumption that instincts are strong, undesirable, and unchangeable, our basic needs, though instinctoid, are weak. To be impulse-aware, to know that we really want and need love, respect, knowledge, a philosophy, self-actualization, etc.—this is a difficult psychological achievement. Not only this, but the higher they are, the weaker and more easily changed and suppressed they are. Finally they are not bad but are either neutral or good. We wind up with the paradox that our human instincts, what is left of them, are so weak that they need protection against culture, against education, against learning—in a word, against being overwhelmed by the environment.

7. Our understanding of the aims of psychotherapy (and of education, of child rearing, of the formation of the good character in general) must shift considerably. To many it still means the acquisition of a set of inhibitions and controls of the intrinsic impulses. Discipline, control, suppression are the watchwords of such a regime.

But if therapy means a pressure toward breaking controls and inhibitions, then our new key words must be spontaneity, release, naturalness, self-acceptance, impulse awareness, gratification, self-choice. If our intrinsic impulses are understood to be admirable rather than detestable, we shall certainly wish to free them for their fullest expression rather than to bind them into straitjackets.

8. If instincts can be weak and if higher needs are seen to be instinctoid in character, and if culture is seen as more, not less, powerful than instinctoid impulses, and if man's basic needs turn out to be good and not bad, then the improvement of man's nature may come about via fostering of instinctoid tendencies as well as through fostering social improvements. Indeed, the point of bettering the culture will be seen as giving man's inner biological tendencies a better chance to actualize themselves.

9. In the finding that living at the higher need level can sometimes become relatively independent of lower need gratification (and even of higher need gratification in a pinch), we may have a solution to an age-old dilemma of the theologians. They have always found it necessary to attempt to reconcile the flesh and the spirit, the angel and the devil—the higher and the lower in the human organism, but no one has ever found a satisfactory solution. Functional autonomy of the higher need life seems to be part of the answer. The higher develops only on the basis of

the lower, but eventually, when well established, may become *relatively* independent of the lower (5).

10. In addition to Darwinian survival-value, we may now also postulate "growth-values." Not only is it good to survive, but it is also good (preferred, chosen, good-for-the-organism) for the person to grow toward full humanness, toward actualization of his potentialities, toward greater happiness, serenity, peak experiences, toward transcendence (317), toward richer and more accurate cognition of reality, etc. No longer need we rest on sheer viability and survival as our only ultimate proof that poverty or war or domination or cruelty are bad, rather than good. We can consider them bad because they also degrade the quality of life, of personality, of consciousness, of wisdom.

8

PSYCHOPATHOGENESIS AND THE THEORY OF THREAT

The conception of motivation so far outlined contains some important cues for understanding the origins of psychopathology as well as the nature of frustration, conflict, and threat.

Practically all theories that propose to explain how psychopathology originates and how it maintains itself rest most heavily on the two concepts of frustration and conflict with which we shall now deal. Some frustrations do produce pathology; some do not. Some conflicts likewise do, and some do not. It will appear that recourse to basic need theory is necessary to unravel this puzzle.

DEPRIVATION, FRUSTRATION, AND THREAT

It is easy in the discussion of frustration to fall into the error of segmenting the human being, i.e., there is still a tendency to speak of the mouth, or stomach being frustrated, or of a need being frustrated. We must remember always that only a whole human being is frustrated, never a part of a human being.

With this in mind, an important distinction becomes apparent, namely, the difference between deprivation and threat to the personality. The usual definitions of frustration are in terms simply of not getting what one desires, of interference with a wish, or with a gratification. Such a definition fails to make the distinction between a deprivation that is unimportant to the organism (easily substituted for, with few serious after effects) and, on the other hand, a deprivation that is at the same time a threat to the personality, that is, to the life goals of the individual, to his defensive system, to his self-esteem, to his self-actualization, i.e., to his basic needs. It is our contention that only a *threatening* deprivation has the multitude of effects (usually undesirable) that are commonly attributed to frustration in general.

A goal object may have two meanings for the individual. First it has its intrinsic meaning, and secondly, it may have also a secondary, symbolic value. Thus a certain child deprived of an ice-cream cone that he wanted may have lost simply an ice-cream cone. A second child, however, deprived of an ice-cream cone, may have lost not only a sensory gratification, but may feel deprived of the love of his mother because she refused to buy it for him. For the second boy the ice-cream cone not only has an intrinsic value, but may also be the carrier of psychological values. Being deprived merely of ice cream qua ice cream probably means little for a healthy individual, and it is questionable whether it should even be called by the same name, i.e., frustration, that characterizes other more threatening deprivations. It is only when a goal object represents love, prestige, respect, or other basic needs, that being deprived of it will have the bad effects ordinarily attributed to frustration in general.

It is possible to demonstrate very clearly this twofold meaning of an object in certain groups of animals and in certain situations. For instance, it has been shown that when two monkeys are in a dominance-subordination relationship a piece of food is (1) an appeaser of hunger and also (2) a symbol of dominance status. Thus if the subordinate animal attempts to pick up food, he will at once be attacked by the dominant animal. If, however, he can deprive the food of its symbolic dominance value, then his dominator allows him to eat it. This he can do very easily by a gesture of obeisance, i.e., sexual presentation as he approaches the food; this is as if to say, "I want this food only to still hunger, I do not want to challenge your dominance. I readily concede your dominance." In the same way we may take a criticism from a friend in two different ways. Ordinarily the average person will respond by feeling attacked and threatened (which is fair enough because so frequently criticism is an attack). He therefore bristles and becomes angry in response. But if he is assured that this criticism is not an attack or a rejection of himself, he will then not only listen to the criticism, but possibly even be grateful for it. Thus if he has already had thousands of proofs that his friend loves him and respects him, the criticism represents only criticism; it does not also represent an attack or threat (304, 313),

Neglect of this distinction has created a great deal of unnecessary turmoil in psychiatric circles. An ever-recurring question is: Does sexual deprivation inevitably give rise to all or any of the many effects of frustration, e.g., aggression, sublimation, etc.? It is now well known that many cases are found in which celibacy has no psychopathological effects. In many other cases, however, it has many bad effects. What factor determines which shall be the result? Clinical work with nonneurotic people gives the clear answer that sexual deprivation becomes pathogenic in a severe sense only when it is felt by the individual to represent rejection by the opposite sex, inferiority, lack of worth, lack of respect, isolation, or other thwarting of basic needs. Sexual deprivation can be borne with relative ease by individuals for whom it has no such implications (of course, there will probably be what Rosenzweig (408) calls need-persistive reactions, but these, though irritating, are not necessarily pathological).

The unavoidable deprivations in childhood are also ordinarily thought of as frustrating. Weaning, elimination control, learning to walk, in fact every new level of adjustment, is conceived to be achieved by forcible pushing of the child. Here, too, the differentiation between mere deprivation and threat to the personality enjoins caution upon us. Observations of children who are completely assured of the love and respect of their parents have shown that deprivations, disciplines, and punishments can sometimes be borne with astonishing ease. There are few frustration effects if these deprivations are not conceived by the child to be threatening to his fundamental personality, to his main life goals, or needs.

From this point of view, it follows that the phenomenon of threatening frustration is much more closely allied to other threat situations than it is to mere deprivation. The classic effects of frustration are also found frequently to be a consequence of other types of threat—traumatization, conflict, cortical damage, severe illness, actual physical threat, imminence of death, humiliation, or great pain.

This leads us to our final hypothesis that perhaps frustration as a single concept is less useful than the two concepts that crosscut it: (1) deprivation of nonbasic needs and (2) threat to the personality, i.e., to the basic needs or to the various coping systems associated with them. Deprivation implies much less than is ordinarily implied by the concept of frustration; threat implies much more. Deprivation is not psychopathogenic; threat is.

CONFLICT AND THREAT

The single concept of conflict can be crosscut by the concept of threat just as we have done for frustration. The types of conflict may be classified as follows.

SHEER CHOICE

This is conflict in the simplest sense of all. The daily life of every human being is filled with numberless choices of this sort. I would conceive the difference between this kind of choice and the next type to be discussed to be as follows. The first type involves a choice between two paths to the same goal, this goal being relatively unimportant for the organism. The psychological reaction to such a choice situation is practically never a pathological one. As a matter of fact, most often there is no subjective feeling of conflict at all.

CHOICE BETWEEN TWO PATHS TO THE SAME (VITAL, BASIC) GOAL

In such a situation the goal itself is important for the organism but there are alternative ways of reaching this goal. The goal itself is not endangered. The importance or nonimportance of the goal is, of course, a matter to be determined for each individual organism. What is important for one may not be for another. An example would be a woman trying to decide whether to wear one pair of shoes or another, one dress or another to a party that happened to be important for her and at which she hoped to make a good impression. When the decision is made here the apparent feeling of conflict usually disappears. It is true, however, that such conflicts may become very intense as in a woman choosing not between two dresses, but between two possible husbands. We are again reminded of Rosenzweig's distinction between need-persistent effects and ego-defensive effects.

THREATENING CONFLICTS

This type of conflict is fundamentally different in kind from conflicts of the first two types. It is still a choice situation but now it is a choice between two different goals, both vitally necessary. Here a choice reaction usually does not settle the conflict, since the decision means giving up something that is almost as necessary as what is chosen. Giving up a necessary goal or need satisfaction is threatening, and even after the choice has been made, threat effects persist. In a word, this sort of choice can eventuate only in chronic thwarting of a basic need. This is pathogenic.

CATASTROPHIC CONFLICT

This might better be called pure threat with no alternative or possibilities of choice. All the choices are equally catastrophic or threatening in their effects or else there is only one possibility and this is a catastrophic threat. Such a situation can be called a conflict situation only by an extension of the meaning of the word. This can be seen readily if we take the example of a man who is to be executed in a few minutes, or the animal who is forced in the direction of a decision that he knows to be a punishing one and in which all possibilities of escape, attack, or substitute behavior are cut off, as is the case in many experiments on animal neurosis (285).

CONFLICT AND THREAT

Speaking from the point of view of psychopathology we must come to the same conclusion that we came to after our analysis of frustration. There are, in general, two types of conflict situations or conflict reactions, non-threatening and threatening. The nonthreatening conflicts are quite unimportant, since they are not ordinarily pathogenic; the threatening types of conflict are important because they very often are pathogenic.[1] Again it would seem that when we speak about a feeling of conflict as an originator of symptoms we should do better to speak rather about threat or threatening conflict, since there are types of conflict that do not create symptoms. Some actually strengthen the organism.

We may then proceed to a reclassification of our concepts in the general field of psychopathogenesis. We may speak first of deprivation, and secondly of choice, and consider them both to be nonpathogenic and therefore unimportant concepts for the student of psychopathology. The one concept that is important is neither conflict nor frustration but the essential pathogenic characteristic of both, namely, threat of thwarting or actual thwarting of the basic needs and self-actualization of the organism.

THE NATURE OF THE THREAT

But again it is necessary to point out that the concept of threat includes phenomena that are subsumed neither under the head of conflict nor frustration as these words have been commonly used. Severe illness of certain types can be psychopathogenic. A person who has had a bad heart attack very frequently behaves in a threatened fashion. Illness or hospital experience in young children is often directly threatening, quite apart from the deprivations that are imposed thereby.

Another kind of patient in which general threat has been demonstrated is the brain-injured patient as studied by Gelb, Goldstein, Scheerer,

---

[1] Threat is not always pathogenic; there are healthy ways of handling it, as well as neurotic or psychotic solutions. Furthermore, an apparently threatening situation may or may not produce feelings of psychological threat in any particular individual. A bombardment or threat to life itself may not be so threatening as a sneer, a snub, the defection of a friend, an illness in one's child, or an act of injustice perpetrated against a total stranger miles away. In addition, threat may have strengthening effects.

and others. The only way in which these patients can ultimately be understood is to assume that they feel threatened. Possibly *all* organic-psychotic
patients of any type may be considered to feel basically threatened. In
these patients the symptoms can be understood only if studied from two
points of view: first, the direct effect on the organism of the damage to
function or loss of function of whatever kind (loss effects), and second, the
dynamic reactions of the personality to these threatening losses (threat
effect).

From Kardiner's monograph on traumatic neuroses (222) we find
that we can add the effect of very basic and severe traumatization to our
list of threat effects that are neither conflict nor frustration.[2] According
to Kardiner these traumatic neuroses are the effect of a basic threat to the
most basic executive functions of life itself—walking, talking, feeding,
and the like. We might paraphrase his argument as follows:

The person who has gone through a very severe accident may conclude that he is not the master of his own fate and that death is ever at
his door. In the face of such an overwhelmingly stronger and more threatening world some men seem to lose confidence in their own abilities, even
the simplest ones. Other milder traumata will of course be less threatening. I would add that such a reaction is to be expected more often in
people with a certain kind of character structure that predisposes them to
threat.

The imminence of death for whatever reasons also may (but not
necessarily) put us in a state of threat for the reason that we may lose our
basic self-confidence here. When we can no longer handle the situation,
when the world is too much for us, when we are not masters of our own
fate, when we no longer have control over the world or over ourselves,
certainly we may speak of feelings of threat. Other situations in which
"there is nothing we can do about it" are also sometimes felt to be threatening. Perhaps severe pain should be added in this category. This is certainly something that we can do nothing about.

Perhaps it is possible to extend the concept to include phenomena
that are ordinarily included in a different category. For instance, we
might speak of sudden intense stimulation, being dropped without fore-
knowledge, losing footing, anything unexplained or unfamiliar, the upset
of routine or rhythm in the child as threatening to the child rather than
as merely emotion-producing.

---

[2] Again it must be pointed out that a traumatic situation is not the same as a feeling
of traumatization, i.e., a traumatic situation *may* be psychologically threatening but it
does not *have* to be. It may indeed be educative and strengthening if well handled.

We must of course also speak of the most nuclear aspects of threat, namely, the direct deprivation, or thwarting, or danger to the basic needs —humiliation, rejection, isolation, loss of prestige, loss of strength—these are all directly threatening. In addition, misuse or nonuse of the capacities threatens self-actualization directly. Finally, danger to the metaneeds or Being-values (293, 314) can be threatening to the highly matured person.

We may summarize by saying that, in general, all the following are felt as threatening in our sense: danger of thwarting or actual thwarting of the basic needs and metaneeds (including self-actualization) or the conditions upon which they rest, threat to life itself, threat to the general integrity of the organism, threat to the integration of the organism, threat to the organism's basic mastery of the world, and threat to the ultimate values.

However we define threat, certainly there is one aspect that we must never neglect. An ultimate definition, no matter what else it might include, must certainly be related to the basic goals, values, or needs of the organism. This means that any theory of psychopathogenesis in turn must rest directly upon theory of motivation.

General dynamic theory, as well as various specific empirical findings, would indicate the necessity for individual definition of threat. That is, we must ultimately define a situation or threat not only in terms of species-wide basic needs but also in terms of the individual organism facing its particular problem. Thus frustration and conflict both have frequently been defined in terms of external situations alone rather than in terms of the organism's internal reaction to or perception of these external situations. Among the most persistent sinners in this respect have been some of the researchers in the so-called animal neuroses.

How shall we know when any particular situation is perceived by the organism as a threat? For the human being, this can easily enough be determined by any technique that is adequate to describe the total personality, as for instance, the psychoanalytic technique. Such techniques allow us to know what the person needs, what he is missing, and what endangers him. But for animals, the situation is more difficult. Here we become involved in circular definition. We know a situation is threatening when the animal responds with symptoms of threat. That is, the situation is defined in terms of responses, and the responses are defined in terms of the situations. Circular definition is ordinarily not held in good repute, but we shall have to learn that along with a generally dynamic psychology must go an increase in respectability of the so-called circular definition. In any case, for practical laboratory work this is certainly not an insuperable obstacle.

A last point that would certainly follow from dynamic theory is that we must always consider the feeling of threat to be in itself a dynamic stimulation to other reactions. No picture of threat is complete in any organism unless we know also what this threat feeling leads to, what it makes the individual do, how the organism reacts to the threat. Certainly in the theory of neuroses it is absolutely necessary to understand both the nature of the feeling of threat and also the reaction of the organism to this feeling.

THE THREAT CONCEPT IN ANIMAL WORK

An analysis of the work on behavior disturbances in animals[3] indicates that it is ordinarily conceived in external or situational rather than in dynamic terms. It is the old mistake of considering that control of the psychological situation is achieved when the external experimental setup or situation is made constant. (See for instance the emotion experiments of 25 years ago.) Ultimately, of course, only that is *psychologically* important which the organism perceives or reacts to, or by which it is affected in one way or another. This fact, as well as the fact that every organism is different from every other, must be recognized not just verbally, but also as it influences the setup of our experiments and the conclusions drawn therefrom. For instance, Pavlov (373) has shown that the basic physiological temperament of the animal must be of a certain kind, or the external conflict situation will not produce any internal conflict. And, of course, we are interested not in conflict situations, but only in feelings of conflict within the organism. We must recognize also that the unique history of the individual animal will produce varying individual reactions to a given external situation, as, for example, in the work of Gantt and of Liddell and his collaborators. We have been shown by the work with white rats that in some cases a peculiarity of the organism is all-important in determining the presence or absence of breakdown to identical external situations. Different species will have different resources with which to perceive, to react to, to be threatened or not threatened by an external situation. Certainly the concepts of conflicts and frustration are used loosely in many of these experiments. Furthermore, because of neglect of the individually defined character of threat to the organism,

---

[3] Obviously the concepts presented in this chapter are so general that they apply to *many* types of experimental work. The sample chosen could be augmented by, for instance, current researches on repression, forgetting, perseveration of incompleted tasks, as well as the more direct researches on conflict and frustration.

certain differences in the reactions of various animals to an identical situation seem unexplainable.

A better phrasing than those ordinarily used in the literature is that given by Scheerer of "requiring the animal to do something that he cannot do." This is a good concept because it does cover all the known animal work, but we should make more explicit some of its implications. For instance, taking away from the animal things that are important for it may produce pathological effects of a kind similar to those produced by asking the organism to do something that it cannot do. In the human being the concept must include, in addition to the factors mentioned, those of the threatening character of certain illnesses and certain damages to the integrity of the organism. In addition, we should explicitly recognize the factor of temperament, which allows an animal to face a situation in which it is required to do something impossible and to which it responds in a nonpathological fashion simply by not caring about the situation, by being placid about it, or perhaps even by refusing to perceive it. Perhaps this sharper character can be achieved in part by adding to Scheerer's phrasing a statement of strong motivation, "Pathological reactions occur when the organism is faced with a task or situation that is impossible for it to solve or cope with, and *which it wants very much to solve or which it must solve.*" Even this, of course, would still fall short because it would not include some of the phenomena that have been mentioned. However, it has the virtue of being a rather practical statement of the threat theory for laboratory purposes.

Another point is that, because of neglecting to distinguish between nonthreatening choice situations and threatening ones in the animal, and between nonthreatening frustrations and threatening ones, the behavior of the animal seems inconsistent. If the animal is conceived to be in a conflict situation at a choice point in the maze, why does it not break down more often? If deprivation of food for 24 hours is conceived to be frustrating for the rat, then why does the animal not break down? Some change in phrasing or conceptualization is clearly necessary. One example of the neglect in differentiation is the failure to distinguish between a choice in which the animal gives up something and a choice in which the animal gives up nothing, one in which the goal remains constant and unthreatened but in which the animal has two or more paths to the same assured goal. If an animal is both thirsty and hungry, it would be more likely to feel threatened if it had to choose between food and water, getting either one or the other but not both.

In a word, we must define the situation or stimulus not *per se* but as incorporated by the subject, animal or human—by its psychological meaning to the particular subject involved in the experiment, dynamically.

THREAT IN THE LIFE HISTORY

Healthy adults are less threatened by external situations in general than are average or neurotic adults. We must remember again that though this adult health has been produced by lack of threat through childhood, or by threats successfully overcome, it becomes more and more impervious to threat as the years go by, i.e., it is practically impossible to threaten the masculinity of the man who is *quite* sure of himself. Withdrawal of love is no great threat to one who has been well loved through his life and who feels loveworthy and lovable. Again the principle of functional autonomy must be invoked.

THREAT AS INHIBITION OF SELF-ACTUALIZATION

It is possible to subsume most individual instances of threat under the rubric "inhibiting or threatening-to-inhibit development toward ultimate self-actualization" as Goldstein has done. This emphasis on future as well as on contemporaneous damage has many serious consequences. As an instance we may cite Fromm's revolutionary conception of the "humanistic" conscience as perception of deviation from the path of growth or self-actualization. This phrasing throws into sharp relief, the relativism and therefore the inadequacy of the Freudian conception of the super-ego.

We should also notice that synonymizing "threat" with "growth-inhibiting" creates the possibility of a situation being at this moment subjectively nonthreatening, but threatening or growth-inhibiting in the future. The child may now wish for gratification which will please him, quiet him, make him grateful, etc., but which will yet be growth-inhibiting. An example is seen in the parental submission to the child which produces the indulged psychopath.

ILLNESS AS UNITARY

Another problem which is created by identifying psychopathogenesis with ultimately faulty development arises from its monistic character. What we have implied is that all or most illnesses come from this single source; i.e., psychopathogenesis seems to be unitary rather than multiple. Where then do separate syndromes of illness come from? Perhaps not only pathogenesis but also psychopathology may be unitary. Perhaps what we now speak of as separate disease entities on the medical model are actually superficial and idiosyncratic reactions to a deeper general illness, as

Horney claimed (197). My test of security-insecurity (294) was built on just such a basic assumption and so far seems to have succeeded fairly well in picking out people who have psychological illness in general rather than hysteria or hypochondria or anxiety neurosis in particular.

Since my only aim here is to indicate that important problems and hypotheses are generated by this theory of psychopathogenesis, no effort will be made now to explore these hypotheses further. It is necessary only to underline its unifying, simplifying possibilities.

9

IS DESTRUCTIVENESS INSTINCTOID?

On the surface, the basic needs (motives, impulses, drives) are not evil or sinful. There is nothing necessarily bad in wanting and needing food, safety, belongingness and love, social approval and self-approval, self-actualization. On the contrary, most people in most cultures would consider these—in one local form or another—to be desirable and praiseworthy wishes. At our most scientifically cautious, we would still have to say that they are neutral rather than evil. Something of the sort is true for most or all of the human species-specific capacities that we know about (the ability to abstract, to speak a grammatical language, to build philosophies, etc.), and for constitutional differences (activity or passivity, mesomorphy or ectomorphy, high or low energy levels, etc.). As for the metaneeds for excellence, truth, beauty, lawfulness, simplicity, etc. (314), it is practically impossible in our culture, and in most cultures that we know, to call them intrinsically bad or evil or sinful.

The raw material of humanness and of human specieshood, therefore, does not in itself explain the huge amount of evil that is obvious in our world, in human history, and within our own individual characters. True, we already know enough to attribute much of what is called evil to sickness of the body and of the personality, to ignorance and stupidity, to immaturity, and to bad social and institutional arrangements. But it cannot be said that we know enough to say *how* much. We know that evil can be reduced by health and by therapy, by knowledge and wisdom, by chronological and psychological maturity, by good political, economic, and other social institutions and systems. But by how much? Can such measures ever reduce evil to zero? It can certainly be granted by now that our knowledge is sufficient to reject any claim that human nature is, in its essence, *primarily, biologically, fundamentally* evil, sinful, malicious, ferocious, cruel, or murderous. But we do not dare to say that there are *no* instinctoid tendencies at all to bad behavior. It is quite clear that we just do not know enough to make such an affirmation and there is at least some evidence to contradict it. In any case it has become just as clear that such knowledge is attainable, and that these questions can be brought into the jurisdiction of a suitably expanded humanistic science (292, 376).

This chapter is a sample of the empirical approach to one crucial question in this area of what has been called good and evil. Even though it makes no effort to be definitive, it is a reminder that knowledge of destructiveness *has* advanced even though not yet to the point of final and conclusive answers.

ANIMAL DATA

First of all, it is true that what looks like primary aggressiveness can be observed in some species of animals; not in all animals, nor even in many, but still in some. Some animals apparently kill for the sake of killing, and are aggressive for no observable external reason. A fox that enters a henhouse may kill more hens than it could eat, and the cat that plays with the mouse is proverbial. Stags and other ungulate animals at rutting will look for fights, sometimes even abandoning their mates to do so. In many animals, even the higher ones, onset of old age seems to make them more vicious for apparently constitutional reasons, and previously mild animals will attack without provocation. In various species killing is not for the sake of food alone.

A well-known study on the laboratory rat shows that it is possible to breed wildness, aggressiveness, or ferocity as one can breed anatomical characteristics. The tendency to ferocity, at least in this one species and possibly in others as well, can be a primarily inherited determinant of behavior. This is made more plausible by the general finding that the adrenal glands in wild and ferocious rats are much larger than in milder, tamer ones. Other species, of course, can be bred by the geneticists in just the opposite fashion, toward mildness and tameness and lack of ferocity. It is such examples and observations as these that permit us to advance and to accept the simplest of all possible explanations, namely, that the behavior in question comes from an *ad hoc* motivation, that there was a hereditary drive to just this particular kind of behavior.

However, many other instances of apparently primary ferocity in animals are not quite what they appear when analyzed more closely. Aggression can be evoked in many ways and by many situations in animals just as in human beings. For example, there is the determinant called territoriality (14), which may be illustrated in birds that nest on the ground. As they select their breeding place, it will be found that they attack any other birds that come within the radius that they have designated for themselves. But they will attack these trespassers and no others. They do not attack in general; they attack only trespassers. Certain species will attack any other animal, even of their own species, that does not have the odor or appearance of their particular group or clan. For example, the howler monkeys form a sort of closed corporation. Any other howler monkey that tries to join the group is repelled by noisy attack. If, however, it lingers long enough, it will eventually become part of the group, to attack in turn any stranger that comes along.

When the higher animals are studied, attacking is found to be correlated more and more with dominance. These studies are too complex to be quoted in detail, but it may be said that this dominance, and the aggressiveness that sometimes evolves from it, does have functional value or survival value for the animal. The animal's place in dominance hierarchy is in part determined by his successful aggression, and his place in the hierarchy determines in turn how much food he will get, whether or not he will have a mate, and other biological satisfactions. Practically all the cruelty manifested in these animals occurs only when it is necessary to validate dominance status, or to make a revolution in dominance status. How true this is for other species, I am not sure. But I do suspect that the phenomenon of territoriality, of attack on strangers, of jealous protection of the females, of attack on the weak or sick, and other phenomena that are often explained by instinctive aggression or cruelty are very often found to have been motivated by dominance rather than by a specific motivation to aggression for its own sake, e.g., this aggression may be means behavior rather than end behavior.

When the infrahuman primates are studied, it is discovered that aggression becomes less and less primary and more and more derived and reactive, more and more functional, more and more a reasonable, understandable reaction to a totality of motivations, of social forces, and immediate situational determinants. By the time one reaches the chimpanzees, that animal of all animals that is closest to the human being, no behavior at all is found that can even be remotely suspected of being aggressive for the sake of aggression. So likable and coöperative and friendly are these animals, especially when young, that in some groups one may not find cruel aggression of any kind for whatever reason. Something similar is true for gorillas as well.

At this point I may say that the whole argument from animal to man must certainly always be held suspect. But if it is accepted for the sake of argument, it must be concluded, if one reasons from the animals that are closest to man, that they prove almost the opposite of what is usually considered to be the case. If man has an animal heritage, it must be largely an anthropoid heritage, and anthropoid apes are more coöperative than aggressive.

This mistake is an instance of a general type of pseudo-scientific thinking that can best be described as illegitimate animal centrism. The correct procedure for making this kind of a mistake is first to construct a theory, or formulate a prejudice, and then to select from the whole evolutionary gamut that one animal that best illustrates the point. Second, one must deliberately blind himself to the behavior of all animals that do not fit into the theory. If one wishes to prove instinctive destructiveness, by all means choose the wolf and forget the rabbit. Third, it is necessary to forget that clear developmental trends can be seen if one studies the whole phyletic scale from low to high, instead of selecting some particular favorite species. For example, ascending the animal scale, appetites become more and more important, and sheer hungers become less and less important (302). Moreover, variability becomes greater and greater; the period between fertilization and adulthood tends, with exceptions, to become longer and longer; and, perhaps most significantly, reflexes, hormones, and instincts become less and less important determiners and are increasingly replaced by intelligence, learning, and social determination.

The evidence from animals may be summarized by saying first that the argument from animal to human is always a delicate task to be executed with the greatest of caution; second, that a primary and inherited tendency to destructive or cruel aggression may be found in some species of animals, although probably in fewer than most people believe. It is missing completely in some species. Third, specific instances of aggressive behavior in animals, when carefully analyzed, are found more often than not to be secondary, derived reactions to various determinants and not just expressions of an instinct of aggressiveness for its own sake. Fourth, the higher the ascent in the phyletic scale and the closer the approach to man, the more clearly the evidence for a putative primary instinct of aggressiveness is seen to become weaker and weaker, until by the time one reaches the apes, it seems to be absent altogether. Fifth, if one studies most carefully the apes, man's closest relatives among all the animals, little or no evidence of primary malicious aggression is found, but instead a great deal of evidence for friendliness. coöperativeness, and even altruism. A final point of importance comes from our tendency to assume motives when all we know is behavior. It is now generally agreed upon by students of animal behavior that most carnivores killing their prey are simply getting food rather than being sadistic, in about the same spirit that we get steaks, for food rather than from the lust to kill. What all this means finally is that henceforth any evolutionary argument about man's animal nature forcing him to aggressiveness or destructiveness for its own sake must be suspected or rejected.

CHILD DATA

Observations and experimental studies and findings of children sometimes seem to resemble a kind of projective method, a Rorschach ink blot upon which adult hostility can be projected. One hears a great deal of talk about the innate selfishness and innate destructiveness of children, and there are far more papers dealing with these than with cooperation, kindness, sympathy, and the like. Furthermore, these latter studies, few in number though they have been, are usually overlooked. Psychologists and psychoanalysts often have conceived of the infant as a little devil, born with original sin and with hatred in his heart. Certainly this undiluted picture is false. I must admit that there is a regrettable lack of scientific material in this area. I base my judgment on only a few excellent studies, particularly that of Lois Murphy, on sympathy in children (352), on my own experience with children, and finally on certain theoretical considerations (301). However, even such scanty evidence seems to me to be enough to throw doubt on the conclusion that children are primarily destructive, aggressive, hostile little animals who have to have some modicum of goodness knocked into them by discipline and punishment.

The facts, experimental and observational, seem to be that normal children are in fact often hostile, destructive, and selfish in a primitive sort of way as has been claimed. But they are also at other times, and perhaps as often, generous, cooperative, and unselfish in the same primitive style. The main principle that determines the relative frequency of the two types of behavior seems to be that the child who is insecure, basically thwarted, or threatened in his needs for safety, love, belongingness, and self-esteem is the child who will show more selfishness, hatred, aggression, and destructiveness. In children who are basically loved and respected by their parents, less destructiveness should be found, and in my opinion what evidence there is shows that less destructiveness actually *is* found. This implies a reactive, instrumental, or defensive interpretation of hostility rather than an instinctive one.

If one looks at a healthy and well-loved and cared-for infant, let us say up to the age of one year and perhaps later, then it is quite impossible to see anything that could be called evil, original sin, sadism, malice, pleasure in hurting, destructiveness, hostility for its own sake, or deliberate cruelty. On the contrary, careful and long-continued observation demonstrates the opposite. Practically every personality characteristic found in self-actualizing people, everything lovable, admirable, and enviable is found in such babies—that is, except knowledge, experience, wisdom. One of the reasons that babies are loved and wanted so much must be just this—that they are without visible evil, hatred, or malice in the first year or two of their lives.

As for destructiveness, I am very doubtful that it ever occurs in normal children as a direct primary expression of a simple destructive drive. One example after another of apparent destructiveness can be analyzed away dynamically as it is examined more closely. The child who pulls the clock apart is not in his own eyes destroying the clock; he is examining the clock. If one must speak of a primary drive here, curiosity would be a much more sensible choice than destructiveness. Many other examples that look like destructiveness to the distraught mother turn out to be not only curiosity but activity, play, exercise of the growing capacities and skills, and even sometimes actual creation, as when a child cuts her father's carefully typed notes into pretty little forms. I doubt that young children are deliberately destructive for the sheer pleasure of malicious destruction. A possible exception is pathological cases; for example, epilepsy and postencephalitis, and even in these so-called pathological examples, to this day it is not known that their destructiveness may not also have been reactive, a response to threats of one kind or another.

Sibling rivalry is a special and sometimes puzzling case. A two-year-old child can be dangerously aggressive to its newborn baby brother. Sometimes the hostile intent is expressed very naively and forthrightly. One reasonable explanation is that a two-year-old is simply not capable of the thought that his mother can love *two* children. He hurts not merely for the sake of hurting but to retain the love of his mother.

Another special case is the psychopathic personality whose aggression often seems unmotivated, i.e., seems to be performed for its own sake. I consider it necessary to invoke a principle here that I first heard enunciated by Ruth Benedict (40) in an effort to explain why secure societies could go to war. Her explanation was that secure, healthy people are not hostile or aggressive against people who are in a broad sense their brothers, people with whom they can identify. If certain ones are *not* seen as human beings, they can be snuffed out quite easily even by kind, loving, healthy people, in the same way that they are completely guiltless about killing annoying insects, or slaughtering animals for food.

I have found it helpful in understanding psychopaths to assume that they have no love identifications with other human beings and can therefore hurt them or even kill them casually, without hate, and without pleasure, precisely as they kill animals who have come to be pests. Some childish reactions that seem cruel probably also come from lack of identification of this sort, i.e., before the child has matured enough to enter into interpersonal relations.

Finally, it seems to me that certain semantic considerations of considerable importance are also involved. To say it as succinctly as possible, aggression, hostility, and destructiveness are all adult words. They mean certain things to adults that they do *not* mean to children, and should therefore not be used without modification or redefinition.

For instance, children in the second year of life can play independently side by side without really interacting with each other (73). When selfish or aggressive interactions do occur in such children, it is not the same kind of interpersonal relationship that can occur between ten-year-olds; it may be without awareness of the other. If one such child then pulls away a toy from the other against resistance, this may be more like wrestling an object from a tight container than like adult selfish aggression.

So also for the active infant who finds the nipple snatched from his mouth and then yells in rage, or the three-year-old who strikes back at the punishing mother, or the angry five-year-old who shrieks, "I wish you were dead," or the two-year-old who persistently roughs up his newborn brother. In none of these cases ought we treat the child as if he were an adult; nor ought we interpret his reaction as we would an adult's reaction.

Most such behaviors, dynamically understood in the child's own frame of reference, must probably be accepted as reactive. This is to say they most likely come from disappointment, rejection, loneliness, fear of loss of respect, fear of loss of protection, i.e., thwarting of basic needs or threat of such thwarting, more than they do from an inherited, per se, drive to hate or hurt. Whether or not this reactive explanation accounts for *all* destructive behavior, and not merely most of it, our knowledge—or rather our lack of knowledge—simply does not permit us to say.

ANTHROPOLOGICAL DATA

A discussion of the comparative data may be amplified through recourse to ethnology. I can say at once that even a cursory survey of the material would prove to any interested reader that the amount of hostility, aggression, or destructiveness in living, primitive cultures is not constant, but varies between the extremes of almost 0 to almost 100 percent. There are peoples like the Arapesh who are so mild, so friendly, so unaggressive that they have to go to extremes to find a man who is even self-assertive enough to organize their ceremonies. At the other extreme one can find people like the Chukchi and the Dobu who are so full of hatred that one wonders what keeps them from killing one another off altogether. Of course, these are descriptions of behavior externally observed. We may still wonder about unconscious impulses that underlie these behaviors and that *may* be different from what we can *see*.

I can speak from direct knowledge[1] of but one Indian group—the Northern Blackfoot—but this, however inadequate, was enough to convince me directly of the fundamental fact that the amount of destructiveness and aggression is largely culturally determined. Here was a group with a constant population of about 800 in which I could get records of only 5 fist fights that had occurred in the last 15 years. Intrasocial hostility, for which I hunted with all the anthropological and psychiatric means at my command, was certainly at a minimum when compared with our larger society.[2] The humor was friendly rather than malicious, the gossip substituted for newspapers rather than for backbiting, the magic, the sorcery, the religion were almost all for the good of the whole group or for healing purposes rather than for destructiveness, aggression, or revenge. During my stay I never observed directed at me a single instance of what might be called cruelty or hostility. Children were rarely punished physically, and the whites were despised for the cruelty with which they treated their children and their fellows. Even alcohol uncovered comparatively little aggression. Under the influence of alcohol the older Blackfoot was more apt to become jovial, expansive, and universally friendly than pugnacious. The exceptions were definitely

[1] I wish to thank the Social Science Research Council who made this field trip possible by a grant-in-aid of research.

[2] These statements apply primarily to the older, less acculturated individuals observed in the year 1939. The culture has changed drastically since then.

exceptions. These were not weak people by any means. The Northern Blackfoot Indians were a prideful, strong, upstanding, self-valuing group. They were simply apt to regard aggression as wrong or pitiful or crazy.

Apparently human beings need not be even as aggressive or destructive as the average man in American society, let alone those of some other parts of the world. There seems to be, in the anthropological evidence, a potent source for considering destructiveness, malice, or cruelty in human beings to be most probably a secondary, reactive consequence of thwarting of or threat to the basic human needs.

SOME THEORETICAL CONSIDERATIONS

As we have seen, a widely held view is that destructiveness or hurting is secondary or derived behavior rather than primary motivation. By this is meant the expectation that hostile or destructive behavior in the human being will practically always be found to result from an assignable reason of some sort, to be a reaction to another state of affairs, to be a product rather than an original source. The view with which this contrasts is that destructiveness is the direct and primary product, in whole or in part, of some instinct of destructiveness.

In any such discussion the most important single distinction that can be made is the one between motivation and behavior. Behavior is determined by many forces, of which internal motivation is only one. I might say very briefly that any theory of determination of behavior must include the study of at least the following determinants: (1) the character structure, (2) the cultural pressures, and (3) the immediate situation or field. In other words, the study of inner motivation is only part of one of three major areas involved in any study of the main determinants of behavior. With these considerations in mind, I may rephrase my question to read, How is destructive behavior determined? Second, Is the only determinant for destructive behavior some inherited, predetermined, *ad hoc* motivation? These questions of course answer themselves at once on an a priori basis alone. All possible motivations taken together, let alone a specific instinct, do not determine in themselves the occurrence of aggression or destructiveness. The culture in general must be involved, and the immediate situation or field in which the behavior occurs must also be considered.

There is still another way of stating the problem. It can be shown certainly for the human being that destructive behavior derives from so many different sources that it becomes ridiculous to speak of any single urge to destructiveness. This can be illustrated by a few examples.

Destructiveness may occur quite incidentally as one sweeps something out of his path to the goal. A child who is trying hard to reach some toy at a distance is not apt to notice that he is trampling other toys in his path (233).

Destructiveness may occur as one of the concomitant reactions to basic threat. Thus any threat of thwarting of the basic needs, any threat to the defensive or coping system, any threat to the general way of life is likely to be reacted to by anxiety-hostility, which means that hostile, aggressive, or destructive behavior may very frequently be expected in such reactions. This is ultimately defensive behavior, counterattack rather than attack for its own sake.

Any damage to the organism, any perception of organic deterioration, will probably arouse in the insecure person similar feelings of threat, and destructive behavior may therefore be expected, as in many cases of brain injury where the patient frantically attempts to support his faltering self-esteem by a diversity of desperate measures.

One reason for aggressive behavior that is customarily overlooked, or if not, then is phrased inaccurately, is the authoritarian (303) view of life. If a person were *actually* to live in a jungle in which all other animals were divided into two classes, those who could eat him and those he could eat, aggression would become a sensible and logical thing. People described as authoritarian must frequently tend unconsciously to envisage the world as just such a jungle. On the principle that the best defense is a good attack, these people are apt to lash out, to strike, to destroy with no apparent reason whatsoever, and the whole reaction remains meaningless until it is realized that this was simply in anticipation of an attack by the other person. There are also many other well-known forms of defensive hostility.

The dynamics of sadistic-masochistic reactions have now been fairly well analyzed, and it is generally understood that what looks like a simple aggression may actually have very complex dynamics behind it. These dynamics make an appeal to some putative instinct of hostility look far too simple. The same is true for the overwhelming drive for power over other people. Analysis by Horney and others has shown clearly that, in this area as well, recourse to instinctual explanation is unnecessary (198, 448). World War II has taught us the lesson that the attack of the gangster and the defense of the righteously indignant are not the same psychologically.

This list could easily be expanded. I cite these few examples to illustrate my point that destructive behavior is very often a symptom, a type of behavior that can result from many factors. If one wishes to be truly dynamic, one must learn to be alert to the fact that these behaviors may appear alike despite the fact that they derive from different sources. The dynamic psychologist is not a camera or mechanical recorder. He is interested in knowing why things happen as well as what happens.

CLINICAL EXPERIENCE

The usual experience reported in the literature of psychotherapy is that violence, anger, hatred, destructive wishes, impulses to vengeance and the like all exist in great quantity in practically everyone, if not visibly then under the surface. Any experienced therapist will refuse to take seriously anyone's claim that he has never felt hatred. He will simply assume that the person has suppressed or repressed it. He expects to find it in everyone.

Yet it is also the general experience in therapy that talking freely about one's violent impulses (without acting them out) tends to purge them, to reduce their frequency, and to eliminate their neurotic, unrealistic components. The general result of successful therapy (or a successful growth and maturing) tends to be approximately what is seen in self-actualizing people: (1) they experience hostility, hatred, violence, malice, destructive aggression much less often than do average people; (2) they do not *lose* their anger or aggression, but its quality tends to be changed into indignation, to self-affirmation, to resistance against being exploited, to anger against injustice, i.e., from unhealthy to healthy aggression; and (3) healthier people seem much less afraid of their own angers and aggressions, and so are able to express them more wholeheartedly when they do express them at all. Violence has two opposites, not just one. The opposite of violence can be less violence, or control of one's violence, or efforts to be nonviolent. *Or* it can be an opposition between healthy and unhealthy violence.

These "data" do not settle our issue however, and it is very instructive to learn that Freud and his loyalist followers consider violence to be instinctive, whereas Fromm, Horney, and other Neo-Freudians conclude that it is not at all instinctive.

DATA FROM ENDOCRINOLOGY, GENETICS, ETC.

Anyone who wanted to put together all that is known about the sources of violence would also have to dig out the data that the endocrinologists have accumulated. Again, the situation is relatively simple in lower animals. There is little doubt that the sex hormones and the adrenal and pituitary hormones are unmistakable determiners of aggression, dominance, passivity, wildness. But because all the endocrine glands are mutually determinative, some of these data are very complex and require special knowledge. This is even more true for the human species, in which the data are even more complex. And yet they dare not be by-passed. Again, there is evidence that the male hormones have something to do with self-affirmation, with readiness and ability to fight, etc. There is some evidence that different individuals secrete different proportions of adrenaline and nonadrenaline, and that these chemicals have some-thing to do with the individual's proneness to fight rather than flee, etc. The new cross-disciplinary science of psychoendocrinology will undoubt-edly teach us much about our problem.

Of course data from genetics, from the chromosomes and genes themselves, will obviously be of very special relevance. For instance, the recent discovery that males with a double male chromosome (a double dose of male heredity) tend to be almost uncontrollably violent, itself makes a pure environmentalism impossible. In the most peaceful of societies, with the most perfect social and economic conditions, *some* people will have to be violent just because of the way they are con-structed. This finding of course brings up the much discussed but not yet finally settled question: does the male, especially the adolescent male, perhaps need some violence, something or someone to fight against, to have conflict with? There is some evidence to indicate that this may be so, not only for human adults but even for babies, and for monkey babies as well. The degree to which this is or is not intrinsically determined we must also leave to future researchers to decide.

I could mention data from history, sociology, management studies, semantics, medical pathologies of all sorts, politics, mythology, psycho-pharmacology, and other sources as well. But no more is necessary to make the point that the questions asked at the beginning of this chapter are *empirical* questions and may therefore be confidently expected to be answerable by further research. Of course the integration of data from many fields makes team research a probability, perhaps even a necessity. In any case, this casual sampling of data available should be enough to teach us to reject the extreme, black–white polarizing into *either* all in-stinct, heredity, biological fate *or else* all environment, social forces, learning. The old hereditarian vs. environmental polemics are not yet dead even though they should be. Clearly the determinants of destruc-tiveness are pluralistic. It is absolutely clear even now that among these determinants we must count culture, learning, environment. It is less clear but still very probable that biological determinants also play an essential role, even though we cannot be quite sure what it is. At the very least, we must accept the inevitability of violence as part of the human essence, if only because basic needs are absolutely doomed to be frustrated at times, and we know that the human species is constructed in such a manner that violence, anger, retaliation are quite common consequences of such frustrations.

Finally it is not necessary to make a choice between all-powerful instincts and all-powerful culture. The position presented in this chapter transcends this dichotomy and makes it unnecessary. Hereditary or other biological determination is not all or none; it is a matter of degree, of little or much. In the human being the preponderance of the evidence indicates that there *are* biological and hereditary determinants, but that in most individuals they are quite weak and easily overwhelmed by learned cultural forces. Not only are they weak but also they are fragmented, remnants and pieces rather than the whole and complete instincts found in lower animals. The human being has no instincts, but he *does* seem to have instinct-remnants, "instinctoid" needs, intrinsic capacities and potentialities. Furthermore, clinical and personological experience generally suggests that these weak instinctoid tendencies are good, desirable, and healthy rather than malign or evil, and that the great effort to save them from annihilation is both feasible and worthwhile, and indeed, that this is a major function of any culture that would be called good.

10

THE EXPRESSIVE COMPONENT OF BEHAVIOR

The distinction between the expressive (noninstrumental) and the coping (instrumental, adaptive, functional, purposive) components of behavior is by now well established (by the writings particularly of G. Allport, Werner, Arnheim, and W. Wolff), but has not yet been properly exploited as a basis for value psychology.[1]

Because contemporary psychology is overly pragmatic, it abdicates from certain areas that should be of great concern to it. In its preoccupation with practical results, with technology and means, it has notoriously little to say, for example, about beauty, art, fun, play, wonder, awe, joy, love, happiness, and other "useless" reactions and end-experiences. It is therefore of little or no service to the artist, the musician, the poet, the novelist, to the humanist, the connoisseur, the axiologist, the theologian, or to other end- or enjoyment-oriented individuals. This is the equivalent of an accusation against psychology that it offers little to the modern man whose most desperate need is a naturalistic or humanistic end or value system.

---

[1] We must be careful here to avoid sharp, either–or dichotomizing. Most acts of behavior have both an expressive and a coping component, e.g., walking has simultaneously a purpose and a style. And yet we do not wish to exclude, as do Allport and Vernon (8), the theoretical possibility of practically pure expressive acts, e.g., sauntering instead of walking; blushing; gracefulness; poor posture; whistling; a child's laughing in glee; private, noncommunicative artistic activity; pure self-actualization, etc.

By exploring and applying the differentiation between expression and coping—which is simultaneously a differentiation between "useless" and "useful" behavior—we may help to extend the jurisdiction of psychology in these desirable directions. This chapter also is conceived as a necessary preliminary to the important task of challenging and calling into question the generally accepted belief that all behavior is motivated. This will be attempted in Chapter 14. More specifically, this chapter discusses the differences between expression and coping and then applies them to some problems of psychopathology.

1. Coping is by definition purposive and motivated; expression is often unmotivated.

2. Coping is more determined by external environmental and cultural variables; expression is largely determined by the state of the organism. A corollary is the much higher correlation of expression with deep-lying character structure. So-called projective tests might more accurately be called "expressive tests."

3. Coping is most often learned; expression is most often unlearned or released or disinhibited.

4. Coping is more easily controlled (repressed, suppressed, inhibited, acculturated); expression is more often uncontrolled and sometimes even uncontrollable.

5. Coping is usually designed to cause changes in the environment and often does; expression is not designed to do anything. If it causes environmental changes, it does so unwittingly.

6. Coping is characteristically means behavior, the end being need gratification or threat reduction. Expression is often an end in itself.

7. Typically, the coping component is conscious (although it may become unconscious); expression is more often not conscious.

8. Coping is effortful; expression is effortless in most instances. Artistic expression is of course a special and in-between case, because one *learns* to be spontaneous and expressive (if one is successful). One can *try* to relax.

COPING AND EXPRESSION

Coping behavior always has among its determinants drives, needs, goals, purposes, functions, or aims. It comes into existence to get something done, e.g., walking to some destination, shopping for food, going to mail a letter, building a set of bookshelves, or doing the work for which we get paid. The term coping itself (296) implies the attempt to solve a problem or at least to deal with it. It therefore implies a reference to something beyond itself; it is not self-contained. This reference may be either to immediate or to basic needs, to means as well as ends, to frustration-induced behavior as well as to goal-seeking behavior.

Expressive behavior of the type so far discussed by psychologists is generally unmotivated, although, of course, it is determined. (That is, though expressive behavior has many determinants, need gratification need not be one of them.) It simply mirrors, reflects, signifies, or expresses some state of the organism. Indeed, it most often is *part* of that state, e.g., the stupidity of the moron, the smile and the springy walk of the healthy person, the benevolent mien of the kind and affectionate, the beauty of the beautiful woman, the slumping posture, lowered tonus, and hopeless expression of the depressed person, the style of handwriting, walking, gesturing, smiling, dancing, etc. These are nonpurposive. They have no aim or goal. They were not elaborated for the sake of need gratification.[2] They are epiphenomenal.

While all this is true as far as it goes, a special problem is raised by what at first glance seems a paradox, namely, the concept of motivated self-expression. The more sophisticated person can *try* to be honest, graceful, kind, or even artless. People who have been through psychoanalysis as well as people at the highest motivational levels know well how this is.

Indeed, it is their most basic single problem. Self-acceptance and spontaneity are among the easiest achievements, e.g., in healthy children, and the most difficult, e.g., in self-questioning, self-improving adults, especially those who have been or still are neurotic. Indeed, for some it is an impossible achievement, e.g., in certain types of neurosis the individual is an actor who has no self at all in the ordinary sense, but only a repertoire of roles from which to choose.

We may take two examples, one simple and the other complex, to demonstrate the (apparent) contradictions involved in the concept of motivated, purposeful spontaneity, of Taoistic yielding and letting go, as with tight muscles or sphincters. The most desirable way to dance, at least for the amateur, is to be spontaneous, fluid, automatically responsive to the rhythm of the music and the unconscious wishes of the partner. A good dancer can let himself go, becoming a passive instrument fashioned by the music and played upon by it. He need have no wish, no criticism, no direction, no will. In a very real and useful sense of the word, he may

---

[2] This statement is independent of any particular phrasing of motivation theory. For instance, it applies as well to simple hedonism; thus we may rephrase our statement to say: Coping behavior is responsive to praise or blame, reward or punishment; expressive behavior is ordinarily not, at least so long as it remains expressive.

become passive, even as he dances to the point of exhaustion. Such passive spontaneity or willing abandon can yield some of life's greatest pleasures, as in allowing the surf to tumble one about, or allowing oneself to be cared for and nursed, massaged, barbered, as in being made love to, or as in the mother who passively allows her baby to suckle, to bite, and to crawl over her. But few people can dance as well as this. Most will try, will be directed, self-controlled, and purposeful, will listen carefully to the rhythm of the music, and by a conscious act of choice, fall in with it. They will be poor dancers from the point of view of the onlooker and from the subjective point of view as well, for they will never enjoy dancing as a profound experience of self-forgetfulness, and voluntary renunciation of control unless they finally transcend trying and become spontaneous.

Many dancers become good without training. And yet education can be a help here too. But it must be a different kind, an education in spontaneity and eager abandon, in being natural, nonvoluntary, noncritical, and passive in the Taoist style, trying not to try. One must "learn" for such purposes to be able to drop inhibitions, self-consciousness, will, control, acculturation, and dignity. ("When once you are free from all seeming, from all craving and lusting, then will you move of your own impulse, without so much as knowing that you move"—Lao Tse.)

More difficult problems are raised by an examination of the nature of self-actualization. Of people who are at this level of motivational development, it may be said that their actions and creations are in a very high degree spontaneous, guileness, open, self-disclosing, and unedited and therefore expressive, (the "Easy State," we might call it, after Asrani). Furthermore, their motivations change in quality so much and are so different from the ordinary needs for safety or love or respect, that they ought not even to be called by the same name. (I have suggested the word "metaneeds" to describe the motivations of self-actualizing people.)

If the wish for love be called a need, the pressure to self-actualize ought to be called by some name other than need because it has so many different characteristics. The one main difference most pertinent to our present task is that love and respect, etc., may be considered as external qualities that the organism lacks and therefore needs. Self-actualization is not a lack or deficiency in this sense. It is not something extrinsic that the organism needs for health, as for example, a tree needs water. Self-actualization is intrinsic growth of what is already in the organism, or more accurately of what *is* the organism itself. Just as our tree needs food, sun, water from the environment, so does the person need safety, love, and respect from the social environment. But as in the first case, so also in the second, this is just where real development, i.e., of individuality, begins. All trees need sunlight and all human beings need love, and yet, once satiated with these elementary necessities, each tree and each human being proceeds to develop in his own style, uniquely, using these universal necessities to his own private purposes. In a word, development then proceeds from within rather than from without, and paradoxically the highest motive is to be unmotivated and nonstriving, i.e., to behave purely expressively. Or, to say it in another way, self-actualization is growth-motivated rather than deficiency-motivated. It is a "second naïvete," a wise innocence, an "Easy State," (295, 314, 315).

One can try to go in the direction of self-actualization by solving the lesser, prerequisite motivational problems. Thereby one consciously and purposefully seeks spontaneity. Thus at the highest levels of human development, the distinction between coping and expression, like so many other psychological dichotomies, is resolved and transcended, and trying becomes a path to nontrying.

INNER AND OUTER DETERMINANTS

Coping behavior is characteristically more determined by relatively external determinants than is expressive behavior. It is most often a functional response to an emergency, a problem or a need whose solution or gratification comes from the physical and/or cultural world. Ultimately, as we have seen, it is an attempt to make up internal deficiencies by external satisfiers.

Expressive behavior contrasts with coping behavior in its more exclusively characterological determination (see below). We may say that coping behavior is essentially an interaction of the character with the nonpsychic world, adjusting each to the other with mutual effect; expression is essentially an epiphenomenon or by-product of the nature of the character structure. In the former, therefore, may be detected the working of both the laws of the physical world and of the inner character; in the latter one detects primarily psychological or characterological laws. An illustration could be the contrast between representational and nonrepresentational art.

Several corollaries follow. (1) It is certain that if one wishes to know about the character structure, the best behavior to study is expressive rather than coping behavior. This is supported by the now extensive experience with projective (expressive) tests. (2) With reference to the perennial debate about what is psychology and what is the best approach to its study, it is clear that adjustmental, purposive, motivated, coping behavior is not the only kind of behavior there is. (3) Our distinction may have some bearing on the question of the continuity or discontinuity of psychology with the other sciences. In principle the study of the natural world should help us to understand coping behavior but probably not expression. The latter seems to be more purely psychological, probably having its own rules and laws and therefore best studied directly rather than through the physical and natural sciences.

RELATION TO LEARNING

Ideal coping behavior is characteristically learned, while ideal expressive behavior is characteristically unlearned. We do not have to learn how to feel helpless or look healthy or be stupid or show anger, while we do ordinarily have to learn how to build bookshelves, ride a bicycle, or dress ourselves. This contrast may be clearly seen in the determinants of reaction to achievement tests on the one hand, and to the Rorschach test on the other. Also coping behavior tends to die out unless rewarded; expression often persists without reward or reinforcement. One is gratification-bent; the other is not.

THE POSSIBILITY OF CONTROL

Differential determination by inner and outer determinants shows itself also in a varying susceptibility to conscious or unconscious control (inhibition, repression, suppression). Spontaneous expression is very difficult to manage, to change, to conceal, to control, or to influence in any way. Indeed, control and expression are by definition antithetical. This is true even for the motivated self-expression spoken of above, for this is the end product of a series of efforts to learn how not to control.

Control of style of handwriting, dancing, singing, speaking, emotional reacting may at best be kept up for only a short time. Supervision or criticism of one's reactions cannot be continuous. Sooner or later because of fatigue, distraction, redirection, or attention, etc., control slips, and deeper, less conscious, more automatic, more characterological determinants take over (6). Expression is not, in the full sense, voluntary behavior. Another aspect of this contrast is the effortlessness of expression. Coping is in principle effortful. (Again, the artist is a special case.)

Some warnings are called for here. An easy mistake here is to think of spontaneity and expressiveness as good always and control of any kind as bad and undesirable. This is not so. Certainly, much of the time, expressiveness *feels* better, is more fun, more honest, effortless, etc., than self-control, so is in this sense desirable both for the person himself and for his interpersonal relationships, as for instance Jourard (217) has shown.

And yet there are several meanings of self-control, or of inhibition, and some of them are quite desirable and healthy, even apart from what is necessary for dealing with the outside world. Control need not mean frustration or renunciation of basic need gratifications. What I would call the "Apollonizing controls" do *not* call the gratification of needs into question at all; they make them *more* rather than less enjoyable by, e.g., suitable delay (as in sex), by gracefulness (as in dancing or swimming) by estheticizing (as with food and drink), by stylizing (as in sonnets), by ceremonializing, sacralizing, dignifying, by doing something well rather than just doing it.

And then too—what has to be repeated again and again—is that the healthy person is not only expressive. He must be able to be expressive when he wishes to be. He must be able to let himself go. He must be able to drop controls, inhibitions, defenses when he deems this desirable. But equally he must have the ability to control himself, to delay his pleasures, to be polite, to avoid hurting, to keep his mouth shut, and to rein his impulses. He must be able to be either Dionysian or Apollonian, Stoic or Epicurean, expressive or coping, controlled or uncontrolled, self-disclosing or self-concealing, able to have fun and able to give up fun, able to think of the future as well as the present. The healthy or self-actualizing person is essentially versatile; he has lost fewer of the human capacities than the average man has. He has a larger armamentarium of responses and moves toward full-humanness as a limit; that is, he has *all* the human capacities.

EFFECTS ON ENVIRONMENT

Coping behavior characteristically originates as an attempt to change the world, and characteristically does so with more or less success. Expressive behavior, on the other hand, often has no effect on the environment. And where it does have such effect, it is not premeditated, willed, or purposed; it is unwitting.

As an example we may take a man in conversation. Conversation has purpose, e.g., he is a salesman trying to get an order, and the conversation is consciously and avowedly brought into being for this reason. But his style of speaking may be unconsciously hostile or snobbish or supercilious and may cause him to lose the order. Thus the expressive aspects of his behavior may have environmental effects, but it is to be noted that the speaker did not want these effects, that he did not try to be supercilious or hostile, and he was not even aware that he gave this impression. The environmental effects of expression, when there are any at all, are unmotivated, unpurposed and epiphenomenal.

MEANS AND ENDS

Coping behavior is always instrumental, always a means to a motivated end. Contrariwise, any means-end behavior (with the one exception discussed above, of voluntarily giving up coping) must be coping behavior.

On the other hand, the various forms of expressive behavior either have nothing to do with either means or ends, e.g., style of handwriting, or else they come close to being ends-in-themselves behavior, e.g., singing, sauntering, painting, extemporizing at the piano, etc.[3] This point will be examined more carefully in Chapter 14.

COPING AND CONSCIOUSNESS

Expression in its purest forms is unconscious, or at least not fully conscious. We are ordinarily unaware of our style of walking, or standing or smiling or laughing. It is true that we may be made aware of them by moving pictures, phonograph records, caricatures, or imitations. But such are apt to be exceptions or at least uncharacteristic. Expressive acts that are conscious, choosing our clothes, furniture, hair style, are seen as special, unusual, or intermediate cases. But coping may be and characteristically is fully conscious. When it is unconscious, this is seen as exceptional or unusual.

RELEASE AND CATHARSIS;
THE INCOMPLETED ACT;
KEEPING SECRETS

There is a special type of behavior which, though essentially expressive, has nevertheless some usefulness to the organism, sometimes even a wished-for usefulness, e.g., what Levy has called release behavior. Perhaps cursing to oneself or similar private expressions of rage are better examples than the more technical ones offered by Levy (271). Cursing is certainly expressive in being a reflection of the state of the organism. It is not coping behavior in the ordinary sense of being produced in order to gratify a

---

[3] In our overpragmatic culture, the instrumental spirit can overtake even the end experiences; love ("It's the normal thing to do."), sport ("Good for the digestion."); education ("Raise your pay."); singing ("It's good for chest development."); hobbies ("Relaxation improves sleep."); beautiful weather (". . . good for business."); reading ("I really should keep up with things."); affection ("Do you want your child to be neurotic?"); kindness ("Bread cast upon the waters. . . ."); science ("National defense!"); art (". . . has definitely improved American advertising."); kindness (". . . if you're not, they'll steal the silver.")

basic need, though it may be satisfying in another sense. It seems rather to produce as a by-product a change in the state of the organism itself.

Probably all such release behaviors can be generally defined as keeping the organism more comfortable, i.e., keeping tension level down, by (1) allowing an incompleted act to be completed; (2) draining off accumulations of hostility, anxiety, excitement, joy, ecstasy, love, or other tension-producing emotions by allowing consummatory motor expression, or (3) permitting simple activity for its own sake of the type indulged in by any healthy organism. The same seems to be true for self-disclosure (217) and keeping secrets.

It is very likely that catharsis, as originally defined by Breuer and Freud, is in essence a more complex variant of release behavior. This, too, is the free (and, in a special sense, satisfying) expression of an impeded, uncompleted act that, like all impeded acts, seems to press for expression. This would seem also to be true for simple confession and disclosing secrets. Perhaps even full psychoanalytic insight, if we knew enough about it, might be found to fit into our series of release or completion phenomena.

It is desirable to keep separated from each other those perseverative behaviors that are a coping response to threat and those that are simply and unemotionally tendencies to complete a half-completed act or series of acts. The former have to do with threat to and gratification of basic, partial, and/or neurotic needs. They are therefore properly in the jurisdiction of motivation theory. The latter are very probably ideomotor phenomena, which in turn are very closely related to such neurological and physiological variables as blood sugar level, adrenalin secretion, autonomic arousal, and reflex tendencies. Thus, in trying to understand the little boy jumping up and down for (pleasant) excitement, it is best to invoke the principle of motor expression of a physiological state of affairs rather than to refer to his motivational life. And of course, putting on an act, not being yourself, concealing your own true nature, must cause the same kind of strain that a spy has to endure. Being yourself, being natural must be less wearing and fatiguing. So also for honesty, relaxing, guilelessness.

REPETITION PHENOMENA; PERSISTENT, UNSUCCESSFUL COPING; DETOXIFICATION

The repetitive nightmare dreams of the traumatic neuroses, the bad dreams of the insecure child (or adult), the child's chronic fascination with just that which frightens him most, tics, rituals, and other symbolic acts, dissociative acts, and neurotic "acting out," are all examples of repetitive phenomena that demand special explanation.[4] How important they are can be judged from the fact that Freud felt it necessary because of such phenomena to overhaul some of his most basic theories. Several recent writers, for example Fenichel (129), Kubie (245), and Kasanin (223), have pointed to what is probably the solution to this problem. They see these behaviors as repeated efforts, sometimes successful, more often not, to solve an almost insoluble problem. Such behavior may be likened to the hopelessly outclassed but desperate fighter who gets up off the floor again and again, only to be knocked down again and again. In short, they seem to be persistent if almost hopeless efforts at mastery of a problem by the organism. In our terms, therefore, they must be considered to be coping behaviors, or at any rate, attempts at coping. They thus differ from simple perseverations, catharsis, or release, since the latter do no more than complete the uncompleted and resolve the unresolved.

A child overwhelmed by repeated stories in which wolves figure will in some cases tend to come back to the problem again, e.g., in play, conversation, questions asked, making up stories, and in paintings. The child may be said to be detoxifying or desensitizing the problem. This result comes to pass because repetition means familiarization, release, and catharsis, working through, ceasing to respond with emergency reactions, slowly building up defenses, trying out various mastery techniques, practicing successful ones, etc.

We may expect the repetition compulsion to disappear with the evaporation of the determinants that brought the compulsion into existence. But what shall we say about the repetitions that do not disappear? It would appear that in such cases the efforts at mastery failed.

Apparently the insecure person cannot accept defeat gracefully. He must keep on trying again and again, useless though this may be. Here we may recall the experiments by Ovsiankina (367) and Zeigarnik (493) on the perseveration of uncompleted tasks, that is to say, unsolved problems. Recent work has shown that this tendency appears only where threat to the personality core is involved, i.e., where failure means loss of

---

[4] We restrict ourselves here to symbolic acts, resisting the temptation to plunge into the fascinating and obviously pertinent problem of symbolism in general. As for dreams, it is obvious that in addition to the type mentioned here, there are also primarily coping dreams (e.g., simple wish fulfillment) and primarily expression dreams (e.g., insecurity dreams, projection dreams). This latter kind of dream should, in theory, be usable as a kind of projective or expressive test for the diagnosis of character structure.

safety, self-esteem, prestige, or the like. On the basis of these experiments it seems reasonable to add to our phrasing a similar qualification. We may expect permanent repetition, i.e., unsuccessful coping, where a basic need of the personality is threatened and where the organism has no successful way of solving this problem.

The distinction between relatively expressive and relatively coping perseverations not only cuts across a single class of acts, but also enlarges each of the newly divided subclasses. We have seen that the rubric "expressive perseveration" or "simple act completion" includes not only releases and catharses but also probably motor restlessness, expressions of excitement, either pleasant or unpleasant, and ideomotor tendencies in general. It is equally possible (or rather fruitful) to include under the rubric "repetitive coping" such phenomena as unresolved feeling of insult or humiliation, unconscious jealousy and envy, persistent compensation for inferiority feelings, the compulsive and persistent promiscuity of latent homosexuals, and other such vain efforts to remove a threat. We could even suggest that with suitable conceptual modifications the neurosis itself could be so conceived.

Of course it is necessary to remind ourselves that the task of differential diagnosis remains, i.e., is this particular repetitive dream in this particular person expressive or coping, or both? See Murray's (353) list below for further examples.[5]

THE DEFINITION OF NEUROSIS

It would now be universally agreed that the classical neurosis as a whole as well as single neurotic symptoms are characteristically coping mechanisms. It was one of Freud's greatest contributions to show that these symptoms had functions, aims, purposes, and that they achieved effects of various sorts (primary gains).

But it is also true that many symptoms have been called neurotic that are not truly coping, functional, or purposive behaviors, but that are rather expressive behaviors. It would seem to be far more fruitful and

---

[5] Unconscious needs commonly express themselves in dreams, in visions, in emotional outbursts and unpremeditated acts, in slips of the tongue and pen, in absent-minded gestures, in laughter, in numberless disguised forms fused with acceptable (conscious) needs, in compulsions, in rationalized sentiments, in projections (illusions, delusions, and beliefs), and in all symptoms (hysterical conversion symptoms particularly), and in such things as children's games, regressions, doll play, making up stories (TAT), finger painting, man drawing, and fantasy productions. And we may one day add to this list rituals, ceremonials, folk tales and the like.

less confusing to call only those behaviors neurotic that are primarily functional or coping; behaviors that are predominantly expressive ought not to be called neurotic but rather by other names (see below).

There is a simple enough test, simple at least in theory, for making the differentiation between symptoms that are truly neurotic, i.e., functional, purposive, or coping, and symptoms that are primarily expressive. If a neurotic symptom does have a function, does do a job for the person, we must assume that the person is better off for having this symptom. If it were possible to rob the patient of a truly neurotic symptom, then, according to theory, he should be hurt in one way or another, i.e., thrown into anxiety or acutely disturbed in some other way. A fair analogy would be ripping away the foundation stone from underneath the house that rests upon it. If the house in reality rests upon it, then it is dangerous to rip it away, even though it may be crumbly or rotten or not so good as some other stone.[6]

If, on the other hand, the symptom is not truly functional, if it does not play some vital role, ripping it away will do no harm, but will only benefit the patient. One of the usual strictures against symptom therapy is based on just this point, i.e., assuming that the symptom that seems to the onlooker to be wholly useless actually plays some important role in the psychic economy of the patient, it therefore ought not to be tampered with until the therapist knows exactly what this role may be.

What is implied here is that while symptom therapy is admittedly dangerous for truly neurotic symptoms, it is not at all dangerous for symptoms that are merely expressive. These latter may be ripped away with no consequence but benefit for the patient. This implies a more important role for symptom therapy than psychoanalysis would now allow (463, 487). Some hypnotherapists and behavior therapists feel very strongly that the dangers of symptom therapy have been much exaggerated.

It also helps to teach us that the neurosis has ordinarily been conceived too simply. In any neurotic person one may find both expressive symptoms and coping symptoms. It is as important to differentiate between them as it is to differentiate between prior and subsequent. Thus a

---

[6] Mekeel has given us a good example of a woman who was hysterically paralyzed and who was told that she was. A few days later she went into complete collapse, but the paralysis disappeared. At the hospital she stayed in collapse. The paralysis never recurred but later she became hysterically blind (private communication). The "behavior therapists" have recently been surprisingly successful at getting rid of symptoms with no further consequences. Perhaps symptom substitution does not occur as often as the psychoanalysts expected.

feeling of helplessness found in a neurotic person ordinarily gives rise to reactions of various sorts by which the person tries to overcome the feeling of helplessness, or at least to live with it. These reactions are truly functional. But the feeling of helplessness itself is primarily expressive; it does the person no good; he never wished it to be that way. It is for him a primal or given fact to which he can do nothing but react.

CATASTROPHIC BREAKDOWN; HOPELESSNESS

Occasionally it happens that all the defensive efforts of the organism fail. This may be either because the dangers that press from the outside are too overwhelming or because the defensive resources of the organism are too weak.

Goldstein's profound analyses of brain-injured patients (160) demonstrated for the first time a differentiation between coping reactions, however feeble, and the catastrophic breakdown that results when coping is made impossible or useless.

The kind of behavior that ensues can be seen in the phobic who is caught in the situation he is afraid of (260), in reactions to overwhelmingly traumatic experiences (222), etc. Perhaps it is even better seen in the frantic disorganized behavior of the so-called neurotic rats (285). These animals are of course not at all neurotic in any rigorous sense of the term. A neurosis is an organized reaction. Their behavior is quite disorganized.

In addition, another characteristic of catastrophic breakdown is that it is functionless, or purposeless; in other words it is expressive rather than coping. It therefore should not be called neurotic behavior but had best be characterized by some special name such as catastrophic breakdown, disorganized behavior, induced behavior disturbance, etc. However, see Klee (233) for another interpretation.

Another example of this kind of expression that should be differentiated from neurotic coping is the deep hopelessness and discouragement sometimes found in people or in monkeys (304) who have been subjected to a long line of disappointments, deprivations, and traumata. Such people may come to the point where they simply give up trying, mostly because they seem to see no use in it. If one hopes for nothing, one fights for nothing. There is, for instance, a possibility that the apathy of the simple schizophrenic may be interpreted as an expression of hopelessness, or discouragement, that is to say, as the giving up of coping rather than as any particular form of it. Apathy can certainly be differentiated as a symptom from the violent behavior of the catatonic or the delusions of the paranoid schizophrenic. These would seem to be true coping reactions and would therefore seem to indicate that the paranoid and catatonic schizophrenic are still fighting, and still hoping. In theory as well as in fact we should then expect better prognosis for them.

A similar differentiation with similar consequences may be observed in suicidal people, on the deathbed, and in patients' reactions to their lesser illnesses. Here, too, the giving up of coping efforts influences prognosis markedly.

PSYCHOSOMATIC SYMPTOMS

Our distinction should be especially useful in the field of psychosomatic medicine. It is in this field that Freud's too-naïve determinism has done the most damage. Freud made the mistake of identifying "determined" with "unconsciously motivated" as if there were no other determinants of behavior, e.g., considering all forgetting, all slips of the tongue, all slips of the pen to be determined by unconscious motivations alone. He stigmatized as nondeterministic anyone who pointed to other possible determinants of forgetting, etc. To this day many psychoanalysts can conceive of no explanation other than unconscious motivation. Such a stand need not be crippling in the field of neurosis because in fact practically all neurotic symptoms do have unconscious motivation (along with other determinants, of course).

In the psychosomatic field this point of view has created a great deal of confusion, for a good many relatively somatic reactions have no goals or functions and are not motivated either consciously or unconsciously. Such reactions as high blood pressure, constipation, gastric ulcers, etc., are more apt to be by-products or epiphenomena of complex chains of psychic and somatic processes. No one has ever, in the beginning at any rate, wished for ulcers, hypertension, or coronary attacks (leaving aside for the moment the question of secondary gain). What a person may wish for— hiding passive tendencies from the world, repressing aggressive tendencies, or living up to a certain ego ideal—may be obtainable only at a somatic price, but this price is always, of course, unanticipated and certainly not wished for. In other words, such symptoms ordinarily do not have any primary gain as the general neurotic symptom does.

An excellent example is seen in the broken bones of Dunbar's accident-prone cases (114). Their carelessness, haste, slipshodness, and hobolike character certainly make broken bones more likely, but these fractures are their fate, not their goal, Such fractures serve no function and do no good.

It is granted that it is possible—even though not probable—that such somatic symptoms as we have mentioned may be produced as a neurotic primary gain. In such a case they had better be labeled for what they are —conversion symptoms, or more broadly, neurotic symptoms. Where somatic symptoms are the unforeseen somatic price or epiphenomena of neurotic processes, they had better be labeled with some other title, e.g., physioneuroses, or as we have suggested, expressive somatic symptoms. The by-products of a neurotic process should not be confused with that process itself.

The most obviously expressive type of symptom may be mentioned before leaving the subject. These are the symptoms that are expressed or are actually part of a very general organismic state of affairs, i.e., depression, good health, activity, apathy, etc. If a person is depressed, he is depressed all over. Constipation in such a person is clearly not coping, but expression (although it is quite clear that it may be a coping symptom in another patient, i.e., the child who withholds his feces as an act of unconscious hostility to an annoying mother). So also for loss of appetite or speech in apathy, for good muscular tone in good health, or for jumpiness in the emotionally insecure person.

A paper by Sontag (433) will serve to demonstrate the various possible alternative interpretations of a psychosomatic disorder. This is a case report of a woman with severe and disfiguring acne of the face. The original appearance of the condition and its recurrence in three separate episodes coincide with severe emotional stress and conflict over sexual problems. The skin disease came in each of the three episodes at just such a time as to prevent the woman from having sexual contact. It might be that the acne was unconsciously elaborated out of a wish to avoid the sexual problem, and perhaps, as Sontag suggests, as a self-imposed punishment for her wrongdoing. In other words, it may have been a purposeful process. It is impossible to be sure of this from the internal evidence; Sontag himself admits the whole thing may have been a series of coincidences.

But it may also have been one expression of a generalized organismic disturbance involving conflict, stress, anxiety, i.e., it may have been an expressive symptom. This paper by Sontag is unusual in one respect. The author recognizes clearly the basic dilemma in this sort of case, namely, that there are alternative possibilities of explaining the acne as an expressive symptom or as a coping symptom. Most writers with no more data than Sontag have permitted themselves to come to a positive conclusion in one direction or another, i.e., being certain in some cases that it was a neurotic symptom, in other cases, just as certain that it was not.

I can think of no better way to drive home the necessity for caution in attributing purposiveness to what may be coincidence than the following case whose source I have unfortunately not been able to trace. The subject was a psychoanalytic patient, a married man undergoing severe guilt reaction because of his clandestine sexual relations with a mistress. He also reported a severe skin rash that developed after each visit to his mistress and at no other time. As affairs stand today in psychosomatic medical circles, many practitioners would assume this to be a neurotic reaction, coping because self-punishing. Examination, however, brought to light a much less esoteric explanation. It turned out that the bed of the patient's mistress was infested with bedbugs!

FREE ASSOCIATION AS EXPRESSION

This same differentiation may be used for the further clarification of the process of free association. If we realize clearly that free association is an expressive phenomenon rather than a purposive, coping one, we can understand far better why free association can do what it does.

If we consider that the huge structure of psychoanalytic theory and all the theories and practices that derive from psychoanalysis rest almost entirely on the one operation of free association, then it seems fantastic that this operation has received so little scrutiny. There is practically no research literature on the subject and there are very few speculations about it. If free association fosters or leads to catharsis and insight, we are forced to say that at this time we do not really know why.

Let us turn to an examination of projective tests like the Rorschach, for here we can examine easily an already well-known example of expression. The perceptions that the patient reports are primarily expressions of his way of looking at the world rather than purposive, functional attempts to solve a problem. Because the situation is primarily an unstructured one, these expressions permit us to make many deductions about the underlying (or emitting) character structure. That is to say, the perceptions reported by the patient are determined almost wholly by the character structure and almost not at all by the demand of the external reality for particular solutions. They exemplify expressing rather than coping.

It is my contention that free association is meaningful and useful for exactly the same reasons that the Rorschach test is meaningful and useful.

Furthermore, free association works best in the unstructured situation just as does the Rorschach test. If we understand free association to be primarily a turning away from the purposeful demands of the outside reality, a reality that demands that the organism subordinate itself to the needs of the situation, and live by physical rather than psychic laws, then we can see why adaptation problems demand a task orientation. That which is good for the solution of the task comes to the fore. The demands of the task serve as the organizing principle under which the various capacities of the organism range themselves in the order that is most efficient for the solution of the externally set problem.

This is what we mean by a structured situation, namely, a situation in which responses are called for and clearly pointed to by the logic of the situation itself. The unstructured situation is very different. The outside world is deliberately made unimportant in the sense that it does not point to certain answers rather than others with a clear demand. Thus we can say that the Rorschach plates are unstructured in the sense that one answer is almost as easy as another. In this sense, of course, they are quite the opposite of the geometry problem in which the situation is so structured that only one answer is possible no matter what the person thinks or feels or hopes.

In this same way and even more intensely than in the Rorschach, for here there are no plates at all, there is no task set in free association except the turning away from task orientation and coping. If the patient finally learns to free associate well, and if he can follow the instruction to report without censorship or realistic logic what passes through his consciousness, these free associations should finally express the character structure of the patient and this should be more and more so as reality becomes less and less determinative and as its demands for adaptation become easier to neglect. The person's responses then become a radium-like emission from within and cease to be responses to external stimuli.

The needs, the frustrations, the attitudes that make up the character structure will then almost wholly determine what is said by the patient in his free associations. This holds true for the dream as well, which we must also consider expressive of the character structure, for in the dream, reality and structure are even less important as determiners than they are in the Rorschach test. Tics, nervous habits, Freudian slips, and forgetting are more functional but not entirely so; they too express.

The next effect of these expressions is to allow us to see the character structure more and more nakedly. Task orientation, problem solving, coping, purposive seeking all belong to the adapting surface of the personality. The character structure is more removed from reality, more determined by its own laws than by the laws of physics and logic. It is surface personality, Freud's ego, that deals more directly with reality and that must then, in order to be successful, be determined by *its* (reality's) laws.

In principle the way to get at the character structure is to remove as much as possible the determining force of reality and logic. This is exactly what we do with the quiet room, the psychoanalytic couch, the permissive atmosphere, and the abdication of the psychoanalyst as well as the patient from all their responsibilities as representatives of the culture. When the patient has learned to express rather than to cope with his words, all the desirable consequences of free association may ensue.

Of course, a special theoretical problem confronts us with the recognition that deliberate and voluntary expressive acts may have a kind of feedback on the character structure itself. For instance, I have often enough found, with suitably selected persons, that having them *act as if* they were bold, or affectionate, or angry could finally make it easier for them to *be* truly bold, affectionate, or angry. One selects for such therapeutic experiments people in whom one feels that the boldness, etc., is there but suppressed. Then willed expressing can change the person.

Perhaps one last word should be said about the superiority of art as an expression of the unique personality. Any scientific fact or theory could have been presented by someone else, as could any invention or any machine. But only Cézanne could have painted Cézannes. *Only* the artist is not replaceable. In this sense, any scientific experiment is more determined by the world than is an original work of art.

11

SELF-ACTUALIZING PEOPLE: A STUDY OF PSYCHOLOGICAL HEALTH

PERSONAL FOREWORD

The study to be reported in this chapter is unusual in various ways. It was not planned as an ordinary research; it was not a social venture but a private one, motivated by my own curiosity and pointed toward the solution of various personal moral, ethical, and scientific problems. I sought only to convince and to teach myself rather than to prove or to demonstrate to others.

Quite unexpectedly, however, these studies have proved to be so enlightening to me, and so laden with exciting implications, that it seems fair that some sort of report should be made to others in spite of its methodological shortcomings.

In addition, I consider the problem of psychological health to be so pressing, that *any* suggestions, *any* bits of data, however moot, are endowed with great heuristic value. This kind of research is in principle so difficult—involving as it does a kind of lifting oneself by one's own norms —that if we were to wait for conventionally reliable data, we should have to wait forever. It seems that the only manly thing to do is not to fear mistakes, to plunge in, to do the best that one can, hoping to learn enough from blunders to correct them eventually. At present the only alternative is simply to refuse to work with the problem. Accordingly, for whatever use can be made of it, the following report is presented with due apologies to those who insist on conventional reliability, validity, sampling, etc.

149

SUBJECTS AND METHODS

The subjects were selected from among personal acquaintances and friends, and from among public and historical figures. In addition, in a first research with young people, three thousand college students were screened, but yielded only one immediately usable subject and a dozen or two possible future subjects ("growing well").

I had to conclude that self-actualization of the sort I had found in my older subjects perhaps was not possible in our society for young, developing people.

Accordingly, in collaboration with E. Raskin and D. Freedman, a search was begun for a panel of *relatively* healthy college students. We arbitrarily decided to choose the healthiest 1 percent of the college population. This research, pursued over a two-year period as time permitted, had to be interrupted before completion, but it was, even so, very instructive at the clinical level.

It was also hoped that figures created by novelists or dramatists could be used for demonstration purposes, but none were found that were usable in our culture and our time (in itself a thought-provoking finding).

The first clinical definition, on the basis of which subjects were finally chosen or rejected, had a positive as well as a merely negative side. The negative criterion was an absence of neurosis, psychopathic personality, psychosis, or strong tendencies in these directions. Possibly psychosomatic illness called forth closer scrutiny and screening. Wherever possible, Rorschach tests were given, but turned out to be far more useful in revealing concealed psychopathology than in selecting healthy people. The positive criterion for selection was positive evidence of self-actualization (SA), as yet a difficult syndrome to describe accurately. For the purposes of this discussion, it may be loosely described as the full use and exploitation of talents, capacities, potentialities, etc. Such people seem to be fulfilling themselves and to be doing the best that they are capable of doing, reminding us of Nietzsche's exhortation, "Become what thou art!" They are people who have developed or are developing to the full stature of which they are capable (148, 160, 347, 398). These potentialities may be either idiosyncratic or species-wide.

This criterion implies also gratification, past or present, of the basic needs for safety, belongingness, love, respect, and self-respect, and of the cognitive needs for knowledge and for understanding, or in a few cases, conquest of these needs. This is to say that all subjects felt safe and unanxious, accepted, loved and loving, respect-worthy and respected, and that they had worked out their philosophical, religious, or axiological bearings. It is still an open question as to whether this basic gratification is a sufficient or only a prerequisite condition of self-actualization.

In general, the technique of selection used was that of *iteration,* previously used in studies of the personality syndromes of self-esteem and of security and described in Appendix B. This consists briefly in starting with the personal or cultural nontechnical state of belief, collating the various extant usages and definitions of the syndrome, and then defining it more carefully, still in terms of actual usage (what might be called the lexicographical stage), with, however, the elimination of the logical and factual inconsistencies customarily found in folk definitions.

On the basis of the corrected folk definition, the first groups of subjects are selected, a group who are high in the quality and a group who are low in it. These people are studied as carefully as possible in the clinical style, and on the basis of this empirical study the original corrected folk definition is further changed and corrected as required by the data now in hand. This gives the first clinical definition. On the basis of this new definition, the original group of subjects is reselected, some being retained, some being dropped, and some new ones being added. This second level group of subjects is then in its turn clinically, and if possible, experimentally and statistically studied, which in turn causes modification, correction, and enrichment of the first clinical definition, with which in turn a new group of subjects is selected and so on. In this way an originally vague and unscientific folk concept can become more and more exact, more and more operational in character, and therefore more scientific.

Of course, external, theoretical, and practical considerations may intrude into this spiral-like process of self-correction. For instance, early in this study, it was found that folk usage was so unrealistically demanding that no living human being could possibly fit the definition. We had to stop excluding a possible subject on the basis of single foibles, mistakes, or foolishness; or to put it in another way, we could not use perfection as a basis for selection, since no subject was perfect.

Another such problem was presented by the fact that in all cases it was impossible to get full and satisfactory information of the kind usually demanded in clinical work. Possible subjects, when informed of the purpose of the research, became self-conscious, froze up, laughed off the whole effort, or broke off the relationship. As a result, since this early experience, all older subjects have been studied indirectly, indeed almost surreptitiously. Only younger people can be studied directly.

Since living people were studied whose names could not be divulged, two desiderata or even requirements of ordinary scientific work became impossible to achieve: namely, repeatability of the investigation and public availability of the data upon which conclusions were made. These difficulties are partly overcome by the inclusion of public and historical figures, and by the supplementary study of young people and children who could conceivably be used publicly.

The subjects have been divided into the following categories:

Cases:	7 fairly sure and 2 highly probable contemporaries (interviewed) 2 fairly sure historical figures (Lincoln in his last years and Thomas Jefferson) 7 highly probable public and historical figures (Einstein, Eleanor Roosevelt, Jane Addams, William James, Schweitzer, Aldous Huxley and Spinoza)
Partial Cases:	5 contemporaries who fairly certainly fall short somewhat but who can yet be used for study
Potential or Possible Cases: Cases suggested or studied by others:	G. W. Carver, Eugene V. Debs, Thomas Eakins, Fritz Kreisler, Goethe, Pablo Casals, Martin Buber, Danilo Dolci, Arthur E. Morgan, John Keats, David Hilbert, Arthur Waley, D. T. Suzuki, Adlai Stevenson, Sholom Aleichem, Robert Browning, Ralph Waldo Emerson, Frederick Douglass, Joseph Schumpeter, Bob Benchley, Ida Tarbell, Harriet Tubman, George Washington, Karl Muenzinger, Joseph Haydn, Camille Pissarro, Edward Bibring, George William Russell (A. E.), Pierre Renoir, Henry Wadsworth Longfellow, Peter Kropotkin, John Altgeld, Thomas More, Edward Bellamy, Benjamin Franklin, John Muir, Walt Whitman[1]

GATHERING AND PRESENTATION OF THE DATA

Data here consist not so much in the usual gathering of specific and discrete facts as in the slow development of a global or holistic impression of the sort that we form of our friends and acquaintances. It was rarely possible to set up a situation, to ask pointed questions, or to do any testing with my older subjects (although this *was* possible and was done with younger subjects). Contacts were fortuitous and of the ordinary social sort. Friends and relatives were questioned where this was possible.

[1] See also (58, p. 97), (68, pp. 264–276) and the Manual and Bibliography for Shostrom's POI Test of Self-Actualization (425, 426).

Because of this and also because of the small number of subjects as well as the incompleteness of the data for many subjects, any quantitative presentation is impossible: only composite impressions can be offered for whatever they may be worth.

The holistic analysis of these total impressions yields, as the most important and useful whole characteristics of self-actualizing people for further clinical and experimental study, the following:

MORE EFFICIENT PERCEPTION OF REALITY AND MORE COMFORTABLE RELATIONS WITH IT

The first form in which this capacity was noticed was as an unusual ability to detect the spurious, the fake, and the dishonest in personality, and in general to judge people correctly and efficiently. In an informal experiment with a group of college students, a clear tendency was discerned for the more secure (the more healthy) to judge their professors more accurately than did the less secure students, i.e., high scorers in the S-I test (294).

As the study progressed, it slowly became apparent that this efficiency extended to many other areas of life—indeed *all* areas that were observed. In art and music, in things of the intellect, in scientific matters, in politics and public affairs, they seemed as a group to be able to see concealed or confused realities more swiftly and more correctly than others. Thus an informal survey indicated that their predictions of the future from whatever facts were in hand at the time seemed to be more often correct, because less based upon wish, desire, anxiety, fear, or upon generalized, character-determined optimism or pessimism.

At first this was phrased as good taste or good judgment, the implication being relative and not absolute. But for many reasons (some to be detailed below), it has become progressively more clear that this had better be called perception (not taste) of something that was absolutely there (reality, not a set of opinions). It is hoped that this conclusion—or hypothesis—can one day be put to the experimental test.

If this is so, it would be impossible to overstress its importance. Money-Kyrle (338), an English psychoanalyst, has indicated that he believes it possible to calle a neurotic person not only *relatively* but *absolutely* inefficient, simply because he does not perceive the real world so accurately or so efficiently as does the healthy person. The neurotic is not emotionally sick—he is cognitively *wrong!* If health and neurosis are, respectively, correct and incorrect perceptions of reality, propositions of fact and propositions of value merge in this area, and in principle, value propositions should then be empirically demonstrable rather than merely matters of taste or exhortation. For those who have wrestled with this problem it will be clear that we may have here a partial basis for a true science of values, and consequently of ethics, social relations, politics, religion, etc.

It is definitely possible that maladjustment or even extreme neurosis would disturb perception enough to affect acuity of perception of light or touch or odor. But it is *probable* that this effect can be demonstrated in spheres of perception removed from the merely physiological, e.g., *Einstellung* experiment (279), etc. It should also follow that the effects of wish, desire, prejudice, upon perception as in many recent experiments should be very much less in healthy people than in sick. A priori considerations encourage the hypothesis that this superiority in the perception of reality eventuates in a superior ability to reason, to perceive the truth, to come to conclusions, to be logical and to be cognitively efficient, in general.

One particularly impressive and instructive aspect of this superior relationship with reality will be discussed as length in Chapter 13. It was found that self-actualizing people distinguished far more easily than most the fresh, concrete, and idiographic from the generic, abstract, and rubricized. The consequence is that they live more in the real world of nature than in the man-made mass of concepts, abstractions, expectations, beliefs, and stereotypes that most people confuse with the world, They are therefore far more apt to perceive what is there rather than their own wishes, hopes, fears, anxieties, their own theories and beliefs, or those of their cultural group. "The innocent eye," Herbert Read has very effectively called it.

The relationship with the unknown seems to be of exceptional promise as another bridge between academic and clinical psychology. Our healthy subjects are generally unthreatened and unfrightened by the unknown, being therein quite different from average men. They accept it, are comfortable with it, and, often are even *more* attracted by it than by the known. They not only tolerate the ambiguous and unstructured (135); they like it. Quite characteristic is Einstein's statement, "The most beautiful thing we can experience is the mysterious. It is the source of all art and science."

These people, it is true, are the intellectuals, the researchers, and the scientists, so that perhaps the major determinant here is intellectual power. And yet we all know how many scientists with high IQ, through timidity, conventionality, anxiety, or other character defects, occupy themselves exclusively with what is known, with polishing it, arranging and rearranging it, classifying it, and otherwise puttering with it instead of discovering, as they are supposed to do.

Since for healthy people, the unknown is not frightening, they do not have to spend any time laying the ghost, whistling past the cemetery, or otherwise protecting themselves against imagined dangers. They do not neglect the unknown, or deny it, or run away from it, or try to make believe it is really known, nor do they organize, dichotomize, or rubricize it prematurely. They do not cling to the familiar, nor is their quest for the truth a catastrophic need for certainty, safety, definiteness, and order, such as we see in an exaggerated form in Goldstein's brain-injured or in the compulsive-obsessive neurotic. They can be, when the total objective situation calls for it, comfortably disorderly, sloppy, anarchic, chaotic, vague, doubtful, uncertain, indefinite, approximate, inexact, or inaccurate (all, at certain moments in science, art, or life in general, quite desirable).

Thus it comes about that doubt, tentativeness, uncertainty, with the consequent necessity for abeyance of decision, which is for most a torture, can be for some a pleasantly stimulating challenge, a high spot in life rather than a low.

ACCEPTANCE (SELF, OTHERS, NATURE)

A good many personal qualities that can be perceived on the surface and that seem at first to be various and unconnected may be understood as manifestations or derivatives of a more fundamental single attitude, namely, of a relative lack of overriding guilt, of crippling shame, and of extreme or severe anxiety. This is in direct contrast with the neurotic person who in every instance may be described as crippled by guilt and/or shame and/or anxiety. Even the normal member of our culture feels unnecessarily guilty or ashamed about too many things and has anxiety in too many unnecessary situations. Our healthy individuals find it possible to accept themselves and their own nature without chagrin or complaint or, for that matter, even without thinking about the matter very much.

They can accept their own human nature in the stoic style, with all its shortcomings, with all its discrepancies from the ideal image without feeling real concern. It would convey the wrong impression to say that they are self-satisfied. What we must say rather is that they can take the frailties and sins, weaknesses, and evils of human nature in the same unquestioning spirit with which one accepts the characteristics of nature.

One does not complain about water because it is wet, or about rocks because they are hard, or about trees because they are green. As the child looks out upon the world with wide, uncritical, undemanding, innocent eyes, simply noting and observing what is the case, without either arguing the matter or demanding that it be otherwise, so does the self-actualizing person tend to look upon human nature in himself and in others. This is of course not the same as resignation in the eastern sense, but resignation too can be observed in our subjects, especially in the face of illness and death.

Be it observed that this amounts to saying in another form what we have already described; namely, that the self-actualized person sees reality more clearly: our subjects see human nature as it *is* and not as they would prefer it to be. Their eyes see what is before them without being strained through spectacles of various sorts to distort or shape or color the reality (46).

The first and most obvious level of acceptance is at the socalled animal level. Those self-actualizing people tend to be good animals, hearty in their appetites and enjoying themselves without regret or shame or apology. They seem to have a uniformly good appetite for food; they seem to sleep well; they seem to enjoy their sexual lives without unnecessary inhibition and so on for all the relatively physiological impulses. They are able to accept themselves not only on these low levels, but at all levels as well; e.g., love, safety, belongingness, honor, self-respect. All of these are accepted without question as worth while, simply because these people are inclined to accept the work of nature rather than to argue with her for not having constructed things to a different pattern. This shows itself in a relative lack of the disgusts and aversions seen in average people and especially in neurotics, e.g., food annoyances, disgust with body products, body odors, and body functions.

Closely related to self-acceptance and to acceptance of others is (1) their lack of defensiveness, protective coloration, or pose, and (2) their distaste for such artificialities in others. Cant, guile, hypocrisy, front, face, playing a game, trying to impress in conventional ways: these are all absent in themselves to an unusual degree. Since they can live comfortably even with their own shortcomings, these finally come to be perceived, especially in later life, as not shortcomings at all, but simply as neutral personal characteristics.

This is not an absolute lack of guilt, shame, sadness, anxiety, defensiveness; it is a lack of unnecessary or neurotic (because unrealistic) guilt, etc. The animal processes, e.g., sex, urination, pregnancy, menstruation, growing old, etc., are part of reality and so must be accepted. Thus no healthy woman need feel guilty or defensive about being female or about any of the female processes.

What healthy people *do* feel guilty about (or ashamed, anxious, sad, or regretful) are (1) improvable shortcomings, e.g., laziness, thoughtlessness, loss of temper, hurting others; (2) stubborn remnants of psychological ill health, e.g., prejudice, jealousy, envy; (3) habits, which, though relatively independent of character structure, may yet be very strong, or (4) shortcomings of the species or of the culture or of the group with which they have identified. The general formula seems to be that healthy people will feel bad about discrepancies between what is and what might very well be or ought to be (2, 148, 199).

SPONTANEITY; SIMPLICITY; NATURALNESS

Self-actualizing people can all be described as relatively spontaneous in behavior and far more spontaneous than that in their inner life, thoughts, impulses, etc. Their behavior is marked by simplicity and naturalness, and by lack of artificiality or straining for effect. This does not necessarily mean consistently unconventional behavior. If we were to take an actual count of the number of times that the self-actualizing person behaved in an unconventional manner the tally would not be high. His unconventionality is not superficial but essential or internal. It is his impulses, thought, consciousness that are so unusually unconventional, spontaneous, and natural. Apparently recognizing that the world of people in which he lives could not understand or accept this, and since he has no wish to hurt them or to fight with them over every triviality, he will go through the ceremonies and rituals of convention with a good-humored shrug and with the best possible grace. Thus I have seen a man accept an honor he laughed at and even despised in private, rather than make an issue of it and hurt the people who thought they were pleasing him.

That this conventionality is a cloak that rests very lightly upon his shoulders and is easily cast aside can be seen from the fact that the self-actualizing person infrequently allows convention to hamper him or inhibit him from doing anything that he considers very important or basic. It is at such moments that his essential lack of conventionality appears, and not as with the average Bohemian or authority-rebel, who makes great issues of trivial things and who will fight against some unimportant regulation as if it were a world issue.

This same inner attitude can also be seen in those moments when the person becomes keenly absorbed in something that is close to one of his main interests. He can then be seen quite casually to drop off all sorts of rules of behavior to which at other times he conforms; it is as if he has to make a conscious effort to be conventional; as if he were conventional voluntarily and by design.

Finally, this external habit of behavior can be voluntarily dropped when in the company of people who do not demand or expect routine behavior. That this relative control of behavior is felt as something of a burden is seen by our subjects' preference for such company as allows them to be more free, natural, and spontaneous, and that relieves them of what they find sometimes to be effortful conduct.

One consequence or correlate of this characteristic is that these people have codes of ethics that are relatively autonomous and individual rather than conventional. The unthinking observer might sometimes believe them to be unethical, since they can break down not only conventions but laws when the situation seems to demand it. But the very opposite is the case. They are the most ethical of people even though their ethics are not necessarily the same as those of the people around them. It is this kind of observation that leads us to understand very assuredly that the ordinary ethical behavior of the average person is largely conventional behavior rather than truly ethical behavior, e.g., behavior based on fundamentally accepted principles (which are perceived to be true).

Because of this alienation from ordinary conventions and. from the ordinarily accepted hypocrisies, lies, and inconsistencies of social life, they sometimes feel like spies or aliens in a foreign land and sometimes behave so.

I should not give the impression that they try to hide what they are like. Sometimes they let themselves go deliberately, out of momentary irritation with customary rigidity or with conventional blindness. They may, for instance, be trying to teach someone or they may be trying to protect someone from hurt or injustice or they may sometimes find emotions bubbling up from within them that are so pleasant or even ecstatic that it seems almost sacrilegious to suppress them. In such instances I have observed that they are not anxious or guilty or ashamed of the impression that they make on the onlooker. It is their claim that they usually behave in a conventional fashion simply because no great issues are involved or because they know people will be hurt or embarrassed by any other kind of behavior.

Their ease of penetration to reality, their closer approach to an animal-like or childlike acceptance and spontaneity imply a superior awareness of their own impulses, desires, opinions, and subjective reactions in general (148, 388, 392). Clinical study of this capacity confirms beyond a doubt the opinion, e.g., of Fromm (145) that the average normal, well-adjusted person often has not the slightest idea of what he is, of what he wants, of what his own opinions are.

It was such findings as these that led ultimately to the discovery of a most profound difference between self-actualizing people and others; namely, that the motivational life of self-actualizing people is not only quantitatively different but also qualitatively different from that of ordinary people. It seems probable that we must construct a profoundly different psychology of motivation for self-actualizing people, e.g., meta-motivation or growth motivation, rather than deficiency motivation. Perhaps it will be useful to make a distinction between living and *preparing* to live. Perhaps the ordinary concept of motivation should apply *only* to nonself-actualizers. Our subjects no longer strive in the ordinary sense, but rather develop. They attempt to grow to perfection and to develop more and more fully in their own style. The motivation of ordinary men is a striving for the basic need gratifications that they lack. But self-actualizing people in fact lack none of these gratifications; and yet they have impulses. They work, they try, and they are ambitious, even though in an unusual sense. For them motivation is just character growth, character expression, maturation, and development; in a word self-actualization. Could these self-actualizing people be more human, more revealing of the original nature of the species, closer to the species type in the taxonomical sense? Ought a biological species to be judged by its crippled, warped, only partially developed specimens, or by examples that have been overdomesticated, caged, and trained?

PROBLEM CENTERING

Our subjects are in general strongly focused on problems outside themselves. In current terminology they are problem centered rather than ego centered. They generally are not problems for themselves and are not generally much concerned about themselves; e.g., as contrasted with the ordinary introspectiveness that one finds in insecure people. These individuals customarily have some mission in life, some task to fulfill, some problem outside themselves which enlists much of their energies (72, 134).

This is not necessarily a task that they would prefer or choose for themselves; it may be a task that they feel is their responsibility, duty, or obligation. This is why we use the phrase "a task that they must do" rather than the phrase "a task that they want to do." In general these tasks are nonpersonal or unselfish, concerned rather with the good of mankind in general, or of a nation in general, or of a few individuals in the subject's family.

With a few exceptions we can say that our objects are ordinarily concerned with basic issues and eternal questions of the type that we have learned to call philosophical or ethical. Such people live customarily in the widest possible frame of reference. They seem never to get so close to the trees that they fail to see the forest. They work within a framework of values that are broad and not petty, universal and not local, and in terms of a century rather than the moment. In a word, these people are all in one sense or another philosophers, however homely.

Of course, such an attitude carries with it dozens of implications for every area of daily living. For instance, one of the main presenting symptoms originally worked with (bigness, lack of smallness, triviality, or pettiness) can be subsumed under this more general heading. This impression of being above small things, of having a larger horizon, a wider breadth of vision, of living in the widest frame of reference, *sub specie aeternitatis,* is of the utmost social and interpersonal importance; it seems to impart a certain serenity and lack of worry over immediate concerns that make life easier not only for themselves but for all who are associated with them.

THE QUALITY OF DETACHMENT; THE NEED FOR PRIVACY

For all my subjects it is true that they can be solitary without harm to themselves and without discomfort. Furthermore, it is true for almost all that they positively *like* solitude and privacy to a definitely greater degree than the average person.

It is often possible for them to remain above the battle, to remain unruffled, undisturbed by that which produces turmoil in others. They find it easy to be aloof, reserved, and also calm and serene; thus it becomes possible for them to take personal misfortunes without reacting violently as the ordinary person does. They seem to be able to retain their dignity even in undignified surroundings and situations. Perhaps this comes in part from their tendency to stick by their own interpretation of a situation rather than to rely upon what other people feel or think about the matter. This reserve may shade over into austerity and remoteness.

This quality of detachment may have some connection with certain other qualities as well. For one thing it is possible to call my subjects more objective (in *all* senses of that word) than average people. We have seen that they are more problem centered than ego centered. This is true even when the problem concerns themselves, their own wishes, motives, hopes, or aspirations. Consequently, they have the ability to concentrate to a degree not usual for ordinary men. Intense concentration produces as a by-product such phenomena as absent-mindedness, the ability to forget and to be oblivious of outer surroundings. Examples are the ability to sleep soundly, to have undisturbed appetite, to be able to smile and laugh through a period of problems, worry, and responsibility.

In social relations with most people, detachment creates certain troubles and problems. It is easily interpreted by "normal" people as coldness, snobbishness, lack of affection, unfriendliness, or even hostility. By contrast, the ordinary friendship relationship is more clinging, more demanding, more desirous of reassurance, compliment, support, warmth, and exclusiveness. It is true that self-actualizing people do not need others in the ordinary sense. But since this being needed or being missed is the usual earnest of friendship, it is evident that detachment will not easily be accepted by average people.

Another meaning of autonomy is self-decision, self-government, being an active, responsible, self-disciplined, deciding agent rather than a pawn, or helplessly "determined" by others, being strong rather than weak. My subjects make up their own minds, come to their own decisions, are self-starters, are responsible for themselves and their own destinies. It is a subtle quality, difficult to describe in words, and yet profoundly important. They taught me to see as profoundly sick, abnormal, or weak what I had always taken for granted as humanly normal; namely that too many people do not make up their own minds, but have their minds made up for them by salesmen, advertisers, parents, propagandists, TV, newspapers and so on. They are pawns to be moved by others rather than self-moving, self-determining individuals. Therefore they are apt to feel helpless, weak, and totally determined; they are prey for predators, flabby whiners rather than self-determining, responsible persons. What this nonresponsibility means for self-choice politics and economics is of course obvious; it is catastrophic. Democratic self-choice society must have self-movers, self-deciders, self-choosers who make up their own minds, free agents, free-willers.

The extensive experiments by Asch (20) and by McClelland (326–328) permit us to guess that self-determiners come to perhaps 5 percent to 30 percent of our population depending on the particular circumstances. Of my self-actualizing subjects, 100 percent are self-movers.

Finally I must make a statement even though it will certainly be disturbing to many theologians, philosophers, and scientists: self-actualizing individuals have more "free will" and are less "determined" than average people are. However the words "free will" and "determinism" may come to be operationally defined, in this investigation they are empirical realities. Furthermore, they are degree concepts, varying in amount; they are not all-or-none packages.

AUTONOMY; INDEPENDENCE OF CULTURE AND ENVIRONMENT; WILL; ACTIVE AGENTS

One of the characteristics of self-actualizing people, which to a certain extent crosscuts much of what we have already described, is their relative independence of the physical and social environment. Since they are propelled by growth motivation rather than by deficiency motivation, self-actualizing people are not dependent for their main satisfactions on the real world, or other people or culture or means to ends or, in general, on extrinsic satisfactions. Rather they are dependent for their own development and continued growth on their own potentialities and latent resources. Just as the tree needs sunshine and water and food, so do most people need love, safety, and the other basic need gratifications that can come only from without. But once these external satisfiers are obtained, once these inner deficiencies are satiated by outside satisfiers, the true problem of individual human development begins, e.g., self-actualization.

This independence of environment means a relative stability in the face of hard knocks, blows, deprivations, frustrations, and the like. These people can maintain a relative serenity in the midst of circumstances that would drive other people to suicide; they have also been described as "self-contained."

Deficiency-motivated people *must* have other people available, since most of their main need gratifications (love, safety, respect, prestige, belongingness) can come only from other human beings. But growth-motivated people may actually be *hampered* by others. The determinants of satisfaction and of the good life are for them now inner-individual and *not* social. They have become strong enough to be independent of the good opinion of other people, or even of their affection. The honors, the status, the rewards, the popularity, the prestige, and the love they can bestow must have become less important than self-development and inner growth (209, 360, 388, 403). We must remember that the best technique we know, even though not the only one, for getting to this point of relative independence from love and respect, is to have been given plenty of this very same love and respect in the past.

CONTINUED FRESHNESS OF APPRECIATION

Self-actualizing people have the wonderful capacity to appreciate again and again, freshly and naïvely, the basic goods of life, with awe, pleasure, wonder, and even ecstasy, however stale these experiences may have become to others—what C. Wilson has called "newness" (483). Thus for such a person, any sunset may be as beautiful as the first one, any flower may be of breath-taking loveliness, even after he has seen a million flowers. The thousandth baby he sees is just as miraculous a product as the first one he saw. He remains as convinced of his luck in marriage thirty years after his marriage and is as surprised by his wife's beauty when she is sixty as he was forty years before. For such people, even the casual workaday, moment-to-moment business of living can be thrilling, exciting, and ecstatic. These intense feelings do not come all the time; they come occasionally rather than usually, but at the most unexpected moments. The person may cross the river on the ferry ten times and at the eleventh crossing have a strong recurrence of the same feelings, reaction of beauty, and excitement as when he rode the ferry for the first time (115).

There are some differences in choice of beautiful objects. Some subjects go primarily to nature. For others it is primarily children, and for a few subjects it has been primarily great music; but it may certainly be said that they derive ecstasy, inspiration, and strength from the basic experiences of life. No one of them, for instance, will get this same sort of reaction from going to a night club or getting a lot of money or having a good time at a party.

Perhaps one special experience may be added. For several of my subjects the sexual pleasures and particularly the orgasm provided, not passing pleasure alone, but some kind of basic strengthening and revivifying that some people derive from music or nature. I shall say more about this in the section on the mystic experience.

It is probable that this acute richness of subjective experience is an aspect of closeness of relationship to the concrete and fresh, *per se* reality discussed above. Perhaps what we call staleness in experience is a consequence of rubricizing or ticketing off a rich perception into one or another category or rubric as it proves to be no longer advantageous, or useful, or threatening or otherwise ego involved (46).

I have also become convinced that getting used to our blessings is one of the most important nonevil generators of human evil, tragedy, and suffering. What we take for granted we undervalue, and we are therefore too apt to sell a valuable birthright for a mess of pottage, leaving behind regret, remorse, and a lowering of self-esteem. Wives, husbands, children, friends are unfortunately more apt to be loved and appreciated after they have died than while they are still available. Something similar is true for physical health, for political freedoms, for economic well-being; we learn their true value after we have lost them.

Herzberg's studies of "hygiene" factors in industry (193), Wilson's observations on the St. Neot's margin (481, 483), my study of "low grumbles, high grumbles and metagrumbles" (291) all show that life could be vastly improved if we could count our blessings as self-actualizing people can and do, and if we could retain their constant sense of good fortune and gratitude for it.

THE MYSTIC EXPERIENCE; THE PEAK EXPERIENCE

Those subjective expressions that have been called the mystic experience and described so well by William James (212) are a fairly common experience for our subjects though not for all. The strong emotions described in the previous section sometimes get strong enough, chaotic, and widespread enough to be called mystic experiences. My interest and attention in this subject was first enlisted by several of my subjects who described their sexual orgasms in vaguely familiar terms which later I remembered had been used by various writers to describe what *they* called the mystic experience. There were the same feelings of limitless horizons opening up to the vision, the feeling of being simultaneously more powerful and also more helpless than one ever was before, the feeling of great ecstasy and wonder and awe, the loss of placing in time and space with, finally, the conviction that something extremely important and valuable had happened, so that the subject is to some extent transformed and strengthened even in his daily life by such experiences.

It is quite important to dissociate this experience from any theological or supernatural reference, even though for thousands of years they have been linked. Because this experience is a natural experience, well within the jurisdiction of science, I call it the peak experience. We may also learn from our subjects that such experiences can occur in a lesser degree of intensity. The theological literature has generally assumed an absolute, qualitative difference between the mystic experience and all others. As soon as it is divorced from supernatural reference and studied as a natural phenomenon, it becomes possible to place the mystic experience on a quantitative continuum from intense to mild. We discover then that the *mild* mystic experience occurs in many, perhaps even most individuals, and that in the favored individual it occurs often, perhaps even daily.

Apparently the acute mystic or peak experience is a tremendous intensification of *any* of the experiences in which there is loss of self or transcendence of it, e.g., problem centering, intense concentration, muga behavior, as described by Benedict (40), intense sensuous experience, self-forgetful and intense enjoyment of music or art. Further studies of peak experiences are set forth in (252, 293, 295, 310, 315).

I have learned through the years since this study was first begun in 1935 (it is still going on) to lay far greater stress than I had at first on the differences between "peakers" and "nonpeakers." Most likely this is a difference of degree or amount, but it is a very important difference. Some of its consequences are set forth in considerable detail in (315). If I had to sum it up very briefly, I would say that the nonpeaking self-actualizers seem so far to tend to be practical, effective people, meso-morphs living in the world and doing very well in it. Peakers seem *also* to live in the realm of Being; of poetry, esthetics; symbols; transcendence; "religion" of the mystical, personal, noninstitutional sort; and of end-experiences. My prediction is that this will turn out to be one of the crucial characterological "class differences," crucial especially for social life because it looks as though the "merely healthy" nonpeaking self-actualizers seem likely to be the social world improvers, the politicians, the workers in society, the reformers, the crusaders, whereas the transcending peakers are more apt to write the poetry, the music, the philosophies, and the religions.

GEMEINSCHAFTSGEFÜHL

This word, invented by Alfred Adler (2), is the only one available that describes well the flavor of the feelings for mankind expressed by self-actualizing subjects. They have for human beings in general a deep feeling of identification, sympathy, and affection in spite of the occasional anger, impatience, or disgust described below. Because of this they have a genuine desire to help the human race. It is as if they were all members of a single family. One's feelings toward his brothers would be on the whole affectionate, even if these brothers were foolish, weak, or even if they were sometimes nasty. They would still be more easily forgiven than strangers.

If one's view is not general enough and if it is not spread over a long period of time, then one may not see this feeling of identification with mankind. The self-actualizing person is after all very different from other people in thought, impulse, behavior, emotion. When it comes down to it, in certain basic ways he is like an alien in a strange land. Very few really understand him, however much they may like him. He is often saddened, exasperated, and even enraged by the shortcomings of the average person, and while they are to him ordinarily no more than a nuisance, they sometimes become bitter tragedy. However far apart he is from them at times, he nevertheless feels a basic underlying kinship with these creatures whom he must regard with, if not condescension, at least the knowledge that he can do many things better than they can, that he can see things that they cannot see, that the truth that is so clear to him is for most people veiled and hidden. This is what Adler called the older-brotherly attitude.

INTERPERSONAL RELATIONS_SA

Self-actualizing people have deeper and more profound interpersonal relations than any other adults (although not necessarily deeper than those of children). They are capable of more fusion, greater love, more perfect identification, more obliteration of the ego boundaries than other people would consider possible. There are, however, certain special characteristics of these relationships. In the first place, it is my observation that the other members of these relationships are likely to be healthier and closer to self-actualization than the average, often *much* closer. There is high selectiveness here, considering the small proportion of such people in the general population.

One consequence of this phenomenon and of certain others as well is that self-actualizing people have these especially deep ties with rather few individuals. Their circle of friends is rather small. The ones that they love profoundly are few in number. Partly this is for the reason that being very close to someone in this self-actualizing style seems to require a good deal of time. Devotion is not a matter of a moment. One subject expressed it like this: "I haven't got time for many friends. Nobody has, that is, if they are to be *real* friends." The only possible exception in my group was one woman who seemed to be especially equipped socially. It was almost as if her appointed task in life was to have close and warm and beautiful relations with all the members of her family and their families as well as all her friends and theirs. Perhaps this was because she was an uneducated woman who had no formal task or career. This exclusiveness of devotion can and does exist side by side with a wide-spreading *Gemeinschaftsgefühl*, benevolence, affection, and friendliness (as qualified above). These people *tend* to be kind or at least patient to almost everyone. They have an especially tender love for children and are easily touched by them. In a very real even though special sense, they love or rather have compassion for all mankind.

This love does not imply lack of discrimination. The fact is that they can and do speak realistically and harshly of those who deserve it, and especially of the hypocritical, the pretentious, the pompous, or the self-inflated. But the face-to-face relationships even with these people do not always show signs of realistically low evaluations. One explanatory statement was about as follows: "Most people, after all, do not amount to much but they *could* have. They make all sorts of foolish mistakes and wind up being miserable and not knowing how they got that way when their intentions were good. Those who are not nice are usually paying for it in deep unhappiness. They should be pitied rather than attacked."

Perhaps the briefest possible description is to say that their hostile reactions to others are (1) deserved, (2) for the good of the person attacked or for someone else's good. This is to say, with Fromm, that their hostility is not character based, but is reactive or situational.

All the subjects for whom I have data show in common another characteristic that is appropriate to mention here, namely, that they attract at least some admirers, friends or even disciples or worshippers. The relation between the individual and his train of admirers is apt to be rather one-sided. The admirers are apt to demand more than our individual is willing to give. And furthermore, these devotions can be rather embarrassing, distressing, and even distasteful to the self-actualizing person, since they often go beyond ordinary bounds. The usual picture is of our subject being kind and pleasant when forced into these relationships, but ordinarily trying to avoid them as gracefully as possible.

THE DEMOCRATIC CHARACTER STRUCTURE

All my subjects without exception may be said to be democratic people in the deepest possible sense. I say this on the basis of a previous analysis of authoritarian (303) and democratic character structures that is too elaborate to present here; it is possible only to describe some aspects of this behavior in short space. These people have all the obvious or superficial democratic characteristics. They can be and are friendly with anyone of suitable character regardless of class, education, political belief, race, or color. As a matter of fact it often seems as if they are not even aware of these differences, which are for the average person so obvious and so important.

They have not only this most obvious quality but their democratic feeling goes deeper as well. For instance they find it possible to learn from anybody who has something to teach them—no matter what other characteristics he may have. In such a learning relationship they do not try to maintain any outward dignity or to maintain status or age prestige or the like. It should even be said that my subjects share a quality that could be called humility of a certain type. They are all quite well aware of how little they know in comparison with what *could* be known and what *is* known by others. Because of this it is possible for them without pose to be honestly respectful and even humble before people who can teach them something that they do not know or who have a skill they do not possess. They give this honest respect to a carpenter who is a good carpenter; or for that matter to anybody who is a master of his own tools or his own craft.

The careful distinction must be made between this democratic feeling and a lack of discrimination in taste, of an undiscriminating equalizing of any one human being with any other. These individuals, themselves elite, select for their friends elite, but this is an elite of character, capacity, and talent, rather than of birth, race, blood, name, family, age, youth, fame, or power.

Most profound, but also most vague is the hard-to-get-at-tendency to give a certain quantum of respect to *any* human being just because he is a human individual; our subjects seem not to wish to go beyond a certain minimum point, even with scoundrels, of demeaning, of derogating, of robbing of dignity. And yet this goes along with their strong sense of right and wrong, of good and evil. They are *more* likely rather than less likely to counterattack against evil men and evil behavior. They are far less ambivalent, confused or weak-willed about their own anger than average men are.

DISCRIMINATION BETWEEN MEANS AND ENDS, BETWEEN GOOD AND EVIL

I have found none of my subjects to be chronically unsure about the difference between right and wrong in his actual living. Whether or not they could verbalize the matter, they rarely showed in their day-to-day living the chaos, the confusion, the inconsistency, or the conflict that are so common in the average person's ethical dealings. This may be phrased also in the following terms: these individuals are strongly ethical, they have definite moral standards, they do right and do not do wrong. Needless to say, their notions of right and wrong and of good and evil are often not the conventional ones.

One way of expressing the quality I am trying to describe was suggested by Dr. David Levy, who pointed out that a few centuries ago these would all have been described as men who walk in the path of God or as godly men. A few say that they believe in a God, but describe this God more as a metaphysical concept than as a personal figure. If religion is defined only in social–behavioral terms, then these are all religious people, the atheists included. But if more conservatively we use the term *religion* to stress the supernatural element and institutional orthodoxy (certainly the more common usage) then our answer must be quite different, for then very few of them are religious.

Self-actualizing people most of the time behave as though, for them, means and ends are clearly distinguishable. In general, they are fixed on ends rather than on means, and means are quite definitely subordinated to these ends. This, however, is an overly simple statement. Our subjects make the situation more complex by often regarding as ends in themselves many experiences and activities that are, for other people, only means. Our subjects are somewhat more likely to appreciate for its own sake, and in an absolute way, the doing itself; they can often enjoy for its own sake the getting to some place as well as the arriving. It is occasionally possible for them to make out of the most trivial and routine activity an intrinsically enjoyable game or dance or play. Wertheimer pointed out that most children are so creative that they can transform hackneyed routine, mechanical, and rote experiences, e.g., as in one of his experiments, transporting books from one set of shelves to another, into a structured and amusing game of a sort by doing this according to a certain system or with a certain rhythm.

PHILOSOPHICAL, UNHOSTILE SENSE OF HUMOR

One very early finding that was quite easy to make, because it was common to all my subjects, was that their sense of humor is not of the ordinary type. They do not consider funny what the average man considers to be funny. Thus they do not laugh at hostile humor (making people laugh by hurting someone) or superiority humor (laughing at someone else's inferiority) or authority-rebellion humor (the unfunny, Oedipal, or smutty joke). Characteristically what they consider humor is more closely allied to philosophy than to anything else. It may also be called the humor of the real because it consists in large part in poking fun at human beings in general when they are foolish, or forget their place in the universe, or try to be big when they are actually small. This can take the form of poking fun at themselves, but this is not done in any masochistic or clownlike way. Lincoln's humor can serve as a suitable example. Probably Lincoln never made a joke that hurt anybody else; it is also likely that many or even most of his jokes had something to say, had a function beyond just producing a laugh. They often seemed to be education in a more palatable form, akin to parables or fables.

On a simple quantitative basis, our subjects may be said to be humorous less often than the average of the population. Punning, joking, witty remarks, gay repartee, persiflage of the ordinary sort is much less often seen than the rather thoughtful, philosophical humor that elicits a smile more usually than a laugh, that is intrinsic to the situation rather than added to it, that is spontaneous rather than planned, and that very often can never be repeated. It should not be surprising that the average man, accustomed as he is to joke books and belly laughs, considers our subjects to be rather on the sober and serious side.

Such humor can be very pervasive; the human situation, human pride, seriousness, busy-ness, bustle, ambition, striving and planning can all be seen as amusing, humorous, even funny. I once understood this attitude, I thought, in a room full of "kinetic art," which seemed to me to be a humorous parody of human life, with the noise, movement, turmoil, hurry and bustle, all of it going no place. This attitude also rubs off on professional work itself, which in a certain sense is also play, and which, though taken seriously, is somehow also taken lightly.

CREATIVENESS$_{SA}$

This is a universal characteristic of all the people studied or observed. There is no exception. Each one shows in one way or another a special kind of creativeness or originality or inventiveness that has certain peculiar characteristics. These special characteristics can be understood more fully in the light of discussion later in this chapter. For one thing, it is different from the special-talent creativeness of the Mozart type. We may as well face the fact that the so-called geniuses display ability that we do not understand. All we can say of them is that they seem to be specially endowed with a drive and a capacity that may have rather little relationship to the rest of the personality and with which, from all evidence, the individuals seem to be born. Such talent we have no concern with here since it does not rest upon psychic health or basic satisfaction. The creativeness of the self-actualized man seems rather to be kin to the naïve and universal creativeness of unspoiled children. It seems to be more a fundamental characteristic of common human nature —a potentiality given to all human beings at birth. Most human beings lose this as they become enculturated, but some few individuals seem either to retain this fresh and naïve, direct way of looking at life, or if they have lost it, as most people do, they later in life recover it. Santayana called this the "second naïveté," a very good name for it.

This creativeness appears in some of our subjects not in the usual forms of writing books, composing music, or producing artistic objects, but rather may be much more humble. It is as if this special type of creativeness, being an expression of healthy personality, is projected out upon the world or touches whatever activity the person is engaged in. In this sense there can be creative shoemakers or carpenters or clerks. Whatever one does can be done with a certain attitude, a certain spirit that arises out of the nature of the character of the person performing the act. One can even *see* creatively as the child does.

This quality is differentiated out here for the sake of discussion, as if it were something separate from the characteristics that precede it and follow it, but this is not actually the case. Perhaps when we speak of creativeness here we are simply describing from another point of view, namely, from the point of view of consequences, what we have described above as a greater freshness, penetration, and efficiency of perception. These people seem to see the true and the real more easily. It is because of this that they seem to other more limited men creative.

Furthermore, as we have seen, these individuals are less inhibited, less constricted, less bound, in a word, less enculturated. In more positive terms, they are more spontaneous, more natural, more human. This too would have as one of its consequences what would seem to other people to be creativeness. If we assume, as we may from our study of children, that all people were once spontaneous, and perhaps in their deepest roots still are, but that these people have in addition to their deep spontaneity a superficial but powerful set of inhibitions, then this spontaneity must be checked so as not to appear very often. If there were no choking-off forces, we might expect that every human being would show this special type of creativeness (10, 307).

RESISTANCE TO ENCULTURATION; THE TRANSCENDENCE OF ANY PARTICULAR CULTURE

Self-actualizing people are not well adjusted (in the naïve sense of approval of and identification with the culture). They get along with the culture in various ways, but of all of them it may be said that in a certain profound and meaningful sense they resist enculturation (295) and maintain a certain inner detachment from the culture in which they are immersed. Since in the culture-and-personality literature very little has been said about resistance to molding by the culture, and since, as Riesman (398) has clearly pointed out, the saving remnant is especially important for American society, even our meager data are of some importance.

On the whole the relationship of these healthy people with their much less healthy culture is a complex one; from it can be teased out at least the following components.

1. All these people fall well within the limits of apparent conventionality in choice of clothes, of language, of food, of ways of doing things in our culture. And yet they are not *really* conventional, certainly not fashionable or smart or chic.

The expressed inner attitude is usually that it is ordinarily of no great consequence which folkways are used, that one set of traffic rules is as good as any other set, that while they make life smoother they do not really matter enough to make a fuss about. Here again we see the general tendency of these people to accept most states of affairs that they consider unimportant or unchangeable or not of primary concern to them as individuals. Since choice of shoes, or style of haircut or politeness, or manner of behaving at a party are not of primary concern to any of the individuals studied, they are apt to elicit as a reaction only a shrug of the shoulders. These are not moral issues.

But since this tolerant acceptance of harmless folkways is not warm approval with identification, their yielding to convention is apt to be rather casual and perfunctory, with cutting of corners in favor of directness, honesty, saving of energy, etc. In the pinch, when yielding to conventions is too annoying or too expensive, the apparent conventionality reveals itself for the superficial thing that it is, and is tossed off as easily as a cloak.

2. Hardly any of these people can be called authority rebels in the adolescent or hot sense. They show no active impatience or moment-to-moment, chronic, long-time discontent with the culture or preoccupation with changing it quickly, although they often enough show bursts of indignation with injustice. One of these subjects, who was a hot rebel in his younger days, a union organizer in the days when this was a highly dangerous occupation, has given up in disgust and hopelessness. As he became resigned to the slowness of social change (in this culture and in this era) he turned finally to education of the young. All the others show what might be called a calm, long-time concern with culture improvement that seems to me to imply an acceptance of slowness of change along with the unquestioned desirability and necessity of such change.

This is by no means a lack of fight. When quick change is possible or when resolution and courage are needed, it is available in these people. Although they are not a radical group of people in the ordinary sense, I think they easily *could* be. First of all, this is primarily an intellectual group (it must be remembered who selected them), most of whom already have a mission, and feel that they are doing something really important to improve the world. Second, they are a realistic group and seem to be unwilling to make great but useless sacrifices. In a more drastic situation it seems very likely that they would be willing to drop their work in favor of radical social action, e.g., the anti-Nazi underground in Germany or in France. My impression is that they are not against fighting but only against ineffective fighting.

Another point that came up very commonly in discussion was the desirability of enjoying life and having a good time. This seems to all but one to be incompatible with hot and full-time rebelliousness. Furthermore, it seems to them that this is too great a sacrifice to make for the small returns expected. Most of them have had their episodes of fighting, impatience, and eagerness in youth, and in most cases have learned that their optimism about quick change was unwarranted. What they settled down to as a group was an accepting, calm, good-humored everyday effort to improve the culture, usually from within, rather than to reject it wholly and fight it from without.

3. An inner feeling of detachment from the culture is not necessarily conscious but is displayed by almost all, particularly in discussions of the American culture as a whole, in various comparisons with other cultures, and in the fact that they very frequently seem to be able to stand off from it as if they did not quite belong to it. The mixture of varying proportions of affection or approval and hostility or criticism indicated that they select from American culture what is good in it by their lights and reject what they think bad in it. In a word they weigh it, assay it, taste it, and then make their own decisions.

This is certainly very different from the ordinary sort of passive yielding to cultural shaping displayed for instance by the ethnocentric subjects of the many studies of authoritarian personalities. It is also different from the total rejection of what after all is a relatively good culture, that is, when compared with other cultures that actually *exist*, rather than fantasied heavens of perfection (or as one lapel button put it, Nirvana *Now!*).

Detachment from the culture is probably also reflected in our self-actualizing subjects' detachment from people and their liking for privacy, which has been described above, as also in their less than average need for the familiar and customary.

4. For these and other reasons they may be called autonomous, i.e.,

ruled by the laws of their own character rather than by the rules of society. It is in this sense that they are not only or merely Americans, but also to a greater degree than others, members at large of the human species. To say that they are above or beyond the American culture would be misleading if interpreted strictly, for after all they speak American, act American, have American characters, etc.

And yet if we compare them with the oversocialized, the robotized, or the ethnocentric, we are irresistibly tempted to hypothesize that this group is not simply another subcultural group, but rather less encul-turated, less flattened out, less molded. This implies degree, and placing on a continuum that ranges from relative acceptance of the culture to relative detachment from it.

If this turns out to be a tenable hypothesis, at least one other hypoth-esis can be deduced from it, that those individuals in different cultures who are more detached from their own culture should not only have less national character but also should be more like each other in certain respects than they are like the less developed members of their own societies.

In summary the perennial question, Is it possible to be a good or healthy man in an imperfect culture? has been answered by the observa-tion that it *is* possible for relatively healthy people to develop in the American culture. They manage to get along by a complex combination of inner autonomy and outer acceptance that of course will be possible only so long as the culture remains tolerant of this kind of detached with-holding from complete cultural identification.

Of course this is not ideal health. Our imperfect society clearly forces inhibitions and restraints upon our subjects. To the extent that they have to maintain their little secrecies, to that extent is their spontaneity lessened and to that extent are some of their potentialities not actualized. And since only few people can attain health in our culture (or perhaps in *any* culture), those who do attain it are lonely for their own kind and are therefore less spontaneous and less actualized.[1]

THE IMPERFECTIONS OF
SELF-ACTUALIZING PEOPLE

The ordinary mistake that is made by novelists, poets, and essayists about the good human being is to make him so good that he is a caricature, so

[1] I am indebted to Dr. Tamara Dembo for her help with this problem.

that nobody would like to be like him. The individual's own wishes for perfection, and his guilt and shame about shortcomings are projected upon various kinds of people from whom the average man demands much more than he himself gives. Thus teachers and ministers are sometimes conceived to be rather joyless people who have no mundane desires and who have no weaknesses. It is my belief that most of the novelists who have attempted to portray good (healthy) people did this sort of thing, making them into stuffed shirts or marionettes or unreal projections of unreal ideals, rather than into the robust, hearty, lusty individuals they really are. Our subjects show many of the lesser human failings. They too are equipped with silly, wasteful, or thoughtless habits. They can be boring, stubborn, irritating. They are by no means free from a rather superficial vanity, pride, partiality to their own productions, family, friends, and children. Temper outbursts are not rare.

Our subjects are occasionally capable of an extraordinary and unexpected ruthlessness. It must be remembered that they are very strong people. This makes it possible for them to display a surgical coldness when this is called for, beyond the power of the average man. The man who found that a long-trusted acquaintance was dishonest cut himself off from this friendship sharply and abruptly and without any observable pangs whatsoever. Another woman who was married to someone she did not love, when she decided on divorce, did it with a decisiveness that looked almost like ruthlessness. Some of them recover so quickly from the death of people close to them as to seem heartless.

Not only are these people strong but also they are independent of the opinions of other people. One woman, extremely irritated by the stuffy conventionalism of some individuals she was introduced to at a gathering, went out of her way to shock these people by her language and behavior. One might say it was all right for her to react to irritation in this way, but another result was that these people were completely hostile not only to the woman but to the friends in whose home this meeting took place. While our subject *wanted* to alienate these people, the host and hostess did not.

We may mention one more example that arises primarily from the absorption of our subjects in an impersonal world. In their concentration, in their fascinated interest, in their intense concentration on some phenomenon or question, they may become absent-minded or humorless and forget their ordinary social politeness. In such circumstances, they are apt to show themselves more clearly as essentially not interested in chatting, gay conversation, party-going, or the like, they may use language or behavior that may be very distressing, shocking, insulting, or hurtful to others. Other undesirable (at least from the point of view of others) consequences of detachment have been listed above.

Even their kindness can lead them into mistakes, e.g., marrying out of pity, getting too closely involved with neurotics, bores, unhappy people, and then being sorry for it, allowing scoundrels to impose on them for a while, giving more than they should so that occasionally they encourage parasites and psychopaths, etc.

Finally, it has already been pointed out that these people are *not* free of guilt, anxiety, sadness, self-castigation, internal strife, and conflict. The fact that these arise out of nonneurotic sources is of little consequence to most people today (even to most psychologists) who are therefore apt to think them *un*healthy for this reason.

What this has taught me I think all of us had better learn. *There are no perfect human beings!* Persons can be found who are good, very good indeed, in fact, great. There do in fact exist creators, seers, sages, saints, shakers, and movers. This can certainly give us hope for the future of the species even if they *are* uncommon and do *not* come by the dozen. And yet these very same people can at times be boring, irritating, petulant, selfish, angry, or depressed. To avoid disillusionment with human nature, we must first give up our illusions about it.

VALUES AND SELF-ACTUALIZATION

A firm foundation for a value system is automatically furnished to the self-actualizer by his philosophic acceptance of the nature of his self, of human nature, of much of social life, and of nature and physical reality. These acceptance values account for a high percentage of the total of his individual value judgments from day to day. What he approves of, disapproves of, is loyal to, opposes or proposes, what pleases him or displeases him can often be understood as surface derivations of this source trait of acceptance.

Not only is this foundation automatically (and universally) supplied to *all* self-actualizers by their intrinsic dynamics (so that in at least this respect fully developed human nature may be universal and cross-cultural); other determiners are supplied as well by these same dynamics. Among these are (1) his peculiarly comfortable relationships with reality, (2) his *Gemeinschaftsgefühl,* (3) his basically satisfied condition from which flow, as epiphenomena, various consequences of surplus, of wealth, overflowing abundance, (4) his characteristically discriminating relations to means and ends, etc. (see above).

One most important consequence of this attitude toward the world

—as well as a validation of it—is the fact that conflict and struggle, ambivalence and uncertainty over choice lessen or disappear in many areas of life. Apparently much so-called "morality" is largely an epiphenomenon of nonacceptance or dissatisfaction. Many problems are seen to be gratuitous and fade out of existence in the atmosphere of pagan acceptance. It is not so much that the problem is solved as that it becomes clearly seen that it never was an intrinsic problem in the first place, but only a sick-man-created one, e.g., card-playing, dancing, wearing short dresses, exposing the head (in some churches) or *not* exposing the head (in others), drinking wine, or eating some meats and not others, or eating them on some days but not on others. Not only are such trivialities deflated; the process also goes on at a more important level, e.g., the relations between the sexes, attitudes toward the structure of the body and toward its functioning, and toward death itself.

The pursuit of this finding to more profound levels has suggested to the writer that much else of what passes for morals, ethics, and values may be simple by-products of the pervasive psychopathology of the average. Many conflicts, frustrations, and threats (which force the kind of choice in which value is expressed), evaporate or resolve for the self-actualizing person in the same way as do, let us say, conflicts over dancing. For him the seemingly irreconcilable battle of the sexes becomes no conflict at all but rather a delightful collaboration. The antagonistic interests of adults and children turn out to be not so antagonistic after all. Just as with sex and age differences, so also is it with natural differences, class and caste differences, political differences, role differences, religious differences, etc. As we know, these are each fertile breeding grounds for anxiety, fear, hostility, aggression, defensiveness, and jealousy. But it begins to appear that they *need not be,* for our subjects' reaction to differences is much less often of this undesirable type. They are more apt to enjoy differences than to fear them.

To take the teacher-student relationship as a specific paradigm, our teacher subjects behaved in a very unneurotic way simply by interpreting the whole situation differently, e.g., as a pleasant collaboration rather than as a clash of wills, of authority, of dignity, etc.; the replacement of artificial dignity—that is easily and inevitably threatened—with the natural simplicity that is *not* easily threatened; the giving up of the attempt to be omniscient and omnipotent; the absence of student-threatening authoritarianism; the refusal to regard the students as competing with each other or with the teacher; the refusal to assume the professor stereotype and the insistence on remaining as realistically human as, say, a plumber or a carpenter; all of these create a classroom atmosphere in which suspicion, wariness, defensiveness, hostility, and anxiety tend to disappear. So also do similar threat responses tend to disappear in marriages, in families and in other interpersonal situations when threat itself is reduced.

The principles and the values of the desperate man and of the psychologically healthy man must be different in at least some ways. They have profoundly different perceptions (interpretations) of the physical world, the social world and the private psychological world, whose organization and economy is in part the responsibility of the person's value system. For the basically deprived man the world is a dangerous place, a jungle, an enemy territory populated by (1) those whom he can dominate and (2) those who can dominate him. His value system is of necessity, like that of any jungle denizen, dominated and organized by the lower needs, especially the creature needs and the safety needs. The basically satisfied person is in a different case. He can afford out of his abundance to take these needs and their satisfaction for granted and can devote himself to higher gratifications. This is to say that their value systems are different, in fact *must* be different.

The topmost portion of the value system of the self-actualized person is entirely unique and idiosyncratic-character-structure-expressive. This must be true by definition, for self-actualization is actualization of a self, and no two selves are altogether alike. There is only one Renoir, one Brahms, one Spinoza. Our subjects had very much in common, as we have seen, and yet at the same time were more completely individualized, more unmistakably themselves, less easily confounded with others than any average control group could possibly be. That is to say, they are simultaneously very much alike and very much unlike each other. They are more completely individual than any group that has ever been described, and yet are also more completely socialized, more identified with humanity than any other group yet described. They are closer to *both* their species-hood and to their unique individuality.

THE RESOLUTION OF DICHOTOMIES
IN SELF-ACTUALIZATION

At this point we may finally allow ourselves to generalize and underscore a very important theoretical conclusion derivable from the study of self-actualizing people. At several points in this chapter—and in other chapters as well—it was concluded that what had been considered in the past to be polarities or opposites or dichotomies were so *only in less healthy people*. In healthy people, these dichotomies were resolved, the polarities disappeared, and many oppositions thought to be intrinsic merged and coalesced with each other to form unities. But see also (82).

For example the age-old opposition between heart and head, reason and instinct, or cognition and conation was seen to disappear in healthy people where they become synergic rather than antagonists, and where conflict between them disappears because they say the same thing and point to the same conclusion. In a word in these people, desires are in excellent accord with reason. St. Augustine's "Love God and do as you will" can easily be translated, "Be healthy and then you may trust your impulses."

The dichotomy between selfishness and unselfishness disappears altogether in healthy people because in principle every act is *both* selfish and unselfish (312). Our subjects are simultaneously very spiritual and very pagan and sensual even to the point where sexuality becomes a *path* to the spiritual and "religious." Duty cannot be contrasted with pleasure nor work with play when duty *is* pleasure, when work *is* play, and the person doing his duty and being virtuous is simultaneously seeking his pleasure and being happy. If the most socially identified people are themselves also the most individualistic people, of what use is it to retain the polarity? If the most mature are also childlike? And if the most ethical and moral people are also the lustiest and most animal?

Similar findings have been reached for kindness-ruthlessness, concreteness-abstractness, acceptance-rebellion, self-society, adjustment-maladjustment, detachment from others-identification with others, serious-humorous, Dionysian-Apollonian, introverted-extraverted, intense-casual, serious-frivolous, conventional-unconventional, mystic-realistic, active-passive, masculine-feminine, lust-love, and Eros-Agape. In these people, the id, the ego, and the superego are collaborative and synergic; they do not war with each other nor are their interests in basic disagreement as they are in neurotic people. So also do the cognitive, the impulsive and the emotional coalesce into an organismic unity and into a non-Aristotelian interpenetration. The higher and the lower are not in opposition but in agreement, and a thousand serious philosophical dilemmas are discovered to have more than two horns, or, paradoxically, no horns at all. If the war between the sexes turns out to be no war at all in matured people, but only a sign of crippling and stunting of growth, who then would wish to choose sides? Who would deliberately and knowingly choose psychopathology? Is it necessary to choose between the good woman and the bad, as if they were mutually exclusive, when we have found that the really healthy woman is both at the same time?

In this, as in other ways, healthy people are so different from average ones, not only in degree but in kind as well, that they generate two very different kinds of psychology. It becomes more and more clear that the study of crippled, stunted, immature, and unhealthy specimens can yield only a cripple psychology and a cripple philosophy. The study of self-actualizing people must be the basis for a more universal science of psychology.

12

LOVE IN SELF-ACTUALIZING PEOPLE

It is amazing how little the empirical sciences have to offer on the subject of love. Particularly strange is the silence of the psychologists, for one might think this to be their particular obligation. Probably this is just another example of the besetting sin of the academicians, that they prefer to do what they are easily able rather than what they ought, like the not-so-bright kitchen helper I knew who opened every can in the hotel one day because he was so *very* good at opening cans.

I must confess that I understand this better now that I have undertaken the task myself. It is an extraordinarily difficult subject to handle in any tradition. And it is triply so in the scientific tradition. It is as if we were at the most advanced position in no man's land, at a point where the conventional techniques of orthodox psychological science are of very little use. (As a matter of fact, it was this inadequacy that made necessary the development of new methods of getting information about this and other uniquely human reactions. These in turn have led on toward a different philosophy of science (292, 376).

Our duty is clear here. We *must* understand love; we must be able to teach it, to create it, to predict it, or else the world is lost to hostility and to suspicion. The importance of the goal lends worth and dignity even to such unreliable data as are herein offered. The research, the subjects, and the major findings have already been described in the previous chapter. The specific question before us now is, what have these people to teach us about love and sex?

A PRELIMINARY DESCRIPTION OF
SOME CHARACTERISTICS OF LOVE
BETWEEN THE SEXES

We shall mention first some of the better-known characteristics of love between the sexes and then proceed to the more special findings of our study of self-actualizing people.

The core of the description of love must be subjective or phenomenological rather than objective or behavioral. No description, no words can ever communicate the full quality of the love experience to one who has himself never felt it. It consists primarily of a feeling of tenderness and affection with great enjoyment, happiness, satisfaction, elation, and even ecstasy in experiencing this feeling (if all is going well). There is a tendency to want to get closer, to come into more intimate contact, to touch and embrace the loved person, to yearn for him. This person furthermore is perceived in some desirable way, whether as beautiful, as good, or as attractive; in any case, there is pleasure in looking at and being with the loved one and distress and depression in separation from him. Perhaps from this comes the tendency to focus attention upon the loved person, along with the tendency to forget other people, and to narrow perception in such a way that many things are not noticed. It is as if the loved person were in himself attractive, and *pulled* the attention and perception of the loving person. This feeling of pleasure in contact and in being with, shows itself also in the desire to be together with the loved one as much as possible in as many situations as possible; in work, in play, during aesthetic and intellectual pursuits. There is often expressed a desire to share pleasant experiences with the loved person so that it is often reported that the pleasant experience is more pleasant because of the presence of the sweetheart.

Finally, of course, there is a special sexual arousal in the lover. This, in the typical instance, shows itself directly in genital changes. The beloved person seems to have a special power that nobody else in the world has to the same degree of producing erection and secretion in the partner, of arousing specific conscious sexual desire, and of producing the usual pricklings and tinglings that go with sexual arousal. And yet this is not essential, since love can be observed in people who are too old for sexual intercourse.

The desire for intimacy is not only physical but also psychological. It expresses itself frequently as a special taste for privacy for the pair. In addition to this, I have observed often the growth in a pair who love each other of a secret language, secret sexual words that other people cannot understand, and of special tricks and gestures that only the lovers understand.

Quite characteristic is the feeling of generosity, of wanting to give and to please. The lover gets special pleasure from doing things for and making gifts to the loved one.[1]

Very common is the desire for a fuller knowledge of one another, a yearning for a kind of psychological intimacy and psychological proximity and of being fully known to each other. Special delight in sharing secrets is common. Perhaps these are subexamples that come under the broader heading of personality fusion, of which we shall speak below.

A common example of the tendency to generosity and to do things for the one who is loved are the very common fantasies in which a person will imagine himself making great sacrifices for the sake of his sweetheart. (There are of course other love relationships, for example between friends, brothers, parent and child. I must at least mention my suspicion, arrived at in the course of these investigations, that the purest love for the Being of the other—B-love—is found in some grandparents.)

DROPPING OF DEFENSES IN
SELF-ACTUALIZING LOVE RELATIONSHIPS

Theodor Reik (393, p. 171) has defined one characteristic of love as the absence of anxiety. This is seen with exceptional clearness in healthy individuals. There is little question about the tendency to more and more complete spontaneity, the dropping of defenses, the dropping of roles, and of trying and striving in the relationship. As the relationship continues, there is a growing intimacy and honesty and self-expression, which at its height is a rare phenomenon. The report from these people is that with a beloved person it is possible to be oneself, to feel natural; "I can

---

[1] Self-actualizing love, or B-love, tends to be a free giving of oneself, wholly and with abandon, without reserve, withholding, or calculation of the kind exemplified in the following statements collected from college women: "Don't give up too easily." "Make it hard to get." "Make him uncertain." "He shouldn't be too sure of me." "I keep him guessing." "Don't give yourself too fast or too completely." "If I love him too much he's the boss." "In love one must love more than the other; whoever does is the weaker." "Let him worry a little."

let my hair down." This honesty also includes allowing one's faults, weaknesses, and physical and psychological shortcomings to be freely seen by the partner.

There is much less tendency to put the best foot forward in the healthy love relationship. This goes so far as to make less likely the hiding even of physical defects of middle and old age, of false teeth, braces, girdles, and the like. There is much less maintenance of distance, mystery, and glamour, much less reserve and concealment and secrecy. This complete dropping of the guard definitely contradicts folk wisdom on the subject, not to mention some of the psychoanalytic theorists. For instance, Reik believes that being a good pal and being a good sweetheart are mutually exclusive and contradictory. My data, or rather my impressions seem to indicate the contrary.

My data definitely contradict also the age-old theory of intrinsic hostility between the sexes. This hostility between the sexes, this suspicion of the opposite sex, this tendency to identify with one's own sex is an alliance against the other sex, even the very phrasing of "opposite" sex is found often enough in neurotic people and even in average citizens in our society, but it is definitely not found in self-actualizing people, at least with the resources for investigation that I had at my disposal.

Another finding that contradicts folk wisdom and also some of the more esoteric theorists on sexuality and love, is the definite indication that in self-actualizing people the quality of the love satisfactions and the sex satisfactions may both improve with the length of the relationship. It seems quite clear that even the strictly sensual and physical satisfactions can be improved by familiarity with the partner rather than by novelty in healthy people. Of course, there is little doubt that novelty in the sexual partner is very exciting and attractive for many people, but our data make it very unwise to make any generalization about this, and certainly not for self-actualizing people.

We may sum up this characteristic of self-actualizing love in the generalization that healthy love is in part an absence of defenses, that is to say, an increase in spontaneity and in honesty. The healthy love relationship tends to make it possible for two people to be spontaneous, to know each other, and still to love each other. Of course, this implies that as one gets to know another person more and more intimately and profoundly, one will like what one sees. If the partner is profoundly bad rather than good, increasing familiarity will produce not increasing preference but increasing antagonism and revulsion. This recalls a finding that I made in a little study of the effects of familiarization on paintings. My finding was that good paintings become more and more preferred and enjoyed with increasing familiarization, but that bad paintings become less and less preferred. The difficulty of deciding at that time on some objective criterion of good and bad in paintings was so great that I preferred not to publish the finding. But if I may be permitted this amount of subjectivism, I will say that the better people are, the more they will be loved with greater familiarity; the worse people are the *less* they will be liked as familiarity increases.

One of the deepest satisfactions coming from the healthy love relationship reported by my subjects is that such a relationship permits the greatest spontaneity, the greatest naturalness, the greatest dropping of defenses and protection against threat. In such a relationship it is not necessary to be guarded, to conceal, to try to impress, to feel tense, to watch one's words or actions, to suppress or repress. My people report that they can be themselves without feeling that there are demands or expectations upon them; they can feel psychologically (as well as physically) naked and still feel loved and wanted and secure.

Rogers has described this well (401a, p. 159). " 'Loved' has here perhaps its deepest and most general meaning—that of being deeply understood and deeply accepted. . . . We can love a person only to the extent that we are not threatened by him; we can love only if his reactions to us, or to those things which affect us, are understandable to us. . . . Thus, if a person is hostile toward me, and I can see nothing in him at the moment except the hostility, I am quite sure that I will react in a defensive way to the hostility."

Menninger (335a, p. 22) describes the reverse side of the coin. "Love is impaired less by the feeling that we are not appreciated than by a dread, more or less dimly felt by everyone, lest others see through our masks, the masks of repression that have been forced upon us by convention and culture. It is this that leads us to shun intimacy, to maintain friendships on a superficial level, to underestimate and fail to appreciate others lest they come to appreciate us too well." These conclusions are further supported by the greater freedom of hostility and anger expression in our subjects as well as in their lowered need for conventional politeness with each other.

THE ABILITY TO LOVE
AND TO BE LOVED

My subjects were loved and were loving, and are loved and are loving. In practically all (not quite all) my subjects where data were available, this tended to point to the conclusion that (all other things being equal) psychological health comes from being loved rather than from being deprived of love. Granted that the ascetic path is a possible one, and that frustration has some good effects, yet basic need gratification seems to be much more the usual precursor or *Anlage* of health in our society. This seems to be true not only for being loved but for loving as well. (That *other* requirements are also necessary is proven by the psychopathic personality, especially as exemplified by Levy's (264) indulged psychopath.)

It is also true of our self-actualizing people that they *now* love and are loved. For certain reasons it had better be said that they have the power to love and the ability to *be* loved. (Even though this may sound like a repetition of the sentence, before, it is really not.) These are clinically observed facts, and are quite public and easily confirmed or disconfirmed.

Menninger (335a) makes the very acute statement that human beings really *do* want to love each other but just do not know how to go about it. This is much less true for healthy people. *They* at least know how to love, and can do so freely and easily and naturally and without getting wound up in conflicts or threats or inhibitions.

However, my subjects used the word love warily and with circumspection. They applied it only to a few rather than to many, tending to distinguish sharply between loving someone and liking him or being friendly or benevolent or brotherly. It described for them an intense feeling, not a mild or disinterested one.

SEXUALITY IN SELF-ACTUALIZING LOVE

We can learn a very great deal from the peculiar and complex nature of sex in the love life of self-actualizing people. It is by no means a simple story; there are many interwoven threads. Nor can I say that I have many data. Information of this sort is hard to come by in private people. On the whole, however, their sex life, as much as I know of it, is characteristic and can be described in such a way as to make possible guesses, both positive and negative, about the nature of sex as well as about the nature of love.

For one thing it can be reported that sex and love can be and most often are more perfectly fused with each other in healthy people. Although it is perfectly true that these are separable concepts, and although no purpose would be served in confusing them with each other unnecessarily (393, 442), still it must be reported that in the life of healthy people, they tend to become joined and merged with each other. As a matter of fact we may also say that they become less separable and less separate from each other in the lives of the people we have studied. We cannot go so far as some who say that any person who is capable of having sexual pleasure where there is no love must be a sick man. But we can certainly go in this direction. It is certainly fair to say that self-actualizing men and women tend on the whole not to seek sex for its own sake, or to be satisfied with it alone when it comes. I am not sure that my data permit me to say that they would rather not have sex at all if it came without affection, but I am quite sure that I have a fair number of instances in which for the time being at least sex was given up or rejected because it came without love or affection.[2]

Another finding already reported in Chapter 11 is the very strong impression that the sexual pleasures are found in their most intense and ecstatic perfection in self-actualizing people. If love is a yearning for the perfect and for complete fusion, then the orgasm as sometimes reported by self-actualizing people becomes the attainment of it. Experiences described in reports that I have obtained have indeed been at so great a level of intensity that I felt it justifiable to record them as mystic experiences. Such phrases as too big to assimilate, too good to be true, too good to last, etc., have been coupled with reports of being swept away completely by forces beyond control. This combination of very perfect and intense sexuality along with other characteristics to be reported produces several seeming paradoxes that I now wish to discuss.

In self-actualizing people the orgasm is simultaneously more important and less important than in average people. It is often a profound and almost mystical experience, and yet the absence of sexuality is more easily tolerated by these people. This is not a paradox or a contradiction. It follows from dynamic motivation theory. Loving at a higher need level makes the lower needs and their frustrations and satisfactions less important, less central, more easily neglected. But it also makes them more wholeheartedly enjoyed when gratified.

An excellent parallel may be made between this and the attitude of these people toward food. Food is simultaneously enjoyed and yet regarded as relatively unimportant in the total scheme of life by self-actualizing people. When they do enjoy it, they can enjoy it wholeheartedly and without the slightest tainting with bad attitudes toward

2 Schwarz, Oswald, *The Psychology of Sex*, Penguin Books, 1951, p.. 21: "Although totally different in nature, sexual impulse and love are dependent on, and complementary to, each other. *In a perfect, fully mature human being only this inseparable fusion of sexual impulse and love exists.* This is the fundamental principle of any psychology of sex. If there be anyone capable of experiencing the purely physical gratification of sex, he is stigmatized as sexually subnormal (immature or otherwise)."

animality and the like. And yet ordinarily feeding oneself takes a relatively unimportant place in the total picture. These people do not *need* sensuality; they simply enjoy it when it occurs.

Certainly also food takes a relatively unimportant place in the philosophy of Utopia, in Heaven, in the good life, in the philosophy of values and ethics. It is something basic, to be taken for granted, to be used as a foundation stone upon which higher things are built. These people are very ready to recognize that the higher things cannot be built until the lower ones are built, but once these lower needs are satisfied, they recede from consciousness, and there is little preoccupation with them.

The same seems to be true of sex. Sex can be, as I said, wholeheartedly enjoyed, enjoyed far beyond the possibility of the average person, even at the same time that it does not play any central role in the philosophy of life. It is something to be enjoyed, something to be taken for granted, something to build upon, something that is very basically important like water or food, and that can be enjoyed as much as these; but gratification should be taken for granted. I think such an attitude as this resolves the apparent paradox in the self-actualizing person's simultaneously enjoying sex so much more intensely than the average person, yet at the same time considering it so much less important in the total frame of reference.

It should be stressed that from this same complex attitude toward sex arises the fact that the orgasm may bring on mystical experiences, and yet at other times may be taken rather lightly. This is to say that the sexual pleasure of self-actualizing people may be very intense or not intense at all. This conflicts with the romantic attitude that love is a divine rapture, a transport, a mystic experience. It is true that it may be also a delicate pleasure rather than an intense one, a gay and light-hearted, playful sort of thing rather than a serious and profound experience or even a neutral duty. These people do not always live on the heights— they usually live at a more average level of intensity, and lightly and mildly enjoy sex as a titillating, pleasant, playful, enjoyable, tickling kind of experience instead of a plumbing of the most intense depths of ecstatic emotionality. This is especially true when the subjects are relatively fatigued. Under such circumstances, the lighter kind of sex may take place.

Self-actualizing love shows many of the characteristics of self-actualization in general. For instance, one characteristic is that it is based on a healthy acceptance of the self and of others. So much can be accepted by these people that others would not accept. For example, in spite of the fact that these people are relatively less driven to love affairs outside the marriage, yet they are much more free than the average to admit to the fact of sexual attraction to others. My impression is that there tends to be a rather easy relationship with the opposite sex, along with casual acceptance of the phenomenon of being attracted to other people, at the same time that these individuals do rather less about this attraction than other people. Also it seems to me that their talk about sex is considerably more free and casual and unconventional than the average. Now what this sums up to is an acceptance of the facts of life, which, going along with the more intense and profound and satisfying love relationship, seems to make it less *necessary* to seek for compensatory or neurotic sex affairs outside the marriage. This is an interesting instance in which acceptance and behavior do not correlate. The easier acceptance of the facts of sexuality seems to make it *easier* rather than harder to be relatively monogamous.

In one instance, where the woman had long since separated from her husband, whatever information I was able to get from her indicated that she went in for what would be called promiscuity. She had sexual affairs and was very definite about how she enjoyed them. This was a fifty-five-year-old woman. I was never able to get more details than her statements that she did have such affairs and that she enjoyed sex very much. There was no slight element of guilt or anxiety or of the feeling of doing anything wrong in her conversation about this matter. Apparently the tendency to monogamy is not the same as the tendency to chastity, or a rejection of sexuality. It is just that the more profoundly satisfying the love relationship, the less necessity there is for all sorts of compulsions for sex affairs with people other than the wife or husband.

Of course, this acceptance of sexuality is also a main basis for the intensity of enjoyment of sexuality that I find in self-actualizing people. Another characteristic I found of love in healthy people is that they made no really sharp differentiation between the roles and personalities of the two sexes. That is, they did not assume that the female was passive and the male active, whether in sex or love or anything else. These people were all so certain of their maleness or femaleness that they did not mind taking on some of the cultural aspects of the opposite sex role. It was especially noteworthy that they could be both active and passive lovers and this was the clearest in the sexual act and in physical love-making. Kissing and being kissed, being above or below in the sexual act, taking the initiative, being quiet and receiving love, teasing and being teased— these were all found in both sexes. The reports indicated that both were enjoyed at different times. It was considered to be a shortcoming to be limited to just active love-making or passive love-making. Both have their particular pleasures for self-actualizing people.

This can go pretty far, almost to the point of reminding us of sadism and masochism. There can be a joy in being used, in subjection and passivity, even in accepting pain, in being exploited. Also, there can be an active and positive pleasure in squeezing and hugging and biting and in being violent and even in inflicting and receiving pain, so long as this does not go beyond a certain point.

Since this is very probably related to the lack of doubt about their maleness or femaleness, their masculinity or femininity, so also is it my strong impression that healthier men are more apt to be *attracted* by intelligence, strength, competence, etc., in their women rather than threatened by it, as is so often the case with the uncertain male.

Here again we have an instance of the way in which common dichotomies are so often resolved in self-actualization, appearing to be valid dichotomies only because people are not healthy enough.

This agrees with D'Arcy's (103) thesis that erotic and agapean love are basically different but merge in the best people. He speaks about two kinds of love, which are ultimately masculine or feminine, active or passive, self-centered or self-effacing, and it is true that in the general public these seem to contrast and to be at opposite poles. However, it is different in healthy people. In these individuals the dichotomies are resolved, and the individual becomes both active and passive, both selfish and unselfish, both masculine and feminine, both self-interested and self-effacing. D'Arcy acknowledges that this occurs, though with extreme rarity.

One negative conclusion that our data, limited though they are, permit us to make with considerable confidence is that the Freudian tendency to derive love from sex or to identify them is a bad mistake.[3] Of course Freud is not alone in this error—it is shared by many less thoughtful citizens—but he may be taken as its most influential exponent in western civilization. There are strong indications here and there in Freud's writings that he had different thoughts about the matter occasionally. Once, for example, he spoke about the child's feeling for the mother as deriving from the self-preservation instincts, i.e., a kind of feeling akin to gratitude for being fed and cared for: "It (affection) springs from the very earliest years of childhood, and was formed on the founda-

---

[3] Balint, M., "On genital love," *Int. J. Psychoanal.*, 1948, 29, 34–40: "If one reads the psychoanalytical literature for references to genital love, to one's surprise two striking facts emerge: (a) much less has been written on genital love than on pre-genital love; (b) almost everything that has been written on genital love is negative." See also Balint, M., "The final goal of psychoanalytic treatment," *Int. J. Psychoanal.*, 1936, 17, 206–216, p. 206.

tion provided by the interests of the self-preservation instinct" (139, p. 204). In another place he interprets it as reaction formation (p. 252); again, as the mental side of the sexual impulse (p. 259). In a lecture reported by Hitschmann (195, pp. 2–3) he considered all love to be repetition of the infant's love for the mother. ". . . the sucking of the child at the breast of the mother (is) the model of every love-relation. The finding of the object is indeed a refinding."

On the whole, however, the most widely accepted of the various theories put forth by Freud is that tenderness is aim-inhibited sexuality.[4] That is, to put it very bluntly, it is, for Freud, deflected and disguised sexuality. When we are forbidden to fulfill the sexual aim of coupling, and when we keep on wanting to and do not dare admit to ourselves that we are, the compromise product is tenderness and affection. Contrariwise, when we meet with tenderness and affection we have no Freudian recourse but to regard this as aim-inhibited sexuality. Another deduction from this premise that seems unavoidable is that if sex were never inhibited, and if everyone could couple with anyone else, then there would be no tender love. Incest taboos and repression—these are what breed love, according to Freud. For other views see Refs. 27, 213.

Another kind of love discussed by the Freudians is genital love, frequently defined with exclusive emphasis on genital and without any reference to love. For instance, it is often defined as the power to be potent, to have a good orgasm, to have this orgasm from penile-vaginal coupling without the *necessity* of recourse to clitoris, anus, sadism, masochism, etc. Of course, more sophisticated statements are also found though rarely. The best statements in the Freudian tradition I have been able to find are the ones by Michael Balint[5] and by Edward Hitschmann (195).

---

[4] Freud, Sigmund, *Civilization and Its Discontents:* "These people make themselves independent of their object's acquiescence by transferring the main value from the fact of being loved to their own act of loving; they protect themselves against loss of it by attaching their love not to individual objects but to all men equally, and they avoid the uncertainties and disappointments of genital love by turning away from its sexual aim and modifying the instinct into an impulse with an *inhibited aim*. The state which they induce in themselves by this process—an unchangeable, undeviating, tender attitude—has little superficial likeness to the stormy vicissitudes of genital love, from which it is nevertheless derived" (p. 22).

[5] Balint, M., "On genital love," *Int. J. Psychoanal.*, 1948, 29, 34–40: "To avoid this pitfall (emphasis on negative qualities) let us examine an ideal case of such postambivalent genital love that has no traces of ambivalency and in addition no traces of pre-genital object relationship; (a) there should be no greediness, no insatiability, no wish to devour the object, to deny it any independent existence, i.e., there should be no oral features; (b) there should be no wish to hurt, to humiliate, to boss, to dominate

How tenderness is involved in genital love remains a mystery, for in sexual intercourse there is, of course, no inhibition of the sexual aim (it *is* the sexual aim). Nothing has been said by Freud of aim-*gratified* sexuality. If tenderness is found in genital love, then some source other than aim inhibition must be found, a nonsexual source, it would seem. Suttie's analysis (442) very effectively reveals the weakness of this position. So also do those of Reik (393), Fromm (145, 148), DeForest (106), and others in the revisionist-Freudian tradition. Adler (13) as far back as 1908 affirmed that the need for affection was not derived from sex.

CARE, RESPONSIBILITY, THE POOLING OF NEEDS

One important aspect of a good love relationship is what may be called need identification, or the pooling of the hierarchies of basic needs in two persons into a single hierarchy. The effect of this is that one person feels another's needs as if they were his own and for that matter also feels his own needs to some extent as if they belonged to the other. An ego now expands to cover two people, and to some extent the two people have become for psychological purposes a single unit, a single person, a single ego.

This principle, probably first presented in technical form by Alfred

---

the object, etc., i.e., no sadistic features; (c) there should be no wish to defile the partner, to despise him (or her) for his (her) sexual desires and pleasures. There should be no danger of being disgusted by the partner or being attracted only by some unpleasant features of him, etc., and there should be no remnants of anal traits; (d) there should be no compulsion to boast about the possession of a penis, no fear of the partner's sexual organs, no fear for one's own sexual organs, no envy of the male or female genitalia, no feeling of being incomplete or of having a faulty sexual organ, or of the partner having a faulty one, etc. There should be no trace of the phallic phase or of the castration complex. . . . What is then 'genital love' apart from the absence of all the enumerated pregenital traits? Well, we love our partner (1) because he or she can satisfy us; (2) because we can satisfy him or her; because we can experience a full orgasm together nearly or quite simultaneously. . . . Genital satisfaction is apparently only a necessary and not a sufficient condition of genital love. What we have learned is that genital love is much more than gratitude for or contentment about the partner being available for genital satisfaction. Further that it does not make any difference whether this gratitude or contentment is one-sided or mutual. What is this? We find in addition to the genital satisfaction in a true love relation (1) idealization; (2) tenderness; (3) a special form of identification. To sum up: Genital love in man is really a misnomer. . . . What we call genital love is a fusion of disagreeing elements, genital satisfaction and pregenital tenderness . . . the reward for fearing the strain of this fusion is the possibility of regressing periodically for some happy moments to a really infantile stage of *no* reality testing . . ." (p. 34).

Adler (2, 13), has been very well phrased by Erich Fromm (148), particularly in his book *Man for Himself,* in which love is defined (pp. 129–130):

> Love, in principle is indivisible as far as the connection between 'objects' and one's own self is concerned. Genuine love is an expression of productiveness and implies care, respect, responsibility, and knowledge. It is not an 'affect' in the sense of being affected by somebody, but an active striving for the growth and happiness of the loved person, rooted in one's own capacity to love.

Schlick (413a, p. 186) has also phrased this well:

> The social impulses are those dispositions of a person by virtue of which the idea of a pleasant or unpleasant state of *another* person is itself a pleasant or unpleasant experience (also the mere perception of another creature, his presence alone, can by virtue of such an impulse, elicit feelings of pleasure). The natural effect of these inclinations is that their bearer establishes the joyful states of others as ends of his conduct. And, upon realization of these ends he enjoys the resultant pleasure; for not only the idea, but also the actual perception of the expression of joy pleases him.

The ordinary way in which this need identification shows itself to the eyes of the world is in terms of taking on responsibility, of care, of concern for another person. The loving husband can get as much pleasure from his wife's pleasure as he can from his own. The loving mother would rather cough herself than hear her child cough, and as a matter of fact would willingly take on to her own shoulders the disease of her child, since it would be less painful for her to have it than to see and hear her child have it. A good example of this is seen in the differential reactions in good marriages and in bad marriages to illnesses and the consequently necessary nursing. An illness in the good couple is an illness of the couple rather than a misfortune of one of the pair. Equal responsibility is automatically taken, and it is as if they were both simultaneously struck. The primitive communism of the loving family shows itself in this way and not only in the sharing of food or of money. It is here that one sees at its best and purest the exemplification of the principle: from each according to his abilities and to each according to his needs. The only modification that is here necessary is that the needs of the other person *are* the needs of the lover.

If the relationship is a very good one, the sick or weak one can throw himself upon the nursing care and the protectiveness of the loving partner with the same abandonment and lack of threat and lack of self-consciousness that a child shows in falling asleep in his parent's arms. It is often enough observed in less healthy couples that illness makes a strain in the couple. For the strong man whose masculinity is practically identified with physical strength, illness and weakness is a catastrophe in the same way. For the woman who defines femininity in terms of physical attractiveness of the beauty contest style, illness or weakness or anything else that lessens her physical attractiveness is for her a tragedy, and for the man as well if he defines femininity in the same way. Our healthy people are almost completely exempted from this mistake.

If we remember that human beings are in the last analysis isolated from each other and encapsulated, each one in his own little shell, and if we agree that also in the last analysis people can never really know each other as they know themselves, then every intercourse between groups and individuals is like an effort of "two solitudes to protect, and touch and greet each other" (Rilke). Of all such efforts that we know anything about, the healthy love relationship is the most effective way of bridging the unbridgeable gap between two separate human beings.

In the history of theorizing about love relations as well as about altruism, patriotism, etc., much has been said about the transcendence of the ego. An excellent modern discussion of this tendency at the technical level is afforded in a book by Angyal (12), in which he discusses various examples of a tendency to what he calls homonomy, and which he contrasts with the tendency to autonomy, to independence, to individuality, and the like. More and more clinical and historical evidence accumulates to indicate that Angyal was right in demanding that some room be made in a systematic psychology for these various tendencies to go out beyond the limits of the ego. Furthermore, it seems quite clear that this need to go out beyond the limits of the ego may be a need in the same sense that we have needs for vitamins and minerals, i.e., that if the need is not satisfied, the person becomes sick in one way or another. I should say that one of the most satisfying and most complete examples of ego transcendence is a healthy love relationship. See also (182, 314).

FUN AND GAIETY IN THE HEALTHY LOVE RELATIONSHIP

The concepts of Erich Fromm and Alfred Adler that were mentioned above stress productiveness, care, responsibility. This is all very true, but Fromm, Adler, and the others who write in the same vein strangely omit one aspect of the healthy love relationship that was very clear in my subjects: namely, fun, merriment, elation, feeling of well-being, gaiety. It is quite characteristic of self-actualizing people that they can enjoy themselves in love and in sex. Sex very frequently becomes a kind of a game in which laughter is quite as common as panting. The way in which Fromm and other serious thinkers on the subject have described the ideal love relationship is to make it into something of a task or a burden rather than a game or a pleasure. When Fromm (148, p. 110) says: "Love is the productive form of relatedness to others and to oneself. It implies responsibility, care, respect and knowledge, and the wish for the other person to grow and develop. It is the expression of intimacy between two human beings under the condition of the preservation of each other's integrity," it must be admitted that this sounds a little like a pact or a partnership of some kind rather than a spontaneous sportiveness. It is not the welfare of the species, or the task of reproduction, or the future development of mankind that attracts people to each other. The love and sex life of healthy people, in spite of the fact that it frequently reaches great peaks of ecstasy, is nevertheless also easily compared to the games of children and puppies. It is cheerful, humorous, and playful. We shall point out in greater detail below that it is not primarily a striving, as Fromm implies; it is basically an enjoyment and a delight, which is another thing altogether.

ACCEPTANCE OF THE OTHER'S INDIVIDUALITY; RESPECT FOR THE OTHER

All serious writers on the subject of ideal or healthy love have stressed the affirmation of the other's individuality, the eagerness for the growth of the other, the essential respect for his individuality and unique personality. This is confirmed very strongly by the observation of the self-actualizing people, who have in unusual measure the rare ability to be pleased rather than threatened by the partner's triumphs. They do indeed respect their partners in a very profound and basic way that has many, many implications. As Overstreet says quite well (366a, p. 103), "The love of a person implies, not the possession of that person, but the affirmation of that person. It means granting him, gladly, the full right to his unique manhood."

Fromm's statement on the subject is also very impressive (145, p. 261): "Love is the foremost component of such spontaneity; not love as the dissolution of the self in another person, but love as a spontaneous affirmation of others, as the union of the individual with others on the basis of the preservation of the individual himself." A most impressive example of this respect is the ungrudging pride of such a man in his wife's achievements, even where they outshine his. Another is the absence of jealousy.

This respect shows itself in many ways which, incidentally, should be differentiated from the effects of the love relationship *per se*. Love and respect are separable, even though they often go together. It is possible to respect without loving, even at the self-actualizing level. I am not quite so sure that it is possible to love without respecting, but this too may be a possibility. Many of the characteristics that might be considered aspects or attributes of the love relationship are very frequently seen to be attributes of the respect relationship.

Respect for another person acknowledges him as an independent entity and as a separate and autonomous individual. The self-actualizing person will not casually use another or control him or disregard his wishes. He will allow the respected person a fundamental irreducible dignity, and will not unnecessarily humiliate him. This is true not only for interadult relationships but also in a self-actualizing person's relationship to children. It is possible for him, as for practically nobody else in our culture, to treat a child with real respect.

One amusing aspect of this respect relationship between the sexes is that it is very frequently interpreted in just the opposite way, i.e., as a lack of respect. For example, we know well that a good many of the so-called signs of respect for ladies are in fact hangovers from a nonrespecting past, and possibly even at this time are for some unconscious representations of a deep contempt for women. Such cultural habits as standing up when a lady enters a room, giving a lady the chair, helping her with her coat, allowing her to go first through the door, giving her the best of everything and the first choice of everything—these all imply historically and dynamically the opinion that the woman is weak and incapable of taking care of herself, for these all imply protection, as for the weak and incapable. Generally women who respect themselves strongly tend to be wary of these signs of respect, knowing full well that they may mean just the opposite. Self-actualizing men who tend really and basically to respect and to like women as partners, as equals, as pals, and as full human beings rather than as partial members of the species, are apt to be much more easy and free and familiar and impolite in the traditional sense. I have seen this make for trouble, and I have actually seen self-actualizing men accused of lack of respect for women.

LOVE AS END EXPERIENCE;
ADMIRATION; WONDER; AWE

The fact that love has many good effects does not mean that it is motivated by those effects or that people fall in love *in order* to achieve them.

The love that is found in healthy people is much better described in terms of spontaneous admiration and of the kind of receptive and undemanding awe and enjoyment that we experience when struck by a fine painting. There is too much talk in the psychological literature of rewards and purposes, of reinforcements and gratifications, and not nearly enough of what we may call the end experience (as contrasted with the means experience) or awe before the beautiful that is its own reward.

Admiration and love in my subjects are most of the time *per se*, undemanding of rewards and conducive to no purposes, experienced in Northrop's Eastern sense (361), concretely and richly, for their own sake, idiographically (6).

Admiration asks for nothing and gets nothing. It is purposeless and useless. It is more passive than active and comes close to simple receiving in the Taoistic sense. The awed perceiver does little or nothing to the experience; rather it does something to him. He watches and stares with the innocent eye, like a child who neither agrees nor disagrees, approves nor disapproves, but who, fascinated by the intrinsic attention-attracting quality of the exeprience, simply lets it come in and achieve its effects. The experience may be likened to the *eager* passivity with which we allow ourselves to be tumbled by waves just for the fun that is in it; or perhaps better, to the impersonal interest and awed, unprojecting appreciation of the slowly changing sunset. There is little we can inject into a sunset. In this sense we do not project ourselves into the experience or attempt to shape it as we do with the Rorschach. Nor is it a signal or symbol for anything; we have not been rewarded or associated into admiring it. It has nothing to do with milk, or food, or other body needs. We can enjoy a painting without wanting to own it, a rosebush without wanting to pluck from it, a pretty baby without wanting to kidnap it, a bird without wanting to cage it, and so also can one person admire and enjoy another in a nondoing or nongetting way. Of course awe and admiration lie side by side with other tendencies that *do* involve individuals with each other; it is not the *only* tendency in the picture, but it is definitely part of it.

Perhaps the most important implication of this observation is that we thereby contradict most theories of love, for most theorists assume that people are *driven* into loving another rather than *attracted* into it. Freud (138) speaks of aim-inhibited sexuality, Reik (393) speaks of aim-inhibited power, and many speak of dissatisfaction with the self forcing us to create a projected hallucination, an unreal (because overestimated) partner.

But it seems clear that healthy people fall in love the way one reacts to one's first appreciative perception of great music—one is awed and overwhelmed by it and loves it. This is so even though there was no prior need to be overwhelmed by great music. Horney in a lecture has defined unneurotic love in terms of regarding others as *per se,* as ends in themselves rather than as means to ends. The consequent reaction is to enjoy, to admire, to be delighted, to contemplate and appreciate, rather than to use. St. Bernard said it very aptly: "Love seeks no cause beyond itself and no limit; it is its own fruit, its own enjoyment. I love because I love; I love in order that I may love . . ." (209).

Similar statements are available in abundance in the theological literature (103). The effort to differentiate godly love from human love was often based on the assumption that disinterested admiration and altruistic love could be only a superhuman ability and not a natural human one. Of course, we must contradict this; human beings at their best, fully grown, show *many* characteristics once thought, in an earlier era, to be supernatural prerogatives.

It is my opinion that these phenomena are best understood in the framework of various theoretical considerations presented in previous chapters. In the first place, let us consider the differentiation between deficiency motivation and growth motivation (295). I have suggested that self-actualizers can be defined as people who are no longer motivated by the needs for safety, belongingness, love, status, and self-respect because these needs *have already been satisfied.* Why then should a love-gratified person fall in love? Certainly not for the same reasons that motivate the love-deprived person, who falls in love because he needs and craves love, because he lacks it, and is impelled to make up this pathogenic deficiency (D-love).[6]

Self-actualizers have no serious deficiencies to make up and must now be looked upon as freed for growth, maturation, development, in a word, for the fulfillment and actualization of their highest individual and species nature. What such people do emanates from growth and expresses it without striving. They love because they are loving persons, in the same way that they are kind, honest, natural, i.e., because it is their nature to be so spontaneously, as a strong man is strong without willing to be, as a rose emits perfume, as a cat is graceful, or as a child is childish. Such epiphenomena are as little motivated as is physical growth or psychological maturation.

There is little of the trying, straining, or striving in the loving of

6 See (295, pp. 42–43) for the differentiation between B-love and D-love.

the self-actualizer that so dominates the loving of the average person. In philosophical language, it is an aspect of being as well as of becoming and can be called B-love, that is, love for the Being of the other.

DETACHMENT AND INDIVIDUALITY

A paradox seems to be created at first sight by the fact that self-actualizing people maintain a degree of individuality, of detachment, and autonomy that seems at first glance to be incompatible with the kind of identification and love that I have been describing above. But this is only an apparent paradox. As we have seen, the tendencies to detachment and to need identification and to profound interrelationships with another person can coexist in healthy people. The fact is that self-actualizing people are simultaneously the most individualistic and the most altruistic and social and loving of all human beings. The fact that we have in our culture put these qualities at opposite ends of a single continuum is apparently a mistake that must now be corrected. These qualities go together and the dichotomy is resolved in self-actualizing people.

We find in our subjects a healthy selfishness, a great self-respect, a disinclination to make sacrifices without good reason.

What we see in the love relationship is a fusion of great ability to love and at the same time great respect for the other and great respect for oneself. This shows itself in the fact that these people cannot be said in the ordinary sense of the word to *need* each other as do ordinary lovers. They can be extremely close together and yet go apart when necessary without collapsing. They do not cling to each other or have hooks or anchors of any kind. One has the definite feeling that they enjoy each other tremendously but would take philosophically a long separation or death, that is, would remain strong. Throughout the most intense and ecstatic love affairs, these people remain themselves and remain ultimately masters of themselves as well, living by their own standards even though enjoying each other intensely.

Obviously, this finding, if confirmed, will necessitate a revision or at least an extension in the definition of ideal or healthy love in our culture. We have customarily defined it in terms of a complete merging of egos and a loss of separateness, a giving up of individuality rather than a strengthening of it. While this is true, the fact appears to be at this moment that the individuality is strengthened, that the ego is in one sense merged with another, but yet in another sense remains separate and strong as always. The two tendencies, to transcend individuality and to sharpen and strengthen it, must be seen as partners and not as contradictories. Furthermore, it is implied that the best way to transcend the ego is via having a strong identity.

THE GREATER TASTE AND PERCEPTIVENESS OF HEALTHY LOVERS

One of the most striking superiorities reported of self-actualizing people is their exceptional perceptiveness. They can perceive truth and reality more efficiently than the average run of people, whether it is structured or unstructured, personal or nonpersonal.

This acuity manifests itself in the area of love relations primarily in an excellent taste (or perceptiveness) in sexual and love partners. The close friends, husbands, and wives of our subjects make a far finer group of human beings than random sampling would dictate.

This is not to say that *all* the observed marriages and choices of sexual partner were at the self-actualizing level. Several mistakes can be reported, and although they can be to some extent explained away, they testify to the fact that our subjects are not perfect or omniscient. They have their vanities and their own special weaknesses. For example, at least one man of those I studied married more out of pity than out of equalitarian love. One married a woman much younger than himself, in the face of the inevitable problems. A measured statement would then stress that their taste in mates, while far better than average, is by no means perfect.

But even this is enough to contradict the generally held belief that love is blind or, in the more sophisticated versions of this mistake, that the lover necessarily overestimates his partner. It is quite clear that, though this probably is true for average people, it need not be true for healthy individuals. Indeed, there are even some indications that the perceptions of healthy people are *more* efficient, more acute when in love than when not. Love may make it possible to see qualities in the loved person of which others are completely oblivious.[7] It is easy enough to make this mistake because healthy people can fall in love with people whom others would not love for very definite faults. However, this love

---

[7] Schwarz, Oswald, *The Psychology of Sex*, Penguin, 1951: "It cannot be emphasized strongly enough that this miraculous capacity which love bestows on the lovers consists in the power to discover in the object of love virtues which it actually possesses but which are invisible to the uninspired; they are not invented by the lover, who decorates the beloved with illusory values: love is no self-deception" (pp. 100–101). "No doubt there is a strong emotional element in it but essentially love is a cognitive act, indeed the only way to grasp the innermost core of personality" (p. 20).

is not blind to the faults; it simply overlooks these perceived faults, or else does not regard them as shortcomings. Thus physical imperfections, as well as economic, educational, and social shortcomings, are far less important to healthy people than are character defects. As a consequence, it is easily possible for self-actualizing people to fall deeply in love with homely partners. This is called blindness by others, but it might much better be called good taste or perceptiveness.

I have had the opportunity of watching the development of this good taste in several relatively healthy young college men and women. The more mature they become, the less attracted they were by such characteristics as handsome, good-looking, good dancer, nice breasts, physically strong, tall, handsome body, good necker, and the more they spoke of compatibility, goodness, decency, good companionship, considerateness. In a few cases, it could actually be seen that they fell in love with individuals with characteristics considered specifically distasteful a few years before, e.g., hair on the body, too fat, not smart enough. In one young man, I have seen the number of potential sweethearts grow fewer year by year until, from being attracted to practically any female, and with exclusions being solely on a physical basis (too fat, too tall), he could think of making love with only two girls from among all that he knew. These were now spoken of in characterological rather than in physical terms.

I think research will show that this is more characteristic of increasing health than simply of increasing age.

Two other common theories are contradicted by our data. One is that opposites attract, and the other is that like marries like (homogamy). The facts of the matter are that in healthy people homogamy is the rule with respect to such character traits as honesty, sincerity, kindliness, and courage. In the more external and superficial characteristics, e.g., income, class status, education, religion, national background, appearance, the extent of homogamy seems to be significantly less than in average people. Self-actualizing people are not threatened by differences nor by strangeness. Indeed, they are rather intrigued than otherwise. They need familiar accents, clothes, food, customs, and ceremonies much less than do average people.

As for opposites attracting, this is true for my subjects to the extent that I have seen honest admiration for skills and talents that they themselves do not possess. Such superiorities make a potential partner *more* rather than less attractive to my subjects, whether in man or in woman.

Finally, I wish to call attention to the fact that the last few pages supply us with another example of resolution or denial of an age-old dichotomy, i.e., between impulse and reason, between head and heart. The people with whom my subjects fall in love are soundly selected by *either* cognitive or conative criteria. That is, they are *intuitively, sexually, impulsively* attracted to people who are right for them by cold, intellectual, clinical calculation. Their appetites agree with their judgments, and are synergic rather than antagonistic.

This reminds us of Sorokin's efforts (434) to demonstrate that the true, the good, and the beautiful are positively interrelated. Our data seem to confirm Sorokin, but *only for healthy people*. With respect to neurotic people, we must remain circumspect on this question. See also (449).

13

COGNITION
OF THE INDIVIDUAL
AND OF THE GENERIC

INTRODUCTION

All experience, all behavior, all individuals can be reacted to by the psychologist in either of two ways: He may study an experience or a behavior in its own right, as unique and idiosyncratic, i.e., as different from any other experience or person or behavior in the whole world. Or he may respond to the experience not as unique, but as typical, i.e., as an example or representative of one or another class, category, or rubric of experience. This is to say that he does *not* in the strictest sense examine, attend to, perceive, or even experience the event; his reaction is rather like that of the file clerk who perceives only enough of the page to be able to file it under A or B, etc. For this activity the name "rubricizing" might be suggested. For those who dislike neologisms the term "abstracting $_{BW}$" might be preferable. The subscript letters B and W stand for Bergson (461)[1] and Whitehead (475), the two thinkers who

---

[1] "Even where it (reason) confesses that it does not know the object presented to it, it believes that its ignorance consists only in not knowing which one of its time-honored categories suits the new object. In what drawer, ready to open, shall we put it? In what garment, already cut out, shall we clothe it? Is it this, or that, or the other thing? And 'this,' and 'that,' and 'the other thing' are always something already conceived, already known. The idea that for a new object we might have to create a new concept, perhaps a new method of thinking, is deeply repugnant to us. The history of philosophy is there, however, and shows us the eternal conflict of systems, the impossi-

have contributed most to our understanding of dangerous abstracting.[2]

Such a distinction is a natural by-product of any serious concern with the basic theories that underlie psychology. In general, most American psychological activity proceeds as if reality were fixed and stable rather than changing and developing (a state rather than a process), and as if it were discrete and additive rather than interconnected and patterned. This blindness to the dynamic and holistic aspects of reality is responsible for many of the weaknesses and failures of academic psychology. Even so, it is not necessary to create a dichotomy of opposition, or to choose up sides to do battle. There are stability as well as change, similarities as well as differences, and holism-dynamicism can be as one-sided and doctrinaire as atomism-staticism. If we emphasize the one at the expense of the other in this chapter, it is because this is necessary to round out the picture and restore balance.

In this chapter we shall discuss some of the problems of cognition in the light of these theoretical considerations. The writer especially hopes to communicate some of his conviction that much of what passes for cognition is actually a substitute for it, a second-hand trick made necessary by the exigencies of living in a flux-and-process reality without being willing to acknowledge this fact. Because reality is dynamic, and because the average Western mind can cognize well only what is static,

bility of satisfactorily getting the real into the readymade garments of our ready-made concepts, the necessity of making to measure. But, rather than go to this extremity, our reason prefers to announce once for all, with a proud modesty, that it has to do only with the relative, and that the absolute is not in its province. This preliminary declaration enables it to apply its habitual method of thought without any scruple, and thus, under pretense that it does not touch the absolute, to make absolute judgments upon everything. Plato was the first to set up the theory that to know the real consists in finding its Idea, that is to say, in forcing it into a pre-existing frame already at our disposal—as if we implicitly possessed universal knowledge. But this belief is natural to the human intellect, always engaged as it is in determining under what former heading it shall catalogue any new object; and it may be said that, in a certain sense, we are all born Platonists." (46, pp. 55–56).

2 The interested reader may be referred here to the psychological writers who have made differentiations more or less similar to the one presented in this chapter. Kurt Lewin's (274) contrast between the Aristotelian and Galilean approaches to science, Gordon Allport's (6) plea for an "idiographic" as well as a "nomothetic" approach to the science of personality, and most recently, the general semanticists' stress on the differences rather than the likenesses between experiences (215), all overlap the thesis of this chapter and have been used freely in its preparation. We shall also mention below several of the interesting questions raised by Kurt Goldstein's abstract-concrete dichotomy (160). Also relevant is Itard's *Wild Boy of Aveyron*.

much of our attending, perceiving, learning, remembering, and thinking actually deals with staticized abstractions from reality or with theoretical constructions rather than with reality itself.

Lest this chapter be taken as a polemic against abstractions and concepts, let me make it clear that we cannot possibly live without concepts, generalizations, and abstractions. The point is that they must be experientially based rather than empty or helium-filled. They must be rooted in concrete reality and tied to it. They must have meaningful content rather than being mere words, mere labels, mere abstractions. This chapter deals with pathological abstracting, "reduction to the abstract," and with the dangers of abstracting.

RUBRICIZING IN ATTENTION

In so far as the concept of attending differs at all from the concept of perceiving, it is in a relatively greater stress on selective, preparatory, organizing, and mobilizing actions. These need not be pure and fresh responses that are determined entirely by the nature of the reality attended to. It is a commonplace that attending is determined as well by the nature of the individual organism, by the person's interests, motives, prejudices, past experiences, etc.

What is more to our point, however, is the fact that it is possible to discern in the attending responses the difference between fresh, idiosyncratic attending to the unique event, and stereotyped, rubricized recognition in the outside world of a set of categories that already exist in the mind of the attending person. That is, attending may be no more than a recognition or discovery in the world of what we ourselves have already put there—a sort of prejudging of experience before it happens. It may be, so to speak, a rationalization for the past, or an attempt to maintain the *status quo,* rather than a true recognition of change, novelty, and flux. This can be achieved by attending only to that which is already known, or by forcing the new into the shape of the familiar.

The advantages and disadvantages for the organism of this stereotyping of attention are equally obvious. It is evident that full attention is not needed for mere rubricizing or class placing of an experience, which in turn means saving of energy and effort. Rubricizing is definitely less fatiguing than whole-hearted attending. Furthermore, rubricizing does not call for concentration, it does not demand *all* the resources of the organism. Concentrated attention, which is necessary for the perceiving and understanding of an important or novel problem is, as we all know, extremely wearing, and is therefore relatively rare. Testimony for this conclusion is found in the common preference for streamlined reading, condensed novels, digest magazines, stereotyped movies, cliché-laden conversation, and in general, avoidance of real problems, or at least a strong preference for stereotyped pseudosolutions.

Rubricizing is a partial, token, or nominal response rather than a total one. This makes possible automaticity of behavior, i.e., doing several things at the same time, which in turn means making possible higher activities by permitting lower activities to be carried on in a reflexlike fashion. In a word, we do not have to notice or pay attention to the familiar elements of experience. Thus we need not perceive as individuals, waiters, doormen, elevator operators, street cleaners, men in any sort of uniform, etc.[3]

There is a paradox involved here, for it is simultaneously true that we tend (1) *not* to notice that which does not fit into the already constructed set of rubrics, i.e., the strange, and (2) it is the unusual, the unfamiliar, the dangerous, or threatening that are *most* attention compelling. An unfamiliar stimulus may be either dangerous (a noise in the dark) or not (new curtains on the windows). Fullest attention is given to the unfamiliar-dangerous; least attention is given to the familiar-safe; an intermediate amount is given to the unfamiliar-safe or else it is transformed into the familiar-safe, i.e., rubricized.[4]

There is an interesting speculation that proceeds from the curious tendency that the novel and strange either attract no attention at all or attract it overwhelmingly. It would seem that a large proportion of our (less healthy) population responds with attention only to threatening experiences. It is as if attention were to be regarded only as a response to danger and as a warning of the necessity for an emergency response. These people brush aside experiences that are nonthreatening and not dangerous, as therefore not being worthy of attention or any other response, cognitive or emotional. For them, life is either a meeting of dangers or relaxation between dangers.

But there are some people for whom this is not so. These are the people who will respond not only to dangerous situations. Probably feel-

---

[3] For more experimental examples, see Bartlett's excellent study (33).

[4] "Nothing is more congenial from babyhood to the end of life than to be able to assimilate the new to the old, to meet each threatening violator or burster of our well known series of concepts, as it comes in, see through its unwontedness and ticket it off as an old friend in disguise. . . . We feel neither curiosity nor wonder concerning things so far beyond us that we have no concepts to refer them to or standards by which to measure them." (211, Vol. II, p. 110.)

ing more secure and self-confident, they can afford the luxury of responding to, noticing, and even thrilling with experiences that are not dangerous but pleasantly exciting, etc. It has been pointed out that this positive response, whether mild or strong, whether a slight titillation or an overwhelming ecstasy, is, like the emergency response, a mobilization by the autonomic nervous system, involving the viscera and the rest of the organism. The main difference between these experiences is that one seems to be felt introspectively as pleasant, the other as unpleasant. With this observation, we see that the human being not only adapts to the world in a passive way but also enjoys it and even imposes himself upon it actively. The factor whose variation seems to account for most of these differences is what may loosely be called mental health. For relatively anxious people, attending is more exclusively an emergency mechanism, and the world tends somewhat to be divided simply into the dangerous and the safe.

The truest contrast with rubricizing attention is probably furnished by Freud's concept of "free floating attention."[5] Observe that Freud recommends passive rather than active attending on the grounds that active attention tends to be an imposition of a set of expectations upon the real world. Such expectations can drown out the voice of reality, if it be weak enough. Freud recommends that we be yielding, humble, passive, interested only in finding out what reality has to say to us, concerned only to allow the intrinsic structure of the material to determine that which we perceive. This all amounts to saying that we must treat

---

[5] "For as soon as attention is deliberately concentrated in a certain degree, one begins to select from the material before one; one point will be fixed in the mind with particular clearness and some other consequently disregarded, and in this selection one's expectations of one's inclinations will be followed. This is just what must not be done, however; if one's expectations are followed in this selection there is the danger of never finding anything but what is already known, and if one follows one's inclinations anything which is to be perceived will most certainly be falsified. It must not be forgotten that the meaning of the thing one hears is, at all events, for the most part, only recognizable later on.

"It will be seen, therefore, that the principle of evenly-distributed attention is the necessary corollary to the demand on the patient to communicate everything that occurs to him without criticism or selection. If the physician behaves otherwise he is throwing aside most of the advantage to be gained by the patients' obedience to the 'fundamental rule of psycho-analysis.' For the physicians the rule may be expressed thus: All conscious exertion is to be withheld from the capacity for attention, and one's 'unconscious memory' is to be given full play; or to express it in terms of technique, pure and simple: One has simply to listen and not to trouble to keep in mind anything in particular." (139, pp. 324–325.)

the experience as if it were unique and unlike anything else in the world and that our only effort must be to apprehend it in its own nature, rather than to try to see how it fits into our theories, our schemes, and our concepts. This is in the most complete sense a recommendation to problem centering and against ego centering. To the fullest extent possible the ego, its experiences, and its preconceptions, its hopes, and its fears are to be put aside if we are to apprehend the *per se* intrinsic nature of the experience before us.

It may be helpful to make the familiar (even stereotyped) contrast between the approach to an experience by the scientist and by the artist. If we may allow ourselves to think of such abstractions as the true scientist and the true artist, it is probably accurate to contrast their approach to any experience by saying that the scientist fundamentally seeks to classify the experience, to relate it to all other experiences, to put it into its place in a unitary philosophy of the world, to look for the respects in which this experience is similar to and different from all other experiences. The scientist tends to put a name or a label upon the experience, he tends to put it into its place, in a word, to classify it. The artist, that is, if he is what an artist should be, according to Bergson, Croce, et al., is most interested in the unique and idiosyncratic character of his experience. He must treat the experience as an individual. Each apple is unique, different, and so also each model, each tree, each head—no one is quite like any other. As a critic said of a certain artist, "He sees what others only look at." He is in no way interested in classifying the experience or placing it in any mental card catalog that he may have. It is his task to see the experience fresh, and then if he has the talent, to freeze the experience in some way so that perhaps less perceptive people may also see it fresh. Simmel said it nicely, "The scientist *sees* something because he *knows* something—the artist, however, *knows* something because he *sees* it."[6]

Perhaps another parallel may help to drive the difference home. These same people whom I have called true artists are different from ordinary people in at least one other characteristic. To put it as briefly as I can, they seem to be able to see each sunset, each flower, or each tree with the same delight and awe and full attention and strong emotional reaction as if this were the first sunset or flower or tree they had ever

[6] Like all stereotypes, these are dangerous. It is an implied point of this chapter that scientists would do well to become more intuitive, more artistic, and more appreciative and respectful of raw, direct experience. Likewise, the study and understanding of reality as seen by science should deepen the artist's reactions to the world, in addition to making them more valid and adult. The injunction to both artist and scientist is actually the same: "See reality whole."

seen. The average person will respond in a commonplace fashion to any miracle, however wonderful, if only he has seen the miracle happen five times before. An honest artist can retain the sense of the miraculous even after these thousand experiences. "He sees the world with the greater clarity of those for whom it is continuously new."

RUBRICIZING IN PERCEPTION

Stereotyping is a concept that can apply not only to the social psychology of prejudice, but also to the basic process of perceiving. Perceiving may be something other than the absorption or registration of the intrinsic nature of the real event. It is more often a classifying, ticketing, or labeling of the experience rather than an examination of it, and ought therefore to be called by a name other than true perceiving. What we do in stereotyped or rubricized perceiving is parallel to the use of clichés and hackneyed phrases in speaking.

For instance, it is possible in being introduced to another human being to react to him freshly, to try to understand or to perceive this individual as a unique individual, not quite like anybody else living. More often what we do, however, is to ticket or label or place the man. We place him in a category or a rubric, regard him not as a unique individual, but as an example of some concept or as a representation of a category. For instance, he is a Chinaman, rather than Lum Wang who has dreams and ambitions and fears that are quite different from those of his brother. Or he is labeled as a millionaire or a member of society or a dame or a child or a Jew or a something.[7] In other words, the person engaged in stereotyped perceiving ought to be compared, if we wish to be honest, to a file clerk rather than a camera. The file clerk has a drawer full of folders, and her task is to put every letter on the desk into its appropriate folder under the A's or B's or whatever.

Among the many examples of rubricizing in perceiving, we may cite the tendency to perceive:

1. The familiar and hackneyed rather than the unfamiliar and fresh
2. The schematized and abstract rather than the actual

[7] "Such (cheap) fiction represents verbal rigidity in all its forms: content, formal, and evaluational. The plots, characters, action, situations, and 'morals' are relatively standardized. In large measure too, the stories involve standardized words and phrases; it is on this basis, to a considerable extent, that the characters, who are not individuals but *types,* are recognizable as the gun moll, the detective, the poor working girl, the boss's son, etc." (215, p. 259).

The general semanticist would also point out that once an individual has been placed in a category, others tend to react to the category rather than to the individual.

3. The organized, structured, the univalent rather than the chaotic, unorganized, and ambiguous
4. The named or namable rather than the unnamed and unnamable
5. The meaningful rather than the meaningless
6. The conventional rather than the unconventional
7. The expected rather than the unexpected

Furthermore, where the event is unfamiliar, concrete, ambiguous, unnamed, meaningless, unconventional, or unexpected, we show a strong tendency to twist or force or shape the event into a form that is more familiar, more abstract, more organized, etc. We tend to perceive events more easily as representatives of categories than in their own right, as unique and idiosyncratic.

Numerous illustrations of each of these tendencies can be found in the Rorschach test, the literatures of Gestalt psychology, of projective testing, and of the theory of art. Hayakawa (99, p. 103), in this last area, cites the example of an art teacher who "is in the habit of telling his pupils that they are unable to draw any individual arm because they think of it as *an* arm; and because they think of it as an arm they think they know what it ought to be." Schachtel's book is full of fascinating examples (410).

It is obvious that one needs to know less about a stimulus object for the purpose of filing it in an already constructed system of categories than for the purpose of understanding and appreciating it. True perception, which would encompass the object as unique, play over all of it, soak it in, and understand it, would obviously take infinitely more time than the fraction of a second that is all that is necessary for labeling and cataloging.

It is also probable that rubricizing is far less efficient than the fresh perception, mostly because of this already mentioned characteristic of being possible in a fraction of a second. Only the most outstanding characteristics can then be used to determine the reaction, and these can very easily give a false lead. Rubricizing perception then is an invitation to mistakes.

These mistakes become doubly important because rubricizing perception also makes it less probable that any original mistake will be corrected. One who has already been put into a rubric tends very strongly to be kept there, because any behavior that contradicts the stereotype of the rubric can be regarded simply as an exception that need not be taken seriously. For instance, if we have become convinced for some reason that a person is dishonest, and if then, in one particular card game, we try to catch him, only to fail, we ordinarily continue to call him a thief, as-suming that he was honest for *ad hoc* reasons, perhaps out of fear of detection or out of laziness or the like. If we are profoundly enough con-vinced of his dishonesty, it may make no difference if we *never* catch him in a dishonest act. He might then be regarded simply as a thief who happens to be afraid to be dishonest with us. Or contradictory behavior may be regarded as interesting, in the sense of being not characteristic of the essence of the person but rather only superficially put on. If we are perfectly convinced that Chinese are inscrutable, then to find one who laughs does not change our stereotype of the Chinese, but we are rather apt to regard him simply as a queer or exceptional or peculiar Chinese. Indeed it may be that the concept of stereotyping or rubricizing may furnish us with a good part of the answer to the age-old problem of how people can continually believe in falsehood even when truth stares them in the face year after year. I know it is customary to consider this imperviousness to evidence as entirely explained by repression, or in general, motivational forces. There is no doubt that this statement is also true. The question is whether it is the whole truth, and in and of itself, a sufficient explanation. Our discussion indicates that there are also other reasons for being blind to evidence.

We can get some inkling of the violence that can be done to an object if we ourselves are on the receiving end of a stereotyping attitude. Of course, any Negro or any Jew could attest to this but it is also true at times of everyone else. See, for instance, such expressions as "Oh, it's just the waiter," or "It is another of those Joneses," etc. We ordinarily feel insulted and unappreciated if we are thus casually put into a parcel with a lot of other people from whom we feel different in many ways. But it is impossible to improve on William James's statement on the subject: "The first thing the intellect does with an object is to class it along with something else. But any object that is infinitely important to us and awakens our devotion feels to us also as if it must be *sui generis* and unique. Probably a crab would be filled with a sense of personal outrage if it could hear us class it without ado or apology as a crustacean, and thus dispose of it. 'I am no such thing,' it would say; 'I am *myself, myself alone*' " (212, p. 10).

RUBRICIZING IN LEARNING

A habit is an attempt to solve a present problem by using a previously successful solution. This implies that there must be (1) a placing of the present problem in a certain category of problems, and (2) a selection of the most efficient problem solution for this particular category of problems. Classification, i.e., rubricization, is therefore inevitably involved.

The phenomenon of habit illustrates best a point that is also true of rubricized attention, perceiving, thinking, expression, etc., namely that all rubricizing is, in effect, an attempt to "freeze the world."[8] In actuality, the world is a perpetual flux and all things are in process. In theory, nothing in the world is static (even though for *practical* purposes, many things are). If we are to take theory quite seriously, then each experience, each event, each behavior is in some way or other (whether important or unimportant) different from every other experience, behavior, etc. that has occurred in the world before or will ever occur again.[9]

It would seem reasonable then, as Whitehead has repeatedly pointed out, to base our theories and philosophies of science and common sense squarely on this basic and unavoidable fact. The truth is that most of us do not do this. Even though our most sophisticated scientists and philosophers have long ago discarded the old concepts of empty space and enduring things pushed around aimlessly in it, these verbally discarded concepts still live on as a basis for all our less intellectual reactions. Though

[8] "Intellect therefore instinctively selects in a given situation whatever is like something already known; it seeks this out, in order that it may apply its principle that 'like produces like.' In just this does the prevision of the future by common sense consist. Science carries this faculty to the highest possible degree of exactitude and precision, but does not alter its essential character. Like ordinary knowledge, science is concerned only with the aspect of *repetition*. Though the whole be original, science will always manage to analyze it into elements or aspects that are approximately a reproduction of the past. Science can work only on what is supposed to repeat itself. . . ." (46, pp. 34–35.) It should be mentioned again (see Chapters 1 and 2 above and also Appendix B) that there is now available the beginnings of another philosophy of science, another conception of knowledge and of cognizing, which includes the holistic (as well as the atomistic), the unique (as well as the repetitive), the human and personal (as well as the mechanical), the changing (as well as the stable), the transcendent (as well as the positivistic). See (292, 376) and the bibliographical references therein.

[9] "No two things are alike, and no one thing stays the same. If you are clearly aware of this, it is quite all right to act as though some things were alike, and to act as though some things stayed the same—to act according to habit. It is all right, because a difference to be a difference, must make a difference, and some differences don't, sometimes. So long as you realize that there always are differences nonetheless, and that you have to judge whether they do make any difference, you can be trusted with a habit, because you will know when to set it aside. No habit is foolproof. Habits are useful to people who do not depend on them or insist on following them, regardless of circumstances; for less judicious individuals, habits tend to make for inefficiency, stupidity, and danger." (215, p. 199.)

the world of change and growth is and must be accepted, this is rarely done emotionally and with enthusiasm. We are still deeply Newtonian (287).

All reactions that may be labeled rubricized may then be redefined as "efforts to freeze or staticize or stop the motion of a moving, changing process world in order to be able to handle it," for it is as if we could handle this world only when it is not in motion. An example of this tendency is the ingenious trick that static-atomistic mathematicians have invented in order to treat motion and change in a motionless way, i.e., the calculus. For the purposes of this chapter, psychological examples are more pertinent, however, and it is necessary to pound home the thesis that habits, and indeed all reproductive learning, are examples of this tendency by statically minded people to freeze a process world into temporary immobility, since they cannot manage or cope with a world in a flux.

Habits are then conservative mechanisms, as James long ago pointed out (211). Why is this so? For one thing, because any learned reaction, merely by existing, blocks the formation of other learned reactions to the same problem. But there is another reason, just as important, but ordinarily neglected by the learning theorists, namely, that learning is not only of muscular responses but of affective preferences as well. Not only do we learn to speak English but we learn to like and prefer it (309).[10] Learning is not then a completely neutral process. We cannot say, "If this reaction is a mistake, it is easy enough to unlearn it or replace it with the right reaction," for by learning, we have, to some degree, committed ourselves and our loyalties. Thus if it is our desire to learn to speak French well, it may be better not to learn it at all if the only available teacher has a bad accent; it could be more efficient to wait until a

---

10 *Anthologistics*

> "Since one anthologist put in his book
> Sweet things by Morse, Bone, Potter, Bliss and Brook,
> All subsequent anthologists, of course,
> Have quoted Bliss, Brook, Potter, Bone and Morse.
> For, should some rash anthologist make free
> To print selections, say, from you and me,
> Omitting with a judgment all his own
> The classic Brook, Morse, Potter, Bliss and Bone,
> Contemptuous reviewers, passing by
> Our verses, would unanimously cry,
> 'What manner of anthology is this
> That leaves out Bone, Brook, Potter, Morse and Bliss!' "
> —Arthur Guiterman (167)

good teacher is available. For this same reason we must disagree with those in science who are very airy in their attitude toward hypotheses and theories. "Even a false theory is better than none," they say. The true situation is not as simple as this, if the foregoing considerations have any validity. As a Spanish proverb says, "Habits are at first cobwebs, then cables."

These criticisms by no means apply to all learning; they apply only to atomistic and reproductive learning, i.e., recognition and recall of isolated *ad hoc* reactions. Many psychologists write as if this were the only way in which the past could have an influence upon the present, or in which the lessons of past experience may profitably be used to solve present problems. This is a naïve assumption, for much of what is actually learned in the world, i.e., the most important influences of the past, is neither atomistic nor reproductive. The most important influence of the past, the most influential type of learning, is what we may call character or intrinsic learning (311a), i.e., all the effects on character of all our experiences. Thus, experiences are not acquired by the organism one by one like so many coins; if they have any deep effect at all, they change the whole person. Thus the influence of some tragic experience would be to change him from an immature person to a more mature adult, wiser, more tolerant, more humble, better able to solve *any* of the problems of adult life. The contrasting theory would be that he had changed in no way except by the *ad hoc* acquisition of a technique of managing or solving such and such a particular type of problem, e.g., the death of his mother. Such an example is far more important, far more useful, far more paradigmatic than the usual examples of blind association of one nonsense syllable with another, which experiments, in my opinion, have to do with nothing in the world except other nonsense syllables.[11]

If the world is in process, every moment is a new and unique one.

---

[11] "Memory, as we have tried to prove, is not a faculty of putting away recollections in a drawer, or of inscribing them in a register. There is no register, no drawer; there is not even, properly speaking, a faculty, for a faculty works intermittently, when it will or when it can, whilst the piling up of the past upon the past goes without relaxation. . . .

"But, even though we may have no distinct idea of it, we feel vaguely that our past remains present to us. What are we, in fact, what is our *character*, if not the condensation of the history that we have lived from our birth—nay, even before our birth, since we bring with us prenatal dispositions? Doubtless we think with only a small part of our past, but it is with our entire past, including the original bent of our soul, that we desire, will and act. Our past, then, as a whole, is made manifest to us in its impulse; it is felt in the form of idea." (46, pp. 7–8.)

Theoretically speaking, *all* problems must be novel. The typical problem, according to process theory, is the problem that has never been faced before and that is, in essential ways, unlike any other problem. That problem that very much resembles past problems is then, according to this theory, to be understood as a special case rather than a paradigmatic one. If this is so, recourse to the past for *ad hoc* solutions is as likely to be dangerous as helpful. My belief is that actual observation will show this to be practically as well as theoretically true. In any case, nobody, whatever his theoretical bias, will argue about the fact that at least *some* of the problems of life are novel and must therefore have novel solutions.[12]

From the biological point of view, habits play a double role in adaptation because they are simultaneously necessary and dangerous. They necessarily imply something which is not true, i.e., a constant, unchanging, static world, and yet are commonly regarded as one of the human being's most efficient tools of adaptation, which certainly implies a changing, dynamic world. A habit is an already formed reaction to a situation or answer to a problem. Because it is already formed, it develops a certain inertia and resistance to change.[13] But when a situation changes, our reaction to it should also change or be ready to change quickly. Therefore, the presence of a habit may be worse than no reaction at all, since the habit guarantees resistance to and delay in building up the newly necessary reaction to the new situation. In a similar connection, Bartlett speaks of the "challenge of the external environment which partially changes and in part persists, so that it demands a variable adjustment yet never permits an entirely new start." (33, p. 224).

It may help to make this clearer if we describe this paradox from another point of view. We may then say that habits are built up to save time, effort, and thought in dealing with recurrent situations. If a problem comes up again and again in similar form, we certainly can save a

12 "Precisely because it is always trying to reconstitute, and to reconstitute with what is given, the intellect lets what is *new* in each moment of a history escape. It does not admit the unforeseeable. It rejects all creation. That definite antecedents bring forth a definite consequent, calculable as a function of them, is what satisfies our intellect. That a definite end calls forth definite means to attain it, is what we also understand. In both cases we have to do with the known, which is combined with the known, in short, with the old which is repeated." (46, p. 180.)

13 "The capacity to be influenced by past reactions, often—but very likely somewhat inaccurately—called 'modification by experience,' on the whole conflicts with the demand, issued by a diverse, and constantly changing environment, for adaptability, fluidity, and variety of response. Its general effect is twofold: to lead to stereotyped behavior and to produce relatively fixed serial reactions." (33, p. 218)

good deal of thought by having available some habitual answer that can automatically be trotted out to deal with this recurrent problem whenever it arises. Thus a habit is a response to a repetitive, unchanging, familiar problem. This is why it is possible to say that a habit is an as-if reaction—"as if the world were static, unchanging, and constant." This interpretation is borne out, of course, by the uniform stress upon repetition by those psychologists who are impressed with the primary importance of habit as an adjustive mechanism.

A good deal of the time this is just as it should be, for there is no doubt that many of our problems are actually repetitive, familiar, and relatively unchanging. The man who is engaged in what are called the higher activities, thinking, inventing, creating, finds that these activities demand, as a prerequisite, elaborate sets of innumerable habits that automatically solve the petty problems of everyday life, so that the creator is free to give his energy to the so-called higher problems. But a contradiction is involved—even a paradox. In actual fact, the world is not static, familiar, repetitive, and unchanging. Instead, it is constantly in flux, ever new, always developing into something else, shifting, and changing. We need not argue as to whether this is a fair characterization of every aspect of the world; we can avoid unnecessary metaphysical debate by assuming for the sake of argument that some aspects of the world are constant, while some are not. If this is granted, then it must also be granted that however useful habits may be for the constant aspects of the world, they are positively a hindrance and an impediment when the organism has to deal with the changing, fluctuating aspects of the world with problems which are unique, novel, never before met with.[14]

---

[14] "The picture is one of human beings confronted by a world in which they can live and be masters only as they learn to match its infinite diversity by increasing delicacy of response, and as they discover ways to escape from the complete sway of immediate circumstances." (46, p. 301).

"Our freedom, in the very moments by which it is affirmed, creates the growing habits that will stifle it if it fails to renew itself by a constant effort: it is dogged by automatism. The most living thought becomes frigid in the formula that expresses it. The word turns against the idea. The letter kills the spirit." (46, p. 141.)

"Habit can be an accessory to progress, but it is not the chief means to it. It should be regulated from that point of view. It is an accessory to progress insofar as it saves time and conserves energy—but there is no progress, even so, unless the time so saved and the energy so conserved are used in the intelligent modification of other behavior. The more habitual shaving becomes for you, for example, the more free you are, while shaving, to consider problems that are of some importance to you. There is much advantage in this—unless, in considering these problems, you always arrive at the same conclusions." (215, p. 198.)

Here then we have the paradox. Habits are simultaneously necessary and dangerous, useful and harmful. They undoubtedly save us time, effort, and thought, but at a big expense. They are a prime weapon of adaptation and yet they hinder adaptation. They are problem solutions and yet in the long run they are the antonyms of fresh, unrubricized thinking, that is to say, of solutions to new problems. Though useful in adjusting ourselves to the world, they often hinder us in our inventiveness and creativeness, which is to say they tend to prevent our adjusting the world to ourselves. Finally, they tend to *replace,* in a lazy way, true and fresh attending, perceiving, learning, and thinking.[15]

It might be added finally that reproductive memory is much more difficult *unless* a set of rubrics (frame of reference) is available. The interested reader is referred to Bartlett's excellent book (33) for experimental support for this conclusion. Schachtel (410) is brilliant on the subject. We might add one other example here that fortunately can also be easily checked. The writer found during a summer's field work with an Indian tribe that he could not remember the Indian songs that he liked very much, however often he tried. It was possible to sing the song along with the Indian singer perhaps a dozen times, and then only five minutes later not be able to repeat it alone. For any person with a good musical memory this can be a baffling experience, understandable only when it is realized that Indian music is so different in basic organization and quality that there is no frame of reference against which to remember it. A simpler example that everyone will have met with is the difference in difficulty for an English-speaking person in learning, let us say, Spanish on the one hand and, on the other hand, some Slavic language like Russian. Most words in Spanish or French or German have cognates that the English-speaking person can use as a frame of reference. But since these cognates are almost entirely missing in Russian, learning the language becomes extraordinarily difficult.

---

15 "Thus the four factors mentioned—natural laziness or simian reluctance, fondness of assimilating the new to the old, tradition and success—have contributed to keep our thought undeveloped. The periods of really intense intellectual ferment and tradition-shattering thinking have been extraordinarily few within the historical period. The thinking of Plato and Aristotle sufficed from Greek times to the Renaissance, and the thinking of Galileo and Descartes at the Renaissance has furnished natural science with a stock of fundamental notions that have needed little revision until recent times. Thus during most of the intervening times thinking has chiefly been a process of working out. . . ."

RUBRICIZING IN THINKING

In this area rubricizing consists of: (1) having only stereotyped problems, or in failing to perceive new ones, or in reshaping them, in a Procrustean fashion, so that they may be classified as familiar rather than novel, and/or (2) using only stereotyped and rote habits and techniques for solving these problems, and/or (3) having, in advance of all life's problems, sets of ready-made, cut and dried solutions and answers. These three tendencies add up to an almost complete guarantee against creativeness or inventiveness.[16]

But they impel us so strongly that so profound a psychologist as Bergson was impelled mistakenly to define intellect as though it could do nothing more than rubricize, e.g., "Intellect (is) . . . the faculty of connecting the same with the same, of perceiving and also of producing repetition." (46, p. 59). "Explaining it always consists in resolving it, it the unforeseeable and new, into elements of old or known, arranged in a different order. The intellect can no more admit complete novelty than real becoming; that is to say, here again it lets an essential aspect of life escape . . ." (46, p. 181). ". . . we treat the living like the lifeless and think all reality however fluid, under the form of the sharply defined solid. We are at ease only in the discontinuous, in the immobile, in the dead. *The intellect is characterized by a natural inability to comprehend life*" (46, p. 182). But Bergson's own intellect refuted this over-generalization.

STEREOTYPED PROBLEMS

To start with, the first effort of that person who tends strongly to rubricize will ordinarily be to avoid or overlook problems of any kind. In most extreme form this is exemplified by those compulsive-obsessive patients who regulate and order every corner of their lives because they dare not face anything unexpected. Such people are severely threatened by any

---

[16] ". . . clarity and orderliness enable the possessor to deal with foreseen situations. They are necessary foundations for the maintenance of existing social situations. And yet they are not enough. Transcendence of mere clarity and order is necessary for dealing with the unforeseen, for progress, for excitement. Life degenerates when enclosed within the shackles of mere conformation. A power of incorporating vague and disorderly elements of experience is essential for the advance into novelty." (475, p. 108.)

"The essence of life is to be found in the frustrations of established order. The Universe refuses the deadening influence of complete conformity. And yet in its refusal, it passes toward novel order as a primary requisite for important experience. We have to explain the aim at forms of order, and the aim at novelty of order, and the measure of success, and the measure of failure." (475, p. 119.)

problem that demands more than a ready-made answer, i.e., that demands self-confidence, courage, security.

If the problem *must* be perceived, the first effort is to place the problem and to see it as a representative of a familiar category (since the familiar does not produce anxiety). The attempt is to discover, "Into which class of previously experienced problems can this particular one be placed?" or "Into which category of problems does this fit—or can it be squeezed?" Such a placing reaction is possible, of course, only on the basis of perceived resemblances. I do not wish to go into the difficult problem of similarity; it is sufficient to point out that this perception of resemblances need not be a humble, passive registration of the intrinsic nature of the realities perceived. This is proved by the fact that various individuals, classifying in terms of idiosyncratic sets of rubrics, can nevertheless *all* be successful in rubricizing the experience. Such people do not like to be at a loss and will classify all experiences that cannot be overlooked, even if they find it necessary to cut, squeeze, or distort the experience.

One of the best pieces I know on this subject is that of Crookshank (97) on the problems involved in medical diagnosis. Psychologists will be more familiar with the strictly taxonomical attitude of many psychiatrists toward their patients.

STEREOTYPED TECHNIQUES

Generally, one of the main advantages of rubricizing is that along with successful placing of the problem goes an automatically available set of techniques for handling this problem. This is not the only reason for rubricizing. That the tendency to place a problem is very deeply motivated is seen, e.g., in the physician who feels more easy in the presence of a known, though incurable, disease than in the presence of a completely mysterious set of symptoms.

If one has handled this same problem many times before, the proper machinery will be well oiled and ready to use. Of course, this means a strong tendency to do things as they have been done before, and as we have seen, habitual solutions carry disadvantages as well as advantages. As advantages we may cite again ease of execution, energy saving, automaticity, affective preference, anxiety saving, etc. The main disadvantages are loss of flexibility, adaptability, and creative inventiveness, i.e., the usual consequences of assuming that this dynamic world can be treated as if it were static.

An excellent example of the effects of stereotyped thinking techniques is furnished by Luchins' interesting experiments on *Einstellung* (279).

STEREOTYPED CONCLUSIONS

Probably the best-known example of this process is rationalization. This and similar processes may be defined for our purposes as having a ready-made idea or foregone conclusion and then devoting a good deal of intellectual activity to supporting this conclusion or finding evidence for it. ("I don't like that fellow and I'm going to find a good reason why.") This is the kind of activity that has only a thinking-like façade. It is not thinking in the best sense because it comes to its conclusions irrespective of the nature of the problem. The knitting of the brow, the heated discussions, the straining after evidence are all so many smoke screens; the conclusion was fated before the thinking ever began. Often enough even the façade is lacking; people may simply *believe* without even making the gesture of seeming to think. This takes even less effort than rationalizing.

Every psychologist knows that it is possible for a person to live by a set of ready-made ideas that were acquired complete and entire during the first decade of life and that have never and shall never be changed in the slightest degree. It is true that such a man may have a high IQ. He may therefore be able to spend a good deal of his time in intellectual activity, selecting out from the world whatever bits of evidence support his ready-made ideas. We cannot deny that this sort of activity may occasionally be of some use to the world, and yet it seems clearly desirable for the psychologist to make some sort of verbal differentiation between productive, creative thinking on the one hand and even the most skillful rationalizing on the other. The occasional advantages of rationalizing are a small matter when weighed against the more impressive phenomena of blindness to the real world, imperviousness to new evidence, distortion in perceiving and remembering, the loss of modifiability and adaptability to a changing world, and other indications that the mind has ceased to develop.

But rationalization need not be our only example. It is also rubricizing when the problem is used as a stimulus to associations from among which are chosen those which best fit the particular occasion.

It would seem that rubricized thinking has a special affinity for and relationship to reproductive learning. The three types of processes that we have listed could easily be dealt with as special forms of habit activity. There is clearly involved a special reference to the past. Problem solving becomes little more than a technique of classifying and solving any new problem in the light of past experience. Thinking of this type then often amounts to no more than a shuffling about and rearrangement of previously acquired habits and memories of the reproductive type.

The contrast with more holistic-dynamic thinking can be seen more clearly when we understand that this latter type of thinking is more clearly allied to the perceptual processes than to the memory processes (225, 465). The main effort in holistic thinking is perceiving as clearly as possible the intrinsic nature of the problem with which one is confronted, as Wertheimer stresses in his recent book (465) and which Katona (225) phrases as "the effort to perceive *in* a problem its solution."[17] It is examined carefully in its own right and in its own style almost as if no other such problem had been met before. The effort is to ferret out its own intrinsic, *per se* nature, whereas in associative thinking it is rather to see how this problem relates to or resembles other problems previously experienced.[18]

This is not to imply that past experience is not used in holistic thinking. Of course it is. The point is that it is used in a different way, as has been described in the discussion above of so-called intrinsic learning, or learning to become the Person you are potentially (311a).

That associative thinking occurs there is no doubt. The debate is rather over which kind of thinking shall be used as the centering point, as the paradigm, as the ideal model. The contention of the holistic-dynamic theorists is that thinking activity, if it carries any meaning at all,

[17] It is interesting to observe that the thinking of the Gestalt psychologists parallels in this respect that of various modern philosophers who are often apt to think of a problem solution as identical or tautologous with the problem itself, e.g., "When there is a full understanding, any particular item belongs to what is already clear. Thus it is merely a repetition of the known. In that sense, there is tautology" (475, p. 71). I believe that the logical positivists also maintain such a position, or at least did.

[18] In a practical sense, in terms of behavior, this principle can be reduced to a sort of motto: 'I don't know—let's see.' That is to say, whenever one is confronted by a new situation one does not unhesitatingly respond to it in some way definitely decided upon in advance. It is rather as though one were to say, 'I don't know—let's see,' with a sensitiveness to any respects in which *this* situation might be different from previous ones, and with a readiness to make appropriate reactions accordingly.

"It is to be clearly recognized that such an approach to new situations does not involve indecisiveness. It does not represent failure to 'make up one's mind.' Rather it represents a method for making up one's mind without going off half-cocked. It provides a measure of insurance against the blunders we make in judging people by first impressions, in applying to individual woman drivers our attitude toward *the* woman driver, in condemning a person—or in committing ourselves to his support— on the basis of hearsay or on the basis of very brief acquaintance. We make such blunders by reacting to the individual, different and variable, but as though he were merely a member of a type and the same as all other members of that type—and then we react inappropriately because we are so very sure of our opinion of the type." (212, pp. 187–188.)

by definition has the meaning of creativeness, uniqueness, ingenuity, and inventiveness. Thinking is the technique whereby mankind creates something new, which in turn implies that thinking must be revolutionary in the sense of occasionally conflicting with what has already been concluded. If it conflicts with an intellectual *status quo* it is then the *opposite* of habit, or memory, or what we have already learned, for the simple reason that it must *by definition* contradict what we have already learned. If our past learning and our habits work well, we can respond automatically, habitually, and familiarly. That is to say, we do not have to think. From this point of view, thinking is seen as the opposite of learning, rather than as a type of learning. If we were permitted a slight exaggeration, thinking might almost be defined as the ability to *break* our habits and to *disregard* our past experiences.

Another dynamic aspect is involved in the kind of truly creative thinking exemplified by the great achievements of human history. This is its characteristic boldness, daring, and courage. If these words are not *quite* apropos in this connection, they come close enough, as we can see if we think of the contrast between a timid child and a brave child. The timid child must cling closer to his mother who represents safety, familiarity, and protection; the holder child is freer to venture forth and can go farther from home base. The thinking process that parallels the timid clinging to the mother is the equally timid clinging to habit. The bold thinker—which is almost a redundancy, like saying a thinking thinker— must be able to break the *Einstellung,* to be able to be free of the past, of habit, expectation, learning, custom, and convention, and to be free of anxiety whenever venturing out of the safe and familiar harbor.

Another type of stereotyped conclusion is furnished by those instances in which individuals' opinions are formed by imitation and/or prestige suggestion. These are generally considered to be underlying and basic trends in healthy human nature. It would probably be more accurate to consider them examples of mild psychopathology, or at least something very close to it. When important enough problems are involved, they are primarily responses to an unstructured situation, which has no fixed frame of reference, by overanxious, overconventionalized, or overlazy people (people without an opinion of their own, people who do not know what their opinion is, people who mistrust their own opinions).[19]

It would seem that a fairly large proportion of the conclusions and

---

[19] An excellent discussion of the dynamics of the situation is found in Fromm (145). This same theme is also discussed in novel form in *The Fountainhead,* by Ayn Rand (388). In this connection, *1066 and All That* (490) is both funny and instructive.

problem solutions that we come to in the most basic areas of life seem to be of this sort, in which, while we think, we look out of the corner of our eyes to see what conclusion the other people are coming to so that we can also come to it. Obviously such conclusions are not thoughts in the truest sense of the word, i.e., dictated by the nature of the problem, but rather stereotyped conclusions picked up whole from other people whom we trust more than ourselves.

As might be expected, such a position has certain implications for helping us to understand why conventional education in this country falls so far short of its goals. We shall stress only one point here, namely, that education makes little effort to teach the individual to examine reality directly and freshly. Rather it gives him a complete set of prefabricated spectacles with which to look at the world in every aspect, e.g., what to believe, what to like, what to approve of, what to feel guilty about. Rarely is each person's individuality made much of, rarely is he encouraged to be bold enough to see reality in his own style, or to be iconoclastic or different. Proof for the contention of stereotyping in higher education can be obtained in practically any college catalog, in which all of shifting, ineffable, and mysterious reality is neatly divided into three credit slices which, by some miraculous coincidence, are exactly fifteen weeks long, and which fall apart neatly, as a tangerine does, into completely independent and mutually exclusive departments.[20] If ever there was a perfect example of a set of rubrics imposed *upon* reality rather than *by* reality, this is it. (There is beginning to be available what might be called a "parallel educational establishment" or "humanistic education," which attempts to remedy these defects of the conventional educational establishment. Names, addresses, etc., may be found in "The Eupsychian Network" in (295, pp. 237–240).

This is all obvious enough, but what is less obvious is what to do about it. One idea strongly suggested by an examination of rubricized thinking is a decreased absorption with rubrics and an increased concern with fresh experiences, with concrete and particular realities. On this point we cannot improve on Whitehead's statements.

---

[20] "Science is taught as something fixed and stable, not as a system of knowledge whose life and value depends on its mobility and readiness to revise at a moment's notice its most cherished constructions when new facts or a new point of view suggests the possibility of alternative ones".

> "I am Master of this College;
> And what I know not,
> Is not knowledge." (475, p. 59.)

My own criticism of our traditional educational methods is that they are far too much occupied with intellectual analysis, and with the acquirement of formularized information. What I mean is, that we neglect to strengthen habits of concrete appreciation of the individual facts in their full interplay of emergent values, and that we merely emphasize abstract formulations which ignore this aspect of the interplay of diverse values.

At present our education combines a thorough study of a few abstractions, with a slighter study of a large number of abstractions. We are too exclusively bookish in our scholastic routine. The general training should aim at eliciting our concrete apprehensions, and should satisfy the itch of youth to be doing something. There should be some analysis even here, but only just enough to illustrate the ways of thinking in diverse spheres. In the Garden of Eden, Adam saw the animals before he named them: in the traditional system, children named the animals before they saw them.

This professional training can only touch one side of education. Its centre of gravity lies in the intellect, and its chief tool is the printed book. The centre of gravity of the other side of training should lie in intuition without an analytical divorce from the total environment. Its object is immediate apprehension with the minimum of eviscerating analysis. The type of generality, which above all is wanted, is the appreciation of variety of value. (475, pp. 284–286.)

STEREOTYPING AND NONHOLISTIC THEORIZING

It is by now generally accepted that theory building customarily implies selection and rejection, which in turn means that a theory must be expected to make some aspects of the world *more* clear and other aspects *less* clear. One characteristic of most nonholistic theories is that they are sets of rubrics or classes. But no one has ever devised a set of rubrics into which *all* phenomena fit easily; there are always some left out, some that fall in between the rubrics, and some that seem to belong simultaneously in various rubrics.

Furthermore, this kind of theory is almost always abstractive, that is to say, it emphasizes certain qualities of phenomena as more important than others or at least more worthy of notice. Thus any such theory, or any other abstraction for that matter, is apt to derogate or neglect or overlook some of the qualities of phenomena, i.e., to omit part of the truth. Because of these principles of rejection and selection, any theory must be expected to give no more than a partial, pragmatically biased view of the world. It is probably true, also, that all theories combined never give a full view of phenomena and of the world. The full subjective richness of an experience seems to come more often to artistically and emotionally sensitive people than to theorizers and intellectuals. It may even be that the so-called mystic experience is the perfect and extreme expression of this sort of full appreciation of all the characteristics of the particular phenomenon.

These considerations should by contrast show up another characteristic of particularized, individual experience, namely, its nonabstractive character. This is not the same as saying it is concrete in Goldstein's sense. The brain-injured patient, when he behaves concretely, is actually *not* seeing all the sensuous characteristics of an object or experience. He sees and is able to see only one such characteristic, that determined by the particular context, e.g., a bottle of wine is *just* that and nothing else, not for instance, a weapon, or a decoration, or a paperweight, or a fire extinguisher. If we define abstracting as selective attention, for any of various reasons, to some rather than others of the numberless characteristics of an event, Goldstein's patients might actually be said to be abstracting.

There is then a certain contrast between classifying experiences and appreciating them, between using them and enjoying them, between cognizing them in one way and cognizing them in another way. All writers on the mystic and religious experiences have emphasized this as few technical psychologists have. For instance, Aldous Huxley says: "As the individual grows up, his knowledge becomes more conceptual and systematic in form, and its factual, utilitarian content is enormously increased. But these gains are offset by a certain deterioration in the quality of immediate apprehension, a blunting and a loss of intuitive power" (209, p. vii).[21]

However, since appreciation is certainly not our only relationship with nature, being in fact the least pressing biologically of all such relationships, we must not maneuver ourselves into the foolish position of stigmatizing theories and abstractions because of their dangers. Their advantages are great and obvious, especially from the point of view of communication and of practical manipulation of the world. If it were our function to make recommendations, we should probably phrase it in some such fashion as this: The ordinary cognitive processes of the working intellectual, the scientist, etc. can be made even more powerful than they are if it be remembered that these processes are not the only possible weapons in the armory of the researchers. There are others as well. If they have ordinarily been relegated to the poet and the artist this is because it was not understood that these neglected styles of cognition gave access

[21] For references on mysticism, see Aldous Huxley's *The Perennial Philosophy* (209) and William James's *The Varieties of Religious Experience* (212).

to that portion of the real world which is hidden from the exclusively abstracting intellectual.

Furthermore, as we shall see in Appendix B, holistic theorizing is also possible, in which things are not dissected and separated from each other, but are seen intact in their interrelations as facets of a whole, contained within it, seen as figure against ground, or at different levels of magnification.

LANGUAGE AND NAMING

Language is primarily an excellent means of experiencing and communicating nomothetic information, i.e., rubricizing. Of course, it attempts also to define and communicate the idiosyncratic or idiographic, but for ultimate theoretical purposes, it often fails.[22] All it can do with the idiosyncratic is to give it a name, which after all does not describe it or communicate it, but only labels it. The only way to know the idiosyncratic fully is to experience it fully and to experience it oneself. Even naming the experience may screen it off from further appreciation, as one pro-

---

[22] For instance, see the writing of James Joyce or various contemporary discussions of the theory of poetry. Poetry is an attempt to communicate, or at least express, an idiosyncratic experience that most people "have no art to say." It is a putting into words of emotional experiences that are in essence wordless. It is an attempt to describe a fresh and unique experience with schematizing labels that are themselves neither fresh nor unique. About all the poet can do in such a hopeless situation is to use these words to make parallels, figures of speech, new word patterns, etc., with which, though he cannot describe the experience itself, he hopes to touch off a similar experience in the reader. That he sometimes succeeds is simply a miracle. If he attempts to make the words themselves unique, then communication is impaired as in James Joyce and as in modern nonrepresentational art. An effective expression of these points is found in the following introduction to an unusual story by V. Lincoln in *The New Yorker*, Sept. 28, 1946.

"Why are we never prepared, why do all the books and all the wisdom of our friends avail us nothing in the final event? How many deathbed scenes we have read, how many stories of young love, of marital infidelity, of cherished ambition, fulfilled or defeated. There is nothing that can happen to us that has not happened again and again, that we have not read over a thousand times, closely, carefully, accurately recorded; before we are fully launched on life, the story of the human heart has been opened for us again and again with all the patience and skill of the human mind. But the event, when it comes, is never anything like the description; it is strange, infinitely strange and new, and we stand helpless before it and realize that the words of another convey nothing, nothing.

"And still we cannot believe that personal life is, in its essence, incommunicable. We, too, having lived the moment, are impelled to convey it, to speak the words so honest in intent, so false in the final effect."

fessor discovered when walking down a country road with his artist wife. Upon seeing some lovely flower for the first time, he asked its name. He was thereupon scolded by his wife. "What good does the name do you? When you learn its name, you're satisfied and don't bother enjoying the flower any more."[23]

To the extent that language forces experiences into rubrics, it is a screen between reality and the human being. In a word, we pay for its benefits. Therefore, while using language, as we must of necessity, we should be aware of its shortcomings and we should try to get around them.[24]

If all this is true for language at its theoretical best, the situation must be far worse when language gives up altogether the struggle to be idiosyncratic, and degenerates completely into the use of stereotypes, platitudes, mottoes, slogans, clichés, battle cries, and epithets. It is then very obviously and frankly a means for obviating thought, for dulling the perceptions, stunting mental growth, and stultifying the human being. Language then has in truth "the function of concealing thought rather than of communicating it."

---

[23] "This is to be seen with unusual clearness in what I have called evaluative labeling. This term is designed to emphasize our common tendency to evaluate individuals and situations according to the names we apply to them. After all, this is a way of saying that the way in which we classify something determines in large measure the way in which we react to it. We classify largely by naming. Having named something, we tend to evaluate it and so to react to it in terms of the name we have given it. We learn in our culture to evaluate names, or labels, or words, quite independently of the actualities to which they might be applied." (215, p. 261.)

". . . consider the differences in social status and self-esteem that exist between two sets of public servants who perform simliar menial tasks, 'airline hostesses' and 'Pullman porters' " (187); see also Ref. 490.

[24] One suggestion would be that the scientist learn to respect the poet, at least the great poet. The scientist usually thinks of his own language as being exact and of other languages as being inexact, but often the poet's language is paradoxically, if not more exact, at any rate more true. Sometimes it is even more exact. For instance, it is possible to say, if one is talented enough, in a very condensed way what the intellectual professor needs ten pages to say. The following story, attributed to Lincoln Steffens (25, p. 222) illustrates this point:

'Satan and I,' said Steffens, 'were walking down Fifth Avenue together when we saw a man stop suddenly and pick a piece of Truth out of the air—right out of the air—a piece of living Truth.'

" 'Did you see that?,' I asked Satan.

" 'Doesn't it worry you? Don't you know that it is enough to destroy you?'

" 'Yes, but I am not worried. I'll tell you why. It is a beautiful living thing now, but the man will first name it, then he will organize it, and by that time it will be dead. If he would let it live, and live it, it would destroy me. I'm not worried.' "

One other characteristic of language that helps to make trouble is that it is outside of space-time—or at least particular words may be. The word England over a period of 1000 years does not grow, age, develop, evolve, or change as the nation itself does. And yet such words as this are all we have to describe events in space-time. What does it mean to say, "There will always be an England"? As Johnson has it, "The moving finger of actuality writes faster than the tongue can herald. The structure of language is less fluid than the structure of reality. Just as the thunder we hear is no longer sounding, so the reality we speak about exists no more." (215, p. 119.)

14

UNMOTIVATED
AND PURPOSELESS
REACTIONS

In this chapter we shall grope further toward a scientifically usable differentiation between striving (doing, coping, achieving, trying, purposiveness) and being-becoming (existing, expressing, growing, self-actualization). This distinction is, of course, a familiar one in Eastern cultures and religions, e.g., Taoism, and, in our culture, among some philosophers, theologians, aestheticians, students of mysticism, and increasingly among "humanistic psychologists," existential psychologists, etc.

Western culture generally rests on the Judaic-Christian theology. The United States particularly is dominated by the Puritan and pragmatic spirit which stresses work, struggle and striving, soberness and earnestness, and above all, purposefulness.[1] Like any other social institution, science

---

[1] ". . . idle associations, superfluous images, involved dreams, random explorations, play a part in development that could never be justified, in origin, on any principle of economy or by any direct expectation of usefulness. In a mechanistic culture like our own, these important activities have been either undervalued or overlooked. . . .

"Once we rid ourselves of the unconscious bias of mechanism, we must recognize that the 'superfluous' is just as essential to human development as the economic: that beauty, for example, has played as large a part in evolution as use and cannot be explained, as Darwin sought to, merely as a practical device for courtship or fertilization. In short, it is just as permissible to conceive nature, mythologically, as a poet, working in metaphors and rhythms, as to think of nature as a cunning mechanic, trying to save material, make both ends meet, do the job efficiently and cheaply. The in general and psychology in particular is not exempt from these cultural climate and atmosphere effects. American psychology, by participation, is overpragmatic, over-Puritan, and overpurposeful. This is evident not only in its effects and avowed purposes but also in its gaps, in what it neglects. No textbooks have chapters on fun and gaiety, on leisure and meditation, on loafing and puttering, on aimless, useless, and purposeless activity, on aesthetic creation or experience, or on unmotivated activity. That is to say, American psychology is busily occupying itself with only half of life to the neglect of the other—and perhaps more important—half!

From the point of view of values, this may be described as a preoccupation with means to the exclusion of concern with ends. This philosophy is implicit in practically all American psychology (including orthodox and revisionist psychoanalysis), which uniformly neglects *per se* activity and end experience (which gets nothing done) in favor of coping, changing, effective, purposeful activity that gets something useful done.[2]

Mechanistic interpretation is quite as subjective as the poetic one; and up to a point each is useful." (347, p. 35.)

Gordon Allport stresses strongly and correctly that "being" is as effortful and active as is striving. His suggestions would lead us to contrast striving-to-make-up-deficiencies with striving-to-self-actualize rather than striving with being. This correction also serves to remove the too easily acquired impression that "being," unmotivated reactions and purposeless activity are easier, less energetic and less effortful than coping with external problems. That this *dolce far niente* interpretation of self-actualization is misleading is easily demonstrated by such examples of struggling self-development as Beethoven.

[2] "Existence for each individual may be seen as a continual struggle to satisfy needs, relieve tensions, maintain equilibrium." "In terms of our molar unit, then, the behavior of the individual is always concerned with needs and goals. If, in any given instance, this unit does not appear to be the most meaningful or useful, we must first reexamine the validity of our observations rather than the usefulness of this unit. Often a behavior may seem unmotivated because we have failed to identify concretely the need or goal involved, or because we have artificially abstracted a part of the individual's behavior from its integrated context." "At the present time, we recognize that every reaction of a living being must be purposive in the sense of being adapted to the preservation of the species if the latter is to survive in the struggle for existence." ". . . all action is motivated and expresses some purpose." "Laziness, like all other human activities, serves a purpose." "All behavior is evoked by the pressure of need—the kinds of needs which have already been mentioned. Behavior is the reaction of the organism in its efforts to effect a reduction of these needs through commerce with its environment. All conduct, therefore, is dictated by need-derived interest." "All human behavior is directed toward the satisfaction of needs." "All behavior is motivated and all learning involves reward." "Needs are determined by the report of a person experiencing them, and, on the assumption that all behavior satisfies some conscious or unconscious needs, by inference from an individual's behavior." "All behavior is thus goal directed . . ."

The culmination of this philosophy may be found in a quite explicit form in John Dewey's *Theory of Valuation* (108) in which the possibility of ends is in effect denied; they are themselves only means to other means, to other means . . . , etc. (although in other of his writings, he *does* accept the existence of ends).

At a clinical level, we have alrady discussed various aspects of this differentiation in the following ways:

1. In Appendix B it may be noticed that a holistic emphasis is necessary to stress coexistence and mutual interdependence in addition to the successiveness of causality theory, especially of the atomistic variety. In chain causality, as in Dewey's value theory, one thing leads to another, which leads to another, which leads to another . . . , etc. This is a natural acompaniment of the theory that nothing is important for its own sake. Causality theory is a quite suitable, even necessary tool for the life of achievement and technological accomplishment, but is completely useless for the life that stresses intensive perfection, aesthetic experience, contemplation of ultimate values, enjoyment, meditativeness, connoisseurship, and self-actualization.

2. In Chapter 3 it was recognized that motivated is not synonymous with determined. There are determinants other than motives as demonstrated by, e.g., constitutional changes like sunburn or glandular activity, maturational changes, situational and cultural determinants, as well as for psychological changes like retroactive and proactive inhibition or latent learning.

Although it was Freud (141) who originally confounded the two concepts, his mistake has been so widely followed by psychoanalysts that they now automatically look for motives only no matter what change occurs, e.g., eczema, gastric ulcer, slips of the pen, forgetting, etc.

3. In Chapter 5 many psychological phenomena were shown to be unmotivated, epiphenomenal consequences of need gratification rather than purposeful, motivated, learned changes as has usually been assumed.

". . . most, if not all, of the movements, or responses, which an individual makes have the immediate net effect of either rewarding or punishing him." "Some behavior leads us at once to infer the operation of some drive or motive, while other behavior sequences are—relatively, at least—devoid of motivation. Probably no human action above the simplest reflexes is completely unmotivated." "This principle hold that all behavior is fundamentally motivated by the physiologic requirements of the organism, whether the urges to activity arising from such needs be labeled instincts, drives or goal-directed strivings. . . ." The fact that most of these writers are speaking of *lower*, more material needs alone makes it even worse.

That this is no small mistake is apparent at once from the list of phenomena that were claimed to be wholly or partially gratification effects, e.g., psychotherapy, attitudes, interests, tastes and values, happiness, good citizenship, attitudes toward the self, a host of character traits, and dozens of other psychological effects as well. Need gratification permits the emergence of relatively unmotivated behavior, e.g., "immediately after satiation, the organism allows itself to give up pressure, tension, urgency and necessity, to loaf, laze and relax, to putter, to be passive, to enjoy the sun, to ornament, to decorate and polish the pots and pans (rather than to use them), to play and have fun, to observe idly what is of no importance, to be casual and aimless."

4. An experiment on the effects of familiarity in 1937 (309) demonstrated that simple, unrewarded, repetitive contact tended finally to produce preference for the familiar object, or word, or activity even when it was initially distasteful. Since this constitutes a pure case of learning by unrewarded contiguity, it must be considered unmotivated change by the reward, tension-reduction, and reinforcement theorists at least.

5. Chapter 13 demonstrates the important difference for various fields of psychology between stereotyped or rubricized cognition and fresh, humble, receptive, Taoistic cognition of the concrete, the idiosyncratic, the unique, innocent cognition without preconceptions and expectations, and without the intrusion of wishes, hopes, fears, or anxieties. Most acts of cognition, it would seem, are stale, careless recognitions and catalogings of stereotypes. Such a lazy classifying under preëxisting rubrics is profoundly different from actual, concrete perceiving with full and undivided attention of the many-sidedness of the unique phenomenon. It is only from such cognition that full appreciation and savoring of any experience can come. To the extent that rubricizing is a premature freezing of conclusions, because the person is afraid of the unknown, it is motivated by the hope of anxiety reduction and avoidance. The person who has comfortable relations with the unknown, or what is almost the same thing, can tolerate ambiguity (135), is therefore less motivated in his perceptions. It was also suggested in this chapter that the close tie found by Murphy, Bruner, Ansbacher, Murray, Sanford, McClelland, Klein, and many others, between motivation and perception had best be regarded as a somewhat psychopathological phenomenon, rather than as healthy. Very bluntly put, this tie is symptomatic of a slightly sick organism. In self-actualizing people it is at a minimum; in neurotic and psychotic people it is at a maximum, as in delusions and hallucinations. One way of describing this difference is to say that cognition in the healthy is relatively unmotivated; in the sick it is relatively motivated. Latent learning in human beings is

an instance of unmotivated cognition that could test this clinical finding.

6. Our study of self-actualizing people made clear the necessity for distinguishing somehow between their motivational life and that of more average people. They were clearly living a self-fulfilling, value-enjoying, self-perfecting life, rather than seeking for the basic need gratification that the average citizen lacks, i.e., growth motivation or metamotivation rather than deficiency motivation. Thus they were being themselves, developing, growing, and maturing, not going anywhere (in the sense, e.g., of social climbing), not striving in the ordinary sense of straining and trying for a state of affairs other than that in which they were. The distinction between deficiency motivation and growth motivation implies that self-actualizing itself is not a motivated change, unless motivation be understood in a wholly new sense. Self-actualization, the coming to full development and actuality of the potentialities of the organism, is more akin to growth and maturation than it is to habit formation or association via reward, that is, it is not acquired from without but is rather an unfolding from within of what is, in a subtle sense, already there. Spontaneity at the self-actualizing level—being healthy, natural—is unmotivated; indeed it is the contradiction of motivation.

7. Finally, in Chapter 10 the expressive determinant of behavior and of experience was discussed at some length, especially in its implications for theory of psychopathology and psychosomatics. It was strongly stressed that expression must be called relatively unmotivated, by contrast with coping, which is both motivated and purposive. The only alternative to this contrast is a complete semantic and conceptual revolution in the vocabulary of motivation.

In this chapter, depression, Goldsteinian catastrophic breakdown, Maier's frustration-instigated behavior, and catharsis and release phenomena in general were also shown to be expressive, i.e., relatively unmotivated. So also were Freudian slips, tics, and free association seen to be expressive as well as motivated.

8. Behavior, with rare exceptions discussed below, is means rather than end, i.e., it gets things done in the world. It is a question whether the exclusion of subjective states as a legitimate object of psychological study does not, a priori, make difficult or even impossible the solution of the problem we are discussing. Ends as I see them are very frequently subjective experiences of satisfaction. Without reference to the fact that most instrumental behaviors have human worth only because they bring about these subjective end-experiences, the behavior itself often becomes scientifically senseless (492). Behaviorism itself may be understood better if it is seen as one cultural expression of the general Puritan striving and

achieving point of view we have already mentioned. This implies that to its various other failings must now be added ethnocentrism.

EXAMPLES OF RELATIVELY UNMOTIVATED REACTIONS

So far then we have listed several broad categories of phenomena that must be considered to be more or less unmotivated, depending on the various definitions of the word that are possible. There are also many other such reactions, and these we shall now discuss briefly. It should be observed that they are all relatively neglected areas of psychology, an excellent illustration for the student of science of the way in which a limited outlook on life creates a limited world. For the carpenter who is *only* a carpenter, the world is made of wood.

ART

The creation of art may be relatively motivated, i.e., when it seeks to communicate, to arouse emotion, to show, to do something to another person, or it may be relatively unmotivated, i.e., when it is expressive rather than communicative, intrapersonal rather than interpersonal. The fact that expression may have unforeseen interpersonal effects (secondary gain) is beside the point.

Very much to the point, however, is the question, "Is there a *need* for expression?" If there is, then artistic expression, as well as cathartic and release phenomena are as motivated as food seeking or love seeking. I have indicated at various points in earlier chapters that I think the evidence will soon force us to recognize such a need to express in action whatever impulses have been aroused in the organism. That this will make paradoxes is clear from the fact that *any* need or *any* capacity is an impulse and therefore seeks expression. Should it then be called a separate need or impulse or should it rather be considered to be a universal characteristic of *any* impulse?

At this point we need not opt for one or another of these alternatives, since our only purpose is to show that they are *all* neglected. Whichever one turns out to be most fruitful will force a recognition of (1) the category of unmotivation or (2) a tremendous reconstruction of all motivation theory.

Quite as important for the sophisticated person is the question of aesthetic experience. This is so rich and valuable an experience for so many people that they will simply scorn or sneer at any psychological theory that denies or neglects it, no matter what scientific grounds there may be for such neglect. Science must account for *all* reality, not only the impoverished and bloodless portions of it. The fact that the aesthetic response is useless and purposeless, and that we know nothing about its motivations, if indeed, there *are* any in the ordinary sense, should indicate to us only the poverty of our official psychology.

Even the aesthetic perception, cognitively speaking, may be seen as relatively unmotivated by comparison with ordinary cognitions. We have seen in Chapter 13 that rubricizing perception was at best partial; not so much an examination of all the attributes of an object, as a classification of it on the basis of those few attributes that are useful to us, relevant to our concerns, or need gratifying or need threatening. Taoistic, disinterested perceiving of the many-sidedness of a phenomenon (with especial reference not to usefulness but to its efficacy in producing end experiences) is one characteristic of the aesthetic perception.[3]

I have found useful as a jumping-off point for thinking about just being, analysis of the concept of waiting. The cat in the sun does *not* wait any more than a tree waits. Waiting implies wasted, unappreciated time that is empty of significance for the organism, and is a by-product of a too exclusively means-oriented attitude toward life. It is most often a stupid, inefficient, and wasteful response, since (1) impatience usually does no good, even from the point of view of efficiency, and (2) even means experiences and means behaviors can be enjoyed, savored, and appreciated for their own sake at, so to speak, no extra charge. Travel is an excellent example of the way in which a piece of time can be either

---

[3] "The brain serves to bring about this choice: it actualizes the useful memories, it keeps in the lower strata of the consciousness those which are of no use. One could say as much for perception. The auxiliary of action, it isolates *that part of reality as a whole that interests us; it shows us less the things themselves than the use we can make of them.* It classifies, it labels them beforehand; we scarcely look at the object, it is enough for us to know to which category it belongs. But now and then, by a lucky accident, men arise whose senses or whose consciousness are less adherent to life. Nature has forgotten *to attach their faculty of perceiving to their faculty of acting.* When they look at a thing, *they see it for itself, and not for themselves. They do not perceive simply with a view to action; they perceive in order to perceive—for nothing, for the pleasure of doing so.* In regard to a certain aspect of their nature, whether it be their consciousness or one of their senses, they are born *detached;* and according to whether this detachment is that of a certain particular sense, or of consciousness, they are painters or sculptors, musicians or poets. It is therefore a much more direct vision of reality that we find in the different arts; and *it is because the artist is less intent on utilizing his perception that he perceives a greater number of things.*" (46, pp. 162–163.)

enjoyed as end experience or completely wasted. Education is another instance. So also are interpersonal relations in general.

Involved here also is a certain inversion of the concept of wasted time. For the use-oriented, purposeful, need-reducing kind of person that time is wasted that achieves nothing and serves no purpose. While this is a perfectly legitimate usage, we may suggest that an equally legitimate usage might be to consider that time wasted that does not carry end experience with it, i.e., that is not ultimately enjoyed. "Time you enjoy wasting is not wasted time." "Some things that are not necessary may yet be essential."

An excellent illustration of the way in which our culture is unable to take its end experiences straight may be seen in strolling, canoeing, golfing, etc. Generally these activities are extolled because they get people into the open, close to nature, out into the sunshine, or into beautiful surroundings. In essence, these are ways in which what *should be* unmotivated end activities and end experiences are thrown into a purposeful, achieving, pragmatic framework in order to appease the Western conscience.

APPRECIATION, ENJOYMENT, WONDER, ZEST, CONNOISSEURSHIP, END EXPERIENCE

Not only the aesthetic experience but many others also are passively received and enjoyed by the organism. This enjoyment itself can hardly be said to be motivated; if anything it is the end or purpose of motivated activity, the epiphenomenon of need gratification.

The mystic experience, the experience of awe, of delight, of wonder, of mystery, and of admiration are all subjectively rich experiences of the same passive, aesthetic sort, experiences that beat their way in upon the organism, flooding it as music does. These too are end experiences, ultimate rather than instrumental, changing the outside world not at all. All this is true for leisure as well, if it is properly defined (375).

Perhaps it is appropriate to speak here of two such ultimate pleasures: (1) K. Bühler's function pleasure, and (2) the pleasure of sheer living (biopleasure, zestful experiencing). Especially can we see these in the child who repeats and repeats his newly perfected skill out of sheer delight that comes with good and skillful functioning. Dancing may also be a good example. As for the basic life pleasure, any ailing or dyspeptic or nauseated person can testify to the reality of that most ultimate biological pleasure (zestful experiencing) that is an automatic, unsought-for, unmotivated by-product of being alive and healthy.

STYLE AND TASTES

In Chapter 10, the *style* of behavior, as contrasted with its functions and purposes, was listed as an example of expression, following among others, Allport, (8), Werner (464), and Wertheimer (465, 467).

I wish to add here some data reported in 1939 (305) that should illustrate and support this thesis. In this research I attempted to discover the various ways in which high-dominance with high self-esteem, women (strong, self-confident, self-assertive characters) differed from low-dominance women (with low self-esteem, passive, shy, or retreating characters). So many differentiations were discovered that it finally became relatively easy to make diagnosis (and therefore validation) by simply watching them walk, talk, etc. Character structure showed itself in tastes, in clothes, party behavior, etc. as well as in overt functional, purposeful, motivated behavior. A few examples will suffice.

The stronger person shows this strength by choosing foods that are saltier, sourer, and more bitter, more sharp and of stronger taste, e.g., strong cheeses rather than milder ones; foods that taste good even though ugly and unattractive, e.g., shellfish; foods that are novel and unfamiliar, e.g., fried squirrel, snails. They are less finicky, less easily nauseated, less fussy about unattractive or sloppily prepared food. And yet they are more sensuous and hearty and lusty about good food than are the low-dominance women.

By a kind of physiognomical isomorphism (464) these same qualities show themselves in other areas, e.g., their language is tougher, stronger, harder; the men they choose are tougher, stronger, harder; their reactions to exploiters, leeches, and other people who try to take advantage of them is stronger, tougher, and harder.

Eisenberg's studies (118) very strongly supported these conclusions in various other ways. For instance, the high scorers in my test of dominance-feeling or self-esteem (294), were more apt to come late to appointments with the experimenter, to be less respectful, more casual, more forward, more condescending, less tense, anxious, and worried, more apt to accept an offered cigarette, much more apt to make themselves comfortable without bidding or invitation.

In still another research (311), their sexual reactions were found to be even more sharply different. The stronger woman is much more apt to be pagan, permissive, and accepting in all sexual realms. She is less apt to be a virgin, more apt to have masturbated, more apt to have had sexual relations with more than one man, much more apt to have tried such experiments as homosexuality, cunnilingus, fellatio, and anal sexuality.

In other words here too she is apt to be more forward, less inhibited, tougher, harder, stronger. See also De Martino (107).

An unpublished experiment by Carpenter (79) on the different musical tastes of high- and low-scoring women comes to a foreseeable conclusion, namely, that high scorers (high self-esteem) are more open to strange, wild, unfamiliar music, to cacophony, and to lack of melody, to the powerful rather than the sweet.

Meadow (335) showed that low scorers (shy, timid, less confident) deteriorated intellectually more than did high scorers when put under stress, i.e., they were less strong. See (297a) for parallels with work of McClelland and his collaborators on the need for achievement.

The value of these examples for our thesis lies in the clearly observable fact that these are all unmotivated choices, all expressive of a type of character structure in the same way that all of Mozart's music is Mozartian somehow, or that Renoir's copy of a Delacroix painting looks more like Renoir than like Delacroix.

These are all expressive in the same way that the style of writing is, or that TAT stories or Rorschach protocols are, or that doll play is.

PLAY

Play may be either coping or expressive or both (see page 70) as is now quite clear from the literature on play therapy and play diagnosis. It seems quite probable that this general conclusion will supplant the various functional, purposive, motivational theories of play put forward in the past. Since there is nothing to prevent us from using the coping-expressive dichotomy with animals, we may also reasonably look forward to more useful and realistic interpretations of animal play as well. All we have to do to open up this new area for research is to admit the possibility that play may be useless and unmotivated, a phenomenon of being rather than of striving, end rather than means. The same may probably be affirmed of laughter, hilarity, gaiety, having fun, joy, ecstasy, euphoria, etc.

IDEOLOGY, PHILOSOPHY, THEOLOGY, COGNITION

This is another area that has resisted the tools of official psychology. I think this is partly so because thinking in general has been automatically regarded since Darwin and Dewey as problem solving, i.e., as functional and as motivated.

What little data we have to contradict this assumption come mostly from the analysis of the larger thought products—philosophical systems —whose correlations with individual character structure are easy enough to establish (192). That a pessimist like Schopenhauer should produce a pessimistic philosophy seems very understandable. To consider it purely rationalization or defense or security device is surely naïve after all we have learned from TAT stories or the art products of children. In any case, to take a parallel expressive production, how could Bach's music or Rubens's painting be defensive or rationalization?

Remembering also may be relatively unmotivated, as is clearly seen in the phenomenon of latent learning, which is found in greater or lesser degree, in all human beings. The to-do among the researchers over this problem is really irrelevant since it is of no concern to us whether rats show latent learning or not. Human beings in their daily lives do beyond a doubt.

The finding of Ansbacher (13) that insecure people tend strongly to have insecure early memories, and my own finding that insecure people tend strongly to have manifestly insecure dreams are also instances in point. These seem to be obvious expressions of attitude toward the world. I cannot conceive how they could be, without straining, interpreted as solely need gratifying, rewarding, or reinforcing.

The truth or the correct answer is in any case often simply perceived without effort, rather than struggled for and sought. The fact that in most experiments motivation of some sort is necessary before problems can be solved may easily be a function of the triviality or arbitrariness of the problems rather than proof that *all* thinking must be motivated. In the good life lived by the healthy person, thinking, like perceiving, may be spontaneous and passive reception or production, an unmotivated, effortless, happy expression of the nature and existence of the organism, a *letting* things happen rather than making them happen, as much an example of being as the perfume of a flower or the apples on a tree.

15

PSYCHOTHERAPY, HEALTH, AND MOTIVATION

It is amazing that experimental psychologists have not turned to the study of psychotherapy as to an unworked gold mine. As a result of successful psychotherapy, people perceive differently, think differently, learn differently. Their motives change, as do their emotions. It is the best technique we have ever had for laying bare men's deepest nature as contrasted with their surface personalities. Their interpersonal relations and attitudes toward society are transformed. Their characters (or personalities) change both superficially and profoundly. There is even some evidence that their appearance changes, that physical health is improved, etc. In some cases, even the IQ goes up. And yet, the word is not even listed in the index of most books on learning, perception, thinking, motivation, social psychology, physiological psychology, etc.

To take a single example, there is no question whatsoever that the theory of learning would, to say the least, profit by the study of the learning effects of such therapeutic forces as marriage, friendship, free association, resistance analysis, success in a job, not to mention tragedy, trauma, conflict, and suffering.

Another equally important set of unsolved problems is turned up by examining the psychotherapeutic relationships as simply a subexample of social or interpersonal relationships, i.e., as a branch of social psychology. We can now describe at least three ways in which patients and therapists can relate to each other, the authoritarian, the democratic, the laissez-faire, each having its special usefulness at various times. But precisely these three types of relationships are found in the social atmosphere of boys' clubs and in styles of hypnosis, in types of political theory, in mother–child relationships (300) and in kinds of social organization found in infrahuman primates (306).

Any thorough study of the aims and goals of therapy must expose very quickly the inadequate development of current personality theory, call into question the basic scientific orthodoxy that values have no place in science, lay bare the limitations of medical notions of health, disease, therapy, and cure, and reveal clearly that our culture still lacks a usable value system. No wonder people are afraid of the problem. Many other examples could be adduced to prove that psychotherapy is an important department of general psychology.

We may say that psychotherapy takes place in seven main ways: (1) by expression (act completion, release, catharsis), as exemplified in Levy's release therapy (271); (2) by basic need-gratification (giving support, reassurance, protection, love, respect); (3) by removing threat (protection, good social, political, and economic conditions; (4) by improved insight, knowledge, and understanding; (5) by suggestion or authority; (6) by direct attack on the symptoms, as in the various behavior therapies; and (7) by positive self-actualization, individuation, or growth. For the more general purposes of personality theory, this also constitutes a list of the ways in which personality changes in culturally and psychiatrically approved directions.

We are here specially interested in tracing a few of the interrelationships between the data of therapy and the theory of motivation so far presented in this book. It will be seen that gratification of the basic needs is an important (perhaps the *most* important) step along the path to the ultimate, positive goal of all therapy, namely, self-actualization.

It will also be pointed out that these basic needs are mostly satisfiable *only by other human beings,* and that therefore therapy must take place mostly on an interpersonal basis. The sets of basic needs whose gratifications constitute the basic therapeutic medications, e.g., safety, belongingness, love, and respect, can be obtained only from other people.

May I say at once that my own experience has been almost entirely confined to the briefer therapies. Those whose experience is primarily with psychoanalytic (deeper) therapy are much more likely to come to the conclusion that insight rather than need gratification is *the* important medicine. This is so because seriously sick people are incapable of accepting or assimilating satisfactions of basic needs until they have given up their infantile interpretations of self and others and become capable of perceiving and accepting personal and interpersonal reality as it is.

We could debate the matter if we wished, pointing out that the purpose of insight therapy is to make possible the acceptance of good interpersonal relations and the need gratifications that go with them. We know insight has been effective only because these motivational changes come to pass. However, acceptance for the time being of a crude differentiation between the simpler, briefer, need-gratification therapy and the deeper, longer, more laborious insight therapy has considerable heuristic value. As we shall see, need gratification is possible in many nontechnical situations, such as marriages, friendship, collaboration, teaching, etc. This opens a theoretical road to a much wider extension of therapeutic skills to all sorts of laymen (lay therapy). At present, insight therapy is definitely a technical matter, for which much training is necessary. The relentless pursuit of the theoretical consequences of this dichotomy between lay therapy and technical therapy will demonstrate its varied usefulness.

It is possible also to hazard the opinion that, although the deeper insight therapies involve additional principles, they too can best be understood if we choose as our beginning point the study of the effects of thwarting and gratifying of man's basic needs. This is directly contrary to the practice now extant, of deriving an explanation of the shorter therapies from a study of one or another variety of psychoanalysis (or other insight therapy). One by-product of this latter approach has been to make the study of psychotherapy and personal growth an isolated area in psychological theory, more or less sufficient unto itself, and governed by special or autochthonous laws peculiar to this field alone. This chapter explicitly rejects such implications, and proceeds from the conviction that there are no *ad hoc* laws in psychotherapy. That we have proceeded as if there were is due not only to the fact that most professional therapists have been trained medically rather than psychologically, but also to the curious blindness of experimental psychologists to the repercussions upon their own picture of human nature of the phenomena of psychotherapy. In short, we may contend not only that psychotherapy must ultimately base itself squarely on sound, general psychological theory, but also that psychological theory must enlarge itself to become adequate to this responsibility. Accordingly we shall deal first with the simpler therapeutic phenomena, postponing the problems of insight to a later part of this chapter.

SOME PHENOMENA THAT SUPPORT THE VIEW OF PSYCHOTHERAPY AND PERSONAL GROWTH AS NEED-GRATIFICATION VIA INTERPERSONAL RELATIONS

We know of many facts that, taken together, make impossible (1) any purely cognitive, or (2) any purely impersonal theory of psychotherapy, but that are quite compatible with need-gratification theory and with an interpersonal approach to therapy and growth.

1. Psychotherapy has always existed wherever there was a society. The shaman, the medicine man, the witch, the wise old woman of the community, the priest, the guru, and more recently in Western civilization, the physician, have always been able to achieve in some cases what we call today psychotherapy. Indeed the great religious leaders and organizations have been validated as such, by their cures, not only of gross and dramatic psychopathology, but also of subtler character and value disturbances. The explanations that these people offered for these achievements have nothing in common with each other and need not be considered seriously. We must accept the fact that though these miracles could be performed, the performers did not know *why* or *how* they were achieved.

2. This discrepancy between theory and practice exists today also. The various schools of psychotherapy all disagree with each other, sometimes very violently. And yet a psychologist in clinical work will, in a long enough period of time, run across patients who have been cured by representatives of each of these schools of thought. These patients will then be grateful and loyal proponents of the one or another brand of theory. But it is just as easy to collect instances of failure for each of these schools of thought. And to make the matter triply confusing, I have seen patients cured by physicians or even by psychiatrists who, to my certain knowledge, had never had any training of any kind in what could fairly be called psychotherapy (not to mention schoolteachers, ministers, nurses, dentists, social workers, etc.).

It is true that we can criticize these various theoretical schools on empirical and scientific grounds and arrange them in a crude hierarchy of relative validity. And we may expect that in the future we shall be able to gather suitable statistics to show that one theoretical training produces a higher percentage of cure or growth than another, even though neither fails or succeeds all the time.

At this moment, however, we must accept the fact that therapeutic results may occur to some degree independently of theory, or for that matter, with no theory at all.

3. Even within the confines of one school of thought, let us say classical Freudian psychoanalysis, it is well known and commonly admitted by the analysts that there are wide differences from analyst to analyst, not only in ability as ordinarily defined, but also in sheer efficacy at curing. Some brilliant analysts who make important contributions in teaching and writing, who admittedly know a great deal and who are sought after as teachers and lecturers, and as training analysts, yet too often fail to cure their patients. And there are others, who never write anything or make few if any discoveries, who yet cure their patients most of the time. Of course there is clearly some degree of positive correlation in these abilities to be brilliant and to cure patients, and yet the exceptions remain to be explained.[1]

4. There are through history some well-known cases in which the master of a school of therapeutic thought, while himself extraordinarily capable as a therapist, yet largely failed in teaching this ability to his students. If it were only a matter of theory, content, or knowledge, and if the personality of the therapist made no difference, students should

[1] One simple way of approaching this as a research problem is to interview people who have been psychoanalyzed or given other therapeutic treatment. I have such data for 34 individuals, interviewed a year or more after the close of therapy. Twenty-four of them give a flat, unqualified approval of their experience, considering it to have been worth while beyond the shadow of a doubt, and usually expressing themselves with great enthusiasm. Of the remaining ten, two were dissatisfied with their therapists, dropped them, and chose others for whom they then express unqualified approval. Four were diagnosed as psychotic or with strong psychotic trends. Of these, one stuck with her psychiatrist over a period of several years without any benefit that she could see. Another one broke off his analysis and disappeared. A third one broke off after a time and now expresses strong disapproval for all previous three, but approval of the current one. The seventh of this group of ten thinks his analysis did him some good, but at too great a cost of time and money. He may be said to be cured, but feels that he achieved this by his own efforts subsequent upon the analysis. The eighth person, a confirmed homosexual, driven to the therapist by the police, remained uncured according to the therapist himself. The ninth, himself a psychoanalyst, analyzed a long time ago, says that it was a very bad analysis by current standards and he therefore considers himself unanalyzed. The last of the ten, a young epileptic, was forced into an unwanted analysis by parental pressure.

In the present context, what is of most interest to us is that the 71 percent who express unqualified approval were treated by a variety of psychoanalyists and non-analytic therapists ranging the whole gamut of theory, doctrine, and method, and as nearly as I can make out, were equally benefited!

eventually do as well or better than their teachers, if they were equally intelligent and assiduous.

5. It is a common enough experience for any type of therapist to see a patient for the first time, discuss a few external details with him, e.g., procedure, hours, etc., and have him report or demonstrate improvement by the time of the second contact. In terms of what was overtly said or done, this result is absolutely incomprehensible.

6. Sometimes therapeutic results occur without the therapist saying a word. In one instance, a college girl wanted advice about a personal problem. At the end of one hour, during which she talked and I said *not a single word,* she had settled the problem to her own satisfaction, thanked me gratefully for my advice, and left.

7. For cases that are young enough, and that are not too serious, the ordinary major life experiences can be therapeutic in the fullest sense of the word. A good marriage, success in a suitable job, developing good friendships, having children, facing emergencies, and overcoming difficulties—I have occasionally seen all of these produce deep character changes, get rid of symptoms, etc. without the help of a technical therapist. As a matter of fact, a case could be made for the thesis that good life circumstances are among the *ultimate* therapeutic agents and that technical psychotherapy often has the task only of enabling the individual to take advantage of them.

8. Many psychoanalysts have observed that their patients progressed during gaps in their analysis and also after the analysis was completed.

9. It has also been reported that one sign of successful therapy is to be found in concomitant improvement of the wife or husband of the person under therapy.

10. Perhaps most challenging of all is the very peculiar situation existing today in which the vast majority of cases are treated or at least handled by people who were never trained to be therapists or were inadequately trained. I can illustrate best by citing my own experience in this area, an experience that must be paralleled by hundreds of other individuals in the field of psychology and in other fields.

The training of the large majority of graduate students in psychology during the twenties and thirties was (and still is to a lesser extent) limited, sometimes to the point of sterility. The student, coming into psychology because he liked human beings and wanted to understand and help them, found himself initiated into a peculiar cultlike atmosphere in which most of his time was spent on the phenomena of sensation, the ramifications of the conditioned reflex, and the nonsense syllable, and the peregrinations of white rats through mazes. Along with this came a more useful, but still philosophically limited and naïve training in experimental and statistical methods.

And yet, to the layman, a psychologist was a psychologist, a target for all the major life questions, a technician who was supposed to know why divorces occur, why hatred develops, or why people become psychotic. Often he had to answer the best way he could. Especially was this true in the smaller cities and towns that had never seen a psychiatrist and never heard of psychoanalysis. The only alternative to a psychologist was a favorite aunt, the family physician or minister. Thus it was possible for an untrained psychologist to assuage his guilty conscience. Also he could put his efforts down to necessary training.

What I wish to report, however, is that these fumbling efforts so often worked, to the complete amazement of the young psychologist. He was well enough prepared for his failures, which of course were more frequent, but how to explain successful results that he had not even hoped for?

Some experiences were even more unexpected. In the course of various researches in which I had to collect intimate and detailed case histories of various types of personality, I was completely unprepared by my training for the occasional occurrence of a cure of the very personality distortion I was examining when I had done nothing but ask questions about the personality and life history!

It has also happened once in a while that, upon being asked for the usual advice by a student, I would advise him to seek professional psychotherapy and explain why I thought this desirable, what was wrong with him, the nature of psychological illness, etc. In some cases, this alone was sufficient to remove the presenting symptoms.

Such phenomena as these are less often seen by the professional therapist than by the amateur. Indeed, it has become quite clear that some psychiatrists are simply not ready to believe the reports of such happenings as these. But this can all easily be checked and confirmed, since such experiences are common among psychologists and social workers, not to mention ministers, teachers, and physicians.

How to explain these phenomena? It seems to me that we can understand them only with the aid of a motivational, interpersonal theory. It is necessary apparently to stress not what was consciously said or done, but what was unconsciously done and unconsciously perceived. The therapist in all the cases cited was interested in the patient, concerned about him, was trying to help him, thereby proving to the patient that he had worth in the eyes of at least one person. Since the therapist was in all cases someone who was perceived as wiser, older, stronger, or healthier, the patient could also feel more safe and protected and therefore less vulnerable and less anxious. The willingness to listen, the lack of scolding, the encouragement of frankness, the acceptance and approval even after sinful revelations, gentleness and kindness, the feeling given to the patient of having somone on his side, all these in addition to the factors listed above, help to produce in the patient the unconscious realization of being liked, protected, and respected. As has been pointed out already, these are all gratifications of basic needs.

It seems quite clear that if we supplement the better-known therapeutic determinants (suggestion, catharsis, insight, and more recently, the behavior therapies, etc.) by assigning a much larger role to basic need gratifications, we can explain much more than we could with these known processes alone. Some therapeutic phenomena occur with these gratifications as their only explanation—presumably less serious cases. Others—more serious—which are sufficiently explained by the more complex therapeutic techniques alone *can* be even more fully understood by adding, as a determinant, the basic need gratifications, which come almost automatically in good interpersonal relationships (291).

PSYCHOTHERAPY AS A GOOD HUMAN RELATIONSHIP

Any ultimate analysis of human, interpersonal relationships, e.g., friendship, marriage, etc., will show (1) that basic needs can be satisfied *only* interpersonally, and (2) that the satisfactions of these needs are precisely those we have already spoken of as the basic therapeutic medicines, namely, the giving of safety, love, belongingness, feeling of worth, and self-esteem.

We should inevitably in the course of an analysis of human relations find ourselves confronted with the necessity, as well as the possibility, of differentiating good from poor relationships. Such a differentiation can very fruitfully be made on the basis of the degree of satisfaction of the basic needs brought about by the relationship. A relationship—friendship, marriage, parent-child relation—would then be defined (in a limited fashion) as psychologically good to the extent that it supported or improved belongingness, security, and self-esteem (and ultimately self-actualization) and bad to the extent that it did not.

These cannot be satisfied by trees, mountains, or even dogs. Only from another human being can we get fully satisfying respect and protection and love, and it is only to other human beings that we can give these in the fullest measure. But these are precisely what we find good friends, good sweethearts, good parents and children, good teachers and students giving to each other. These are the very satisfactions that we seek for from good human relationship of *any* kind. And it is precisely these need gratifications that are the *sine qua non* preconditions for the production of good human beings, which in turn is the ultimate (if not immediate) goal of all psychotherapy.

The sweeping implications of our system of definitions would then be that (1) psychotherapy is not at its base a unique relationship, for some of its fundamental qualities are found in *all* "good" human relationship,[2] and (2) if this is so, this aspect of psychotherapy must be subjected to a more thoroughgoing critique than it has ordinarily received, from the viewpoint of its nature as a good or bad human interpersonal relation.[3]

1. Taking then the good friendships (whether between wife and husband, parent and child, or man and man) as our paradigms of the good interpersonal relations, and examining them a bit more closely, we find that they offer many more satisfactions than even those we have spoken of. Mutual frankness, trust, honesty, lack of defensiveness, can all be seen as having in addition to their face value, an additional expressive, cathartic release value (see Chapter 10). A sound friendship permits also the expression of a healthy amount of passivity, relaxation, childishness, and silliness, since if there is no danger and we are loved and respected for ourselves rather than for any front we put on or role we play, we can be as we really are, weak when we feel weak, protected when we feel confused, childish when we wish to drop the responsibilities of adulthood. In addition, a really good relationship improves insight even in the Freudian sense, for a good friend or husband is one who feels free enough to offer the equivalent of analytic interpretations for our consideration.

Nor have we spoken enough yet of what may broadly be called the educational value of a good human relationship. We have desires not only to be safe and to be loved, but also to know more and more, to be curious, to unfold every wrapping and to unlock every door. Beyond this, we have to reckon also with our basically philosophical impulses to structure the world, to understand it deeply, and to have it make sense. While

---

2 Just as the major values of a good friendship may be entirely unconscious without much diminishing their worth, so can these same qualities be unconscious in a therapy relation without removing their influence. This is not a contradiction of the undoubted fact that a full awareness of these qualities with a conscious and voluntary direction of their use would increase their value tremendously.

3 These conclusions are more readily acceptable if we confine ourselves for the moment to those milder cases who can receive love and respect directly (who are in a majority in our population, I believe). The question of neurotic-need gratifications and their consequences must be postponed because of its great complexity.

a fine friendship or parent-child relation should offer much in this area, these satisfactions are or should be achieved to a special degree in a good therapeutic relationship.

Finally it might we well to say a word about the obvious (and therefore neglected) fact that it is as great a delight to love as to be loved.[4] The open impulse to affection is a severely inhibited in our culture as the sexual and the hostile impulses—perhaps even more (442). We are allowed open expression of affection in extraordinarily few relationships, perhaps in only three, the parent–child pair, the grandparent–grandchild pair, and in married people and sweethearts, and even in these we know how easily they can become strangulated and mixed with embarrassment, guilt, defensiveness, playing a role, and with a struggle for dominance.

It is not enough stressed that a therapeutic relationship permits, even encourages, open verbal expression of love and affection impulses. Only here (as well as in the various "personal growth" groups) are they taken for granted and expected, and only here are they consciously purged of their unhealthy admixtures and then, thus cleansed, put to the best of uses. Such facts as these point unmistakably to the necessity of reevaluating the Freudian concepts of transference and countertransference. These concepts rose out of a study of sickness, and are much too limited for dealing with health. They must be enlarged to include the sound as well as the crippled, the rational as well as the irrational.

2. There can be differentiated at least three different qualities of human relationship, the dominant–subordinate, the equalitarian, and the aloof or laissez-faire. These have been demonstrated in diverse areas (300), including the therapist–patient relationship.

A therapist can consider himself the active, deciding, managing boss of his patient, or he can relate himself to the patient as a partner in a common task, or finally, he can transform himself into a calm, emotionless mirror to the patient, never becoming involved, never coming humanly close, but always remaining detached. This last is the type that Freud recommended, but the other two types of relationship are the ones that actually prevail most often although officially, the only label available for any normal human feelings for the analysand is countertransference, i.e., irrational, sick.

Now, if the relationship between the therapist and the patient is the

---

[4] I am particularly struck with this inexplicable oversight in the literature of child psychology. "The child must be loved," "The child will behave well in order to keep the love of his parents," etc. can all read with equal validity, "The child must love," "The child will behave well *because* he loves his parents," etc.

medium through which the patient is to obtain his necessary therapeutic medicines—as the water is the medium in which the fish finds all his need objects—it must be considered, not per se, but rather in the light of which medium is best for which patient. We must guard ourselves against choosing one for loyal backing, to the exclusion of others. There is no reason why all three, as well as others, perhaps yet to be discovered, should not be found in the armamentarium of the good therapist.

While it follows from what has been presented above that the average patient would thrive best in a warm, friendly, democratic partnership relation, there are too many for whom it will *not* be the best atmosphere to allow us to make it into a rule. This is particularly true for more serious cases of chronic stabilized neurosis.

Some more authoritarian characters, who will identify kindness with weakness, must not be allowed to develop an easy contempt for the therapist. Holding the reins tight, and setting very definite limits to permissiveness, may be desirable for the patient's ultimate good. This has been especially stressed by the Rankeans in their discussions of the limits of the therapeutic relation.

Others, who have learned to regard affection as a snare and a trap, will recoil with anxiety to anything but aloofness. The deeply guilty may *demand* punishment. The rash and the self-destructive may need positive orders to keep them from harming themselves irreparably.

But there can be no exception to the rule that the therapist ought to be as conscious as possible of the relationship he forms with his patient. Granted that he will spontaneously tend to one type rather than another because of his own character, he should be able to hold himself in check when his patient's good is concerned.

In any case, if the relationship is bad, whether in general terms or in the terms of the individual patient, it is doubtful that any of the other resources of psychotherapy can have much effect. This is largely so because such a relationship is apt never to be entered into or soon broken off. But even if the patient stays with someone he deeply dislikes or resents or is anxious with, time is too apt to be taken with self-defense, with defiance, with the patient tempted to take as his main goal *dis*pleasing the therapist.

To sum up, even though forming a satisfactory human relationship may not be an end in itself but rather a means to an end, it must still be regarded as a necessary or highly desirable precondition for psychotherapy, since it is usually the best medium for dispensation of the ultimate psychological medicines that all human beings need.

There are yet other interesting implications of this point of view. If psychotherapy consists, in ultimate essence, of supplying to a sick human being just those qualities that he should have gotten from other good human relations, this amounts to defining the psychologically sick person as one who has never had enough good relationships with other people. This does not contradict our previous definition of the sick man as one who has not got enough of love, respect, etc., since he can get these only from other people. Though these definitions are thus shown to be tautologous, each leads us off in different directions and opens our eyes to different aspects of therapy.

One consequence of this second definition of sickness is that it throws the psychotherapeutic relationship into another light. It is by most considered to be a desperate measure, a last recourse, and because mostly sick people enter into it, it has come to be regarded as itself weird, abnormal, sick, unusual, an unfortunate necessity, like surgery, even by the therapists themselves.

Surely this is not the attitude with which people enter into other beneficial relationships like marriage, friendship, or partnership. But, by theory at least, psychotherapy is as similar to friendship as it is to surgery. It ought then to be looked upon as a healthy, desirable relation, even to some extent and in some respects, as one of the *ideal* relationships between human beings. By theory, it ought to be looked forward to, eagerly entered upon. This is what *should* follow from previous considerations. In actuality, however, we know that this is not the case very often. This contradiction, of course, is well recognized but is not fully explained by the neurotic's necessity for hanging on to his illness. It must also be explained by misunderstanding of the fundamental nature of therapeutic relations, not only by patients, but also by many therapists. I have found potential patients more ready to go into therapy when it was explained to them as I have done above than when the explanation was of the more usual sort.

Another consequence of an interpersonal definition of therapy is that it makes it possible to phrase one of its aspects as training in the technique of establishing a good human relationship (something a chronic neurotic cannot do without special help), of proving this to be a possibility, of discovering how enjoyable and fruitful it is. The hope would be then that he could now form deeply good friendships with others, by a kind of transfer of training. Presumably, he could then get all necessary psychological medicines, as most of us do, from our friendships, our children, our wives or husbands, and our colleagues. From this point of view, therapy can be defined in still another way, namely, as preparing the patient to set up on his own the good human relationships that all human beings want and in which relatively healthy people get many of the psychological medicines that they need.

Another deduction from foregoing considerations would be that patients and therapists ideally should *choose* each other and that furthermore this choice should be made, not alone on the basis of reputation, size of fee, technical training, and skill, etc., but also on the basis of ordinary human liking for each other. It could easily be demonstrated logically that this should at least shorten the time necessary for treatment, make it easier for both patient and therapist, make possible a closer approach to ideal cure, and make the whole experience more rewarding for both. Various other corollaries of such a conclusion would be that the backgrounds, level of intelligence, experiences, religion, politics, values, etc, of both should be more rather than less similar, ideally.

It must by now be clear that the personality or character structure of the therapist is, if not all-important, certainly one of the crucial considerations. He must be an individual who can enter easily into the ideally good human relationship that is psychotherapy. Furthermore, he must be able to do this with many different kinds of people or even with all human beings. He must be warm and sympathetic, and he must be sure enough of himself to be able to give respect to other human beings. He ought to be an essentially democratic person, in the psychological sense that he looks on other human beings with essential respect simply because they are human and unique. In a word, he should be emotionally secure and he should have healthy self-esteem. In addition his life situation ought *ideally* to be so good that he is not absorbed with his own problems. He should be happily married, be financially successful, have good friends, like life, and generally be capable of having a good time.

Finally, all this implies that we might very well throw open for additional consideration the prematurely closed question (by the psychoanalysts) of continued social contacts between therapist and patient after the formal therapeutic sessions are closed or even while they are going on.

GOOD HUMAN RELATIONS AS PSYCHOTHERAPEUTIC

Because we have expanded and generalized the phrasing of the ultimate goals of psychotherapy, and the specific medicines that produce these end effects, we have become logically committed to an obliteration of the walls that fence off psychotherapy from other human relationships and life happenings. Those happenings and those relationships in the life of the ordinary individual that help him make progress toward the ultimate ends of technical psychotherapy may fairly be called psychotherapeutic even though they occur outside an office and without benefit of a professional therapist. It follows that a wholly proper part of the study of psychotherapy is examination of the everyday miracles produced by good marriages, good friendships, good parents, good jobs, good teachers, etc. An example of a theorem deriving directly from such consideration would be that technical therapy ought to rely much more than it has on steering patients into just such therapeutic relationships as soon as the patient can accept and handle them.

Certainly we need not be afraid as professionals of putting into the hands of amateurs these important psychotherapeutic tools: protection, love and respect for other human beings. While they are certainly powerful tools, they are not therefore dangerous ones. We may expect that ordinarily we cannot hurt anybody by loving and respecting him (except occasional neurotic individuals, who are, in any case, badly off already). It is fair to expect that care, love, and respect are forces almost always for good and not for harm.

Accepting this, it must be our clear conviction that not only is every good human being potentially an unconscious therapist, but also we must accept the conclusion that we should approve of this, encourage it, teach it. At least these fundamentals of what we may call lay psychotherapy can be taught from childhood on to any human being at all. One clear task for public psychotherapy (using the analogy of contrast between public health and private medicine) is to teach just these facts, to broadcast them far and wide, to be certain that every teacher, every parent, and ideally every human being, be given the chance to understand them and to apply them. Human beings have always gone for advice and help to others whom they respected and loved. There is no reason why this historical phenomenon should not be formalized, verbalized, and encouraged to the point of universality by psychologists as well as religionists. Let people realize clearly that every time they threaten someone or humiliate or hurt unnecessarily or dominate or reject another human being, they become forces for the creation of psychopathology, even if these be small forces. Let them recognize also that every man who is kind, helpful, decent, psychologically democratic, affectionate, and warm, is a psychotherapeutic force even though a small one.[5]

---

[5] I suppose it is necessary again to append the proper cautions to such sweeping statements. The reader who has not had experience with chronic, stabilized neuroses must find it difficult to believe that such individuals cannot come within the scope of the

PSYCHOTHERAPY AND THE GOOD SOCIETY

As a parallel to the previously discussed definition of good human relationships, we can explore the implications of the, by now, obviously
called-for definition of the good society as one that gives to its members
the greatest possibility of becoming sound and self-actualizing human
beings. This in turn means that the good society is the one that has its
institutional arrangements set up in such a way as to foster, encourage,
reward, produce a maximum of good human relationships and a minimum of bad human relationships. A corollary from foregoing definitions
and identities would be that good society is synonymous with psychologically healthy society, while bad society would be synonymous with
psychologically sick society, which in turn means basic-need gratifying
and basic-need thwarting respectively, i.e., not enough love, affection, protection, respect, trust, truth, and too much hostility, humiliation, fear, contempt, and domination.

It should be stressed that social and institutional pressures *foster*
therapeutic or pathogenic consequences (make them easier, more advantageous, more probable, give them greater primary and secondary gains).
They do not absolutely *fate* them or make them absolutely inevitable. We
know enough of the range of personality in both simple and complex
societies to respect, on the one hand, the plasticity and resilience of human
nature, and on the other hand, the peculiar stubbornness of the already
formed character structure in exceptional individuals which makes it possible for them to resist and even flout social pressures (see Chapter 11).
Always the anthropologist seems to be able to find one kind man in the
cruel society, one fighter in the pacific society. We know enough now not
to blame *all* human ills on social arrangements à la Rousseau, nor dare
we hope that all human beings can be made happy, healthy, and wise by
social improvements alone.

So far as our society is concerned we can look at it from various
points of view, all useful for one or another purpose. For instance we can
strike a sort of average for our or any other society and label it fairly sick,
extremely sick, etc. More useful for us, however, would be a gauging and
balancing against each other of the sickness-fostering and the health-
fostering forces. Our society clearly has much of both teetering in a pre-

---

foregoing recommendation. Yet every experienced therapist knows this to be so (1).
Along with an increasing respect for lay psychotherapy must go an increasing realization of the necessity for technical psychotherapists. These latter might be defined as
those who take up where the therapeutic life processes fail.

carious balance, with control going now to one set of forces, now another. There is no reason why these forces should not be measured and experimented with.

Leaving such general considerations and turning to the individual-psychological ones, we deal first with the fact of subjective interpretation of the culture. From this point of view, we may fairly say of the neurotic person that, *for him,* the society is sick, for he sees in it preponderantly danger, threat, attack, selfishness, humiliation, and coldness. It is of course understood that his neighbor, looking at the same culture, the same people, may find the society to be a healthy one. These conclusions do not contradict each other *psychologically.* They can both exist psychologically. Thus every deeply sick person lives subjectively in a sick society. The conclusion from the conjoining of this statement and our previous discussion of the psychotherapeutic relationship is that therapy may be phrased as an attempt to set up a miniature good society.[6] This same phrasing may be used even where the society is sick from the point of view of a large majority of its members.

Theoretically then, psychotherapy socially amounts to running counter to the basic stresses and tendencies in a sick society. Or in a more generalized form, no matter what the degree of general health or sickness of a society, therapy amounts to fighting against the sickness-producing forces in that society on an individual scale. It tries, so to speak, to turn the tide, to bore from within, to be revolutionary or radical in an ultimate etymological sense. Every psychotherapist, then, is or should be fighting in the small rather than in the large, the psychopathogenic forces in his society, and if these be fundamental and primary, he is actually fighting his society.

Clearly if psychotherapy could be tremendously extended, if, instead of dealing with a few dozen patients a year, psychotherapists could deal with several million patients a year, then these small forces against the nature of our society would become quite perceptible to the naked eye. That the society would change there can be no doubt. First would come changes here and there in the flavor of human relationships with respect to such qualities as hospitality, generosity, friendliness, and the like, but when enough people became more hospitable, more generous, more kind, more social, then we may rest assured that they would force legal, political, economic, and sociological changes as well (347). Perhaps the rapid spread

---

[6] We must beware of a too extreme subjectivism here. The society that is sick for the sick patient is also bad in a more objective sense (even for healthy people), if only because it can produce neurotic people.

of T-groups, encounter groups, and many other kinds of "personal growth" groups and classes may have perceptible effects on the society.

It seems to me that no society, however good, could completely elim-inate sickness. If threats do not come from other human beings, they will always come from nature, from death, from frustration, from sickness, even from the mere fact that by living together in a society, though we advantage ourselves thereby, we must also necessarily modify the form of satisfying our desires. Nor dare we forget that human nature itself generates much evil, if not from inborn malice, then from ignorance, stupidity, fear, miscommunications, clumsiness, etc. See Chapter 9.

This is a terribly complicated set of interrelations and it is very easy to be misunderstood or to say things in such a way as to invite misunder-standing. Perhaps I can guard against this, without writing at very great length, by referring the reader to a paper I prepared for my students in a seminar on Utopian Social Psychology (311b). It stresses the empirical, the actually attainable (rather than unattainable fantasies) and it also insists on statements of degree rather than either/or statements. The task is structured by the questions: How good a society does human nature permit? How good a human nature does society permit? How good a human nature can we hope for considering the built-in limitations of human nature that we already know about? How good a society dare we hope for in view of the difficulties inherent in the very nature of society itself?

My personal judgments are that no perfect human being is possible or even conceivable, but that human beings are *far* more improvable than most people believe. As for the perfect society, this seems to me to be an impossible hope, especially in view of the obvious fact that it is close to impossible even to make a perfect marriage, a friendship, or parent–child relationship. If untainted love is so difficult to achieve in a pair, a family, a group, how much more difficult for 200 million? For 3 billion? And yet again, it is clear that pairings, groupings and societies, though not perfect-ible, are very clearly improvable and can range from very good to very bad.

Furthermore, I feel we know enough about improving pairs, groups, and societies to reject the likelihood of quick or easy changes. Improving a single person—so that it lasts—can be a matter of years of therapeutic work, and even then the main aspect of the "improvement" is that it permits him to go about the lifelong task of improving himself. Instant self-actualization, in a great moment of conversion or insight or awaken-ing *does* happen, but it is extremely rare and should not be counted upon. The psychoanalysts have long since learned not to rely on insight alone, but now stress "working through," the long, slow, painful, repeated effort to use and to apply the insights. In the East, spiritual teachers and guides will generally also make this same point, that to improve oneself is a life-long effort. The same lesson is now slowly dawning upon the more thoughtful and sober of the leaders of T-groups, basic encounter groups, personal growth groups, affective education, etc., who are now in the painful process of giving up the "Big Bang" theory of self-actualization.

All formulations in this area would have to be degree formulas of course, as in the following examples. (1) The healthier the general society, the less necessity there should be for individual psychotherapy, since fewer individuals would be sick. (2) The healthier the general society, the more likely will it be that a sick person can be helped or cured without technical therapeutic intervention, i.e., by the good life experiences. (3) The healthier the general society, the easier will it be for the therapist to cure the sick patient, since simple gratification therapy is more likely to be acceptable to the patient. (4) The healthier the general society, the easier will it be for insight therapy to cure, because there will be so many supporting good life experiences, good relationships, etc., as well as relative absence of war, unemployment, poverty, etc., and other sociopathogenic influences. Obviously, dozens of theorems of this easily testable sort are possible.

Some such phrasing of the relationship between individual sickness, individual therapy, and the nature of the society is necessary to help solve the often stated pessimistic paradox, "How can health or improvement of health be possible in a sick society that created the ill health in the first place?" Of course the pessimism implied in this dilemma is contradicted by the very presence of self-actualizing people, and by the existence of psychotherapy, which proves its possibility by actually existing. It is helpful, even so, to supply a theory of *how* it is possible, if only to throw the whole question open to empirical research.

THE ROLE OF TRAINING AND THEORY IN MODERN PSYCHOTHERAPY

As illness becomes more and more severe, it becomes less and less accessible to benefit from need gratification. There comes a point in this continuum where (1) basic need gratifications are often not even sought for or wanted, having been given up in favor of neurotic-need gratifications, and (2) even when they are offered, the patient cannot use them. It is no use offering him affection, for he is afraid of it, mistrusts it, misinterprets it, and finally refuses it.

It is at this point that professional (insight) therapy becomes not only necessary but irreplaceable. No other therapy will do, neither suggestion, nor catharsis, nor symptom cure, nor need-gratification. Therefore, beyond this point, we enter, so to speak, into other country—an area governed by its own laws, an area in which all principles so far discussed in this chapter cease to apply unless modified and qualified.

The differences between technical and lay therapy are vast and important. Thirty or forty years ago we should not have had to add anything to the above discussion. Today it is necessary to do so, for psychological developments in this century, starting with the revolutionary discoveries of Freud, Adler, etc., have been transforming psychotherapy from an unconscious art into a consciously applied science. There are now available psychotherapeutic tools that are not automatically available to the good human being, but are available only to people of sufficient intellect who have in addition been rigorously trained to use these new techniques. They are artificial techniques, not spontaneous or unconscious ones. They can be taught in a way that is to some extent independent of the character structure of the psychotherapist.

I wish to speak here only about the most important, the most revolutionary of these techniques, i.e., the bringing of insight to the patient, that is, making consciously available to him his unconscious desires, impulses, inhibitions, and thoughts (genetic analysis, character analysis, resistance analysis, analysis of the transference). It is primarily this tool that gives the professional psychotherapist who also has the requisite good personality his tremendous advantage over the man who has merely the good personality and not the professional techniques.

How is this insight brought about? So far most of not all the techniques for bringing it about have not gone very much beyond those that Freud elaborated. Free associations, dream interpretation, interpretation of the meaning behind everyday behavior, are the major paths by which therapists help the patient to gain conscious insight into himself.[7] A few other possibilities are ready to hand but they are much less important. Relaxation techniques and various techniques that induce some form of dissociation and then take advantage of it are not so important as the

---

[7] Group therapies of various types rely largely upon Freudian theories and methods but promise to add to our repertoire of insight techniques (1) educational techniques of explanation, direct imparting of information, etc., and (2) lifting of milder repressions by hearing other patients ventilate similar ones of their own. This discussion is less relevant to the various behavior therapies.

so-called Freudian techniques, even though they might very well be used more than they are today.

Within limits these techniques can be acquired by anybody with a decent intelligence who is willing to go through a suitable course of training provided by psychiatric and psychoanalytical institutes, graduate departments of clinical psychology, etc. It is true that, as we might have expected, there are individual differences in the efficiency of their use. Some students of insight therapy seem to have better intuition than others. We may suspect also that the kind of man we have labeled as the good personality will be able to use them far more efficiently than the therapist who does not have this kind of personality. All institutes of psychoanalysis include a personality requirement for their students.

Another new and great discovery given to us by Freud is the recognition of the necessity for self-understanding by the psychotherapist himself. While the necessity for this kind of insight by the therapist is recognized by the psychoanalysts, it is not yet formally recognized by psychotherapists of other persuasions. This is a mistake. It follows from the theory presented here that any force that will make the therapist into a better personality will thereby make him a better therapist. Psychoanalysis or other profound therapy of the therapist *can* help to do this. If it sometimes fails to cure altogether, at least it can make the therapist aware of what is likely to threaten him, of the major areas of conflict and frustration within him. Consequently, when he deals with his patients, he can discount these forces within himself, and correct for them. Being always conscious of them, he can make them subject to his intelligence.

In the past, as we have said, the character structure of the therapist was far more important than any theories he held, or even more important than the conscious techniques that he used. But this must become less and less so as technical therapy becomes more and more sophisticated. In the total picture of the good psychotherapist his character structure for the last decade or two has slowly receded in importance and will certainly continue to do so in the future, while his training, his intelligence, his techniques, his theories have steadily become more and more important until, we may rest assured, some time in the future they will become all-important. We have lauded the wise old woman technique of psychotherapy for the simple reasons that in the past these were the only psychotherapists available, and second because even in the present and in the future they will always be important in what we have called lay psychotherapy. No longer, however, is it sensible or justified to toss a coin to decide whether to go to the minister or to the psychoanalyst. The good professional psychotherapist has left the intuitive helper far behind.

We may expect that in the not too distant future, especially if the society improves, the professional psychotherapist will not be used for purposes of reassurance, support, and other need gratifications, because we will get these from our fellow laymen. An individual will come for maladies that lie beyond the reach of simple gratification therapy or release therapy, but that are accessible only to professional techniques that are not used by the layman.

Paradoxically a completely contrary deduction is also possible from the foregoing theories. If relatively healthy people are so much more readily touched by therapy, it is quite possible that much technical therapeutic time will be reserved for the most healthy instead of the least healthy on the sensible grounds that improving ten people a year is better than improving one, especially if these few are themselves in key lay therapeutic positions, e.g., teachers, social workers, physicians. This is already happening to a considerable extent. A large proportion of the time of experienced psychoanalysts and existential analysts is occupied with training and teaching and analyzing young therapists. It is also very common now for a therapist to be teaching physicians, social workers, psychologists, nurses, ministers, and teachers.

Before leaving the subject of insight therapy, I think it well to resolve the dichotomy so far implied between insight and need gratification. Purely cognitive or rationalistic insight (cold, unemotional knowledge about) is one thing; organismic insight is another. The full insight that the Freudians sometimes speak about is a recognition of the fact that mere knowledge about one's symptoms, even when we add knowledge about where they come from and the dynamic role they play in the contemporary psychic economy, is frequently not in itself curative. There ought to be an emotional experience simultaneously, an actual reliving of the experience, a catharsis, a reaction. That is, a full insight is not only a cognitive but also an emotional experience.

Somewhat more subtle is the contention that this insight is often a conative, need-gratifying, or frustrating experience as well, an actual feeling of being loved, or abandoned, or despised, or rejected or protected. The emotion that the analysts speak of then is better seen as the reaction to realization, e.g., that father really loved him after all as one vividly relives a twenty-year-old experience, repressed or wrongly understood until now, or that he suddenly realizes, by actually experiencing the appropriate emotion, that he hated the mother he had always assumed he loved.

This rich experience, simultaneously cognitive, emotional, and conative, we may call the organismic insight. But supposing we have been studying *emotional* experiences primarily? Again we should have to expand the experience more and more to include conative elements, and we should ultimately find ourselves speaking of the organismic or holistic emotion, etc. So also for the conative experience; it too would expand to a nonfaculty experience of the total organism. The final step would be to realize that there was no difference between organismic insight, organismic emotion, and organismic conation except the angle of approach of the student, and the original dichotomies would be clearly seen to be artifacts of a too atomistic approach to the subject.

SELF-THERAPY; COGNITIVE THERAPY

It is one implication of the theory presented here that self-therapy has at the same time greater possibilities and also greater limitations than have been commonly realized. If every human being learns to know what he lacks, learns what his fundamental desires are, learns in broad outline the symptoms that indicate the lack of satisfaction of these fundamental desires, he can consciously go about trying to make up for these lacks. We may fairly say that by this theory most human beings have within their own power greater possibility than they have realized for curing themselves of the multitude of mild maladjustments which are so common in our society. Love, safety, belongingness, and respect from other people are almost panaceas for the situational disturbances and even for some of the mild character disturbances. If the individual knows that he should have love, respect, self-respect, etc., he can consciously seek them out. Certainly everyone will agree that seeking them out consciously will be better and more effective than trying to make up for their lack unconsciously.

But at the same time that this hope is offered to a good many individuals, and that they are given a wider possibility for self-therapy than has ordinarily been thought to be possible, there are certain problems for which they must necessarily seek help only from professional hands. For one thing, in severe character disturbances or existential neuroses, a clear understanding of the dynamic forces originating, precipitating, and maintaining the disturbance are absolutely necessary before anything can be done for the patient beyond mere amelioration. It is here that all the tools that are necessary to bring conscious insight must be used, tools for which there are as yet no substitutes, and that are at present usable only by professionally trained therapists. Once a case is recognized as severe, help from the layman, from the wise old woman becomes in nine cases out of ten completely useless so far as permanent cure is concerned. This is the essential limitation upon self-therapy.[8]

GROUP THERAPY: PERSONAL GROWTH GROUPS

A final implication of our approach of psychotherapy is a greater respect for group therapies as well as T-groups, etc. We have stressed so much the fact that psychotherapy and personal growth is an interpersonal relationship that on a priori grounds alone we should feel that an extension from pairing into a larger grouping might very well be beneficial. If ordinary therapy may be conceived of as a miniature ideal society of two, then group therapy may be seen as a miniature ideal society of ten. We already have a strong motivation for experimenting with group therapy, viz., economy of money and time, and a wider availability of psychotherapy to more and more patients. But in addition we now have empirical data that indicate that group therapy and T-groups can do some things that individual psychotherapy cannot. We know already that it is very easy to get rid of the sense of uniqueness, of isolation, of guilt or sin when patients find out that the other members of the group are made of about the same kind of stuff as they are, that their goals, their conflicts, their satisfactions and dissatisfactions, their hidden impulses and thoughts are apt to be almost universal in the society taken at large. This reduces the psychopathogenic effect of these secretive conflicts and impulses.

Another therapeutic expectation is also borne out by actual practice. In individual psychotherapy the patient learns to make a good human relationship with at least one individual—the therapist. It is then hoped that he can transfer this ability over to his social life in general. Often he can, but sometimes he cannot. In group therapy he not only learns how to establish this good relationship with at least one person, but actually proceeds under the eye of the therapist to practice this ability with a

---

[8] Since this was first written, the interesting books on self-analysis by Horney (200) and Farrow (127) have appeared. Their contention is that the individual, by his own efforts, can come to achieve the kind—but not the degree—of insight achieved by professional analysis. This is not denied by most analysts, but is considered impracticable because of the extraordinary drive, patience, courage, and persistence required of such a patient. Something similar is true, I believe, for the many books on personal growth (63, 189, 365, 366, 368, 374, 415, 446). They can certainly be helpful but must not be counted on for great transformations without help from a professional or from a "guide," guru, leader, etc.

whole group of other people as well. In general the results from experiments already available, while not startling, are certainly encouraging.

It is because of such empirical data as well as because of deductions from theory that we should urge more research with group psychotherapy, not only because it is a promising lead for technical psychotherapy, but also because it will surely teach us much about general psychological theory and even about broad social theory as well.

So also for T-groups, basic encounter groups, sensitivity training, and all the other kinds of groups now categorized as personal growth groups or affective education seminars and workshops. Though quite different in procedure, they may yet be said to have the same *far* goals of all psychotherapies, that is, self-actualization, full-humanness, fuller use of species and personal potentials, etc. Like any of the psychotherapies, they can do wonders when well run by competent people. But we now have enough experience to know that they can be useless or harmful when under bad management. Therefore much more research is needed. This of course is not a startling conclusion because exactly the same is true for surgeons and for all other professionals. Nor have we solved the problem of just *how* a layman or an amateur can choose the competent therapist (or physician or dentist, or guru, guide, or teacher) and avoid the incompetent one.

16

NORMALITY, HEALTH, AND VALUES

The words normal and abnormal cover so many different meanings that they have become just about useless. The strong tendency today is for psychologists and psychiatrists to substitute for these very general words the more specific concepts that are included under these heads. This is what I mean to do in this chapter.

In general the attempts to define normality have been either statistical, or culturally relative, or biological-medical. However, these are the *formal* definitions only, the "company" or Sunday definitions, not the everyday ones. The informal meaning carried by the word is just as definite as the professional ones. Most people have something else in mind when they ask, "What is normal?" For most people, even for the professionals in their informal moments, this is a value question, and in effect asks what we should value, what is good and bad for us, what we shoull worry about, and what we ought to feel guilty or virtuous about. I choose to interpret the title of this chapter in the lay sense as well as in the professional sense. It is my impression that most of the technicians in the field do the same thing although they do not admit it most of the time. There is a good deal of discussion about what normal ought to mean and rather little about what it *does* mean in context, in normal conversation. In my therapeutic work I have always interpreted the question about normality and abnormality in the speaker's context rather than in the technical context. When a mother has asked me whether her child was normal, I understood her to be asking ought she worry about it or not, should she change her efforts to control her child's behavior, or should she let it slide and not bother. When people after a lecture have asked about the normality and abnormality of sexual behavior, I have understood their question in the same way, and my answer very frequently implied, "Do worry about it," or, "Do not worry about it."

I think that the real reason for currently revived interest in this problem among psychoanalysts, psychiatrists, and psychologists is the feeling that this is *the* great value question. When, for instance, Erich Fromm talks about normality, he places it in the context of goodness, desirability, and value. So increasingly have most other writers in this area. This kind of work now and for some time past has been very frankly an effort to construct a psychology of values that might ultimately serve as a practical guide for ordinary people, as well as a theoretical frame of reference for professors of philosophy and other technicians.

I can go even further than this. For many of these psychologists this whole effort is more and more (for most) admitted to be an attempt to do what the formal religions have tried to do and failed to do, that is, to offer people an understanding of human nature in relationship to itself, to other people, to society in general, and to the world in general, a frame of reference in which they could understand when they ought to feel guilty and when they ought not to feel guilty. That is to say, we are working up what amounts to a scientific ethics. I am perfectly willing that my remarks in this chapter be understood as moving in this direction.

DEFINITIONS OF NORMALITY

Now before we get to this important subject let us turn first to the various technical attempts to describe and define normality that have not worked well.

1. Statistical surveys of human behavior tell us simply what is the case and what actually exists, and are supposed to be completely devoid of evaluation. Fortunately, most people, even scientists, are simply not strong enough to resist the temptation to approve of the average, of what is most common and most frequent, especially in our culture, which is so strong for the common man. For instance, Kinsey's excellent survey of sexual behavior is highly useful for the raw information that it gives. But Dr. Kinsey and others simply cannot avoid talking about what is normal (meaning desirable). It is average in our society to have a sick, pathological sexual life (from the psychiatric point of view). This does not make

it desirable or healthy. We must learn to say average when we mean average.

Another example is the Gesell table of norms of baby development, which are certainly useful for scientists and physicians to have. But most mothers are apt to get worried if their baby is below the average in the development of walking or drinking out of a cup, as if this were bad or frightening. Apparently after we find out what is average, we must still ask, "Is the average desirable?"

2. The word normal often is used as an unconscious synonym for tradition or habitual or conventional, and is usually meant to cloak the tradition in approval. I remember the turmoil over women smoking when I went to college. It was not normal, our dean of women said, and forbade it. At that time it was also not normal for college women to wear slacks, or to hold hands in public. Of course what she meant was, "This is not traditional," which was perfectly true, and this implied for her, "This is abnormal, sick, intrinsically pathological," which was perfectly false. A few years later the traditions changed and she was fired, because by that time *her* ways were not "normal."

3. A variant of this usage is to cloak tradition in theological approval. So-called sacred books are interpreted very frequently as setting norms for behavior, but the scientist pays as little attention to these traditions as to any other.

4. Finally, the culturally relative may also be considered to be obsolete as a source of definition of normal, desirable, good, or healthy. The anthropologists of course did us a great service at first in making us aware of our ethnocentrism. We had been as a culture trying to set up as absolute and species-wide criteria all sorts of local cultural habits like wearing pants or eating cows rather than dogs. A wider ethnological sophistication has dispelled many of these notions, and it is generally recognized that ethnocentrism is a serious danger. Nobody can speak for the whole species now unless he knows something about cultural anthropology and something about a half a dozen or a dozen cultures at least, so that he is able to rise above his own culture or stand aside from it, and is thereby more able to judge the human species as a species and not as a neighborhood group.

5. The main variant of this mistake is found in the idea of the well-adjusted man. It may puzzle the lay reader to discover how hostile psychologists have become to this seemingly sensible and obvious idea. After all everyone wants his children to be well adjusted and part of the group, popular, admired, and loved by the friends of their own age. Our big

question is, "Adjusted to *which* group?" Nazis, criminals, delinquents, drug addicts? Popular with whom? Admired by whom? In H. G. Well's wonderful short story, "The Valley of the Blind," where all are blind, the sighted man is maladjusted.

Adjustment means a passive shaping of oneself to one's culture, to the external environment. But supposing it is a sick culture? Or to give another example, we are slowly learning not to prejudge juvenile delinquents as being necessarily bad or undesirable on psychiatric grounds. Crime and delinquency and bad behavior in children may sometimes represent psychiatrically and biologically *legitimate* revolt against exploitation, injustice, and unfairness.

Adjustment is a passive rather than active process; its ideal is attained in the cow or in the slave or anyone else who can be happy without individuality, even, e.g., the well-adjusted lunatic or prisoner.

This extreme environmentalism implies infinite malleability and flexibility in the human being and unchangeability in reality. It is therefore *status quo* and fatalistic. It is also untrue. Human beings are *not* infinitely malleable, and reality *can* be changed.

6. In a completely different tradition is the medical-clinical custom of applying the word normal to the absence of lesion, disease, or obvious malfunctions. The internist who cannot find anything physically wrong after a thorough examination will say the patient is normal, even though he is in pain still. What he means is, "By *my* techniques I cannot discover what is wrong with you."

The physician with some psychological training, the so-called psychosomaticist, can see still more and will use the word normal much less often. Indeed many psychoanalysts go so far as to say no one is normal, meaning completely free of sickness. That is to say, no one is without blemish. Which is true enough, but again does not help us much in our ethical pursuit.

NEW CONCEPTS OF NORMALITY

What is taking the place of these various conceptions that we have learned to reject? The new frame of reference that this chapter is concerned with is still in process of development and construction. It cannot be said to be clearly seen yet or reliably supported by incontestable evidence at the moment. It is fair to characterize it rather as a slowly developing concept or theory that seems more and more probably to be the true direction of future development.

Specifically my prediction or guess about the future of the normality idea is that some form of theory about generalized, species-wide, psychological health will soon be developed, which will hold for all human beginning of Christianity has been dominated by some four successive is taking place on empirical as well as on theoretical grounds. This new form of thinking has been forced by new facts, new data of which I shall speak later.

Drucker (113) has presented the thesis that western Europe since the beginning of Christianity has been dominated by some four successive ideas or concepts as to the ways in which individual happiness and welfare should be sought. Each of these concepts or myths held up a certain type of man as ideal, and generally assumed that if only this ideal were followed, individual happiness and welfare would be sure to result. The spiritual man was regarded as ideal during the middle ages, the intellectual man during the Renaissance. Then with the rise of capitalism and Marxism, the economic man has tended to dominate ideal thinking. More recently, and especially in the fascist countries, it might also be fair to speak of a similar and parallel myth, namely, that of heroic man (heroic in the Nietzchean sense).

It looks now as if all these myths have failed, and are now giving way to a new one that is slowly developing in the minds of the most advanced thinkers and researchers on the subject, and that may fairly be expected to come into flower in the next decade or two, namely, the concept of the psychologically healthy man, or the eupsychic man, who is also in effect the "natural" man. I expect that this concept will affect our era as profoundly as have the ones mentioned by Drucker.

Now let me try to present briefly and at first dogmatically the essence of this newly developing conception of the psychologically healthy man. First of all and most important of all is the strong belief that man has an essential nature of his own, some skeleton of psychological structure that may be treated and discussed analogously with his physical structure, that he has some needs, capacities, and tendencies that are in part genetically based, some of which are characteristic of the whole human species, cutting across all cultural lines, and some of which are unique to the individual. These basic needs are on their face good or neutral rather than evil. Second, there is involved the conception that full health and normal and desirable development consist in actualizing this nature, in fulfilling these potentialities, and in developing into maturity along the lines that this hidden, covert, dimly seen essential nature dictates, growing from within rather than being shaped from without. Third, it is now seen clearly that most psychopathology results from the denial or the frustration or the twisting of man's essential nature. By this concept what is good? Anything that conduces to this desirable development in the direction of actualization of the inner nature of man. What is bad or abnormal? Anything that frustrates or blocks or denies the essential nature of man. What is psychopathological? Anything that disturbs or frustrates or twists the course of self-actualization. What is psychotherapy, or for that matter any therapy or growth of any kind? Any means of any kind that helps to restore the person to the path of self-actualization and of development along the lines that his inner nature dictates.

At first blush, this conception reminds us a great deal of the Aristotelian and Spinozist ideas of the past. In truth, we must say that this new conception has much in common with the older philosophies. But we must also point out that we now know a great deal more than Aristotle and Spinoza about the true nature of the human being. We know in any case enough to understand what their mistakes and shortcomings were.

Primarily the kinds of knowledge that these ancient philosophers lacked and that led their theories to have fatal shortcomings have been discovered by the various schools of psychoanalysis. We have acquired from the dynamic psychologists particularly, but also from animal psychologists and others, a greatly increased understanding of man's motivations, especially of his unconscious motivations. Second, we now have a greatly increased knowledge of psychopathology and of the origins of this psychopathology. Finally, we have learned a great deal from the psychotherapists, particularly from the discussions of the processes and the goals of psychotherapy.

What this amounts to saying is that we may agree with Aristotle when he assumed that the good life consisted in living in accordance with the true nature of man, but we must add that he simply did not know enough about the true nature of man. All that Aristotle could do in delineating this essential nature, or inherent design of human nature, was to look about him, to study people, to observe what they were like. But if one observes human beings only on the surface, which was all Aristotle could do, one must ultimately wind up with what amounts to a static conception of human nature. The only thing that Aristotle could do was to build a picture of the good man in his own culture and in that particular period of time. You remember that in his conception of the good life, Aristotle accepted completely the fact of slavery and made the fatal mistake of assuming that just because a man was a slave that this was his essential nature and therefore it was good for him to be a slave. This exposes completely the weakness of resting on a mere surface observation in the attempt to build up the idea of what the good man or the normal man or the healthy man is like.

DIFFERENCES BETWEEN NEWER
AND OLDER CONCEPTS

I suppose that if I had to put into a single phrase the contrast between the Aristotelian theory and the modern conceptions of Goldstein, Fromm, Horney, Rogers, Bühler, May, Grof, Dabrowski, Murray, Sutich, Bugental, Allport, Frankl, Murphy, Rorschach, and many, many others, I would maintain that the essential difference is that we can now see not only what man is, but what he may become. That is to say that we can see not only surface, not only the actualities, but the potentialities as well. We know better now what lies hidden in man, what lies suppressed, neglected, and unseen. We are now able to judge the essential nature of man in terms of what his possibilities, potentialities, and highest possible development may be, instead of relying only on external observations, of what is the case at this moment. This approach sums up to this: history has practically always sold human nature short.

Another advantage that we have over Aristotle is that we have learned from these same dynamic psychologists that self-realization cannot be attained by intellect or rationality alone. You remember that Aristotle had a hierarchy of human capacities in which reason took the top place. Along with this went inevitably the notion that reason contrasted with, struggled with, and was at odds with man's emotional and instinctoid nature. But we have learned from the study of psychopathology and psychotherapy that we must modify considerably our picture of the psychological organism to respect equally rationality, emotionality, and the conative or wishing and driving side of our nature. Furthermore, from our empirical studies of the healthy man we have learned that these are definitely not at odds with each other, that these sides of human nature are not necessarily antagonistic but can be cooperative and synergic. The healthy man is all of a piece, integrated, we might say. It is the neurotic person who is at odds with himself, whose reason struggles with his emotions. The result of this split has been that not only the emotional life and the conative have been misunderstood and badly defined, but that also we realize now that the conception of rationality that we inherited from the past is also wrongly understood and wrongly defined. As Erich Fromm has said, "Reason by becoming a guard set to watch its prisoner, human nature, has become a prisoner itself and thus both sides of human nature, reason and emotion, were crippled" (148). We must all agree with Fromm that the realization of the self occurs not only by acts of thinking but rather by the realization of man's total personality, which includes the active expression not only of his intellectual but also his emotional and instinctlike capacities.

Once granted reliable knowledge of what man *can* be under certain conditions that we have learned to call good, and granted that he is happy, serene, self-accepting, unguilty, and at peace with himself only when he is fulfilling himself and becoming what he can be, it is possible and reasonable to speak about good and right and bad and wrong and desirable and undesirable.

If it is objected by the technical philosopher, "How can you prove that it is better to be happy than unhappy?" even this question can be answered empirically, for if we observe human beings under sufficiently wide conditions, we discover that they, *they* themselves, *not* the observer, choose spontaneously to be happy rather than unhappy, comfortable rather than pained, serene rather than anxious. In a word, human beings choose health rather than illness, all other things being equal (with the proviso that *they* choose for themselves that they be not too sick, and that the conditions be of a kind that will be discussed later).

This answers also the customary philosophical objection to the means-end value propositions with which all are familiar (*If* you want end *x,* you *ought* to do means *y.* "You ought to eat vitamins, if you want to live longer.") We now have a different approach to this proposition. We know *empirically* what the human species wants, e.g., love, safety, absence of pain, happiness, prolongation of life, knowledge, etc. We can then say *not,* "If you wish to be happy, then . . . ," but, "If you are a sound member of the human species, then. . . ."

This is all true in the same empirical sense that we casually say a dog prefers meat to salad, or that goldfish need fresh water, or that flowers prosper best in the sun. I maintain firmly then that we have been making descriptive, scientific statements rather than purely normative ones. (I have suggested the term *fusion words,* where the word is both descriptive and normative (314).

Another word for my philosophical colleagues who distinguish sharply between what we are and what we ought to be. What we *can* be = what we ought to be, and is much better language than ought to be. Observe that if we are being descriptive and empirical, then ought is completely out of place, as can be clearly seen if we ask about flowers or animals, what *they* ought to be. What sense does ought make here (or should)? What *ought* a kitten become? The answer to this question and the spirit in which it is put is the same for human children.

Even a stronger way of saying this is that it is today possible to distinguish in a single moment of time what a man *is* and what he *could* be.

We are all familiar with the fact that the human personality is organized into layers, or depths. That which is unconscious and that which is conscious coexist, even though they may contradict each other. One *is* (in one sense); the other also *is* (in another deeper sense) and *could* one day come to the surface, become conscious, and then *be* in *that* sense.

In this frame of reference, you can understand that people who behave badly may yet be loving deep down. If they manage to actualize this species-wide potentiality they become healthier men, and in this special sense, more normal.

The important difference between man and all other beings is that his needs, his preferences, his instinct remnants are *weak* and not strong, equivocal not unequivocal, that they leave room for doubt, uncertainty, and conflict, that they are all too easily overlaid and lost to sight by culture, by learning, by the preferences of other people.[1] Through the ages we have been used to thinking of instincts as univocal, unmistakable, strong, and powerful (as they *are* in animals) that we never saw the possibility of *weak* instincts.

We *do* have a nature, a structure, a shadowy bone structure of instinctoid tendencies and capacities, but it is a great and difficult achievement to know it in ourselves. To be natural and spontaneous, to know what one is, and what one *really* wants, is a rare and high culmination that comes infrequently, and that usually takes long years of courage and hard work.

MAN'S INNER NATURE

Let us sum up then. What has been affirmed is that man's inherent design or inner nature seems to be not only his anatomy and physiology, but also his most basic needs, yearnings, and psychological capacities. And second, this inner nature is usually not obvious and easily seeen, but is rather hidden and unfulfilled, weak rather than strong.

And how do we know that these needs and constitutional potentialities *are* inherent design? Of the twelve separate lines of evidence and techniques of discovery listed in Chapter 6 and in (298), I shall mention now only the four most important. First, frustration of these needs and capacities is psychopathogenic, i.e., it makes people sick. Second, their gratification is healthy-character-fostering (eupsychogenic), as neurotic

---

[1] Dr. Lucie Jessner has also suggested the possibility that these needs may be kept weak by the specifically human propensity to overgratify or to gratify too soon after a previous gratification.

need gratifications are not. That is, it makes people healthy and better. Third, they spontaneously show themselves as choices under free conditions. Fourth, they can be directly studied in relatively healthy people.

If we wish to differentiate basic from nonbasic, we cannot look alone to introspection of conscious needs or even to description of unconscious needs because, phenomenologically, neurotic needs and inherent needs may all feel much alike. They press equally for gratification, for the monopolizing of consciousness, and their introspected qualities are not different enough from each other to enable the introspector to differentiate them except perhaps at the end of his life and in retrospect (as did Tolstoy's Ivan Ilyitch), or in moments of special insight.

No, we must have some other external variable to correlate with, to covary with. In effect this other variable has been the neurosis-health continuum. We are now pretty well convinced that nasty aggressiveness is reactive rather than basic, effect rather than cause, because as a nasty person gets healthier in psychotherapy, he gets less vicious; and as a healthier person gets more sick, he changes in the direction of *more* hostility, *more* venom, and *more* viciousness.

Furthermore, we know that giving gratification to neurotic needs does *not* breed health as does gratification of basic inherent needs. Giving a neurotic power seeker all the power he wants does not make him less neurotic, nor is it possible to satiate his neurotic need for power. However much he is fed he still remains hungry (because he's really looking for something else). It makes little difference for ultimate health whether a neurotic need be gratified or frustrated.

It is very different with basic needs like safety or love. Their gratification *does* breed health, their satiation *is* possible, their frustration *does* breed sickness.

The same seems to be true for individual potentialities like intelligence, or strong tendency to activity. (The only data we have here are clinical.) Such a tendency acts like a drive that demands fulfillment. Gratify it and the person develops nicely; frustrate it and block it, and various subtle troubles, not yet very well known, develop at once.

The most obvious technique of all, however, is the direct study of people who are *actually* healthy. We certainly know enough now to be able to select *relatively* healthy people. Granted that perfect specimens do not exist, still it may be expected that we can learn more about the nature, for example, of radium when it is relatively concentrated than when it is relatively dilute.

The investigation reported in Chapter 11 has demonstrated the possibility that a *scientist* could study and describe normality in the sense of excellence, perfection, ideal health, the fulfillment of human possibilities. If we *know* what good people are like or can be like, it becomes possible for the human species (who mostly want to be good) to model themselves on these paragons and improve thereby.

The most fully studied example of inherent design is the love need. With this we can illustrate all four of the techniques so far mentioned for differentiating the inherent and universal in human nature from the accidental and local.

1. It is agreed by practically all therapists that when we trace a neurosis back to its beginnings we shall find with great frequency a deprivation of love in the early years. Several semi-experimental studies have confirmed this in infants and babies to such a point that radical deprivation of love is considered dangerous even to the life of the infant. That is to say, the deprivation of love leads to illness.

2. These illnesses, if they have not gone so far as to be irreversible, are now known to be curable, especially in young children, by giving affection and loving kindness. Even in adult psychotherapy and analysis of more serious cases, there is now good reason to believe that one thing that the therapy does is to make it possible for the patient to receive and utilize the love that heals. Also there is a mounting mass of evidence to prove a correlation between affectionate childhood and a healthy adulthood. Such data add up to the generalization that love is a basic need for healthy development of the human being.

3. The child in the situation where he is permitted free choice, and granted that he is not yet warped and twisted, prefers affection to non-affection. We have no true experiments yet to prove this, but we have a huge amount of clinical data and *some* ethnological data to support this conclusion. The common observation that children prefer an affectionate teacher or parent or friend to the hostile or cold teacher or parent or friend illustrates what I mean. The crying of infants tells us that they prefer affection to nonaffection, for instance in the Balinese situation. The adult Balinese does not need love as the adult American does. Balinese children are taught by bitter experiences not to ask for it and not to expect it. But they do not *like* this training; the children weep bitterly while being trained not to ask for love.

4. Finally, what do we find descriptively in healthy adults? That practically all (though not quite all) have led loving lives, have loved and been loved. Furthermore, they are *now* loving people. And finally and paradoxically they *need* love *less* than the average man does, apparently because they already have enough.

A perfect parallel that makes these points more plausible and more common sense is supplied by *any* other of the deficiency diseases. Supposing an animal lacks salt. First this produces pathology. Second, extra salt taken into the body cures or helps these sicknesses. Third, a white rat or a human that lacks salt when given a choice will prefer salt-laden foods, that is, will eat salt in unusually large quantities and in the case of the human, will report subjective cravings for salt and will report that it tastes especially good. Fourth, we find that healthy organisms, already having enough salt, do *not* specially crave it or need it.

We may therefore say that just as an organism needs salt in order to attain health and avoid illness, so also does it need love for the same reasons. In other words, we can say that the organism is so designed that it needs salt and love, in the same way that automobiles are so designed that they need gas and oil.

We have spoken much of good conditions, of permissiveness, etc. These refer to the special conditions of observation that are so often necessary in scientific work and are the equivalent of saying, "This is true under such and such circumstances."

DEFINITION OF GOOD CONDITIONS

Let us turn to this problem of what constitutes good conditions for the revelation of original nature to see what contemporary dynamic psychology has to offer on the subject.

If the upshot of what we have already said is that the organism has a vaguely delineated, intrinsic nature of its own, it is quite clear that this inner nature is a very delicate and subtle something rather than being strong and overpowering as it is in lower animals, who are never in any doubt about what they are, what they want, and what they do not want. The human needs for love, or for knowledge or for a philosophy, are weak and feeble rather than unequivocal and unmistakable; they whisper rather than shout. And the whisper is easily drowned out.

In order to discover what a human being needs and what he *is*, it is necessary to set up special conditions that foster expression of these needs and capacities that encourage and make them possible. In general these conditions may all be summed up under the one head of permissiveness to gratify and to express. How do we know what is best for pregnant white rats to eat? We give them free choice from among a wide range of possibilities, and we let them eat whatever they want, whenever they want it, and in any quantities or patterns they choose. We know it is best for a human infant to be weaned in an individual fashion, i.e., whenever it is best for *him*. How do we determine this? Certainly we cannot ask the infant, and we have learned not to ask the old-school pediatrician. We give the baby a choice; we let him decide. We offer him both the liquid and the solid food. If the solid food appeals to him he will spontaneously wean himself from the breast. In the same way we have learned to let the child tell us when he needs love, or protection, or respect or control, by setting up a permissive, accepting, gratifying atmosphere. We have learned that this is the best atmosphere for psychotherapy, indeed, the *only* possible one, in the long run. Free choice from among a wide range of possibilities has been found useful in such diverse social situations as choosing roommates in institutions for delinquent girls, choosing teachers and courses in college, choosing bombardier crews, etc. (I leave aside the knotty but important question of *desirable* frustration, of discipline, of setting limits to gratification. I wish to point out only that while permissiveness may be best for our experimental purpose, it need not also be sufficient in itself for teaching consideration of others and awareness of *their* needs or of what may be necessary in the future.)

From the point of view, then, of fostering self-actualization or health, a good environment (in theory) is one that offers all necessary raw materials and then gets out of the way and stands aside to let the (average) organism itself utter its wishes and demands and make its choices (always remembering that it often chooses delay, renunciation in favor of others, etc., and that *other* people also have demands and wishes).

A PSYCHOLOGICAL UTOPIA

It has been my pleasure recently to work up a speculative description of a psychological Utopia in which all men are psychologically healthy. Eupsychia, I call it (pronounced Yew-sigh-key-a). From what we know of healthy people, could we predict the kind of culture that they would evolve if 1000 healthy families migrated to some deserted land where they could work out their own destiny as they pleased? What kind of education would they choose? Economic system? Sexuality? Religion?

I am very uncertain of some things—economics in particular. But of other things I am *very* sure. One of them is that this would almost surely be a (philosophically) anarchistic group, a Taoistic but loving culture, in which people (young people too) would have much more free choice than we are used to, and in which basic needs and meta needs would be respected much more than they are in our society. People would not bother each other so much as we do, would be much less prone to press opinions or religions or philosophies or tastes in clothes or food or art or women on their neighbors. In a word, the inhabitants of

Eupsychia would tend to be more Taoistic, nonintrusive, and basic need-gratifying (whenever possible), would frustrate only under certain conditions that I have not attempted to describe, would be more honest with each other than we are, and would permit people to make free choices wherever possible. They would be far less controlling, violent, contemptuous, or overbearing than we are. Under such conditions, the deepest layers of human nature could show themselves with greater ease.

I must point out that adult human beings constitute a special case. The free-choice situation does not necessarily work for people in general —only for intact ones. Sick, neurotic people make the wrong choices; they do not know what they want, and even when they do, have not courage enough to choose correctly. When we speak of free *choice* in human beings, we refer to sound adults or children who are not yet twisted and distorted. Most of the good experimental work with free choice has been done with animals. We have also learned a great deal about it at the clinical level from the analysis of psychotherapeutic processes.

ENVIRONMENT AND PERSONALITY

There is another important problem that confronts us as we struggle to understand this newer conception of normality and its relationship to environment. One theoretical consequence would seem to be that perfect health needs a perfect world to live in and to make it possible. In actual research, it does not seem to work out that way exactly.

It *is* possible to find extremely healthy individuals in our society, which is very far from perfection. Certainly these individuals are not perfect but they certainly are as fine people as we can now conceive. Perhaps at this time and in this culture we just do not know enough about how perfect people can get.

In any case, research has established an important point in discovering that individuals can be healthier, even *much* healthier, than the culture in which they grow and live. This is possible primarily because of the ability of the healthy man to be detached from his surroundings, which is the same as saying that he lives by his inner laws rather than by outer pressures.

Our culture is democratic and pluralistic enough to give a very wide latitude to individuals to have the characters that they please, so long as their external behavior is not too threatening or frightening. Healthy individuals are not usually externally visible; they are not marked off by unusual clothes, or manners, or behavior. It is an *inner* freedom that they have. So long as they are independent of the approval and disapproval of other people, and seek rather *self*-approval, so long may they be considered to be psychologically autonomous, i.e., relatively independent of the culture. Tolerance and freedom of taste and opinion seem the key necessities.

To sum up, what research we have points to the conclusion that while a good environment fosters good personalities, this relationship is far from perfect, and furthermore, the definition of *good* environment has to change markedly to stress spiritual and psychological as well as material and economic forces.

THE NATURE OF NORMALITY

Now coming back to the question with which we started, the nature of normality, we have come close to identifying it with the highest excellence of which we are capable. But this ideal is not an unattainable goal set out far ahead of us; rather it is actually within us, existent but hidden, as potentiality rather than as actuality.

Furthermore, it is a conception of normality that I claim is discovered rather than invented, based on empirical findings rather than on hopes or wishes. It implies a strictly naturalistic system of values that can be enlarged by further empirical research with human nature. Such research should be able to give us answers to the age-old questions "How can I be a good man?" "How can I live a good life?" "How can I be fruitful?" "Happy?" "At peace with myself?" If the organism tells us what it needs—and therefore what it values—by sickening and withering when deprived of these values, this is the same as telling us what is good for it.

One last point. The key concepts in the newer dynamic psychology are spontaneity, release, naturalness, self-choice, self-acceptance, impulse-awareness, gratification of basic needs. They *used* to be control, inhibition, discipline, training, shaping, on the principle that the depths of human nature were dangerous, evil, predatory, and ravenous. Education, family training, bringing up children, acculturation in general were all seen as a process of bringing the darker forces within us under control.

See how different are the ideal conceptions of society, law, education, and family that are generated by these two different conceptions of human nature. In the one case they are restraining and controlling forces; in the other they are gratifying and fulfilling.[2] Of course, this is

---

[2] Again I must stress that there are two kinds of restraint and control. One kind frustrates basic needs and fears them. The other kind (Apollonizing controls), e.g., delaying the sexual climax, eating elegantly, swimming skillfully, etc., *enhances* the gratification of basic needs.

an oversimple, either-or contrast. It is unlikely that either conception is totally correct or totally incorrect. Yet the contrast of ideal types is useful in sharpening our perceptions.

In any case, if this conception that identifies normality with ideal health holds up, we shall have to change not only our conceptions of individual psychology but also our theories of society.

APPENDIX A.

PROBLEMS GENERATED BY A POSITIVE APPROACH TO PSYCHOLOGY[1]

LEARNING

How do people learn to be wise, mature, kind, to have good taste, to be inventive, to have good characters, to be able to fit themselves to a new situation, to detect the good, to seek the truth, to know the beautiful, and the genuine, i.e., intrinsic rather than extrinsic learning (311a)?

Learning from unique experiences, from tragedy, marriage, having children, success, triumphy, falling in love, being ill, death, etc.

Learning from pain, illness, depression, tragedy, failure, old age, death.

Much that passes for associative learning is actually canalization (225): it is intrinsic and required by reality rather than relative, arbitrary, and fortuitous.

With self-actualizing people, repetition, contiguity, and arbitrary reward become less and less important. Probably advertising of the usual sort is ineffective with them. They are much less susceptible to arbitrary association, to prestige suggestion, to snob appeals and to simple, senseless repetition. Perhaps even they have negative effect, i.e., make them *less* likely to buy rather than more likely.

---

1 I am leaving this appendix with only minor corrections because (1) most of the suggestions are still pertinent and (2) it will be interesting to the student to see just how much progress has been made in these directions in 15 years.

Why does so much of educational psychology concern itself with means, i.e., grades, degrees, credits, diplomas, rather than with ends, i.e., wisdom, understanding, good judgment, good taste?

We do not know enough about the acquisition of emotional attitudes, of tastes, of preferences. The "learning of the heart" has been neglected.

Education in practice too often adapts the child to the convenience of adults by making him less a nuisance and a little devil. More positively oriented education concerns itself more with the growth and future self-actualization of the child. What do we know about teaching children to be strong, self-respecting, righteously indignant, resistant to domination and exploitation, to propaganda and blind enculturation, to suggestion and to fashion?

We know very little about purposeless, unmotivated learning, e.g., latent learning, learning out of sheer, intrinsic interest, etc.

PERCEPTION

Perception is too much the limited study of mistakes, distortion, illusions, and the like. Wertheimer would have called it the study of psychological blindness. Why not add to it the study of intitution, of subliminal perception, of unconscious and preconscious perception? Would not the study of good taste enter here? Of the genuine, of the true, and the beautiful? How about the aesthetic perception? Why do some people perceive beauty and others not? Under this same heading of perception we may also include the constructive manipulation of reality by hope, dreams, imagination, inventiveness, organizing, and ordering.

Unmotivated, disinterested, unselfish perception. Appreciation. Awe. Admiration. Choiceless awareness.

Plenty of studies of stereotypes, but very little scientific study of fresh, concrete, Bergsonian reality.

Free-floating attention of the type that Freud spoke about.

What are the factors that make it possible for healthy people to perceive reality more efficiently, to predict the future more accurately, to perceive more easily what people really are like, that make it possible for them to endure or to enjoy the unknown, the unstructured and ambiguous, and the mysterious?

Why do the wishes and hopes of healthy people have so little power to distort their perceptions?

The healthier people are, the more their capacities are interrelated. This holds also for the sensory modalities that make synaesthesia in principle a more basic study than the isolated study of separate senses. Not only is this so, but the sensory equipment as a whole is related to the motor aspects of the organism. These interrelations need more study: So also do unitive consciousness, B-cognition, illumination, transpersonal and transhuman perceiving, the cognitive aspects of mystic experiences and peak experiences, etc.

EMOTIONS

The positive emotions, i.e., happiness, calm, serenity, peace of mind, contentment, acceptance have not been studied sufficiently. Neither have compassion, pity, charity.

Fun, joy, play, games, sport, are not sufficiently understood.

Ecstasy, elation, zest, exhilaration, gaiety, euphoria, well-being, the mystic experience, the conversion experience in politics and religion, the emotions generated by orgasm.

The difference between the struggle, conflict, frustration, sadness, anxiety, tension, guilt, shame, etc. of the psychopathological person and of the healthy person. In the healthy person these are or can be good influences.

The organizing effects and other good and desirable effects of emotion have been less studied than its disorganizing effects. Under which circumstances does it correlate with *increased* efficiency of perception, of learning, of thinking, etc.?

The emotional aspects of cognition, e.g., the lift that comes with insight, the calming effect of understanding, the acceptance and forgiveness that are products of deeper understanding of bad behavior.

The affective side of love and friendship, the satisfactions and pleasures that they bring.

In healthy people, cognition, conation, and affect are much more synergic than antagonistic or mutually exclusive. We must discover why this is so, and what the underlying mechanical arrangements are, e.g., are hypothalamic-cerebral interrelations different in the healthy? We must learn how, for instance, conative and affective mobilization helps cognition, how cognitive and conative synergic supports affect, emotions, etc. These three aspects of psychic life should be studied in their interrelations, rather than separately.

The connoisseur has been unreasonably neglected by psychologists. Simple enjoyment of eating, of drinking, of smoking, or of the other sensuous gratifications has a definite place in psychology.

What are the impulses behind the construction of utopias? What is hope? Why do men imagine and project and create ideas of heaven, of the good life, of a better society?

What does admiration mean? Awe? Amazement?

Study of inspiration? How can we inspire people to greater efforts? To better goals? etc.

Why does pleasure disappear more rapidly than pain? Are there ways to refreshen pleasure, gratification, happiness? Can we learn to appreciate our blessings instead of taking them for granted?

MOTIVATION

The parental impulses: why do we love our children, why do people want children at all, why do they make so many sacrifices for them? Or rather, why does what looks like a sacrifice to someone else not feel like a sacrifice to the parent? Why are babies lovable?

The study of justice, equality, liberty, the desire for liberty, for freedom, and for justice. Why is it that people will fight for justice at great cost to themselves or even give up their lives? Why is it that some men with nothing to gain for themselves come to the aid of the downtrodden, of the unjustly treated, and the unhappy?

The human being to some extent yearns for his goals, purposes, and ends, *rather* than being driven by blind impulses and drives. The latter of course also happens but not exclusively. The full picture requires both.

So far we have studied only the pathogenic effects of frustration, neglecting its "healthogenic" effects.

Homeostasis, equilibrium, adaptation, self-preservation, defense, and adjustment are merely negative concepts and must be supplemented by positive concepts. "Everything seems directed towards preserving life and very little towards making it worth living." H. Poincaré said that his problem was not to earn his meals but to keep from being bored between them. If we were to define functional psychology as the study of usefulness from the point of view of self-preservation, then by extension a *meta*-functional psychology would study usefulness from the point of view of self-perfection.

The neglect of higher needs and neglect of the differences between lower and higher needs dooms people to disappointment when wanting continues even after a need is gratified. In the healthy person, gratification produces, not cessation of desire, but after a temporary period of contentment, substitution of higher desires and higher frustration levels, along with the same old restlessness and dissatisfaction.

Appetites and preferences and tastes, as well as the brute, life-and-death, desperate hungers.

Urge to perfection, truth, justice (same as straightening a crooked picture? Or completing an incompleted task? Or perseveration of an unsolved problem?). The Utopian impulse, the desire to improve the external world, to set wrong things right.

Neglect of cognitive needs, e.g., by Freud (18), as well as by the academic psychologists.

The conative side of aesthetics, the aesthetic needs.

We do not sufficiently understand the motivations of the martyr, the hero, the patriot, the unselfish man. The Freudian nothing-but, reductive explanations do not explain healthy people.

How about the psychology of right and wrong, the psychology of ethics and of morality?

The psychology of science, of the scientist, of knowledge, of the search for knowledge, of the impulses behind the search for knowledge, of the philosophical impulse.

Appreciation, contemplation, meditation.

Sex is customarily discussed as if it were a problem of avoiding the plague. The preoccupation with the dangers of sex has obscured the obvious that it can be or should be a very enjoyable pastime and possibly also a very profoundly therapeutic and educational one.

INTELLIGENCE

Must we rest content with a definition of intelligence that is derived from what is the case, rather than what should be the case? The whole concept of IQ has nothing to do with wisdom; it is a purely technological concept. For example, Goering had a high IQ but was in a very real sense a stupid man. He was certainly a vicious man. I do not think there is any great harm in separating out the specific concept of high IQ. The only trouble is that in a psychology that limits itself so, the more important subjects— wisdom, knowledge, insight, understanding, common sense, good judgment—are neglected in favor of the IQ because it is technologically more satisfactory. For the humanist, of course, it is a highly irritating concept.

What are the influences that raise the IQ—effective intelligence, common sense, good judgment? We know much about what harms them, little about what improves them. Could there be a psychotherapy of the intelligence.

An organismic conception of intelligence?

To what extent are the intelligence tests culture-bound?

COGNITION AND THINKING

Change of mind. Conversion. Psychoanalytic insight. Sudden understanding. The perception of principle. Illumination. Satori. Awakening.

Wisdom. What are the relations with good taste, with good morals, kindness, etc.?

The characterological and therapeutic effects of sheer knowledge.

The study of creativeness and of productiveness should have an important place in psychology. In thinking we should pay more attention to the study of novelty, of inventiveness, of the production of new ideas, rather than to the finding of solutions to predetermined puzzles of the type so far used in thinking studies. Since thinking at its best is creative, why not study it at its best?

The psychology of science and scientists, of philosophy and philosophers.

Thinking in the healthiest people—if they are also intelligent—is not only of the Dewey type, i.e., stimulated by some disequilibrating problem or nuisance, and disappearing when the problem is solved. It is also spontaneous, sportive, and pleasurable, and *is* often emitted, or produced without effort, automatically, as the liver secretes bile. Such men *enjoy* being thinking animals, they do not have to be harassed into it.

Thinking is not always directed, organized, motivated, or goal-bent. Fantasy, dreaming, symbolism, unconscious thinking, infantile, emotional thinking, psychoanalytic free association, are all productive in their own way. Healthy people come to many of their conclusions and decisions with the aid of these techniques, traditionally opposed to rationality but in actuality synergic with it.

The concept of objectivity. Disinterestedness. Passive response to the nature of reality *per se* without injecting any personal or ego elements. Problem-centered rather than ego-centered cognition. Taistic objectivity, love-objectivity, vs. spectator-objectivity.

CLINICAL PSYCHOLOGY

In general, we should learn to see as psychopathology *any* failure to achieve self-actualization. The average or normal person is just as much a case as the psychotic, even though less dramatic, and less urgent.

The aims and goals of psychotherapy should be positively seen. (This is of course true also for the goals of education, of the family, of medicine, of religion and philosophy.) The therapeutic values of good and successful life experiences should be stressed, as for example, marriage, friendship, economic success, etc.

Clinical psychology is not the same as abnormal psychology. Clinical psychology may be the personal, individual case study of successful and happy and healthy individuals as well. Clinical psychology can study health as well as illness, the strong, the courageous, and the kind as well as the weak, the cowardly, and the cruel.

Abnormal psychology should not be limited to the study of schizophrenia, but should also include such subjects as cynicism, authoritarianism, anhedonia, the loss of values, prejudice, hatred, greed, selfishness, and the like. These are *the* serious diseases from the point of view of values. Dementia praecox, manic depression, obsession-compulsion, and the like are the serious diseases of mankind *from the point of view of technology,* that is, in the sense that they limit efficiency. But it would have been a blessing, not a curse, if Hitler or Mussolini or Stalin had broken down with obvious schizophrenia. What we should study from the point of view of positive and value-oriented psychology are those disturbances that make men bad or limited in the value sense. Cynicism, then, is certainly more important socially than depression.

We spend a great amount of time studying criminality. Why not study also law-abidingness, identification with society, philanthropy, social conscience, *Gemeinschaftsgefühl?*

In addition to studying the psychotherapeutic effects of the good life experiences, such as marriage, success, having children, falling in love, education, etc., we should also study the psychotherapeutic effects of bad experiences, particularly of tragedy, but also, illness, deprivation, frustration, conflict, and the like. Healthy people seem able to turn even such experiences to good use.

The study of interest (as contrasted with the study of boredom). Those who have vitality, wish for life, resistance to death, zest.

Our present knowledge of personality dynamics, of health, and adjustment comes almost entirely from the study of sick people. Not only will the study of healthy people correct this and teach us directly about psychological health, but I am sure it will also teach us much more than we know now about neurosis, psychosis, psychopathy, and psychopathology in general.

The clinical study of ability, capacity, skills, craftsmanship. Vocation, calling, mission.

The clinical study of genius and talent. We spend far more time and money on feeble-minded people than on intelligent people.

Frustration theory as usually conceived is a good example of cripple psychology. In too many theories of child raising, the child is conceived of in the original Freudian fashion, as a completely conservative organism. hanging on to already achieved adjustments; it has no urge to go on to a new adjustment, to grow, and to develop in its own style.

To this day, the psychodiagnostic techniques are used to diagnose pathology, not health. We have no good Rorschach or TAT or MMPI norms for creativeness, ego strength, health, self-actualization, hypnosis, resistance to disease. Most personality questionnaires are still modeled on the original Woodworth model; they list many symptoms of sickness, and a good or healthy score is the *absence* of responses to these list of symptoms.

Since psychotherapy improves people, we miss an opportunity to see people at their best by failing to study the posttherapeutic personality.

The study of peakers and nonpeakers, i.e., those who do and those who do not have peak-experiences.

ANIMAL PSYCHOLOGY

In animal psychology, the stress has been on hunger and thirst. Why not study the higher needs? We actually do not know whether the white rat has anything to compare with our higher needs for love, beauty, understanding, status, and the like. With the techniques now available to animal pschologists, how could we know? We must get over the psychology of the *desperate* rat, the rat who is pushed to the point of starvation, or who is pushed by pain or electric shock into an extreme situation, one so extreme that human beings seldom find themselves in it. (Some such work has been done with monkeys and apes.)

The study of understanding and insight should be more stressed than the study of rote, blind association learning, the higher levels of intelligence as well as the lower, the more complex, as well as the less complex, the higher limits of animal performance have been neglected in favor of averages.

When Husband (204) showed that a rat could learn a maze almost as well as a human being, the maze should have been dropped once and for all as an instrument for the study of learning. We know in advance that the human being learns better than the rat. Any technique that cannot demonstrate this is like measuring people who are bent over in a room with a low ceiling. What we are measuring is the ceiling, not the people. All that a maze does is to measure a low ceiling and not the height to which learning and thinking may go, not even in the rat.

It seems very probable that the use of higher animals rather than lower animals would teach us much more about human psychology.

It should always be kept in mind that the use of animals guarantees in advance the neglect of just those capacities which are uniquely human, for example, martyrdom, self-sacrifice, shame, symbols, language, love, humor, art, beauty, conscience, guilt, patriotism, ideals, the production of poetry or philosophy or music or science. Animal psychology is necessary for learning about those human characteristics that man shares with all primates. It is useless in the study of those characteristics which man does *not* share with other animals or in which he is vastly superior, such as latent learning.

SOCIAL PSYCHOLOGY

Social psychology should be more than a study of imitation, suggestion, prejudice, hatred, hostility. These are minor forces in healthy people.

Theory of democracy, of anarchism. Democratic, interpersonal relationship. The democratic leader. Power in a democracy and among democratic people and in the democratic leader. The motivations of the unselfish leader. Sound people *dislike* having power over other people. Social psychology is too much dominated by a low-ceiling, lower-animal conception of power.

Competition is studied more than cooperation, altruism, friendliness, unselfishness.

The study of freedom and of free men has little or no place in social psychology today.

How is culture improved? What are the good effects of the deviant? We know that culture can never advance or be improved without deviants. Why have they not been more studied? Why are they generally considered to be pathological? Why not healthy?

Brotherhood and equalitarianism deserves as much attention as class and caste and domination in the social sphere. Why not study the religious brotherhoods? The consumers' and producers' coöperatives? Intentional and Utopian communities?

The culture-personality relationship is usually studied as if culture were the prime mover, as if its shaping force were inexorable. But it can be and is resisted by stronger and healthier people. Acculturation and enculturation work only to an extent with some people. The study of freedom *from* the environment is called for.

Opinion polling is based on the uncritical acceptance of a low conception of human possibilities, i.e., the assumption that people's votes will be determined by selfishness or by sheer habit. This is true, but only in the unhealthy 99 percent of the population. Healthy human beings vote or buy or form judgments at least partially on the basis of logic, common sense, justice, fairness, reality, etc., even when this is against their own interests, narrowly and selfishly considered.

Why is there so much neglect of the fact that leadership in democracies is very often sought for the opportunity of service rather than to have power over other people? This has been completely neglected even though it has been a profoundly important force in American history and in world history as well. It is quite clear that Jefferson never wanted power or leadership for any selfish benefits that might come from it, but that he felt rather that he should sacrifice himself because he could do a good job that needed to be done.

The sense of duty, of loyalty, obligation to society, responsibility, the social conscience. The good citizen, the honest man. We spend much time studying the criminal, why not these?

The crusader. The fighter for principle, for justice, for freedom, for equality. The idealist.

The good effects of prejudice, of unpopularity, of deprivation, and of frustration. There is little effort among psychologists to get the full many-sidedness of even pathological phenomena like prejudice. There are certain *good* consequences of excluding or ostracizing. This is especially so if the culture is a doubtful one or a sick or a bad one. Ostracism from such a culture is a good thing for the person, even though it may cost much pain. Self-actualizing people often ostracize themselves by withdrawing from subcultures of which they disapprove.

We do not know as much about the saint, the knight, the do-gooder, the hero, the unselfish leader as we do about the tyrant, the criminal, the psychopath.

Conventionality has its good side and its desirable effects. The good conventions. The contrasting value of conventions in a healthy and in a sick society. The same for "middleclass" values.

Kindness, generosity, benevolence, and charity have too little place in the social psychology textbooks.

The rich liberal, like Franklin Roosevelt, or Thomas Jefferson, who, quite in contradiction to the dictates of his own pocketbook, fights against his own economic interest, in the interest of fairness, and justice, etc.

While there is much written about anti-Semitism, anti-Negroism, racism, and xenophobia, there is very little recognition of the fact that there is also such a thing as philo-Semitism, Negrophilia, sympathy for the underdog, etc. This illustrates how we concentrate more on hostility than on altruism, or sympathy or concern for people who are treated badly.

The study of sportsmanship, of fairness, of the sense of justice, of concern for the other fellow.

In textbooks of interpersonal relations or of social psychology the study of the love, the marriage, the friendliness, and of the therapeutic relationship might very well be paradigmatic for all the chapters that followed. As of today, however, they are rarely taken seriously by extant textbooks.

Sales resistance, advertising resistance, propaganda resistance, opinion-of-other-people resistance, maintenance of autonomy, suggestion resistance, imitation resistance, prestige resistance are all high in healthy people, and low in average people. These symptoms of health should be more extensively studied by applied social psychologists.

Social psychology must shake itself free of that variety of cultural relativism, which stresses too much man's passivity, plasticity, and shapelessness and too little his autonomy, his growth tendencies, and the maturation of inner forces. It should study the active agent as well as the pawn.

Either psychologists and social scientists will supply empirical value systems for humanity or no one will. This task alone generates a thousand problems.

From the point of view of the positive development of human potentiality, psychology was very largely a complete failure during World War II. It was used by very many psychologists as a technology only and was allowed to apply only what was already known. Practically nothing new in psychological theory has come out of the war yet, though there may be later developments. This meant that many psychologists and other scientists allied themeslves with the short sighted people who stressed only the winning of the war and neglected the winning of the peace afterward. They neglected entirely the point of the whole war, making it into a technological game rather than a value struggle which it actually was, or at least was supposed to be. There was little in the body of psychology to prevent them from making this mistake, no philosophy for instance which separated technology from science, no value theory which enabled them to understand clearly what democratic people are really like, what the fighting was all about, and what its emphases were or should have been. They addressed themselves generally to means-questions rather than end-questions and could have been put to as good use by the Nazis as by the democracies. Their efforts were of little avail in preventing the growth of authoritarianism even in our own country.

Social institutions, and indeed culture itself, are customarily studied as shapers, forcers, inhibitors, rather than as need gratifiers, happiness producers, self-actualization fosterers. "Is culture a set òf problems or a set of opportunities?" (A. Meiklejohn). The culture-as-shaper concept is probably a consequence of too exclusive experience with pathological cases. The use of healthier subjects suggests rather culture-as-reservoir-of-gratifications. The same may probably be affirmed for the family which is also seen too often to be a shaping, training, molding force exclusively.

PERSONALITY

The concept of the well-adjusted personality or of good adjustment sets a low ceiling upon the possibility for advancement and for growth. The cow, the slave, the robot may all be well adjusted.

The superego of the child is ordinarily conceived of as introjection of fear, punishment, loss of love, abandonment, etc. The study of children and adults who are safe, loved and respected indicates the possibility of an intrinsic conscience built on love identification, the desire to please and to make others happy, as well as on truth, logic, justice, consistency, right, and duty.

The behavior of the healthy person is less determined by anxiety, fear, insecurity, guilt, shame, and more by truth, logic, justice, reality, fairness, fitness, beauty, rightness, etc.

Where are the researches on unselfishness? Lack of envy? Will power? Strength of character? Optimism? Friendliness? Realism? Self-transcendence? Boldness, courage? Lack of jealousy? Sincerity? Patience? Loyalty? Reliability? Responsibility?

Of course the most pertinent and obvious choice of subject for a positive psychology is the study of psychological health (and other kinds of health, aesthetic health, value health, physical health, and the like). But a positive psychology also calls for more study of the good man, of the secure and of the confident, of the democratic character, of the happy man, of the serene, the calm, the peaceful, the compassionate, the generous, the kind, of the creator, of the saint, of the hero, of the strong man, of the genius, and of other good specimens of humanity.

What produces the socially desirable characteristics of kindliness, social conscience, helpfulness, neighborliness, identification, tolerance, friendliness, desire for justice, righteous indignation?

We have a very rich vocabulary for psychopathology but a very meager one for health or transcendence.

Deprivation and frustration have some good effects. The study of just as well as of unjust discipline is indicated, as is also study of the self-discipline that comes from being allowed to deal directly with reality, learning from its intrinsic rewards and punishments, its feedback.

The study of idiosyncrasy and individuality (*not* individual differences in the classical sense). We must develop an idiographic science of personality.

How do people get to be unlike each other instead of like each other (acculturated, ironed out by the culture, etc.)?

What is dedication to a cause? What produces the dedicated, devoted person who identifies himself with an ego-transcending cause or mission?

The contented, happy, calm, serene, peaceful personality.

The tastes, values, attitudes, and the choices of self-actualizing people are to a great extent on an intrinsic and reality-determined basis, rather than on a relative and extrinsic basis. It is therefore a taste for the right rather than wrong, for the true rather than the false, for the beautiful rather than the ugly. They live within a system of stable values and *not* in a robot world of *no values at all* (only fashions, fads, opinions of others, imitation, suggestion, prestige).

Frustration level and frustration tolerance may very well be *much* higher in self-actualizing people. So also guilt level, conflict level, and shame level.

Child-parent relationships have usually been studied as if they *were* only a set of problems, *only* a chance to make mistakes. They are primarily a pleasure and a delight, and a great opportunity to enjoy. This is true even for adolescence, too often treated as if akin to a plague.

APPENDIX B.

HOLISTIC-DYNAMICS, ORGANISMIC THEORY, SYNDROME DYNAMICS

THE NATURE OF PSYCHOLOGICAL DATA AND METHODS[1]

THE FUNDAMENTAL DATUM OF PSYCHOLOGY

It is difficult to say just what this fundamental datum is, but it is easy to say what it is not. There have been many "nothing but" attempts, but all reductive efforts have failed. We know that the fundamental psychological datum is not a muscle twitch, not a reflex, nor an elementary sensation, nor a neuron, nor even an observable bit of overt behavior. It is a much larger unit, and more and more psychologists think that it is at least as large a unit as an adjustive or coping act, which necessarily involves an organism, a situation, and a goal or purpose. In view of what we have said about unmotivated reactions and pure expression, even this looks too limited.

In a word, we wind up with the paradoxical conclusion that the fundamental datum of psychology is the original complexity that psychologists had set themselves to analyze into elements or fundamental units. If we use the concept of fundamental datum at all, it is certainly a pecu-

---

[1] This appendix presents a set of theoretical conclusions emerging directly from research data on the organization of the human personality, being, so to speak, only one step ahead of the data and firmly based on them.

liar sort of concept, for it refers to a complex and not a simplex, a whole rather than a part.

If we ponder this paradox, we must soon come to understand that the search for a fundamental datum is itself a reflection of a whole world view, a scientific philosophy that assumes an atomistic world—a world in which complex things are built up out of simple elements. The first task of such a scientist then is to reduce the so-called complex to the so-called simple. This is to be done by analysis, by finer and finer separating until we come to the irreducible. This task has succeeded well enough elsewhere in science, for a time at least. In psychology it has not.

This conclusion exposes the essentially theoretical nature of the entire reductive effort. It must be understood that this effort is *not* of the essential nature of science in general. It is simply a reflection or implication in science of an atomistic, mechanical world view that we now have good reason to doubt. Attacking such reductive efforts is then not an attack on science in general, but rather on one of the possible attitudes toward science. We still have, however, the original problem with which we started. Let us now rephrase it so as to ask, not What is the fundamental (irreducible) datum of psychology?, but rather, What is the subject matter of psychological study? and What is the nature of psychological data and how can they be studied?

HOLISTIC-ANALYTIC METHODOLOGY

How shall we study our individual if not by reducing him to his "simple parts"? It can be demonstrated that this is a much simpler problem than it is considered to be by some who reject the reductive effort.

It is necessary to understand first that objection is made not to analysis in general but only to the particular kind of analysis that we have called reduction. It is not at all necessary to deny the validity of the concepts of analysis, of parts, etc. We need simply redefine these concepts so that they may allow us to do our work more validly and more fruitfully.

If we take an example, such as blushing or trembling or stammering, it is easy to see that we may study this behavior in two different ways. On the one hand we may study it as if it were an isolated, discrete phenomenon, self-contained and understandable in itself. On the other hand, we may study it as one expression of the whole organism, attempting to understand it in its richness of interrelationships with the organism and with other expressions of the organism. This distinction can be made clearer if we make the analogy with the two possible ways of studying an organ like the stomach: (1) it can be cut out of the cadaver and laid on the dissecting table, or (2) it can be studied *in situ*, i.e., in the living, functioning organism. The results that are obtained by these two approaches are different in many ways, anatomists now realize. Knowledge obtained by the second approach is more valid and more useful than the results obtained by the equivalent of *in vitro* techniques. Of course dissection and isolated study of the stomach are not stigmatized by modern anatomists. These techniques are used, but only against the broad background of *in situ* knowledge, of knowledge that the human body is not a collection of separate organs, of the realization that organization in the cadaver is not the same as that in the living body. In a word, anatomists do all that was done in the past but (1) they do it with a different attitude, and (2) they do more—they use techniques in addition to those used traditionally.

Just so can we turn to our study of personality with two different attitudes. We can conceive either that we are studying a discrete entity, or that we are studying a part of a whole. The former method we may call reductive-analytic. The latter we may call holistic-analytic. One essential characteristic of holistic analysis of the personality in actual practice is that there be a preliminary study or understanding of the total organism, and that we then proceed to study the role that our part of the whole plays in the organization and dynamics of the total organism.

In the two series of researches upon which this chapter is based (studies of the self-esteem syndrome and of the security syndrome) this holistic-analytic method was used. Actually these results may be phrased not so much as studies of self-esteem or of security in themselves, but as studies of the role of self-esteem or of security in the total personality. In methodological terms this means that the writer found it necessary to understand each subject as a whole, functioning, adjusting individual before he could attempt to find out specifically about the self-esteem of the subject. Thus, before any questions were asked specifically about self-esteem, explorations were made of the subject's relations to his family, to the kind of subculture he lived in, of his general style of adjusting to his main life problems, his hopes for the future, his ideals, his frustrations, and his conflicts. This procedure continued until the writer felt that he understood the subject as well as was possible with the simple techniques being used. Only then did he feel that he could understand the actual psychological meaning for self-esteem of specific bits of behavior.

We can indicate by example the necessity of this background of understanding for proper interpretations of a specific behavior. In general, people with low self-esteem tend to be more religious than people with high self-esteem, but obviously there are many other determinants of religiosity as well. To discover whether, in a specific individual, religious feeling means a necessity to lean on some other source of strength, one must know the individual's religious training, the various external compulsions for and against religion that play on the subject, whether or not his religious feeling is superficial or deep, whether it is external or sincere. In a word, we must understand what religion means for him as an individual. So a person who goes to church regularly may actually be rated as *less* religious than one who does not go to church at all, because perhaps (1) he goes to avoid social isolation, or (2) he goes to please his mother, or (3) religion represents for him not humbleness but a weapon of domination over others, or (4) it marks him as a member of a superior group, or (5) as in Clarence Day's father, "It is good for the ignorant masses and I must play along," or . . . , and so on. He may in a dynamic sense be not at all religious and stil behave as if he were. We must obviously know what religion means for him as an individual before we can assay its role in the personality. Sheer behavioral going to church can mean practically anything, and therefor, for us, practically nothing.

Another example, perhaps more striking, because the same behavior may mean exactly opposite things psychologically, is that of political-economic radicalism. If it is taken *per se*, that is to say behaviorally, discretely, out of context, we get the most confusing results when we study its relation to security feelings. Some radicals are at the extreme of security, others are at the extreme of insecurity. But if we analyze this radicalism in its total context we can learn easily that one person may be a radical because life is not good for him, because he is bitter, disappointed, or frustrated, because he does not have what others have. Careful study of such people often shows them to be very hostile to their fellow men in general, sometimes consciously, sometimes unconsciously. It has been said aptly of this kind of person that he tends to perceive his personal difficulties as a world crisis.

But there is another type of radical who is a very different *kind* of individual even though he votes, behaves, and talks in the same way as the one we have just described. For him, however, radicalism may have a completely different, even opposite motivation or meaning. These people are secure, happy, personally contented people who, however, out of a deep love for their fellow men, feel impelled to improve the lot of the less fortunate, to fight injustice even if it does not touch them directly. Such people may express this urge in any one of a dozen ways: through personal philanthropy, or religious exhortation, or patient teaching, or radical political activity. Their political beliefs tend to be independent of fluctuations of income, of personal calamity, and the like.

In a word, radicalism is a form of expression that may come from completely different underlying motivations, from opposite types of character structure. In one person it may spring essentially from hate for his fellows, in another it may spring essentially from love for his fellows. If radicalism is studied in itself, such a conclusion is not likely to be arrived at.[2]

What remains to be said about holistic analysis can be said much better below after certain other problems have been discussed.

THE HOLISTIC-DYNAMIC POINT OF VIEW

The general point of view that is being propounded here is holistic rather than atomistic, functional rather than taxonomic, dynamic rather than static, dynamic rather than causal, purposive rather than simple-mechanical. In spite of the fact that these opposing factors are ordinarily looked upon as a series of separable dichotomies they are not so considered by the writer. For him they tend strongly to coalesce into two unitary but contrasting world views. This seems to be true for other writers as well, for those who think dynamically find it easier and more natural to think also holistically rather than atomistically, purposively rather than mechanically, and so on. This point of view we shall call the holistic-dynamic point of view. It could also be called organismic in Goldstein's sense.

Opposed to this interpretation is found an organized and unitary viewpoint that is simultaneously atomistic, taxonomic, static, causal, and simple-mechanical. The atomistic thinker finds it much more natural to think also statically rather than dynamically, mechanically rather than purposively, etc. This general point of view I shall call arbitrarily general-atomistic. I have no doubt that it is possible to demonstrate not only that these partial views *tend* to go together but that they *must* logically go together.

A few special remarks on the causality concept are necessary at this point since it is an aspect of the general-atomistic theory that seems to me to be centrally important and that psychological writers have slurred or neglected altogether. This concept lies at the very heart of the general-atomistic point of view and is a natural, even necessary, consequence of

---

[2] A rather commonly used holistic technique (not so labeled ordinarily) is the technique of iteration used in constructing personality tests. I have also used this technique in my investigations of personality syndromes. Starting with a vague grasped whole, we analyze its structure into subdivisions, parts, etc. Through this analysis we discover difficulties with our original conception of the whole. The whole is then reorganized, redefined, and rephrased more exactly and more efficiently, and is, as before, subjected to analysis. Again this analysis makes possible a better, more precise whole, and so on.

it. If one sees the world as a collection of intrinsically independent entities, there remains to be solved the very obvious phenomenal fact that these entities nevertheless have to do with each other. The first attempt to solve this problem gives rise to the notion of the simple billiardball kind of causality in which one separate thing does something to another separate thing, but in which the entities involved continue to retain their essential identity. Such a view is easy enough to maintain, and actually seemed absolute so long as the old physics gave us our world theory. But the advance in physics and chemistry made modification necessary. For instance, the usually more sophisticated phrasing today is in terms of multiple causation. It is recognized that the interrelationships holding within the world are too complex, too intricate to describe in the same way as we do the clicking of billiard balls on a table. But the answer is most often simply a complexifying of the original notion rather than a basic restructuring of it. Instead of one cause, there are many, but they are conceived to act in the same way—separately and independent of each other. The billiard ball is now hit not by one other ball, but by ten simultaneously, and we simply have to use a somewhat more complicated arithmetic to understand what happens. The essential procedures are still addition of separate entities into an "and-sum" to use Wertheimer's phrase. No change is felt to be necessary in the fundamental envisagement of the complex happenings. No matter how complex the phenomenon may be, no essentially new thing is happening. In this way the notion of cause is stretched more and more to fit new needs until sometimes it seems to have no relation but a historical one to the old concept. Actually, however, different though they may seem, they remain in essence the same, since they continue to reflect the same world view.

It is particularly with personality data that the causality theory falls down most completely. It is easy to demonstrate that within any personality syndrome, relationship other than causal exists. That is to say, if we had to use causal vocabulary we should have to say that every part of the syndrome is both a cause and an effect of every other part as well as of any grouping of these other parts, and that furthermore we should have to say that each part is both a cause and effect of the whole of which it is a part. Such an absurd conclusion is the only one that is possible if we use only the causality concept. Even if we attempt to meet the situation by introducing the newer concept of circular or reversible causality we could not completely describe the relations within the syndrome nor the relations of the part to the whole.

Nor is this the only shortcoming of causality vocabulary with which we must deal. There is also the difficult problem of the description of the interaction or interrelation between a syndrome as a whole and all the forces bearing upon it from the "outside." The syndrome of self-esteem, for instance, has been shown to tend to change as a whole. If we try to change Johnny's stammering and address ourselves specifically to this and only this, the chances are very great that we shall find either (1) that we have changed nothing at all, or else (2) that we have changed not Johnny's stammering alone but rather Johnny's self-esteem in general, or even Johnny as a whole individual. External influences usually tend to change the whole human being, not just a bit or a part of him.

There are yet other peculiarities in this situation that defy description by the ordinary causal vocabulary. There is one phenomenon in particular that is very difficult to describe. The nearest I can come to expressing it is to say that it is as if the organism (or any other syndrome) "swallows the cause, digests it, and emits the effect." When an effective stimulus, a traumatic experience let us say, impinges upon the personality, there are certain consequences of this experience. But these consequences practically never bear a one-to-one or a straight-line relationship to the original causal experience. What actually happens is that the experience, if it is effective, changes that whole personality. This personality, now different from what it was before, expresses itself differently and behaves differently than before. Let us suppose that this effect would be that his facial twitch gets a little worse. Has this 10 percent increase of the tic been caused by the traumatic situation? If we say it has, it can be shown that we must, if we wish to be consistent, say that every single effective stimulus that has ever impinged on the organism has also caused this 10 percent increase in the facial tic. For every experience is taken into the organism, in the same sense that food is digested and by intussusception becomes the organism itself. Is the sandwhich I ate an hour ago the cause of the words I now set down, or was it the coffee I drank, or what I ate yesterday, or was it the lesson in writing I got years ago, or the book I read a week ago?

It would certainly seem obvious that any important expression, such as writing a paper in which one is deeply interested, is not caused by anything in particular, but is an expression of, or a creation of the whole personality, which in turn is an effect of almost everything that has ever happened to it. It should seem just as natural for the psychologist to think of the stimulus or cause as being taken in by the personality by means of a readjustment, as to think of it as hitting the organism and pushing it. The net result here would be, not a cause and effect remaining separate, but simply a new personality (new by however little).

Still another way of demonstrating the inadequacy for psychology of conventional cause-effect notions is to show that the organism is not a passive agent to which causes or stimuli *do* something, but that it is an active agent entering into a complex mutual relationship with the cause, doing something to it as well. For readers of the psychoanalytic literature this is a commonplace, and it is necessary only to remind the reader of the facts that we can be blind to stimuli, we can distort them, reconstruct, or reshape them if they are distorted. We can seek them out or avoid them. We can sift them out and select from among them. Or finally, we can even create them if need be.

The causality concept rests on the assumption of an atomistic world with entities that remain discrete, even though they interact. The personality, however, is not separate from its expressions, effects, or the stimuli impinging upon it (causes) and so at least for psychological data it must be replaced by another conception.[3] This conception—holistic-dynamics—cannot be stated simply, since it involves fundamental reorganization of viewpoint, but must be expounded step by step.

DEFINITION OF THE SYNDROME CONCEPT

Granted that a more valid type of analysis is possible, how then can we proceed further in this study of the whole organism? It is clear that the answer to this question must depend on the nature of the organization of the data to be anlayzed and we must now ask: How is the personality organized? As an antecedent to a full answer to this question must come an analysis of the syndrome concept.

In attempting to describe the interrelated characteristics of self-esteem, I have borrowed the term syndrome from medicine. In this field it is used to mean a complex of symptoms that are usually found to occur together and that are therefore given a unifying name. Used thus, the word has its shortcomings as well as its advantages. For one thing it usually connotes disease and abnormality rather than health or normality.

---

[3] More sophisticated scientists and philosophers have now replaced the causality notion with an interpretation in terms of "functional" relationships, i.e., A is a function of B, *or* If A, then B. By so doing, it seem to me that they have given up the nuclear aspects of the concept of cause, that is to say, of necessity, and of acting upon. Simple linear coefficients of correlations are examples of functional statements, which are, however, often used as *contrasting* with cause-effect relationships. It serves no purpose to retain the word "cause" if it means the very opposite of what it used to mean. In any case, we are then left with the problems of necessary or intrinsic relationship, and of the ways in which change comes about. These problems must be solved, not abandoned nor denied nor liquidated.

We shall not use it in any such special sense, considering it rather to be a general concept that refers only to a type of organization without reference to the "value" of this organization.

Further, in medicine it has often been used in a merely additive sense, as a list of symptoms rather than as an organized, interdependent, structured group of symptoms. We shall of course use it in the latter sense. Finally, it has been used in medicine in a causal context. Any syndrome of symptoms was conceived to have a putative, single cause. Once something like this was found, e.g., the microörganism in tuberculosis, researchers tended to rest content and consider their labors finished. By so doing they neglected many problems that we should consider central. Examples of such problems are: (1) the failure of tuberculosis to develop more often in view of the ubiquity of the tuberculosis bacillus, (2) the frequent nonappearance of many of the symptoms of the syndrome, (3) the interchangeability of these symptoms, (4) the unexplained and unpredictable mildness or severity of the disease in specific individuals, etc. In a word, we should demand a study of *all* the factors involved in the production of tuberculosis, not only the most dramatic or the most powerful single one.

Our preliminary definition of a personality syndrome is that it is a structured, organized complex of apparently diverse specificities (behaviors, thoughts, impulses to action, perceptions, etc.) which, however, when studied carefully and validly are found to have a common unity that may be phrased variously as a similar dynamic meaning, expression, "flavor," function, or purpose.

Since these specificities have the same source or function or aim, they are interchangeable and may actually be thought to be psychological synonyms of one another (all "saying the same thing"). For example temper tantrums in one child and enuresis in another may come from the same situation, e.g., rejection, and may be attempts to achieve the same end, e.g., attention or love from the mother. Thus, though they are quite different behaviorally, they may be identical dynamically.[4]

In a syndrome we have a group of feelings and behaviors that seem behaviorally different, or at least have different names, which, however, overlap, intertwine, interdepend, and may be said to be dynamically synonymous. We may thus study them either in their diversity as parts or

---

[4] Interchangeability may be defined in these terms of behavioral difference and dynamic similarity of aim. It may also be defined in terms of probability. If symptoms *a* and *b* have the same probability of being found or not found in syndrome X in an individual case, they may be called interchangeable.

specificities or we may study them in their unity or wholeness. The problem of language is a difficult one here. How shall we label this unity in diversity? There are various possibilities.

We may introduce the concept of "psychological flavor," using as an example a dish composed of different elements and yet having a character of its own, e.g., a soup, a hash, a stew, etc.[5] In a stew we have a concoction of many elements that nevertheless has a unique flavor. Its flavor permeates all the elements of the stew and may be spoken of apart from its isolated ingredients. Or, if we take the human physiognomy we recognize readily that a man may have a misshapen nose, too-small eyes, too-large ears, and still be handsome. (A current witticism says, "He has an ugly face, but on him it looks good.") Here again we may consider either the separate elements taken additively, or the whole, which, though composed of parts, yet has a "flavor" different from anything brought to the whole by any single part. The definition of syndrome that we might derive here is that it is organized of diversities that have a common psychological flavor.

A second approach to the problem of definitions could be in terms of psychological meaning, a concept that is made much of in current dynamic psychopathology. When disease symptoms are said to have the same meaning (night sweating, loss of weight, certain sounds in breathing, etc., all mean tuberculosis) the implication is that they are all diverse expressions of the unifying putative cause spoken of above. Or in psychological discussions the symptoms of feeling of isolation and of feeling of being disliked both mean insecurity because they are seen as being included in this larger, more inclusive concept. That is to say, two symptoms will mean the same thing if they are both parts of the same whole. A syndrome may then be defined in a somewhat circular fashion as an organized collection of diversities, all of which have the same psychological meaning. These concepts of interchangeability, flavor, and meaning, useful though they may be (for instance in the description of the pattern of a culture), have certain specific theoretical and practical difficulties that impel further search for a satisfactory phrasing. Some of these difficulties can be solved if we introduce into our considerations the functional concepts of motivations, goals, purposes, or coping aims. (But still other problems require the concept of expression, or unmotivation for their solution.)

[5] "I have had to tell the story, not as one draws a line from left to right, marking birth at the left, and death at the right; but as one ponders while he turns a relic over and over in his hands." (Taggard, G. *Life and Mind of Emily Dickinson*, Knopf, 1934, p. 15.)

From the point of view of functional psychology the unified organism is seen as always facing problems of certain kinds and attempting to solve them in various ways permitted by the nature of the organism, the culture, and the external reality. The key principle or the centering of all personality organization is then seen by the functional psychologist in terms of the answers of the organism in a world of problems. The alternative phrasing is that the organization of the personality is to be understood in terms of the problems facing it and what it is trying to do about them. Most organized behaviors then must be doing something about something.[6] In the discussion of personality syndromes we should then characterize two specific behaviors as belonging to the same syndrome if they have the same coping aims with respect to a certain problem, that is to say, if they were doing the same thing about the same something. We might then say of the self-esteem syndrome, for instance, that it is the organized answer of the organism to the problem of acquiring, losing, keeping, and defending self-esteem, and similarly for the security syndrome that it is the organism's answer to the problem of gaining, losing, and keeping the love of others.

That we have here no final simple answer is indicated by the fact that the usual finding, when a single behavior is analyzed dynamically, is that it has not one, but several coping aims. Secondly, the organism ordinarily has more than one answer to an important life problem.

We might add also that quite apart from the facts about character expression, purpose cannot, in any case be made a principal characteristic of *all* syndromes.

We cannot speak of the purpose of an organization in the world outside the organism. The Gestalt psychologists have demonstrated abundantly the ubiquity of organization in perceived, learned, and thought-about materials. These materials, of course, cannot all be said to have coping aims in the sense in which we have used the word.

There are certain obvious similarities between our definition of a syndrome and the various definitions of a Gestalt offered by Wertheimer, Köhler, Koffka, and others. The two Ehrenfels criteria are also paralleled in our definition.

Ehrenfels' first criterion of an organized mental phenomenon was that the separate stimuli, e.g., the single notes of a melody, presented singly to a number of persons, would be lacking something that would be experienced by an individual given the organized totality of stimuli, e.g., the whole melody. In other words, the whole is something else than the

---

[6] For exceptions to this rule, see Chapter 14.

additive sum of the parts, So also the syndrome is something else than the additive sum of its isolated reduced parts.[7] But there is also an important difference. In our definition of the syndrome, the main quality that characterizes the whole (meaning, flavor, or aim) can be seen in any of its parts if these parts are understood not reductively, but holistically. Of course this is a theoretical statement and we may expect to find operational difficulties with it. Most of the time we shall be able to discover the flavor or aim of the specific behavior only by understanding the whole of which it is a part. And yet, there are enough exceptions to this rule to convince us that the aim or flavor inheres in the part as well as in the whole. For instance, often we can deduce or infer the whole from a single given part, e.g., we hear a person laugh just once and we are almost certain that he feels insecure; or we can know much about a woman's self-esteem in general simply by her choice of clothes. It is of course granted that such a judgment from a part is usually not so valid as a judgment from the whole.

The second Ehrenfels criterion was that of transposability of elements within a whole. Thus a melody retains its identify even when played in a different key with all the single notes being different in the two cases. This resembles the interchangeability of the elements in a syndrome. Elements that have the same aim are interchangeable or dynamically synonymous with each other; so also are different notes that have the same role in a melody.[8]

In general it may be said that the Gestalt psychologists have agreed with Wertheimer's original definition, that a whole is meaningful when a demonstrable, mutual dependency exists among its parts. The statement that the whole is different from the sum of its parts, while true and very often demonstrable, is less useful as a working laboratory concept and is often felt to be too vague by psychologists of a different tradition, since the problem of definition and characterization of the whole remains even after the demonstration of its existence.

Apparently the problem of a positive definition of a Gestalt cannot be considered completely solved if we also require that this definition be heuristic, workable, and concrete, and that it be capable of forcing acceptance by psychologists of a different tradition (adhering to an atomistic, mechanical world view). There are many reasons for this difficulty, but I

---

[7] It is a question, however, whether the syndrome is something else than the sum of its parts taken holistically. Parts by reduction can add up only to an and-sum; parts of a whole may, however, very well be thought of as adding up to the organized whole if the various terms of this statement are defined in a specific way.

[8] See, however, Köhler's criticism of the Ehrenfels criteria (239, p. 25).

wish to discuss only one, viz., choice of data that have been used. The Gestalt psychologists have worked mostly with the organization of the phenomenal world, of the "field" of "materials" primarily outside the organism. (It should be noted that they usually deny this allegation.) It is, however, the organism itself that is most highly organized and intra-dependent as Goldstein has amply proved. It would seem the best place to seek for the demonstration of the laws of organization and structure. A further advantage to be derived from such a choice of data lies in the fact that the basic phenomena of motivation, purpose, aim, expression, and direction all show up much more clearly in the organism. A definition of the syndrome in terms of coping aims at once creates the possibility of unifying the otherwise isolated theories of functionalism, Gestalt psychology, purposivism (not teleology), the kind of psychodynamics espoused by the psychoanalysts, Adlerians, etc., and the organismic holism of Goldstein. That is to say, the syndrome concept properly defined can be a theoretical basis for the unified world view that we have called the holistic-dynamic point of view and which we contrast with general-atomistic point of view. So could also the Gestalt concept if it were expanded as we have indicated, and if it were more centered upon the human organism and its inner motivations.

CHARACTERISTICS OF PERSONALITY SYNDROMES (SYNDROME DYNAMICS)

INTERCHANGEABILITY

The parts of a syndrome are interchangeable or equivalent in the dynamic sense which has been discussed in previous paragraphs, namely in the sense that two behaviorally different parts or symptoms, since they have the same aim, can subsitute for each other, can do the same job, have equal expectancy of appearing, or may be predicted with equal probability or confidence.

In a hysterical person symptoms are clearly interchangeable in this sense. In the classical cases a paralyzed leg could be "cured" by hypnosis or other suggestion techniques but would almost inevitably be replaced later by some other symptom, a paralyzed arm perhaps. Throughout the Freudian literature as well, there are encountered many examples of symptom equivalents, e.g., fear of a horse may mean, or substitute for, a repressed fear of the father. In a secure person all his behavior expressions are interchangeable in the sense that they all express the same thing, i.e., security. In the example of secure radicalism mentioned before, general desire to help mankind may eventuate *either* in radicalism or philanthropy or kindness to neighbors or in giving nickels to beggars and tramps. In an unknown case, of which we know only that he is secure, one may predict with great certainty that he will show *some* expression of kindness or social interest; but what exactly it will be cannot be predicted. Such equivalent symptoms or expressions may be called interchangeable.

CIRCULAR DETERMINATION

The best descriptions of this phenomenon have come from psychopathological studies, for example, Horney's (197) concept of the vicious circle that is a special case of circular determination. Horney's is one attempt to describe the continual flux of dynamic interaction within a syndrome, whereby any one part is always affecting every other part in some way and is in turn being affected by all other parts, the entire action going on simultaneously.

Complete neurotic dependence implies expectations that must be thwarted. This necessary thwarting creates anger additional to that probably already involved by the admission of weakness and helplessness implicit in complete dependence. This anger, however, tends to be directed against the very person on whom one is dependent and through whose help one hopes to avoid catastrophe, and such anger feelings immediately lead to guilt, anxiety, fear of retaliation, etc. But these states are among the very factors that produced need for complete dependence in the first place. Examination of such a patient will show *at any one moment* most of these factors coexisting in continual flux and mutual reinforcement. While a genetic analysis may show priority of one feature over another in time, a dynamic analysis will never show this. All the factors will be equally causes and effects.

Or an individual may attempt to maintain his security by adopting an overbearing and superior attitude. He would not have taken this attitude unless he felt rejected and disliked (insecure). But this very attitude makes people dislike him more, which in turn reinforces in him the necessity for overbearing attitudes, etc.

In race prejudice we can see this type of circular determination very clearly. The haters will point to certain undesirable traits that excuse their hatred, but these very traits in the disliked group are almost all the product in part of the hatred and rejection.[9]

[9] We are describing in these examples only synchronous dynamics. The question of the origin or determination of the whole syndrome, of how the circular determination ever came to be in the first place is a historical question. Even if such a genetic analysis shows one particular factor to have been first in the chain, this in no way guarantees that this same factor will have basic or prior importance in the dynamic analysis (6).

If we were to use the more familiar cause-effect vocabulary to describe this concept, we should say that A and B cause each other and are effects of each other. Or we could say that they were mutually dependent or mutually supportive or reinforcing variants.

TENDENCY OF THE WELL-ORGANIZED SYNDROME TO
RESIST CHANGE OR TO MAINTAIN ITSELF

No matter what the level of security may be, it is difficult either to raise or to lower it. This phenomenon is something like that described by Freud as resistance but has a much wider and more general application. Thus we find some tendency to hang on to the life style in the healthy as well as in the unhealthy person. The person who tends to believe that all people are essentially good will show the same resistance to change of this belief as will the person who believes all people are essentially bad. Operationally this resistance to change may be defined in terms of the difficulty experienced by the psychological experimenter when he attempts to raise or lower an individual's security level.

Personality syndromes can sometimes maintain a relative constancy under the most surprising conditions of external change. There are many examples of the maintenance of security feelings in emigres who have undergone the most grueling and harrowing experiences. Studies of morale in bombed areas also give us proof of the surprising resistance that most healthy people have to external horrors. Statistics show that depressions and wars do not make for any large increase in the incidence of psychosis.[10] Changes in the syndrome of security are usually in great disproportion to changes in the environment, and sometimes there seems to be almost no personality change at all.

> A German emigre, formally a man of great wealth, came to the United States completely stripped of all his goods. He was diagnosed, however, as a secure personality. Careful questioning showed that his underlying philosophy of human nature had not changed. He still felt that it was essentially sound and good if given a chance, and that the nastiness he had witnessed was explicable in various ways as an externally caused phenomenon. Inter-

---

[10] Such data are usually misinterpreted, since they are often used to refute any environmental or cultural theory of determination of psychopathy. Such a contention simply shows a misunderstanding of dynamic psychology. The real claim that is made is that psychopathy is immediately the result of internal conflicts and threats rather than external calamities. Or at least that external calamities have dynamic influence on the personality only in so far as they relate to the main goals of the individual and to his defensive system.

views with people who had known him in Germany showed that he had been about the same kind of person before his financial downfall.

Many other examples are seen in the resistance of patients to psychotherapy. Sometimes there can be found in a patient, after a period of analysis, a surprising degree of insight into the false basis and the evil consequences of certain of his beliefs. Even so he may hang on to his beliefs with a determined tenacity.

TENDENCY OF THE WELL-ORGANIZED SYNDROME TO
REESTABLISH ITSELF AFTER CHANGE

If a syndrome level has been forced to change, it is often observed that such shift is only temporary. For instance, a traumatic experience very frequently has only a passing effect. There may then be a spontaneous readjustment back to the previous *status quo*. Or else the symptoms created by the trauma are nullified with especial ease (271). Sometimes also this tendency of the syndrome can be inferred as one of the processes in a larger system of changes in which other syndrome tendencies are also involved.

> The following case is typical. A sexually ignorant woman was badly shocked by her first experience after marriage to an equally ignorant man. There was in her a definite shift in the level of the whole security syndrome, i.e., from average to low security. Investigation showed change, as a whole, in most aspects of the syndrome, in her external behavior, philosophy of life, dream life, attitude toward human nature, etc. At this point she was supported and reassured, the situation was discussed in a nontechnical way, and she was given some simple advice over the course of four or five hours. Slowly she changed back, possibly because of these contacts, becoming steadily more secure, but she never quite attained her former level. There remained some slight but permanent effect of her experience, perhaps maintained in part by a rather selfish husband. What was more surprising than this permanent after effect was the strong tendency in spite of everything to think and believe as she had before she was married. A similar picture of sharp change with slow but complete recovery feelings was seen upon remarriage in a woman whose first husband became insane.

It is a tribute to the ubiquity of this tendency that our ordinary expectations in respect to friends who are regarded as normally healthy is that they can recover from any shock at all if only given enough time. The death of a wife or a son, financial ruin, and any other such basic traumatic experiences may throw individuals badly off balance for a while, but they usually recover almost wholly. It is only a chronically bad external or interpersonal situation that is able to create permanent changes in the healthy character structure.

TENDENCY OF THE SYNDROME TO CHANGE AS A WHOLE

This tendency, already discussed above, is perhaps the easiest of all to see. If the syndrome changes at all in any part, the right kind of investigation will practically always show some other concomitant changes in the same direction in other parts of the syndrome. Often enough, such concomitant changes may be seen in almost *all* parts of the syndrome. The reason these change are so often overlooked is simply that they are not expected and therefore not looked for.

It should be emphasized that this tendency to holistic change, like all the other tendencies we have spoken of, is just that—a tendency and not a certainty. There have been cases in which a particular stimulus seemed to have a specific and localized effect with no detectable generalized effect. These cases are rare, however, if we exclude the obviously superficial derangements.

In an unpublished experiment in 1935 on raising self-esteem by external means, a woman was instructed to *behave* in an aggressive fashion in about twenty specific and rather trivial situations. (For instance, she was to insist on a certain brand concerning which her grocer had always overruled her.) She followed instructions, and a wide investigation of personality changes was made three months later.[11] There was no doubt that there had been a generalized shift in her self-esteem. For instance, the character of her dreams had changed. She had bought form-fitting and revealing clothes for the first time. Her sexual behavior had become spontaneous enough for her husband to notice the change. She had gone swimming with other people for the first time, whereas she had always before been too bashful to appear in a swimming suit. And she felt very confident in a variety of other situations. These changes were not suggested, but were spontaneous changes of whose significance she was not at all aware. Change in *behavior* can produce personality change.

A very insecure woman, seen a few years after her very successful marriage, showed a general shift upward in security. When I had first seen her (before her marriage) she had felt alone, unloved and unlovable. Her present husband had finally been able to convince her that he loved her—a difficult task in the case of an insecure woman—and they were married. Now she felt not only that her husband loved her, but also that she was *lovable*. She accepted friendships whereas she had not been able to before. Most of her generalized hatred against human beings had gone. She had developed a kindness and a sweetness of which there was little

---

11 Today this would be called a form of behavior therapy.

trace when I had first seen her. Certain specific symptoms had lessened or disappeared—among others a recurring nightmare, a fear of parties and other groupings of strangers, chronic slight anxiety, a specific fear of the dark, certain undesirable power and cruelty fantasies.

THE TENDENCY TO INTERNAL CONSISTENCY

Even though a person is mostly insecure there may yet persist for various reasons a few specific behaviors, beliefs, or feelings that are characteristic of security. Thus, although a very insecure person more often than not has chronic nightmares, anxiety dreams, or other unpleasant dreams, still in a fair percentage of all such individuals the dream life is not usually unpleasant. In such individuals, however, relatively slight changes in the environment will induce such unpleasant dreams. There seems to be a special tension on these inconsistent elements always acting to pull them into line with the rest of the syndrome.

> People with low self-esteem tend to be modest or bashful. Thus it is usual that many of them will either not appear in a swimming suit or will feel very self-conscious if they do. One girl, however, definitely low in self-esteem, was not only observed at the beach in a swimming suit, but in one that was definitely scanty and revealing. Later a series of interviews revealed that she was very proud of her body, which she considered perfect— an opinion which, for a woman of low self-esteem, is, like her behavior, very unusual. Through her report it was evident, however, that this attitude toward bathing was inconsistent in that she invariably felt self-conscious, that she always had a robe nearby to cover herself with, and that anyone staring at her too openly could drive her from the beach altogether. She had been convinced by various external opinions that her body was attractive; she felt intellectually that she ought to behave a certain way about it, tried very hard to behave in this way, but found it difficult to do so because of her character structure.
>
> Specific fears are often found in very secure persons who are not at all generally fearful. These fears can often be accounted for by specific conditioning experiences. It is very easy to get rid of these fears in such people, I have found. Simple reconditioning, the force of example, exhortation to be strong willed, intellectual explanation, and other such superficial psychotherapeutic measures are often quite sufficient. These simple behavioral techniques, however, should be less successful with fears in definitely insecure people. We might say that the fear that is inconsistent with the rest of the personality is easily removed; the fear that is consistent with the rest of the personality is more tenacious.

In other words, a person who is insecure *tends* to become more perfectly or consistently insecure; a person who is high in self-esteem *tends* to become more consistently high in self-esteem.

THE TENDENCY TO EXTREMENESS OF THE
SYNDROME LEVEL

Side by side with the conserving tendencies we have already described, there is at least one opposing force deriving from the internal dynamics of the syndrome that favors change rather than constancy. It is the tendency for a fairly insecure person to become extremely insecure, for a fairly secure person to become extremely secure.[12]

In a fairly insecure person every external influence, every stimulus impinging on the organism is somewhat more apt to be interpreted insecurely rather than securely. For example, a grin is apt to be seen as a sneer, forgetfulness is apt to be interpreted as insult, indifference is apt to be seen as dislike, and mild affection as indifference. In such persons' worlds then, there are more insecure influences than there are secure ones. We might say that the weight of evidence for him is on the side of insecurity. And so he is pulled steadily, even though slightly in the direction of more and more extreme insecurity. This factor is of course reinforced by the fact that an insecure person tends to behave insecurely, which encourages people to dislike and reject him, which makes him more insecure, which makes him behave still more insecurely—and so on in a vicious circle. Thus he tends, because of his inner dynamics, to bring about just what he fears most.

> The most obvious example is jealous behavior. It springs from insecurity and practically always breeds further rejection and deeper insecurity. A man explained his jealousy as follows: "I love my wife so much that I am afraid that I would collapse if she left me or did not love me. Naturally I am disturbed by her friendliness with my brother." Therefore he took many measures to stop this friendliness, all of them foolish, so that he began to lose the love of both his wife and his brother. This of course made him even more frantic and jealous. The vicious circle was broken with the aid of a psychologist who instructed him first not to behave jealously even if he felt that way, and then started the more important task of relieving the general insecurity in various ways.

TENDENCY OF THE SYNDROME TO CHANGE UNDER EXTERNAL PRESSURES

It is very easy when preoccupied with inner dynamics of syndromes to forget temporarily that all syndromes are of course responsive to the external situation. This obvious fact is mentioned here only for the sake of completeness and as a reminder that the personality syndromes of the organism are not isolated systems.

---

[12] This tendency is closely related to the previously described tendency toward greater internal consistency.

SYNDROME VARIABLES

The most important and most obvious variable is that of *syndrome level*. A person is either high, middle, or low in security, high, middle, or low in self-esteem. We do not necessarily imply that this variation is on a single continuum; we imply only variation from much to little, from high to low. *Syndrome quality* has been discussed chiefly with respect to the self-esteem or dominance syndrome. In the various species of infra-human primates the phenomenon of dominance may be seen in all of them but it will have a different quality of expression in each. In the human being with high self-esteem we have been able to differentiate at least two qualities of high self-esteem that we have chosen to designate on the one hand as strength and on the other hand as power. A person with high self-esteem, who is also secure, shows this feeling of strength of self-confidence in a kind, coöperative, and friendly fashion. The person who is high in self-esteem and is also insecure is interested not so much in helping weaker people as in dominating them and hurting them. Both individuals have high self-esteem, but show it in different ways depending upon other characteristics of the organism. In extremely insecure people there are many ways in which this insecurity can express itself. For instance, it may have the quality of seclusiveness and withdrawal (if he is low in self-esteem), or it may have the quality of hostility, aggressiveness, and nastiness (if he is high in self-esteem).

CULTURAL DETERMINATION OF SYNDROME EXPRESSION

Certainly the relationships between culture and personality are too profound and too complex to treat briefly. More for the sake of completeness than for any other reason it must be pointed out that in general the paths by which the main goals in life are achieved are often determined by the nature of the particular culture. The ways in which self-esteem may be expressed and achieved are in large part, although not completely, culturally determined. The same is true for the love relations. We win the love of other people and express our affections for them through culturally approved channels. The fact that in a complex society, status roles are also in part culturally determined will often shift the expression of personality syndromes. For instance, men with high self-esteem in our society are allowed to express this syndrome much more overtly and in many more ways than are allowed to women with high self-esteem. So also children are given very few opportunities for the direct expression of high self-esteem. It should also be pointed out that there is often a culturally approved syndrome level for each of the syndromes, e.g., security, self-esteem, sociality, activity. This fact can be seen most clearly in cross-cultural comparisons and in historical comparisons. For instance, the average Dobu citizen not only is, but also is expected to be, more hostile than the average Arapesh citizen. The average woman today is expected to be higher in self-esteem than the average woman one hundred years ago.

THE ORGANIZATION OF THE
PERSONALITY SYNDROME

We have so far spoken as if the various parts of the syndrome are homogeneous, like the particles in a fog. Actually this is not the case. Within the syndrome organization we find hierarchies of importance, and clusterings. This fact has already been demonstrated in the simplest possible way for the self-esteem syndrome, namely, by the method of correlation. If the syndrome were undifferentiated, any part of it should correlate as closely with the whole as any other part. Actually, however, self-esteem (measured as a whole) correlates differently with various parts. For instance, the whole self-esteem syndrome as measured by the Social Personality Inventory (313) correlates with irritability $r = -0.39$, with the pagan sexual attitude $r = 0.85$, with a number of conscious inferiority feelings $r = -0.40$, with embarrassability in various situations $r = -0.60$, with a number of conscious fears $r = -0.29$ (305, 311).

Clinical examination of the data also shows this tendency toward a natural clustering of the parts into groups that seem intrinsically to belong close together. For instance, conventionality, morality, modesty, and regard for rules seem to fall together or belong together very naturally, as contrasted with another group of clustering qualities, such as self-confidence, poise, unembarrassability, lack of timidity, and shyness.

This tendency to cluster at once gives us the possibility of classifying within the syndrome, but when we actually attempt to do this we are presented with various difficulties. First of all we are confronted with the common problem of all classifications, that of the principle on which the classifying shall be based. Of course, if we knew all the data and their interrelationships, this would be easy. But when, as in our case, we proceed in partial ignorance, we find that we must be arbitrary at times, no matter how sensitive we try to be to the inner nature of the material. This inner hanging-togetherness gives us, in our case, an initial clue, an indication of general direction. But we can go only so far with such spontaneous groupings, and when we finally come to the point that we fail to perceive them, we must proceed on the basis of our own hypotheses.

Another apparent difficulty is that when we work with syndrome materials we soon find that we can classify any personality syndrome into a dozen main groupings, or a hundred, or a thousand, or ten thousand just as we please, depending on the degree of generality that we have in mind. We suspect that the usual attempt at classification is simply another reflection of the atomistic, connectionistic point of view. Certainly the use of an atomistic tool in dealing with interdepending data cannot get us very far. What is classification ordinarily if not the separation out of different parts, of discrete items? And how then shall we classify if our data are *not* essentially different and separate from each other? Perhaps we shall have to reject atomistic classification and look for some holistic principle of classifying just as we found it necessary to reject reductive analysis in favor of holistic analysis. The following analogies are offered as indications of the direction in which we must probably look for such a holistic technique of classification.

LEVELS OF MAGNIFICATION

This phrase is a physical analogy derived from the way in which a microscope works. In studying a histological slide, one gets the whole character, the general structure, the formation, and interrelationships in their totality by holding the slide up to the light and looking at it with the naked eye, thereby encompassing the whole. With this whole picture held clearly in mind we then examine one portion of this whole at a low magnification, let us say ten times. We are now studying a detail not for its own isolated sake, but with its relationship to the whole in mind. We can then go on to a closer study of this field within the whole by using another objective of still higher magnification, let us say fifty times. Further and finer analysis of the details within the whole are then made possible by using larger and larger magnifications to the practical limits of the instrument.[13]

We might also think of the material as being classified, not in a straight-line series of separated and independent parts which can then be reshuffled in any order, but in terms of "being contained within," perhaps, like a nest of boxes. If we call the whole security syndrome a box,

[13] "But one will never discover that such things as faces exists if one looks through a microscope." (Koffka, K., *Principles of Gestalt Psychology*, Harcourt, Brace & World, 1935, p. 319.)

then the 14 subsyndromes are 14 boxes that are contained with it (294). Within each of these 14 small boxes still other boxes are contained—perhaps 4 in one, 10 in another, 6 in another, etc.

Translating these examples into the terms of syndrome study, we may take the security syndrome and examine it as a whole, that is at level of magnification No. 1. Specifically this means studying the psychological flavor or meaning or aim of the total syndrome as a unity. We may then take one of the 14 subsyndromes of the security syndrome and study it at what we might call level of magnification No. 2. This subsyndrome would then be studied in its particular wholeness, in its interdependence with the 13 other subsyndromes, but always understood as a holistic part of the total security syndrome. As an example we may take the power-submission subsyndrome in the insecure person. The generally insecure person needs power, but this shows itself in many ways and in many different forms, such as overambition, overaggression, possessiveness, hunger for money, overcompetitiveness, tendency to prejudice and hatred, etc., or as their apparent opposites, e.g., bootlicking, submissiveness, masochistic trends, etc. But these characteristics themselves are obviously also general and may be further analyzed and classified. A study of any of these would be at level No. 3. Let us choose, perhaps, the need for or tendency toward prejudice, of which race prejudice is a good example. If we study this correctly, we study it not in itself or in isolation. We could phrase it more fully by saying that we are studying the tendency to prejudice, which is a subsyndrome of the need for power, which is a subsyndrome of the general insecurity syndrome. I need not point out that finer and finer studies would take us to level 4, level 5, and so on. We could take for instance one aspect of this particular complexity, let us say the tendency to seize upon differences, e.g., skin color, shape of nose, language spoken, as a means to bolster one's own need for security. This tendency to seize upon differences is organized as a syndrome and can be studied as a syndrome. To be more specific, in this case it would be classified as a sub-sub-sub-subsyndrome. It is the 5th box in the nest of boxes.

To sum up, such a method of classification, viz., one that is based on the fundamental concept of "being contained within" rather than of "being separate from," can give us the clue for which we have been seeking. It allows us to be sophisticated both about particulars and about wholes without falling into either meaningless particularism or vague and useless generality. It is simultaneously synthetic and analytic, and finally, it allows us to study uniqueness and commonness simultaneously and effectively. It rejects the dichotomies, the Aristotelian division into class A and class Not-A, and yet furnishes us with a theoretically satisfactory principle of classification and analysis.

CONCEPT OF SYNDROME CONCENTRATION

If we look for a heuristic criterion by which to differentiate between syndromes and subsyndromes, we can find it theoretically in the concept of concentration. What is the difference between the natural groupings in the self-esteem syndrome? Conventionality, morality, modesty, and regard for rules were found to cluster together into a group, which could be differentiated from another cluster formed by the characteristics of self-confidence, poise, unembarrassability, and boldness. These clusters or subsyndromes of course correlate with each other and with self-esteem as a whole. Furthermore, within each cluster the various elements correlate with one another. Probably our perception of clustering, the subjective feeling that various elements go together naturally, would be reflected in the correlations that would be obtained if we could get measures of these elements. Probably self-confidence and poise are more closely correlated than are poise and unconventionality. Perhaps a clustering could mean in statistical terms a high average of intercorrelation between all the members of the cluster. This average intercorrelation would presumably be higher than the average of correlation between members of two different clusters. Supposing we assume the intracluster average correlation to be $r = 0.7$, and the average correlation between members of different clusters to be $r = 0.5$, then the new syndrome formed by the merging of the clusters or subsyndromes will have an average correlation higher than $r = 0.5$ and lower than $r = 0.7$, probably closer to $r = 0.6$. As we move from sub-subsyndromes to subsyndromes to syndromes, we may expect that the average correlation will go down. This change we may call change in syndrome concentration, and we may reasonably stress the concept if only because it may furnish us with the working tool with which we may check our clinical findings.[14]

It follows from the basic assumption of a dynamic psychology that what can and should be correlated are *not* behaviors *qua* behaviors, but the meanings of behaviors, e.g., not modest behavior, but the quality of

---

[14] It is the tendency of holistic psychologists to mistrust the correlation technique, but I feel that this is because the technique happens to have been used in an exclusively atomistic way rather than because its essential nature conflicts with holistic theory. Even though, for instance, self-correlations are mistrusted by the average statistician (as if anything else could be expected in the organism!), they *need* not be if certain holistic facts are taken into consideration.

modesty seen intact in its relations to the rest of the organism. Furthermore it must be recognized that even dynamic variables do not necessarily vary along a single continuum, but may at a certain point break sharply into something completely different. An example of this phenomenon may be found in the effects of hunger for affection. If we range young children in a series from fully accepted to fully rejected, we shall find that as we go down the scale, the children hunger more and more frantically for affection, but as we approach the extreme end of the scale—utter rejection from the earliest days of life—we find not a tremendous yearning for love, but a complete coldness and *lack* of desire for affection.

Finally we must of course use holistic data rather than atomistic data, i.e., not the products of reductive analysis but of holistic analysis. In this way, single variables or parts may be correlated without doing violence to the unity of the organism. If we are properly cautious about the data that we correlate, and if we temper all statistics with clinical and experimental knowledge, there is no reason why correlation technique should not be highly useful in a holistic methodology.

THE EXTENT OF THE INTERRELATEDNESS
WITHIN THE ORGANISM

In his book on physical Gestalts, Köhler (239) objects to the overgeneralization of interrelatedness, even to the extent of not being able to choose between a very general monism and a complete atomism. Accordingly, he stresses not only interrelatedness within a Gestalt, but also the fact of separateness of Gestalts. For him most of the Gestalts he works with are (relatively) closed systems. He carries his analysis only to the point of analyzing within the Gestalt; he discusses less often the relations between Gestalts, either physical or psychological.

It must be apparent that when we deal with organismic data we have a different situation. Certainly there are almost no closed systems within the organism. Within the organism everything *does* actually relate with everything else, if only sometimes in the most tenuous and distant fashion. Furthermore, the organism taken as a whole has been shown to be related to and to be fundamentally interdependent with the culture, the immediate presence of other people, the particular situation, physical and geographical factors, etc. So far we may say at least that what Köhler should have done was to restrict his generalization to physical Gestalts and to psychological Gestalts in the phenomenal world, for his strictures certainly do not apply nearly so strongly within the organism.

It is possible to go beyond this minimum statement if we choose to argue about it. Actually a very good case can be made for saying that the whole world is theoretically interrelated. We can find relations of some sort between any part of the universe and any other part if we choose from any of the multitude of relation types that exist. It is only if we wish to be practical, or if we speak in a single realm of discourse rather than in a totality of realms of discourse, that we can assume that systems are relatively independent of one another. For instance, from the psychological point of view, universal interrelatedness breaks up because there are parts of the world that are not *psychologically* related to other parts of the universe, even though they may be related chemically, physically, or biologically. Furthermore the interrelatedness of the world might very well be broken up in a completely different fashion by the biologist or chemist or physicist. It seems to me that the best phrasing possible at the moment is that there are relatively closed systems, but that these closed systems are the product in part of the point of view. What is (or what seems to be) a closed system may not be so a year from now because scientific operations may improve enough next year to demonstrate that there is such relationship. If the reply were to be made that we should have to demonstrate actual physical processes obtaining rather than more theoretical relationships between all the part of the world, then it certainly must be said in reply that the monistic philosophers have never claimed such a universal *physical* interrelatedness but have spoken of many other kinds of interrelatedness. However, since this is not a main point in our exposition, it is not necesary to dwell upon it. It is quite sufficient to point out the phenomenon of (theoretical) universal interrelatedness within the organism.

RELATIONS BETWEEN SYNDROMES

In this area of research we have at least one carefully studied example to offer. Whether this is a paradigm or a special case remains to be discovered by further research.

Quantitatively, that is to say in terms of simple linear correlations, there is a positive but small relationship between the security level and level of self-esteem, $r =$ about 0.2 or 0.3. In the area of individual diagnosis in normal people, it is quite clear that these two syndromes are practically independent variables. In certain groups there may be characteristic relations in the two syndromes: e.g., in Jews there was (in the 1940s), a tendency to be simultaneously high in self-esteem and low in security, while in Catholic women we found often low self-esteem joined with high security. In neurotics both levels were and are apt to be low.

But more startling than this relationship (or lack of it) in level of the two syndromes is the very close relationship between *level* of security (or self-esteem) and the *quality* of self-esteem (or security). This relationship can be demonstrated most easily by contrasting two individuals both high in self-esteem but at opposite ends of the scale in security. Person A (high self-esteem and high security) tends to express his self-esteem in a very different way from person B (high self-esteem and low security). Person A, who has both personal strength and love for his fellow man, will naturally use his strength in a fostering, kindly, or protecting fashion. But B, who has equal strength but has with it hate, contempt, or fear for his fellow man, will more likely use his strength to hurt, to dominate, or to assuage his insecurity. His strength must then be a threat to his fellows. Thus we may speak of an insecure quality of high self-esteem, and we may contrast it with a secure quality of high self-esteem. Similarly we may distinguish insecure and secure qualities of low self-esteem, i.e., the masochist or bootlicker on the one hand, the quiet, sweet, or serving, dependent person on the other hand. Similar differences in security quality correlate with differences in level of self-esteem. For instance, insecure people may be either retiring, withdrawing people or openly hostile and aggressive people accordingly as they are low or high in level of self-esteem. Secure people can be either humble or proud, followers or leaders as their self-esteem levels vary from low to high.

THE PERSONALITY SYNDROMES
AND BEHAVIOR

In a broad fashion, preliminary to more specific analysis, we can say that the relations between the syndromes and overt behavior are about as follows. Each act *tends* to be an expression of the whole integrated personality. This means, more specifically, that each act tends to be determined by each and all of the personality syndromes (in addition to other determinants to be spoken of below). As John Doe laughs and responds to a joke, we can theoretically tease out from among the various determinants of this unitary act his security level, his self-esteem, his energy, his intelligence, etc. Such a viewpoint is in clear contrast to that now obsolete brand of trait theory in which the typical instance is of a single behavior act determined wholly by a single trait. Our theoretical statement gets its best exemplification in certain tasks that are thought of as "more important," like artistic creation. In producing a painting or a concerto, the artist clearly puts himself completely into the task, and accordingly it is an expression of his whole personality. But such an example, or, let us say, any creative response to an unstructured situation—as in the Rorschach test—is at the extreme of the continuum. At the other end is the isolated, specific act that has little or no relation to the character structure. Examples of such are immediate responses to the demands of a momentary situation (getting out of the way of a truck), purely habitual, cultural responses that have long since lost their psychological meaning for most people (getting up when a lady enters the room), or finally, reflex acts. Such behavior can tell us little or nothing about the character, for in these cases it is negligible as a determining factor. Between these extremes we find all sorts of gradations. There are, for example, acts that tend to be almost wholly determined by only one or two syndromes. A particular act of kindness is more closely related to the security syndrome than to any other. The feeling of modesty is largely determined by self-esteem, and so on.

These facts may raise the question why, if all these types of behavior-syndrome relations exist, should it be said at the outset that behavior is generally determined by all the syndromes?

It is obvious that, by a kind of theoretical requiredness, a holistic theory would start with such a statement, while an atomistic approach would start with the selection of an isolated, discrete behavior, cut away from all its connection to the organism—a sensation or conditioned reflex, for instance. Here it is a problem of "centering" (from the point of view of which part is the whole to be organized). For atomistic theory the simplest fundamental datum would be a bit of behavior obtained by reductive analysis, i.e., a behavior cut away from all its relationships to the rest of the organism.

Perhaps more to the point is the contention that the first type of syndrome-behavior relationship is more important. Isolated behaviors tend to be on the fringe of life's main concerns. They are isolated simply *because* they are unimportant, i.e., have nothing to do with the main problems, the main answers, or the main goals of the organism. It is quite true that my leg kicks out when the patellar tendon is struck, or that I eat olives with my fingers, or that I cannot eat boiled onions because I was conditioned against them. It is certainly no truer that I have a certain life philosophy, that I love my family, or that I am drawn to do experiments of a certain kind—but the latter situations are far more important.

While it is true that the inner nature of the organism is a determinant of behavior, it is not the only determinant of behavior. The cultural setting in which the organism behaves, and which has already helped to determine the inner nature of the organism, is also a determinant of behavior. Finally another set of determinants of behavior may be lumped under the head of "the immediate situation." While the goals and aims of the behavior are determined by the nature of the organism, and the paths to the goals are determined by the culture, the immediate situation determines the realistic possibilities and impossibilities: which behavior is wise, which not; which partial goals are available and which not; what offers a threat and what offers a possible tool with which the goals may be achieved.

Conceived thus complexly, it becomes easy to understand why behavior is not always a good index of character structure. For if behavior is as much determined by the external situation and by culture as by character, if it is a compromise formation between three sets of forces, it cannot very well be a perfect indicator of any one of them. Again this is a theoretical statement. Practically there are certain techniques[15] whereby we may "control out" or nullify the influences of culture and situation so that in actual practice, behavior *may* sometimes be a good index of character.

A much higher correlation is found to obtain between character and impulse to behavior. Indeed, this correlation is so high that these impulses to behavior may themselves be considered part of the syndrome. These are far more free of external and cultural compulsions than are overt behavior acts. We may even go so far as to say that we study behavior only as an index of impulse to behavior. If it is a good index, it is worth studying; if it is not a good index, it is not worth studying, if the ultimate object of our studying is the understanding of character.

LOGICAL AND MATHEMATICAL EXPRESSION OF SYNDROME DATA

There is not now extant, so far as I know, any mathematics or logic that is suitable for the symbolic expression and manipulation of syndrome

---

15 For instance, the situation may be controlled out as a determiner of behavior by making it sufficiently vague, as in the various projective tests. Or sometimes the demands of the organism are so overwhelming, as in insanity, that the external world is denied or disregarded and the culture defied. The prime technique for partially ruling out the culture is interview rapport or the psychoanalytic transference. In certain other situations the cultural compulsions may be weakened, as in drunkenness, rage, or other examples of uncontrolled behavior. Again there are many behaviors that culture neglects to regulate, e.g., various subtle, subliminally perceived variations of the culturally determined theme, the so-called expressive movements. Or we may study behavior in relatively uninhibited people, in children in whom cultural compulsions are as yet weak, in animals in which they are almost negligible, or in other societies so that we can rule out cultural influences by contrast. These few examples show that a sophisticated, theoretically sound study of behavior *can* tell us something about inner organization of personality.

data. Such a symbolic system is by no means impossible, for we know that we can construct mathematics or logics to suit our needs. Currently, however, the various logics and mathematical systems that are available are based on and are expressions of the general-atomistic world view that we have already criticized. My own efforts in this direction are much too feeble to present here.

The sharp distinction between A and Not-A introduced by Aristotle as one of the bases of his logic has been carried on to modern logics even where other Aristotelian assumptions have been rejected. So, for instance, we find in Langer's *Symbolic Logic* (250) that this notion, which she describes in terms of complementary classes, is for her one of the basic assumptions that need not be proven but can be taken for granted as common sense. "Every class has a complement; the class and its complement are mutually exclusive and exhaust the universe class between them" (p. 193).

It must by now be obvious that with syndrome data there can be no such sharp cutting away of any part of the data from the whole, or any such sharp division between any single datum and the rest of the syndrome. When we cut A away from the whole, A is no longer A, Not-A is no longer what it was, and certainly simple addition of A and Not-A will not give us back the whole with which we started. Within a syndrome every part of the syndrome overlaps every other part. Cutting away a part is impossible unless we pay no heed to these overlappings. This neglect the psychologist cannot afford. Mutual exclusiveness is possible for data taken in isolation. If they are taken in context, as they must be in psychology, this dichotomizing is quite impossible. It is not, for instance, even conceivable that we could cut away self-esteem behavior from all other behavior, for the very simple reason that there is practically no behavior that is just self-esteem behavior and nothing else.

If we reject this notion of mutual exclusiveness, we call into doubt not only the whole logic that is partially based upon it, but also most of the systems of mathematics with which we are familiar. Most extant mathematics and logic deal with a world that is a collection of mutually exclusive entities, like a pile of apples. Separating one apple from the rest of the pile changes neither the essential nature of the apple, nor the essential nature of the pile. With the organism it is quite different. Cutting away an organ changes the whole organism as well as the part that was cut away.

Another example may be found in the basic arithmetical procedures of addition, subtraction, multiplication, and division. These are all operations that clearly assume atomistic data. Adding an apple to another apple is possible because the nature of apples permits this. The case is different with personality. If we have two people who have high self-esteem and are insecure and we then make one of these people more secure ("add" security), we have one person who probably tends to be coöperative and another who tends to be a tyrant. The high self-esteem in one personality does not have the same quality as the high self-esteem in the other. In the person to whom security has been added there are two changes, not just one. Not only did he acquire security, but the quality of the self-esteem changed, merely by being conjoined with high security. This is a labored example, but it is the closest that we can come to conceiving of anything like the additive processes in personality.

Apparently traditional mathematics and logic, in spite of their unlimited possibilities, seem actually to be handmaidens in the service of an atomistic, mechanical view of the world.

It seems even possible to say that mathematics is lagging behind modern physical sciences in its acceptance of dynamic, holistic theory. Essential changes in the nature of physical theory are made, not by changing the essential nature of mathematics, but by stretching its use, by doing tricks with it, by leaving its essentially static nature unchanged as much as possible. These changes can be made only by making various "as if" assumptions. A good example is found in calculus, which purports to deal with motion and change, but does this only by making the change into a succession of static states. The area under a curve is measured by splitting it into a series of oblongs. Curves themselves are treated "as if" they were polygonal figures with very small sides. That this has been a legitimate procedure with which we can have no ultimate quarrel is proven by the fact that the calculus works and is a highly useful instrument. But what is not legitimate is to forget that it works because of a series of assumptions, of dodges or tricks, of "as if" assumptions that clearly do not deal with the phenomenal world as psychological studies do.

The following quotation is an illustration of our contention that mathematics tends to be static and atomistic. So far as I know its purport has not been challenged by other mathematicians.

> But had we not previously declared quite fervently that we live in a motionless world? And had we not shown at great length, by employing the paradoxes of Zeno, that motion is impossible, that a flying arrow is actually at rest? To what shall we ascribe this apparent reversal of position?
>
> Moreover, if each new mathematical invention rests upon the old-established foundations, how is it possible to extract from the theories of static algebra and static geometry a new mathematics capable of solving problems involving dynamic entities?

As to the first, there has been no reversal of viewpoint. We are still firmly entrenched in the belief that this is a world in which motion as well as change are special cases of the state of rest. There is no state of change, if change implies a state qualitatively different from rest; that which we distinguish as change is merely, as we once indicated, a succession of many different static images perceived in comparatively short intervals of time. . . .

Intuitively convinced that there is continuity in the behavior of a moving body, since we do not actually see the flying arrow pass through every point on its flight, there is an overwhelming instinct to abstract the idea of motion as something essentially different from rest. But this abstraction results from physiological and psychological limitations; it is in no way justified by logical analysis. Motion is a correlation of position with time. Chance is merely another name for *function,* another aspect of that same correlation.

For the rest, the calculus, as an offspring of geometry and algebra, belongs to a static family and has acquired no characteristics not already possessed by its parents. Mutations are not possible in mathematics. Thus, inevitably, the calculus has the same static properties as the multiplication table and the geometry of Euclid. The calculus is but another interpretation, although it must be admitted an ingenious one, of this unmoving world.[16]

Let us say again that there are two ways of looking at elements. For instance, blushing can be blushing *per se* (a reductive element) or it can be blushing in a context (a holistic element). The former involves a kind of "as if" assumption, "as if it were all alone in the world and had no relation to the rest of the world." This is a formal abstraction and in certain scientific areas may be quite useful. In any case certainly no harm can be done by the abstraction so long as it is remembered that it *is* a formal abstraction. Trouble arises only when the mathematician or logician or scientist forgets that he is doing something artificial when he talks about blushing *per se,* for certainly he would admit that there is in the real world no such thing as blushing without a human being to blush, something to blush about, etc. This artificial habit of abstraction, or working with reductive elements, has worked so well and has become so ingrained a habit that the abstractors and the reducers are apt to be amazed at anyone who denies the empirical or phenomenal validity of these habits. By smooth stages they convince themselves that this is the way in which the world is actually constructed, and they find it easy to forget that even though it is useful it is still artificial, conventionalized,

[16] Kasner, E., and Newman, J., *Mathematics and the Imagination,* Simon & Schuster, 1940, pp. 301–304.

hypothetical—in a word, that it is a man-made system that is imposed upon an interconnected world in flux. These peculiar hypotheses about the world have the right to fly in the face of common sense only for the sake of demonstrated convenience. When they are no longer convenient, or when they become hindrances, they must be dropped. It is dangerous to see in the world what we have put into it rather than what is actually there. Let us say this flatly. Atomistic mathematics or logic is, in a certain sense, a theory about the world, and any description of it in terms of this theory the psychologist may reject as unsuited to his purposes. It is clearly necessary for methodological thinkers to proceed to the creation of logical and mathematical systems that are more closely in accord with the nature of the world of modern science.[17]

Research data on which the conclusions expressed in this chapter are based are presented in the following papers and tests by A. H. Maslow. The researches of McClelland and his colleagues is relevant and similar though not identical (297a).

The dominance drive as a determiner of the social and sexual behavior of infra-human primates, I, II, III, IV, *J. genet. Psychol.*, 1936, *48*, 261–277; 278–309 (with S. Flanzbaum); 310–338; 1936, *49*, 161–198.

Dominance-feeling, behavior, and status, *Psychol. Rev.*, 1937, *44*, 404–429.

Dominance-feeling, personality, and social behavior in women, *J. social Psychol.*, 1939, *10*, 3–39.

Individual psychology and the social behavior of monkeys and apes, *Int. J. individ. Psychol.*, 1935, *1*, 47–59.

Dominance-quality and social behavior in infra-human primates, *J. social Psychol.*, 1940, *11*, 313–324.

---

[17] It is possible to extend these remarks to the English language itself. This too tends to reflect the atomistic world theory of our culture. It is not to be wondered that in describing syndrome data and syndrome laws we must resort to the most outlandish analogies, figures of speech, and various other twistings and turnings. We have the conjunction *and* to express the joining of two discrete entities, but we have no conjunction to express the joining of two entities that are not discrete and that when joined form a unit and not a duality. The only substitute that I can think of for this basic conjunction is the clumsy one, "structured with." There are other languages that are more sympathetic to a holistic, dynamic world view. In my opinion the agglutinate languages are more adequate to reflect the holistic world than is the English language. Another point is that our language organizes the world, as most logicians and mathematicians do, into elements and relationships, matter and things done to matter. Nouns are treated as if they were matter, and verbs as if they were actions done by matter to matter. Adjectives describe more accurately the kind of matter, and adverbs describe more accurately the kind of action. A holistic-dynamic view makes no such sharp dichotomy. In any case, words must be strung out in a straight line even when they are trying to describe syndrome data (257).

A test for dominance-feeling (self-esteem) in women, *J. social Psychol.*, 1940, *12*, 255–270.

The dynamics of psychological security-insecurity, *Character and Pers.*, 1942, *10*, 331–344.

Self-esteem (dominance-feeling) and sexuality in women, *J. social Psychol.*, 1942, *16*, 259–294.

A clinically derived test for measuring psychological security-insecurity, *J. gen. Psychol.*, 1945, *33*, 21–51. (with E. Birsh, E. Stein, and I. Honigmann). Published by Consulting Psychologists Press, Palo Alto, Calif., 1952.

Comments on Prof. McClelland's paper. In M. R. Jones (ed.), *Nebraska Symposium on Motivation, 1955,* Lincoln: University of Nebraska Press, 1955.

Some parallels between the dominance and sexual behavior of monkeys and the fantasies of patients in psychotherapy, *J. nervous mental Disease,* 1960, *131,* 202–212 (with H. Rand and S. Newman).

Liberal leadership and personality, *Freedom,* 1942, *2,* 27–30.

The authoritarian character structure, *J. social Psychol.*, 1943, *18,* 401–411.

BIBLIOGRAPHY

1. Ackerman, N., Psychotherapy and "giving love," *Psychiatry*, 1944, 7, 129–137.
2. Adler, A., *Social Interest*, New York: Putnam, 1939.
3. Adler, A., *Superiority and Social Interests: A Collection of Later Writings*, H. L. and R. R. Ansbacher (eds.), Evanston: Northwestern University Press, 1964.
4. Alderfer, C. P., An organization syndrome, *Admin Sci. Quart.* 1967, *12*, 440–460.
5. Allport, G., *Becoming*, New Haven, Conn.: Yale University Press, 1955.
6. Allport, G., *Pattern and Growth in Personality*, New York: Holt, Rinehart and Winston, 1961.
7. Allport, G., *Personality and Social Encounter*, Boston: Beacon, 1960.
8. Allport, G., and Vernon, P. E., *Studies in Expressive Movement*, New York: Macmillan, 1933.
9. Allport, G., Normative compatibility in the light of social science, *in* Maslow, A. H. (ed.), *New Knowledge in Human Values*, New York: Harper & Row, 1959.
10. Anderson, H. H. (ed.), *Creativity and Its Cultivation*, New York: Harper & Row, 1959.
11. Anderson, O. D., and Permenter, R. A., A long term study of the experimental neurosis in the sheep and dog, *Psychosomat. Med. Monogr.*, 1941, *2*, Nos. 3, 4.

12. Angyal, A., *Neurosis and Treatment: A Holistic Theory*, New York: Wiley, 1965.
13. Ansbacher, H., and R., *The Individual Psychology of Alfred Adler*, New York: Basic Books, 1956.
14. Ardrey, R., *The Territorial Imperative*, New York: Atheneum, 1966.
15. Argyris, C., *Interpersonal Competence and Organizational Effectiveness*, Homewood, Ill.: Irwin-Dorsey, 1962.
16. Argyris, C., *Organization and Innovation*, Homewood, Ill.: Irwin, 1965.
17. Aronoff, J., *Psychological Needs and Cultural Systems*, New York: Van Nostrand Reinhold, 1967.
18. Aronoff, J., Freud's conception of the origin of curiosity, *J. Psychol.*, 1962, *54*, 39–45.
19. Asch, S. E., *Social Psychology*, Englewood Cliffs, N. J.: Prentice-Hall, 1952.
20. Asch, S. E., Studies of independence and conformity, *Psycholog. Monogr.*, 1956, *70*, entire No. 416.
21. Assagioli, R., *Psychosynthesis: A Manual of Principles and Techniques*, New York: Hobbs, Dorman, 1965.
22. Axline, V. D., *In Search of Self*, Boston: Houghton Mifflin, 1964.
23. Back, K. W., The game and the myth as two languages of social science, *Behavioral Science*, 1963, *8*, 66–71.
24. Bacon, F., *The Advancement of Learning*, New York: Colonial Press, 1900.
25. Baker, R. S., *American Chronicle*, New York: Scribner's, 1945.
26. Balint, M., The final goal of psychoanalytic treatment, *Int. J. Psychoanal.*, 1936, *17*, 206–216.
27. Balint, M., On genital love, *Int. J. Psychoanal.*, 1948, *29*, 34–40.
28. Banham, K. M., The development of affectionate behavior in infancy, *J. gen. Psychol.*, 1950, *76*, 283–289.
29. Barker, R., Dembo, T., and Lewin, K., *Frustration and Regression: An Experiment with Young Children*, Iowa City: University of Iowa Press, 1941.
30. Barrett, W., *Irrational Man*, New York: Doubleday, 1958.
31. Barron, F., *Creativity and Psychological Health*, New York: Van Nostrand Reinhold, 1963.
32. Barry, J. R., and Malinovsky, M. R., *Client Motivation for Rehabilitation: A Review*, Monogr. No. 1, 1965, Gainesville, Fla.: Regional Rehabilitation Research Institute, University of Florida.
33. Bartlett, F. C., *Remembering*, Cambridge, England: Cambridge University Press, 1932.

34. Bateson, G., and Mead, M., *Balinese Character: A Photo-graphic Analysis,* New York: The New York Academy of Sciences, 1942.

35. Bay, C., *The Structure of Freedom,* New York: Antheneum, 1968.

36. Bay, C., Needs, wants and political legitimacy, *Can. J. pol. Sci.,* 1968, *1,* 241–260.

37. Becker, E., *The Structure of Evil,* New York: Braziller, 1968.

38. Beer, M., *Leadership Employee Needs and Motivation,* Monogr. No. 129, 1966, Columbus, O.: The Ohio State University.

39. Belo, J., *The Trance in Bali,* New York: Columbia University Press, 1960.

40. Benedict, R., Unpublished lectures on *Synergy in Society,* Bryn Mawr, ca 1942. Excerpts to be published, *Amer. Anthropologist,* 1970.

41. Bennett, E., Diamond, M., Krech, D., and Rosenzweig, M., Chemical and anatomical plasticity of brain, *Science,* 1964, *146,* 610–619.

42. Bennis, W., *Changing Organizations,* New York: McGraw-Hill, 1966.

43. Bennis, W., and Slater, P., *The Temporary Society,* New York: Harper & Row, 1968.

44. Bennis, W., Schein, E., Berlew, D., and Steele, F. (eds.), *Interpersonal Dynamics,* 2nd ed., Homewood, Ill.: Dorsey, 1968.

45. Bennis, W., Organizations of the future, *Personnel Administration,* 1967, *30,* 6–24.

46. Bergson, H., *Creative Evolution,* New York: Modern Library, 1944.

47. Bernard, L. L., *Instinct: A Study in Social Psychology,* New York: Holt, Rinehart and Winston, 1924.

48. Berne, E., *Games People Play,* New York: Grove Press, 1964.

49. Bertalanffy, L. V., *Modern Theories of Development,* London: Oxford University Press, 1933.

50. Bertocci, P., and Millard, R., *Personality and the Good,* New York: McKay, 1963.

51. Bettelheim, B., *The Informed Heart,* New York: Free Press, 1960.

52. Bibring, E., The development and problems of the theory of instincts, *Int. J. Psychoanal.,* 1941, *22,* 1–30.

53. Blai, B., Jr., An occupational study of job satisfaction, *J. exptl. Education,* 1964, *32,* 383–388.

54. Blazer, J., An experimental evaluation of "transcendence of environment," *J. humanistic Psychol.,* 1963, *3,* 49–53.

55. Blyth, R. H., *Zen in English Literature and Oriental Classics,* Tokyo: Hokuseido Press, 1942.

56. Bois, J. S., *The Art of Awareness,* Dubuque, Iowa: Brown, 1966.

57. Boisen, A., *The Exploration of the Inner World,* New York: Harper & Row, 1952.

58. Bonner, H., *Psychology of Personality*, New York: Ronald Press, 1961.
59. Bonney, M. E., *The Normal Personality*, Berkeley, Calif.: McCutchan, 1969.
60. Boss, M., *A Psychiatrist Discovers India*, London: Oswald Wolff, 1965.
61. Bossom, J., and Maslow, A. H., Security of judges as a factor in impressions of warmth in others, *J. abnorm. soc. Psychol.*, 1957, *55*, 147–148.
62. Bowlby, J., *Maternal Care and Mental Health*, Geneva: World Health Organization, 1952.
63. Braden, W., *The Private Sea*, Chicago: Quadrangle Books, 1967.
64. Brand, M., *Savage Sleep*, New York: Crown, 1968.
65. Breuer, J., and Freud, S., *Studies in Hysteria*, Boston: Beacon, 1961.
66. Bronowski, J., *Science and Human Values*, New York: Harper & Row, 1956.
67. Brown, G. I., *Now: the Human Dimension*, Monogr. No. 1, 1968, Big Sur, Calif.: Esalen Institute.
68. Bugental, J., *The Search for Authenticity*, New York: Holt, Rinehart and Winston, 1965.
69. Bugental, J. (ed.), *Challenges of Humanistic Psychology*, New York: McGraw-Hill, 1967.
70. Bühler, C., *Psychology for Contemporary Living*, New York: Hawthorn, 1969.
71. Bühler, C., *Values in Psychotherapy*, New York: Free Press, 1962.
72. Bühler, C., and Massarik, F. (eds.), *The Course of Human Life: A Study of Life Goals in the Humanistic Perspective*, New York: Springer, 1968.
73. Bühler, C., Maturation and motivation, *Dialectica*, 1951, *5*, 321–361.
74. Bühler, C., Psychotherapy and the image of man, *Psychotherapy: Theory, Research and Practice*, 1968, *5*, 89–94.
75. Bühler, C., The reality principle, *Am. J. Psychother.*, 1954, *8*, 626–647.
76. Burrow, T., *Preconscious Foundations of Human Experience*, Galt, W. E. (ed.), New York: Free Press, 1964.
77. Burtt, E. A., *In Search of Philosophic Understanding*, London: George Allen and Unwin, 1967.
78. Cannon, W. G., *Wisdom of the Body*. New York: Norton, 1932.
79. Carpenter, J., *Relations between dominance-feeling (self-esteem) and musical tastes*, Unpublished.
80. Carpenter, J., and Eisenberg, P., Some relations between family background and personality, *J. Psychol.*, 1938, *6*, 115–136.
81. Cauffman, J., Motivating university women to positive behavior, *J. Health human Behav.*, 1966, *7*, 295–302.

82. Chenault, J., Syntony: A philosophical premise for theory and research, *in* Sutich, A., and Vich, M. (eds.), *Readings in Humanistic Psychology*, New York: Free Press, 1969.

83. Cheney, S., *Men Who Have Walked With God*, New York: Knopf, 1945.

84. Chiang, Hung-min, and Maslow, A. H., *The Healthy Personality: Readings*, New York: Van Nostrand Reinhold, 1969.

85. Chiang, Hung-min, An experiment in experiential approaches to personality, *Psychologia*, 1968, *11*, 33–39.

86. Child, I., The experts and the bridge of judgment that crosses every cultural gap, *Psychology Today*, 1968, *2*, 24–29.

87. Clark, J. V., Worker Motivation, Alcan, Ltd., Mimeographed copies are available from the author.

88. Clark, J. V., Motivation in work groups: A tentative view, *Human Organization*, 1960, *19*, 199–208.

89. Combs, A., and Snygg, D., *Individual Behavior*, 2nd ed., New York: Harper & Row, 1959.

90. Combs, A. (ed.), *Perceiving, Behaving, Becoming: A New Focus for Education*, Washington, D.C.: Association for Supervision and Curriculum Development, 1962.

91. Combs, A., Soper, D., Gooding, C., Benton, J., Dickman, J., and Usher, R., *Florida Studies in the Helping Professions*, Monogr., Social Sciences, No. 37, 1969, Gainesville, Fla.: Univ. of Florida.

92. Corlis, R. B., and Rabe, P., *Psychotherapy from the Center: A Humanistic View of Change and of Growth*, Scranton, Pa.: International Textbook, 1969.

93. Cortés, J. B., and Gatti, F. M., Physique and motivation, *J. consulting Psychol.*, 1966, *30*, 408–414.

94. Cortés, J. B., and Gatti, F. M., Physique and self-descriptions of temperament, *J. consulting Psychol.*, 1965, *29*, 432–439.

95. Craig, R., Trait lists and creativity, *Psychologia*, 1966, *9*, 107-110.

96. Crawford, M. P., The cooperative solving of problems by young chimpanzees, *Comp. Psychol. Monogr.*, 1937, *14*, No. 68.

97. Crookshank, F. G., The importance of a theory of signs and a critique of language in the study of medicine, *in* Ogden, C. K., and Richards, I. A. (eds.), *The Meaning of Meaning*, New York: Harcourt, Brace & World, 1938.

98. Crutchfield, R., Conformity and character, *Am. Psychologist, 1955, 10,* 191–198.

99. Cummings, L. L., and El Salmi, A. M., Empirical Research on the Bases and Correlates of Managerial Motivation: A review of the literature, *Psycholog. Bull.*, 1968, *70*, 127–141.

100. Dabrowski, K., *Positive Disintegration*, Boston: Little, Brown, 1964.
101. Dailey, C., The effects of premature conclusion upon the acquisition of understanding a person, *J. Psychol.*, 1952, *33*, 133–152.
102. D'Arcy, M. C., *The Meeting of Love and Knowledge*, New York: Harper & Row, 1957.
103. D'Arcy, M. C., *The Mind and Heart of Love*, New York: Holt, Rinehart and Winston, 1947.
104. Davies, J. C., *Human Nature in Politics*, New York: Wiley, 1963.
105. Davies, W. A., The motivation of the underprivileged worker, *in* Whyte, F. W. (ed.), *Industry and Society*, New York: McGraw-Hill, 1946, 84–106.
106. De Forest, I., *The Leaven of Love*, New York: Harper & Row, 1954.
107. De Martino, M. (ed.), *Sexual Behavior and Personality Characteristics*, New York: Grove Press, 1963.
108. Dewey, J., Theory of valuation, *Int. Encycl. Unified Sci.*, 2, No. 4, Chicago: University of Chicago Press, 1939.
109. Dove, W. F., A study of individuality in the nutritive instincts, *Am. Naturalist*, 1935, *69*, 469–544.
110. Drews, E. M., Counseling for self-actualization in gifted girls and young women, *J. counseling Psychol.*, 1965, *12*, 167-175.
111. Drews, E., *The Creative Intellectual Style in Gifted Adolescents, Report II; Report III;* Portland, Ore.: Northwest Regional Educational Research Laboratory, 1966.
112. Driesch, H., *Embryonic Development and Induction*, London: Oxford University Press, 1938.
113. Drucker, P. F., *The End of Economic Man*, New York: John Day, 1939.
114. Dunbar, H. F., *Psychosomatic Diagnosis*, New York: Hoeber, 1943.
115. Eastman, M., *The Enjoyment of Poetry*, New York: Scribner's, 1928.
116. Edel, E. C., A study in managerial motivation, *Personnel Administration*, 1966, *29*, 31–38.
117. Einstein, A., and Infeld, L., *The Evolution of Physics*, New York: Simon and Schuster, 1938.
118. Eisenberg, P., Expressive movements related to feelings of dominance, *Arch. Psychol.*, 1937, *211*, 73.
119. Eisenberg, P., and Lazarsfeld, P., The psychological effects of unemployment, *Psycholog. Bull.*, 1938, *35*, 358–390.
120. Eliade, M., *The Sacred and the Profane*, New York: Harper & Row, 1961.
121. Ellis, W. D. (ed.), *Source Book of Gestalt Psychology*, New York: Harcourt, Brace & World, 1939.

122. Endore, G., *Synanon,* Garden City, N. Y.: Doubleday, 1968.
123. Erikson, E., *Identity and the Life Cycle,* New York: International Universities Press, 1959.
124. Esalen Institute brochures, Big Sur, Calif.: Esalen Institute, 1965–1969.
125. Escalona, S., Feeding disturbances in very young children, *Am. J. Orthopsychiat.,* 1945, *15,* 76–80.
126. Fantini, M., and Weinstein, G., *The Disadvantaged: Challenge to Education,* New York: Harper & Row, 1968.
127. Farrow, E. P., *Psychoanalyze Yourself,* New York: International Universities Press, 1942.
128. Farson, R. (ed.), *Science and Human Affairs,* Palo Alto, Calif.: Science and Behavior Books, 1965.
129. Fenichel, O., *The Psychoanalytic Theory of Neurosis,* New York: Norton, 1945.
130. Feuer, L., *Psychoanalysis and Ethics,* Springfield, Ill.: C. C Thomas, 1955.
131. Fiedler, F. E., The concept of an ideal therapeutic relationship, *J. consulting Psychol.* 1950, *14,* 239–245.
132. Fingarette, H., *The Self in Transformation,* New York: Harper & Row, 1963.
133. Frankl, V., *Man's Search for Meaning,* Boston: Beacon, 1962.
134. Frankl, V., *The Will to Meaning,* New York: World Publishing, 1969.
135. Frenkel-Brunswik, E., Intolerance of ambiguity as an emotional and perceptual personality variable, *J. Pers.,* 1949, *18,* 108–143.
136. Freud, A., *The Ego and the Mechanisms of Defense,* London: Hogarth, 1942.
137. Freud, S., *Beyond the Pleasure Principle,* London: International Psychoanalytic Press, 1922.
138. Freud, S., *Civilization and its Discontents,* New York: Cape and Smith, 1930.
139. Freud, S., *Collected Papers, Vol. II,* London: Hogarth, 1924.
140. Freud, S., Contributions to the psychology of love, Papers XI, XII, XIII *in Collected Papers, Vol. IV,* London: Hogarth, 1925.
141. Freud, S., *General Introduction to Psychoanalysis,* New York: Boni and Liveright, 1920.
142. Freud, S., *The Interpretation of Dreams,* New York: Basic Books, 1956.
143. Freud, S., *New Introductory Lectures on Psychoanalysis,* New York: Norton, 1933.

144. Freud, S., *An Outline of Psychoanalysis,* New York: Norton, 1949.
145. Fromm, E., *Escape from Freedom,* New York: Farrar, Straus & Giroux, 1941.
146. Fromm, E., *The Forgotten Language,* New York: Grove Press, 1957.
147. Fromm, E., *The Heart of Man,* New York: Harper & Row, 1964.
148. Fromm, E., *Man for Himself,* New York: Holt, Rinehart and Winston, 1947.
149. Fromm, E., *Psychoanalysis and Religion,* New Haven, Conn.: Yale University Press, 1950.
150. Fromm, E., *The Sane Society,* New York: Holt, Rinehart and Winston, 1955.
151. Fromm, E., Suzuki, D. T., and De Martino, R., *Zen Buddhism and Psychoanalysis,* New York: Harper & Row, 1960.
152. Gardner, J. W., *Self Renewal: The Individual and the Innovative Society,* New York: Harper & Row, 1963.
153. Ghiselli, E. E., Managerial talent, *Am. Psychologist,* 1963, *18,* 631–642.
154. Glasser, W., *Reality Therapy,* New York: Harper & Row, 1965.
155. Goble, F., *Return to Responsibility,* Pasadena, Calif.: Thomas Jefferson Research Center, 1969.
156. Goldberg, R. T., Need satisfaction and rehabilitation progress of psychotic patients, *J. counseling Psychol.,* 1967, *14,* 253–257.
157. Gourevitch, V., and Feffer, M. H., A study of motivational development, *J. gen. Psychol.,* 1962, *100,* 361–375.
158. Goldfarb, W., Psychological privation in infancy and subsequent adjustment, *Am. J. Orthopsychiat.,* 1945, *15,* 247–255.
159. Goldstein, K., *Human Nature,* Cambridge, Mass.:Harvard University Press, 1940.
160. Goldstein, K., *The Organism,* New York: American Book, 1939.
161. Goodman, R. A., *On the Operationality of the Maslow Need Hierarchy,* Los Angeles: Graduate School of Business Admin., University of California, Los Angeles, 1968, Reprint No. 112.
162. Gordon, D. C., *Self Love,* New York: Verity House, 1968.
163. Guggenheimer, R., *Creative Vision for Art and for Life,* rev. ed., New York: Harper & Row, 1960.
164. Green, H., *I Never Promised You a Rose Garden,* New York: Holt, Rinehart and Winston, 1967.
165. Greening, T. C., and Coffey, H. S., Working with an "impersonal" T group, *J. app. behav. Sci.,* 1966, *2,* 401–411.
166. Grof, S., *Theory and Practice of LSD Psychotherapy,* To be published.

167. Guiterman, A., *Lyric Laughter,* New York: Dutton, 1939. Reprinted by permission.
168. Hall, D. T., and Nougaim, K. E., An examination of Maslow's need hierarchy in an organizational setting, *Organizational Behavior and Human Performance,* 1968, *3,* 12-35.
169. Halmos, P., *The Faith of the Counsellors,* London: Constable, 1965.
170. Halmos, P., *Towards a Measure of Man,* London: Kegan Paul, 1957.
171. Harding, M. E., *Psychic Energy,* New York: Pantheon, 1947.
172. Harlow, H. F., Motivation as a factor in the acquisition of new responses, *in* Jones, R. M. (ed.), *Current Theory and Research in Motivation,* Lincoln, Neb.: University of Nebraska Press, 1953.
173. Harlow, H. F., The heterosexual affectional system in monkeys, *Am. Psychologist,* 1962, *17,* 1–9.
174. Harlow, H. F., Learning motivated by a manipulation drive, *J. exptl. Psychol.,* 1950, *40,* 228–234.
175. Harlow, H. F., Maternal behavior in socially deprived rhesus monkeys, *J. abnorm. soc. Psychol.,* 1964, *69,* 345–354.
176. Harlow, H. F., Primary affectional patterns in primates, *Am. J. Orthopsychiat.,* 1960, *30,* 676–684.
177. Harlow, H. F., and Harlow, M. K., The affectional systems, *in* Schrier, A. M., Harlow, H. F., and Stollnitz, F. (eds.), *Behavior of Non-human Primates,* Vol. 2, New York: Academic Press, 1965.
178. Harlow, H. F., and Harlow, M. K., Learning to love, *Am. Scientist,* 1966, *54,* 244–272.
179. Harlow, H. F., and Harlow, M. K., Social deprivation in monkeys, *Scientific American,* 1962, *207,* 136–146.
180. Harman, W. W., Contemporary social forces and alternative futures, *J. Res. Develop. Education, 2,* Summer 1969, 67–89.
181. Harman, W. W., The new Copernican revolution, *Stanford Today,* Winter 1969, 6–10.
182. Harper, R., *Human Love: Existential and Mystical,* Baltimore: Johns Hopkins Press, 1966.
183. Hartmann, C. G., Endocrine influences on instinctual processes, *Psychosomat. Med.,* 1942, *4,* 206–210.
184. Hartman, R. S., *The Structure of Value: Foundations of Scientific Axiology,* Carbondale, Ill.: Southern Illinois University Press, 1967.

185. Hartmann, H., *Ego Psychology and the Problem of Adaptation*, New York: International Universities Press, 1958.
186. Hattis, R., Love feelings in courtship couples: An analysis, *in* Sutich, A., and Vich, M. (eds.), *Readings in Humanistic Psychology*, New York: Free Press, 1969, 347–385.
187. Hayakawa, S. I., *Language and Thought in Action*, Harcourt, Brace & World, 1949.
188. Hayakawa, S. I., The fully functioning personality, *in* S. I. Hayakawa (ed.), *Our Language & Our World*, New York: Harper & Row, 1959, 202–217.
189. Heard, G., *Training for a Life of Growth*, Santa Monica, Calif.: Wayfarer Press, 1959.
190. Heath, D. H., *Explorations of Maturity: Studies of Mature and Immature College Men*, New York: Appleton-Century-Crofts, 1965.
191. Henle, M. (ed.), *Documents of Gestalt Psychology*, Berkeley, Calif.: University of California Press, 1961.
192. Herzberg, A., *The Psychology of Philosophers*, New York: Harcourt, Brace & World, 1929.
193. Herzberg, F., *Work and the Nature of Man*, New York: World Publishing, 1966.
194. Higgins, M., and Raphael, C. M. (eds.), *Reich Speaks of Freud*, New York: Farrar, Straus & Giroux, 1967.
195. Hitschmann, E., Freud's conception of love, *Int. J. Psychoanal.*, 1952, *33*, 1–8.
196. Hoggart, R., *The Uses of Literacy*, Boston: Beacon, 1961.
197. Horney, K., *The Neurotic Personality of Our Time*, New York: Norton, 1937.
198. Horney, K., *New Ways in Psychoanalysis*, New York: Norton, 1939.
199. Horney, K., *Neurosis and Human Growth*, New York: Norton, 1950.
200. Horney, K., *Self-Analysis*, New York: Norton, 1942.
201. Howells, T. H., The obsolete dogma of heredity, *Psychol. Rev.*, 1945, *52*, 23–34.
202. Howells, T. H., and Vine, D. O., The innate differential in social learning, *J. abnorm. soc. Psychol.*, 1940, *35*, 537–548.
203. Huber, J., *Through an Eastern Window*, Boston: Houghton Mifflin, 1967.
204. Husband, R. W., A comparison of human adults and white rats in maze learning, *J. comp. Psychol.*, 1929, *9*, 361–377.
205. Husserl, E., *Ideas: General Introduction to Pure Phenomenology*, New York: Macmillan, 1952.
206. Huxley, A., *Grey Eminence*, New York: World Publishing, 1959.

207. Huxley, A., *Heaven & Hell,* New York: Harper & Row, 1955.
208. Huxley, A., *Island,* New York: Bantam Books, 1963.
209. Huxley, A., *The Perennial Philosophy,* New York: Harper & Row, 1944.
210. Jahoda, M., *Current Conceptions of Positive Mental Health,* New York: Basic Books, 1958.
211. James, W., *The Principles of Psychology,* New York: Holt, Rinehart and Winston, 1890.
212. James, W., *The Varieties of Religious Experience,* New York: Modern Library, 1943.
213. Jekels, L., and Bergler, E., Transference and love, *Psychoanal. Quart.,* 1949, *18,* 325–350.
214. Jessner, L., and Kaplan, S., "Discipline" as a problem in psychotherapy with children, *The Nervous Child,* 1951, *9,* 147–155.
215. Johnson, W., *People in Quandaries,* New York: Harper & Row, 1946.
216. Jones, R. M., *Fantasy and Feeling in Education,* New York: New York University Press, 1968.
217. Jourard, S. M., *Disclosing Man to Himself,* New York: Van Nostrand Reinhold, 1968.
218. Jung, C., *The Integration of the Personality,* London: Routledge & Kegan Paul, 1950.
219. Jung, C., *Modern Man in Search of a Soul,* New York: Harcourt, Brace & World, 1933.
220. Jung, C., *The Undiscovered Self,* London: Kegan Paul, 1958.
221. Kamiya, J., Conscious control of brain waves, *Psychology Today,* 1968, *1,* 56–61.
222. Kardiner, A., *The Traumatic Neuroses of War,* New York: Hoeber, 1941.
223. Kasanin, S. J., Neurotic "acting out" as a basis for sexual promiscuity in women, *Psychoanal. Rev.,* 1944, *31,* 221–232.
224. Kasner, E., and Newman, J., *Mathematics and the Imagination,* New York: Simon and Schuster, 1940.
225. Katona, G., *Organizing and Memorizing,* New York: Columbia University Press, 1940.
226. Katz, R., Unpublished reports on the Outward Bound program.
227. Kaufman, W., *Nietzsche,* New York: World Publishing, 1956.
228. Kaufman, W. (ed.), *The Portable Nietzsche,* New York: Viking, 1954.
229. Kempf, E. J., *The Autonomic Functions and the Personality,* New York: Nervous and Mental Disease Publishing Co., 1921.

230. Kilby, R. W., Psychoneuroses in times of trouble: evidence for a hierarchy of motives, *J. abnorm. soc. Psychol.*, 1948, *43*, 544–545.

231. King, D. C., The meaning of normal, *Yale J. Biol. Med.*, 1945, *17*, 493–501.

232. Kirkendall, L., *Premarital Intercourse and Interpersonal Relationships*, New York: Julian Press, 1961.

233. Klee, J. B., *Problems of Selective Behavior*, Lincoln, Neb.: University of Nebraska Studies, 1951, New Series No. 7.

234. Klein, M., Dittmann, A., Parloff, M., and Gill, M., *Behavioral Therapy:* Observations and reflections, *J. consult. clin. Psychol.*, 1969, *33*, 259–266.

235. Kluckhohn, C., *Mirror for Man*, New York: McGraw-Hill, 1949.

236. Knutson, J., *Motivation and Political Behavior*, Ph.D. thesis, University of Oregon, 1968.

237. Koestler, A., *The Yogi and the Commissar*, New York: Macmillan, 1945.

238. Kohler, W., *The Place of Values in a World of Facts*, New York: Liveright, 1938.

239. Kohler, W., Gestalt psychology today, *in* Henle, M. (ed.), *Documents of Gestalt Psychology*, Berkeley, Calif.: University of California Press, 1961.

240. Korman, A. K., Self-esteem as a moderator in vocational choice: Replications and extensions, *J. applied Psychol.*, 1969, *53*, 188–192.

241. Korzybski, A., *Science and Sanity: An Introduction to Non-Aristotelian Systems and General Semantics*, 3rd ed., Lakeville, Conn.: International Non-Aristotelian Lib. Pub. Co., 1948.

242. Kris, E., *Psychoanalytic Explorations in Art*, New York: International Universities Press, 1952.

243. Kropotkin, P., *Ethics, Origin and Development*, New York: Dial Press, 1924.

244. Krout, M., Autistic gestures, *Psychol. Monogr.*, 1935, *46*, No. 208.

245. Kubie, L. S., *Neurotic Distortion of the Creative Process*, Lawrence, Kansas: Univ. of Kansas, 1958.

246. Kubie, L. S., Some unsolved problems of the scientific career, *Am. Scientist*, 1953, *41*, 596–613; 1954, *42*, 104–112.

247. Landsman, T., Existentialism in counseling: the scientific view, *Personnel & Guidance Journal*, 1965, *XL*, pp. 568–572.

248. Landsman, T., The beautiful person, *The Futurist*, 1969, *3*, 41–42.

249. Langer, S., *Philosophy in a New Key*, Cambridge, Mass.: Harvard University Press, 1942.

250. Langer, S., *Symbolic Logic,* Boston: Houghton Mifflin, 1937.

251. Lao Tsu, *The Way of Life,* New York: Mentor, 1955.

252. Laski, M., *Ecstasy,* Bloomington, Ind.: Indiana University Press, 1962.

253. Lawler, E. E., III, Job Design and Employee Motivation, *Personnel Psychology,* 1969, *22,* No. 4, 426–435.

254. Lawler, E. E., III, and Porter, L. W., Antecedent attitudes of effective managerial performance, *Organizational Behavior and Human Performance,* 1967, *2,* 122–142.

255. Lawler, E. E., III, and Porter, L. W., The effect of performance on job satisfaction, *Industrial Relations,* 1967, *7,* pp. 20–27.

256. Lee, D., Autonomous motivation, *J. humanistic Psychol.,* 1962, *1,* 12–22.

257. Lee, D., *Freedom & Culture,* Englewood Cliffs, N. J.: Prentice-Hall, 1961.

258. Leeper, R. (ed.), *Humanizing Education,* Washington, D.C.: Association for Supervision and Curriculum Development, 1967.

259. Leeper, R., A motivational theory of emotion to replace "emotion as disorganized response," *Psychol. Rev., 55,* 5–21.

260. Leonard, W. E., *The Locomotive God,* New York: Century Co., 1929.

261. Le Shan, E., *The Conspiracy Against Childhood,* New York: Atheneum, 1967.

262. Le Shan, L., Mobilizing the life force, *The Ethical Forum, 3,* 1966, 1–11.

263. Levy, D. M., *Maternal Overprotection,* New York: Columbia University Press, 1943.

264. Levy, D. M., The deprived and indulged forms of psychopathic personality, *Am. J. Orthopsychiat.,* 1951, *21,* 250–254.

265. Levy, D. M., Experiments on the sucking reflex and social behavior of dogs, *Am. J. Orthopsychiat.,* 1934, *4,* 203–224.

266. Levy, D. M., On instinct-satiations: an experiment on the pecking behavior of chickens, *J. gen. Psychol.,* 1938, *18,* 327–348.

267. Levy, D. M., A note on pecking in chickens, *Psychoanal. Quart.,* 1934, *4,* 612–613.

268. Levy, D. M., On the problem of movement restraint, *Am. J. Orthopsychiat.,* 1944, *14,* 644–671.

269. Levy, D. M., Primary affect hunger, *Am. J. Psychiat.,* 1937, *94,* 643–652.

270. Levy, D. M., Psychic trauma of operations in children, *Am. J. Diseases Children,* 1945, *69,* 7–25.

271. Levy, D. M., Release therapy, *Am. J. Orthopsychiat.*, 1939, *9*, 713–736.

272. Levy, D. M., The strange hen, *Am. J. Orthopsychiat.*, 1950, *19*, 140–144.

273. Levy, D. M., Studies in sibling rivalry, *Amer. Orthopsychiat. Assn., Monogr.*, 1937, No. 2.

274. Lewin, K., *Dynamic Theory of Personality*, New York: McGraw-Hill, 1935.

275. Likert, R., *New Patterns in Management*, New York: McGraw-Hill, 1961.

276. Lorenz, K., *On Aggression*, New York: Harcourt, Brace & World, 1966.

277. Lowen, A., *The Betrayal of the Body*, New York: Macmillan, 1967.

278. Lowen, A., *Love and Orgasm*, New York: Macmillan, 1965.

279. Luchins, A., Mechanization in problem solving: the effect of Einstellung, *Psychol. Monogr.*, 1942, *54*, No. 6.

280. Luchins, A., On recent use of the Einstellung effect as a test of rigidity, *J. consulting Psychology*, 1951, *15*, 89–94.

281. Lyman, E., Occupational differences in the value attached to work, *Am. J. Sociol.*, 1955, *61*, 138–144.

282. Lynd, R., *Knowledge for What?*, Princeton, N. J.: Princeton University Press, 1939.

283. Mahrer, A. H. (ed.), *The Goals of Psychotherapy*, New York: Appleton-Century-Crofts, 1967.

284. Maier, N. R. F., *Frustration*, New York: McGraw-Hill, 1949.

285. Maier, N. R. F., *Studies of Abnormal Behavior in the Rat*, New York: Harper & Row, 1939.

286. Manuel, F. E., *Shapes of Philosophical History*, Stanford, Calif.: Stanford University Press, 1965.

287. Manuel, F. E., *A Portrait of Isaac Newton*, Cambridge, Mass.: Harvard University Press, 1968.

288. Marcuse, H., *Eros and Civilization*, Boston: Beacon, 1955.

289. Marmor, J., The role of instinct in human behavior, *Psychiatry*, 1942, *5*, 509–516.

290. Marrow, A., Bowers, D., and Seashore, S., *Management by Participation*, New York: Harper & Row, 1967.

291. Maslow, A. H., *Eupsychian Management: A Journal*, Homewood, Ill.: Irwin-Dorsey, 1965.

292. Maslow, A. H., *The Psychology of Science: A Reconnaissance*, New York: Harper & Row, 1966.

293. Maslow, A. H., *Religions, Values and Peak Experiences,* Columbus, Ohio: Ohio State University Press, 1964.

294. Maslow, A. H., *The S–I Test: A Measure of Psychological Security–Insecurity,* Palo Alto, Calif.: Consulting Psychologists Press, 1952.

295. Maslow, A. H., *Toward a Psychology of Being,* 2nd ed., New York: Van Nostrand Reinhold, 1968.

296. Maslow, A. H., and Mittelman, B., *Principles of Abnormal Psychology,* rev. ed., New York: Harper & Row, 1951.

297. Maslow, A. H. (ed.), *New Knowledge in Human Values,* New York: Harper & Row, 1959.

297a. Maslow, A. H., Comments on Prof. McClelland's paper *in* Jones, M. R. (ed.), *Nebraska Symposium on Motivation, 1955,* Lincoln, Neb.: University of Nebraska Press, 1955, 65–69.

298. Maslow, A. H., Criteria for judging needs to be instinctoid, *in* Jones, M. R. (ed.), *Human Motivation: A Symposium,* Lincoln, Neb.: Univ. of Nebraska Press, 1965.

299. Maslow, A. H., A philosophy of psychology, *in* Fairchild, J. (ed.), *Personal Problems and Psychological Frontiers,* New York: Sheridan, 1957.

300. Maslow, A. H., Power relationships and patterns of personal development, *in* Kornhauser, A. (ed.), *Problems of Power in American Democracy,* Detroit: Wayne University Press, 1957.

301. Maslow, A. H., and Diaz-Guerrero, R., Juvenile delinquency as a value disturbance, *in* Peatman, J., and Hartley, E. (eds.), *Festschrift for Gardner Murphy,* New York: Harper & Row, 1960.

302. Maslow, A. H., Appetites and hunger in animal motivation, *J. comp. Psychol.,* 1935, *20,* 75–83.

303. Maslow, A. H., The authoritarian character structure, *J. social Psychol.,* 1943, *18,* 401–411.

304. Maslow, A. H., The dominance drive as a determiner of the social and sexual behavior of infra-human primates, I-IV, *J. genet. Psychol.,* 1936, *48,* 261–277, 278–309, 310–338; *49,* 161–190.

305. Maslow, A. H., Dominance-feeling, personality and social behavior in women, *J. social Psychol.,* 1939, *10,* 3–39.

306. Maslow, A. H., Dominance-quality and social behavior in infra-human primates, *J. soc. Psychol.,* 1940, *11,* 313–324.

307. Maslow, A. H., Emotional blocks to creativity, *J. individ. Psychol.,* 1958, *14,* 51–56.

308. Maslow, A. H., The farther reaches of human nature, *J. transpers. Psychol.,* 1969, *1,* 1–10.

309. Maslow, A. H., The influence of familiarization on preference, *J. Exptl. Psychol.*, 1937, *21*, 162–180.
310. Maslow, A .H., Lessons from the peak-experiences, *J. humanistic Psychol.*, 1962, *2*, 9–18.
311. Maslow, A. H., Self-esteem (dominance feeling) and sexuality in women, *J. social Psychol.*, 1942, *16*, 259–294.
311a. Maslow, A. H., Some educational implications of the humanistic psychologies, *Harvard Educational Review*, 1968, *38*, 685–696.
311b. Maslow, A. H., Some fundamental questions that face the normative social psychologist, *J. humanistic Psychol.*, 1968, *8*, 143–153.
312. Maslow, A. H., Synergy in the society and in the individual, *J. individ. Psychol.*, 1964, *20*, 153–164.
313. Maslow, A. H., A test for dominance-feeling (self-esteem) in women, *J. social Psychol.*, 1940, *12*, 255–270.
314. Maslow, A. H., A theory of metamotivation: the biological rooting of the value-life, *J. humanistic Psychol.*, 1967, *7*, 93–127.
315. Maslow, A. H., Theory Z, *J. transpers. Psychol.*, 1969, *1*, 31–47.
316. Maslow, A. H., Toward a humanistic biology, *Am. Psychologist*, 1969, 724–735.
317. Maslow, A. H., Various meanings of transcendence, *J. transpers. Psychol.*, 1969, *1*, 56–66.
318. Maslow, A. H., and Mintz, N. L., Effects of esthetic surroundings: I. Initial short-term effects of three esthetic conditions upon perceiving "energy" and "well-being" in faces, *J. Psychol.*, 1956, *41*, 247–254.
319. Maslow, A. H., Rand, H., and Newman, S., Some parallels between the dominance and sexual behavior of monkeys and the fantasies of psychoanalytic patients, *J. nervous mental Disease*, 1960, *131*, 202–212.
320. Masters, R. D., Review of M. F. A. Montagu (ed.), Man & aggression, *Saturday Review*, October 19, 1968.
321. Matson, F., *The Broken Image*, New York: Braziller, 1964.
322. Matson, F. (ed.), *Being, Becoming and Behavior*, New York: Braziller, 1967.
323. May, R., *Love and Will*, New York: Norton, 1969.
324. May, R., *Psychology and the Human Dilemma*, New York: Van Nostrand Reinhold, 1967.
325. May, R. (ed.), *Existential Psychology*, New York: Random House, 1961.
326. McClelland, D., *The Achieving Society*, New York: Van Nostrand Reinhold, 1961.

327. McClelland, D., *The Roots of Consciousness,* New York: Van Nostrand Reinhold, 1964.

328. McClelland, D., and Winter, D. G., *Motivating Economic Achievement,* New York: Free Press, 1969.

329. McDougall, W., *The Energies of Men,* New York: Scribner's, 1933.

330. McDougall, W., *The Frontiers of Psychology,* New York: Appleton-Century-Crofts, 1935.

331. McDougall, W., *An Introduction to Social Psychology,* rev. ed., Boston: J. W. Luce & Co., 1926.

332. McGregor, D., *The Human Side of Enterprise,* New York: McGraw-Hill, 1960.

333. Mead, M., *Sex and Temperament in Three Primitive Societies,* New York: Morrow, 1935.

334. Mead, M., and Metraux, R., Image of the scientist among high school students, *Science,* 1957, *126,* 384–390.

335. Meadow, A., A relation between dominance–feeling and a classroom test situation, *J. Psychol.,* 1940, *9,* 269–274.

335a. Menninger, K. A., *Love Against Hate,* New York: Harcourt, Brace & World, 1942.

336. Mintz, N. L., Effects of esthetic surroundings: II. Prolonged and repeated experiences in a "beautiful" and an "ugly" room, *J. Psychol.,* 1956, *41,* 459–466.

337. Money-Kyrle, R. E., Some aspects of political ethics from the psychoanalytical point of view, *Int. J. Psychoanal.,* 1944, *25,* 166–171.

338. Money-Kyrle, R. E., Towards a common aim—a psychoanalytical contribution to ethics, *Brit. J. Med. Psychol.,* 1944, *20,* 105–117.

339. Montagu, M. F. A., *The Direction of Human Development,* New York: Harper & Row, 1955.

340. Montagu, M. F. A., *Man and Aggression,* New York: Oxford University Press, 1968.

341. Montagu, M. F. A. (ed.), *The Meaning of Love,* New York: Julian, 1953.

342. Moreno, J. (ed.), *Sociometry Reader,* New York: Free Press, 1960.

343. Moustakas, C., *The Authentic Teacher,* Cambridge, Mass.: Doyle, 1966.

344. Moustakas, C. (ed.), *The Self,* New York: Harper & Row, 1956.

345. Mowrer, O. H., *The New Group Therapy,* New York: Van Nostrand Reinhold, 1964.

346. Mowrer, O. H. (ed.), *Morality and Mental Health,* Chicago: Rand McNally, 1967.
347. Mumford, L., *The Conduct of Life,* New York: Harcourt, Brace & World, 1951.
348. Munroe, R. L., *Schools of Psychoanalytic Thought,* New York: Holt, Rinehart and Winston, 1955.
349. Murphy, G., *Human Potentialities,* New York: Basic Books, 1958.
350. Murphy, G., *Personality,* New York: Harper & Row, 1947.
351. Murphy, G., Psychology in the year 2000, *Am. Psychologist,* 1969, *24,* 521–530.
352. Murphy, L., *Social Behavior and Child Personality,* New York: Columbia University Press, 1937.
353. Murray, H. A., *Explorations in Personality,* New York: Oxford University Press, 1938.
354. Murray, H. A., Prospect for psychology, *Science,* 1962, *136,* 483–488.
355. Murray, H. A., Some basic psychological assumptions and conceptions, *Dialectica,* 1951, *5,* 266–292.
356. Myerson, A., *When Life Loses Its Zest,* Boston: Little, Brown, 1925.
357. Nameche, G., Two pictures of man, *J. humanistic Psychol.,* 1961, *1,* 70–88.
358. Naranjo, C., *The Unfolding of Man,* Menlo Park, Calif.: Stanford Research Institute, 1969.
359. Nielsen, K., On taking human nature as the basis of morality, *Soc. Res.,* 1962, *29,* 157–176.
360. Northrop, F. S. C., *The Logic of the Sciences and the Humanities,* New York: Macmillan, 1947.
361. Northrop, F. S. C., *The Meeting of East and West,* New York: Macmillan, 1946.
362. Olds, J., Physiological mechanisms of reward, *in* Jones, M. R. (ed.), *Nebraska Symposium on Motivation,* Lincoln, Neb.: University of Nebraska Press, 1955.
363. Oppenheimer, M., The "Y" theory: enlightened management confronts alienation, *New Politics,* 1967, *6,* 33–48.
364. Oppenheimer, O., Toward a new instinct theory, *J. social Psychol.,* 1958, *47,* 21–31.
365. Otto, H. (ed.), *Exploration in Human Potentialities,* Sprinfield, Ill.: C. C Thomas, 1966.
366. Otto, H., and Mann, J. (eds.), *Ways of Growth,* New York: Grossman, 1968.
366a. Overstreet, H., *The Mature Mind,* New York: Norton, 1949.

367. Ovsiankina, M., Die Wiederaufnahme unterbrochener Handlungen, *Psychol. Forsch.,* 1928, *11,* 302–379.
368. Owens, C. M., *Discovery of the Self,* Boston: Christopher, 1963.
369. Pahnke, W., Implications of LSD and experimental mysticism, *J. Religion mental Health,* 1966, *5,* 175–208.
370. Paine, F. T., Carroll, S. J., Jr., and Leete, B. A., Need satisfactions of managerial level personnel in a government agency. *J. appl. Psychol.,* 1966, *50,* 247–249.
371. Paine, F. T., Deutsch, D. R., and Smith, R. A., The relationship between family backgrounds to work values, *J. appl. Psychol.,* 1967, 320–323.
372. Pastore, N., *The Nature-Nurture Controversy,* New York: King's Crown, 1949.
373. Pavlov, I. P., *Conditioned Reflexes,* London: Oxford University Press, 1927.
374. Perls, F., Hefferline, R., and Goodman, P., *Gestalt Therapy,* New York: Julian Press, 1951.
375. Pieper, J., *Leisure, the Basis of Culture,* New York: Pantheon, 1964.
376. Polanyi, M., *Personal Knowledge,* Chicago: University of Chicago Press, 1958.
377. Polanyi, M., *Science, Faith and Society,* Chicago: University of Chicago Press, 1964.
378. Polanyi, M., *The Tacit Dimension,* New York: Doubleday, 1966.
379. Porter, L. W., and Lawler, E. E., *Managerial Attitudes and Performance,* Homewood, Ill.: Irwin, 1968.
380. Porter, L. W., A study of perceived need satisfactions in bottom and middle management jobs, *J. appl. Psychol.,* 1961, *45,* 1–10.
381. Porter, L. W., Job attitudes in management: I. Perceived deficiencies in need fulfillment as a function of job level, *J. appl. Psychol.,* 1962, *46,* 375–384.
382. Porter, L. W., Job attitudes in management: II. Perceived importance of needs as a function of job level, *J. appl. Psychol.,* 1963, *47,* 375–384.
383. Porter, L. W., Job attitudes in management: III. Perceived deficiencies in need fulfillment as a function of line versus staff type of job, *J. appl. Psychology,* 1963, *47,* 267–275.
384. Porter, L. W., Job attitudes in management: IV. Perceived deficiencies in need fulfillment as a function of size of company, *J. appl. Psychol.,* 1963, *47,* 386–397.
385. Porter, L. W., and Henry, M., Job attitudes in management: V. Per-

ceptions of the importance of certain personality traits as a function of job level, *J. appl. Psychol.*, 1964, *48*, 31–36.

386. Progoff, I., *Depth Psychology and Modern Man,* New York: Julian Press, 1959.

387. Progoff, I., *Jung's Psychology and Its Social Meaning,* New York: Grove Press, 1953.

388. Rand, A., *The Fountainhead,* Indianapolis: Bobbs-Merrill, 1943.

389. Rapaport, D. (ed.), *Organization and Pathology of Thought,* New York: Columbia University Press, 1951.

390. Reich, W., *Character Analysis,* 3rd ed., New York: Orgone Institute Press, 1949.

391. Reich, W., *The Function of the Orgasm,* New York: Farrar, Straus & Giroux, 1942.

392. Reik, T., *Listening With the Third Ear,* New York: Farrar, Straus & Giroux, 1948.

393. Reik, T., *Of Love and Lust,* New York: Farrar, Straus & Giroux, 1957.

394. Rhinehart, J. B., Barrell, R. P., DeWolfe, A. S., Griffin, J. E., and Spaner, F. E., Comparative study of need satisfactions in governmental and business hierarchies, *J. appl. Psychol.* 1969, *53*, 230–235.

395. Ribble, M., *The Rights of Infants,* New York: Columbia University Press ,1943.

396. Ribot, T. H., *La psychologie des sentiments,* Paris: Alcan, 1896.

397. Richter, C. P., and J. Eckert, Mineral appetites of parathyroidectomized rats, *Am. J. Med. Sci.,* 1939, *198,* 9–16.

398. Riesman, D., *The Lonely Crowd,* New Haven, Conn.: Yale University Press, 1950.

399. Rimmer, R., *The Harrad Experiment,* Bantam, 1966.

400. Ritter, P., and Ritter, J., *The Free Family,* London: Gollancz, 1959.

401. Roe, A., *The Making of a Scientist,* New York: Dodd, Mead, 1953.

401a. Rogers, C., *Client-Centered Therapy,* Boston, Mass.: Houghton Mifflin, 1951.

402. Rogers, C., *Freedom to Learn,* Columbus, O.: Merrill, 1969.

403. Rogers, C., *On Becoming a Person,* Boston, Mass.: Houghton Mifflin, 1961.

404. Rogers, C., *Psychotherapy and Personality Changes,* Chicago: University of Chicago Press, 1954.

405. Rogers, C., and Skinner, B. F., Some issues concerning the control of human behavior: A symposium, *Science,* 1956, *124,* 1057–1066.

406. Rokeach, M., *The Open and Closed Mind,* New York: Basic Books, 1960.
407. Rosenthal, R., *Experimenter Effects in Behavioral Research,* New York: Appleton-Century-Crofts, 1966.
408. Rosenzweig, S., Need-persistive and ego-defensive reactions to frustration, *Psychol. Rev.,* 1941, *48,* 347–349.
409. Ruitenbeek, H. M. (ed.), *Varieties of Personality Theory,* New York: Dutton, 1964.
410. Schachtel, E., *Metamorphosis,* New York: Basic Books, 1959.
411. Scheinfeld, A., *Women and Men,* New York: Harcourt, Brace & World, 1944.
412. Schilder, P., *Goals and Desires of Man,* New York: Columbia University Press, 1942.
413. Schilder, P., *Mind: Perception and Thought in Their Constructive Aspects,* New York: Columbia University Press, 1942.
413a. Schlick, M., *Problems of Ethics,* Englewood Cliffs, N. J.: Prentice-Hall, 1939.
414. Schooland, J. B., Are there any innate behavior tendencies?, *Genet. Psychol. Monogr.,* 1942, *25,* 219–287.
415. Schutz, W., *Joy,* New York: Grove Press, 1968.
416. Schwarz, O., *The Psychology of Sex,* New York: Penguin Books, 1951.
417. Schwitzgebel, R., The self in self-actualization, *Psychologia,* 1961, *4,* 163–169.
418. Seguin, C. A., *Love and Psychotherapy,* New York: Libra, 1965.
419. Severin, F. (ed.), *Humanistic Viewpoints in Psychology,* New York: McGraw-Hill, 1965.
420. Sheldon, W. H., *Psychology and the Promethean Will,* New York: Harper & Row, 1936.
421. Sheldon, W. H. (with the collaboration of E. M. Hartl and E. McDermott), *Varieties of Delinquent Youth,* New York: Harper & Row, 1949.
422. Sheldon, W. H. (with the collaboration of S. S. Stevens), *The Varieties of Temperament,* New York: Harper & Row, 1942.
423. Shils, E., Of plenitude and scarcity, *Encounter,* 1969, *32,* 37–57.
424. Shirley, M., Children's adjustments to a strange situation, *J. abnorm. soc. Psychol.,* 1942, *37,* 201–217.
425. Shostrom, E., *Bibliography for the P.O.I.,* San Diego, Calif.: Educational and Industrial Testing Service, 1968.
426. Shostrom, E., *Personal Orientation Inventory (POI): A Test of Self-*

Actualization, San Diego, California: Educational and Industrial Testing Service, 1963.

427. Simpson, G., Science as morality, *Phil. Sci.,* 1951, *18,* 132–143.

428. Singh, P. N., and Baumgartel, H., Background factors in airline mechanics' work motivations: A research note, *J. appl. Psychol.,* 1966, *50,* 357–359.

429. Singh, P. N., and Wherry, R. J., Ranking of job factors by factory workers in India, *Personnel Psychology,* Spring, 1963, 29–33.

430. Sinnott, E. W., *The Bridge of Life,* New York: Simon and Schuster, 1966.

431. Skeels, H. M., Adult status of children with contrasting early life experiences, *Monographs of the Society for Research in Child Development,* 1966, *31,* entire No. 105.

432. Sohl, J., *The Lemon Eaters,* New York: Dell, 1967.

433. Sontag, L. W., The purpose and fate of a skin disorder, *Psychosomat. Med.,* 1945, *7,* 306–309.

434. Sorokin, P. (ed.), *Exploration in Altruistic Love and Behavior,* Boston: Beacon, 1950.

435. Spemann, H., *Embryonic Development and Induction,* New Haven, Conn.: Yale University Press, 1938.

436. Spitz, R., Hospitalism, *Psychoanal. Study of the Child,* 1945, *1,* 53–74.

437. Stapledon, O., *Odd John,* New York: Galaxy, 1936.

438. Starr, H. E., Promethean Constellations, Parts I and II, *Psychological Clinic,* 1933, *22,* 1–20.

439. Storr, A., *Human Aggression,* London: Allen Lane, The Penguin Press, 1968.

440. Strauss, G., Human relations—1968 style, *Ind. Rel.,* 1968, *7,* 262–276.

441. Sutich, A., and Vich, M., *Readings in Humanistic Psychology,* New York: Free Press, 1969.

442. Suttie, I., *The Origins of Love and Hate,* New York: Julian Press, 1935.

443. Szasz, T. S., The myth of mental illness, *Am. Psychologist,* 1960, *15,* 113–118.

444. Taggard, G., *The Life and Mind of Emily Dickinson,* New York: Knopf, 1934.

445. Tanzer, D., Natural childbirth: Pain or peak experience?, *Psychology Today,* 1968, *2,* 16–21, 69.

446. Tart, C. (ed.), *Altered States of Consciousness,* New York: Wiley, 1969.

447. Tead, O., Toward the knowledge of man, *Main Currents in Modern Thought,* Nov. 1955, *12,* 35–39.
448. Thompson, C., *Psychoanalysis: Evolution and Development,* New York: Hermitage, 1950.
449. Thorndike, E. L., *Human Nature and the Social Order,* New York: Macmillan, 1940.
450. Tillich, P., *The Courage to Be,* New Haven, Conn.: Yale University Press, 1952.
451. Tillich, P., *Love, Power and Justice,* New York: Oxford University Press, 1954.
452. Trotter, W., *Instincts of the Herd in Peace and War,* New York: Macmillan, 1915.
453. Van Doren, C., *Three Worlds,* New York: Harper & Row, 1936.
454. Van Kaam, A. L., *Existential Foundations of Psychology,* Pittsburgh: Duquesne University Press, 1966.
455. Van Kaam, A. L., Phenomenal analysis: Exemplified by a study of the experience of "really feeling understood," *J. individ. Psychol.,* 1959, *15,* 66–72.
456. Vroom, V., *Work and Motivation,* New York: Wiley, 1964.
457. Walder, R., The psychoanalytic theory of play, *Psychoanalyt. Quart.,* 1933, *2,* 208–224.
458. Watson, D. L., *The Study of Human Nature,* Yellow Springs, O.: Antioch Press, 1953.
459. Watts, A. W., *Nature, Man and Woman,* New York: Pantheon, 1958.
460. Watts, A. W., *Psychotherapy: East and West,* New York: Pantheon, 1961.
461. Weisskopf, W., *The Psychology of Economics,* Chicago: University of Chicago Press, 1955.
462. Weisskopf, W., Economic growth and human well-being, *Manas,* August 21, 1963, *16,* 1–8.
463. Wells, W. R., Hypnotic treatment of the major symptoms of hysteria: a case study, *J. Psychol.,* 1944, *17,* 269–297.
464. Werner, H., *The Comparative Psychology of Mental Development,* New York: Harper & Row, 1940.
465. Wertheimer, M., *Productive Thinking,* 2nd ed., New York: Harper & Row, 1959.
466. Wertheimer, M., On truth, *in* Henle, M. (ed.), *Documents of Gestalt Psychology,* Berkeley, Calif.: University of California Press, 1961.
467. Wertheimer, M., Some problems in the theory of ethics, *in* Henle, M. (ed.), *Documents of Gestalt Psychology,* Berkeley, Calif.: University of California Press, 1961.

468. Wheelis, A., *The Quest for Identity,* New York: Norton, 1958.
469. Wheelis, A., *The Seeker,* New York: Random House, 1960.
470. Whitaker, C., and Malone, T., *The Roots of Psychotherapy,* New York: Blakiston, 1953.
471. White, R. W., *Lives in Progress,* New York: Holt, Rinehart and Winston, 1952.
472. White, R. (ed.), *The Study of Lives,* New York: Atherton Press, 1966.
473. White, R., Motivation reconsidered: the concept of competence, *Psychol. Rev.,* 1959, *66,* 297–333.
474. Whitehead, A. N., *The Aims of Education,* New York: New American Library, 1949.
475. Whitehead, A. N., *Modes of Thought,* New York: Macmillan and Cambridge Univ. Press, 1938.
476. Whitehead, A. N., *Science and the Modern World,* New York: Macmillan, 1925.
477. Whiteman, S. L., Associative learning of the college student as a function of need relevant stimuli, Ph.D. Thesis, Case Western Reserve University, 1969.
478. Wienpahl, P., *The Matter of Zen,* New York: New York University Press, 1964.
479. Wilkins, L., and Richter, C., A great craving for salt by a child with cortico-adrenal insufficiency, *J. Am. Med. Assoc.,* 1940, *114,* 866-868.
480. Wilson, C., *Beyond the Outsider,* London: Arthur Barker, 1965.
481. Wilson, C., *Introduction to the New Existentialism,* Boston: Houghton Mifflin, 1967.
482. Wilson, C., *Origins of the Sexual Impulse,* London: Arthur Barker, 1963.
483. Wilson, C., *Voyage to a Beginning,* New York: Crown, 1969.
484. Winthrop, H., *Ventures in Social Interpretation,* New York: Appleton-Century-Crofts, 1968.
485. Witkin, H., Dyk, R., Faterson, H., and Karp, S., *Psychological Differentiation: Studies of Development,* New York: Wiley, 1962.
486. Wolff, W., *The Expression of Personality,* New York: Harper & Row, 1943.
487. Wolpe, J., and Lazarus, A. A., *Behavior Therapy Techniques: A Guide to the Treatment of Neuroses,* New York: Pergamon Press, 1966.
488. Wootton, G., *Workers, Unions and the State,* New York: Schocken, 1967.

489. Yablonsky, L., *The Tunnel Back: Synanon*, New York: Macmillan, 1965.
490. Yeatman, R. J., and Sellar, W. C., *1066 and All That*, New York: Dutton, 1931.
491. Young, P. T., Appetite, palatability and feeding habit; a critical review, *Psychol. Bull.*, 1948, *45*, 289–320.
492. Young, P. T., The experimental analysis of appetite, *Psychol. Bull.*, 1941, *38*, 129–164.
493. Zeigarnik, B., Uber das Behalten von erledigten and unerledigten Handlungen, *Psychol. Forsch.*, 1927, *9*, 1–85.
494. Zinker, J., *Rosa Lee: Motivation and the Crisis of Dying*, Painesville, Ohio: Lake Erie College Studies, 1966.

INDEX OF NAMES

INDEX OF SUBJECTS

71 72 73 7 6 5 4